P9-CCH-469

Assessment Procedures for Counselors and Helping Professionals

SIXTH EDITION

Robert J. Drummond
Late of University of North Florida

Karyn Dayle Jones
University of Central Florida

PEARSON

Merrill
Prentice Hall

Upper Saddle River, New Jersey
Columbus, Ohio

Library of Congress Cataloging-in-Publication Data
Drummond, Robert J.
    Assessment procedures for counselors and helping professionals / Robert J. Drummond
Karyn Dayle Jones.—6th ed.
        p. cm.
    Includes bibliographical references and indexes.
    ISBN 0-13-170784-1
  1. Psychological tests. 2. Educational tests and measurements. 3. Counseling. I.
Jones, Karyn Dayle. II. Title.
    BF176.D78   2006
    150'.28'7—dc22   2005044380

Vice President and Executive Publisher: Jeffery W. Johnston
Publisher: Kevin M. Davis
Editorial Assistant: Sarah N. Kenoyer
Production Editor: Mary Harlan
Production Coordinator: Norine Strang, Carlisle Publishing Services
Design Coordinator: Diane C. Lorenzo
Text Design and Illustrations: Carlisle Publishing Services
Cover Design: Jeff Vanik
Cover Image: SuperStock
Production Manager: Laura Messerly
Director of Marketing: Ann Castel Davis
Marketing Manager: Autumn Purdy
Marketing Coordinator: Brian Mounts

This book was set in Garamond Book by Carlisle Publishing Services. It was printed and
bound by R. R. Donnelley & Sons Company. The cover was printed by The Lehigh Press, Inc.

**Copyright © 2006, 2004, 2000, 1996, 1992, 1988 by Pearson Education, Inc., Upper
Saddle River, New Jersey 07458.** Pearson Prentice Hall. All rights reserved. Printed in the
United States of America. This publication is protected by Copyright and permission should
be obtained from the publisher prior to any prohibited reproduction, storage in a retrieval
system, or transmission in any form or by any means, electronic, mechanical, photocopying,
recording, or likewise. For information regarding permission(s), write to: Rights and
Permissions Department.

Pearson Prentice Hall™ is a trademark of Pearson Education, Inc.
Pearson® is a registered trademark of Pearson plc
Prentice Hall® is a registered trademark of Pearson Education, Inc.
Merrill® is a registered trademark of Pearson Education, Inc.

Pearson Education Ltd.   Pearson Education Australia Pty, Limited
Pearson Education Singapore, Pte. Ltd.   Pearson Education North Asia Ltd.
Pearson Education Canada, Ltd.   Pearson Educación de Mexico, S.A. de C.V.
Pearson Education—Japan   Pearson Education Malaysia, Pte. Ltd.

10 9 8 7 6 5 4 3 2 1
ISBN: 0-13-170784-1

Appreciation of Robert Drummond

Dr. Robert Drummond passed away on March 14, 2005. He was a retired professor and counselor educator at the University of North Florida for 20 years. He was foremost in the field of assessment, and he specialized in educational and psychological testing, career development, models for evaluation, educational research, and personality theory and measurement. Dr. Drummond wrote the first edition of this text in 1988. Now in its sixth edition, the book is the most popular assessment textbook in counseling. I was first introduced to this text as a master's student in counseling, and I used it when I became a counselor educator. I would like to thank Dr. Drummond for helping me and others in the helping professions learn to understand and truly appreciate assessment in counseling.

Karyn Dayle Jones

Preface

The purpose of this text is to help current and future workers in the helping professions become better consumers of psychological and educational tests and assessment procedures. First, users need to know the philosophical and historical background relating to the field of testing. Second, they need to understand the role that statistics plays in testing and assessment. Third, they need to be able to interpret and communicate test scores. Fourth, they need to know how to locate and select the most valid and reliable instruments to aid in their decision making. Finally, they need to be alert to the standards developed by various professional organizations and designed as guidelines for test authors and test users.

In this text, a systems approach is used to organize the knowledge base and the basic skills and competencies needed by test users. The book focuses on six components:

1. *The purpose of testing.* The first chapter presents the historical, philosophical, and social background of the testing movement. It also presents the value of testing as an integral part of the helping professions.
2. *Basic competencies needed.* Chapters 2 through 7 identify the basic measurement, statistical, and research skills needed to select, administer, and interpret tests and assessment information. In addition, ethical considerations in testing are presented.
3. *Types of tests and assessment procedures.* Chapters 8 through 14 introduce the different types of tests and assessment techniques that are commonly used in the helping professions. This portion of the text covers the assessment of learning and cognitive styles and the testing of intelligence, aptitude, interest, and personality. Assessment of the environment and development of the test taker are also discussed.
4. *Special issues in assessment.* Chapter 15 focuses on environmental assessment. Chapter 16 presents information on the use of computers in testing. Chapter 18 focuses on assessment issues in education.

5. *Testing special populations.* Chapter 17 focuses on appraisal procedures and techniques, as well as issues when working with special populations, such as clients with disabilities and multicultural groups.

6. *Communicating test results.* Chapter 19 presents strategies for communicating test results to clients, parents, and other professionals, as well as guidelines for writing test reports.

CHANGES IN THE SIXTH EDITION

For the sixth edition, content is reorganized and chapters are updated. Key changes and content expansions include the following:

1. A new chapter (Chapter 3) focuses on understanding and interpreting test scores.
2. The coverage of validity and reliability is expanded and separated into two chapters (Chapters 4 and 5).
3. Information about discriminant, convergent, and consequential validity is expanded (Chapter 4). In addition, the section on threats to test validity is augmented.
4. Chapter 6, Process and Procedures of Testing, contains expanded and updated information about sources of test information.
5. Information about test user qualifications is new to Chapter 7, Legal and Ethical Concerns and Issues in Testing.
6. Updated information on intelligence tests appears in Chapter 8, Ability and Intelligence Testing.
7. Chapter 13, Clinical Assessment, includes expanded information about unstructured interviews.
8. Validity and reliability information about specific tests is presented throughout.

STRUCTURE OF THE TEXT

Each chapter has a similar format. A chapter overview is followed by learning objectives and a discussion of the topics related to those objectives. A brief summary is included in each chapter, in addition to discussion questions, suggested activities, case studies, and additional readings. Publishers whose tests are cited in the text are listed in the Appendix, and key terms are defined in the glossary. Separate indexes are provided for authors, subjects, and tests.

Myriad tests are presented throughout the text. The annotated lists included in the text are not exhaustive, nor do they represent all the exemplary tests in the field. Their purpose is to indicate the range and scope of tests in each area. The text attempts to encourage the reader's curiosity and interest and stimulate further investigation, research, reading, and experimentation to broaden knowledge, skills, and competencies in measurement and evaluation.

ACKNOWLEDGMENTS

I would like to thank the following colleagues, whose review improved this edition: Aaron W. Hughey, Western Kentucky University; Gerald Juhnke, University of Texas at San Antonio; Jacob J. Levy, University of Southern Mississippi; Edward J. Morris, Western Kentucky University; and Judith S. Rauenzahn, Kutztown University.

Karyn Dayle Jones

Discover the Companion Website
Accompanying This Book

THE PRENTICE HALL COMPANION WEBSITE:
A VIRTUAL LEARNING ENVIRONMENT

Technology is a constantly growing and changing aspect of our field that is creating a need for content and resources. To address this emerging need, Prentice Hall has developed an online learning environment for students and professors alike—Companion Websites—to support our textbooks.

In creating a Companion Website, our goal is to build on and enhance what the textbook already offers. For this reason, the content for each user-friendly website is organized by chapter and provides the professor and student with a variety of meaningful resources.

Common Companion Website features for students include:

- **Chapter Objectives**—Outline key concepts from the text.
- **Interactive Self-quizzes**—Complete with hints and automatic grading that provide immediate feedback for students. After students submit their answers for the interactive self-quizzes, the Companion Website **Results Reporter** computes a percentage grade, provides a graphic representation of how many questions were answered correctly and incorrectly, and gives a question-by-question analysis of the quiz. Students are given the option to send their quiz to up to four email addresses (professor, teaching assistant, study partner, etc.).
- **Essay Questions**—Allow students to respond to themes and objectives of each chapter by applying what they have learned to real classroom situations.
- **Web Destinations**—Links to www sites that relate to chapter content.

To take advantage of the many available resources, please visit the *Assessment Procedures for Counselors and Helping Professionals,* Sixth Edition, Companion Website at

www.prenhall.com/drummond

Research Navigator:
Research Made Simple!

www.ResearchNavigator.com

Merrill Education is pleased to introduce Research Navigator—a one-stop research solution for students that simplifies and streamlines the entire research process. At www.researchnavigator.com, students will find extensive resources to enhance their understanding of the research process so they can effectively complete research assignments. In addition, Research Navigator has three exclusive databases of credible and reliable source content to help students focus their research efforts and begin the research process.

HOW WILL RESEARCH NAVIGATOR ENHANCE YOUR COURSE?

- Extensive content helps students understand the research process, including writing, Internet research, and citing sources.
- Step-by-step tutorial guides students through the entire research process from selecting a topic to revising a rough draft.
- Research Writing in the Disciplines section details the differences in research across disciplines.
- Three exclusive databases—EBSCO's ContentSelect Academic Journal Database, *The New York Times* Search by Subject Archive, and "Best of the Web" Link Library—allow students to easily find journal articles and sources.

WHAT'S THE COST?

A subscription to Research Navigator is $7.50 but is available at no additional cost when used in conjunction with this textbook. To obtain free passcodes for your students, simply contact your local Merrill/Prentice Hall sales representative, and your representative will send you the Evaluating Online Resource Guide, which contains the code to access Research Navigator as well as tips on how to use Research Navigator and how to evaluate research. To preview the value of this Web site to your students, please go to www.educatorlearningcenter.com and use the login name "Research" and the password "Demo."

Brief Contents

Contents

CHAPTER 3

Understanding Test Scores   33

CHAPTER 4

Validity   **51**

CHAPTER 5

Reliability   **64**

CHAPTER 8

Ability and Intelligence Testing   **123**

CHAPTER 9

Aptitude Testing   158

CHAPTER 10

The Assessment of Achievement   175

CHAPTER 11

CHAPTER 12

CHAPTER 13

Clinical Assessment   267

CHAPTER 14

Assessment of Development   287

CHAPTER 15

Environmental Assessment   301

CHAPTER 18

Assessment Issues in Education   369

CHAPTER 19

Communicating Test Results   393

Note: Every effort has been made to provide accurate and current Internet information in this book. However, the Internet and information posted on it are constantly changing, so it is inevitable that some of the Internet addresses listed in this textbook will change.

1 Historical and Philosophical Foundations of Assessment

OVERVIEW

Testing is an integral part of our society. Anyone who has attended grade school or college, served in the military, or applied for a job has taken one or more tests. It is almost impossible to pick up a newspaper, listen to a talk show, or watch a documentary without testing being mentioned. Testing can have significant impact on all our lives. For example, in 2002, President Bush signed into law the No Child Left Behind Act of 2001, containing four basic education reform principles for kindergarten through 12th-grade students. As a result, all 50 states now have testing programs and report testing results to their community. The use of tests should be viewed within the context of the broader concept of assessment. It is vital that counselors and other helping professionals understand the assessment process, the purpose of tests, how to choose appropriate tests, test interpretation, and the use of test results in developing treatment plans or educational plans.

OBJECTIVES

After studying this chapter, you should be able to

✔ Discuss several uses and values of testing

✔ Understand the history of assessment

✔ Discuss current trends and controversial issues in testing

TESTING AND ASSESSMENT

The use of tests has greatly expanded during the 20th century. More than one million standardized tests are used each school day in American schools alone (Lyman, 1998). Add to that the tests given in industry, mental health clinics, the military, government, business, and so on, and that number increases dramatically. The growth in test sales is impressive, from less than $7 million in 1955 to over $263 million in 1997 (Clarke, Madaus, Horn, & Ramos, 2001). Between 1990 and 1997 alone, sales increased by about 50%, or $88 million.

The use of computers to administer and score tests has changed the field of assessment in terms of reducing the time for scoring and analyzing test results and assuring their accuracy. There are tests to measure of a wide variety of attributes including intelligence, achievement, career preferences, personality type, and much more.

Often, the terms *testing* and *assessment* are used interchangeably. It is important to know that the use of tests is only one part of the overall process of assessment. *Assessment* is defined by the American Psychological Association (APA) as a process that integrates test information with information from other sources; a process for evaluating behavior, psychological constructs, and/or characteristics of individuals or groups for the purpose of making decisions regarding classification, selection, placement, diagnosis, or intervention (2000). The term *test* refers to a measurement procedure for assessing psychological characteristics in which a sample of an examinee's behavior is obtained and subsequently evaluated and scored using a standardized process (APA, 2000). Because tests provide only one source of information, professionals may also gather client information from interviews, records, or from other professionals.

A *test user* is the person or persons responsible for the selection, administration, and scoring of tests; for the analysis, interpretation, and communication of test results; and for any decisions or actions that are based, in part, on test scores. Generally, individuals who simply administer tests, score tests, and communicate simple or "canned" test results are not classified as test users.

VALUE OF TESTING

Although testing is a specific task that is different from counseling, it continues to be an important part of the counseling process (Maxmen & Ward, 1995). Though it can occur at several points throughout the counseling relationship, it will almost always occur at the outset of the counseling process (Seligman, 1996). The assessment process is used for the following reasons:

- To obtain information about the client's presenting problem
- To make an accurate diagnosis
- To determine the client's goals for counseling
- To gather information to aid in the development of a treatment plan
- To gather information to aid in the development of an educational plan
- To gather baseline data to measure the client's progress in counseling
- To determine a client's suitability for a certain treatment program or modality

- To assess the effectiveness of an education/counseling program
- To carry out research studies

In addition to providing useful information about clients, test information can be especially valuable in educational decision making because it enhances placement decisions. Public Law 94-142 requires exceptional students to be placed in the least restrictive environment, and test information helps educational personnel place these individuals in environments that will best facilitate their learning. Test data are utilized with different criteria in the selection of students for gifted programs, for admission to colleges and universities, and for admission to vocational and technical programs. Advanced placement (AP) programs and college-level examination programs (CLEPs) are examples of widely used placement programs. Teachers are also aided by test data in their selection of instructional strategies and in their evaluation of curriculum programs.

Another way of looking at the value of test data is to consider how different groups such as administrators, teachers, counselors, psychologists, curriculum experts, students, researchers, the public, and the legislature use the data. All of these groups are consumers of test information.

STANDARDIZED AND NONSTANDARDIZED TESTS

There are several classification systems for tests. Tests can be classified based on their purpose, how they were constructed, their content, or how they are administered, scored, and interpreted (Aiken, 2003). A common classification is standardized and nonstandardized tests. Standardization implies uniformity of procedure in administering and scoring the test; therefore, *standardized tests* will have specific directions for administration, specific instructions for the test taker, and specific scoring procedures. Standardized tests have generally proven *reliability,* or consistency, of scores and *validity,* the ability of the test to measure what it is designed to measure. Some general categories of standardized tests include achievement tests, aptitude tests, intelligence tests, personality inventories, and interest inventories. *Nonstandardized tests* are informally constructed tests without proven reliability or validity. These include interviews, observation, questionnaires, and secondhand information.

HISTORICAL CONTEXTS

Testing is not a new idea, even though the objective test movement began only at the turn of the century (see Table 1.1). Around 2200 B.C., the Chinese used essay examinations to help select civil service employees. The philosophies of Socrates and Plato emphasized the importance of assessing an individual's competencies and aptitudes in vocational selection. Throughout the centuries, philosophers and educators have devised certain scales or items to provide teachers and parents with useful information to help their children. Fitzherbert (1470–1538) identified some items to screen individuals with retardation from those without; for example, being able to count to 20 pence, being able to tell one's age, and being able to identify one's father or mother.

Table 1.1
Major events in testing during the 20th century.

1900 to 1909	Jung Word Association Test		Graduate Record Examinations
	Binet and Simon Intelligence Scale		Wechsler Bellevue Intelligence Scale
	Standardized group tests of achievement		1937 revision of the Stanford-Binet Intelligence Scale
	Stone Arithmetic Test		
	Thorndike Handwriting, Language, Spelling, and Arithmetic Tests		Murray's Thematic Apperception Test
			Bernreuter Personality Inventory
	Spearman's measurement theory		Leiter International Performance Scale
	Pearson's theory of correlation		Kuder Preference Scale Record
	Thorndike's textbook on educational measurement		Lindquist's Iowa Every-Pupil Test
	Goddard's translation of Binet into English		Bender Visual Motor Gestalt Test
			Marino's *Sociometric Techniques*
1910 to 1919	Army Alpha, Army Beta Tests		Piaget's *Origins of Intelligence*
	Stenquist Test of Mechanical Abilities		Tiegs and Clark's Progressive Achievement Test
	Porteous Maze Test		Gesell Maturity Scale
	Seashore Measures of Musical Talents		
	Spearman's *Factors in Intelligence*	1940 to 1949	Minnesota Multiphasic Personality Inventory
	Stanford-Binet Intelligence Scale		Wechsler Intelligence Scale for Children
	Otis Absolute Point Scale		U.S. Employment Service's General Aptitude Test Battery
	Stern's concept of mental quotient		
	Woodworth Personal Data Sheet		Cattell Infant Intelligence Scale
1920 to 1929	Founding of the Psychological Corporation	1950 to 1959	Lindquist's electronic test scoring
	Goodenough Draw-a-Man Test		*Standards for Educational and Psychological Testing*
	Strong Vocational Interest Blank		
	Terman, Kelley, and Ruch's Stanford Achievement Test		Guilford's *The Nature of Human Intelligence*
	Clark's *Aptitude Testing*		Stevenson's *The Study of Behavior: O-Technique and Its Methodology*
	Spearman's *The Abilities of Man: Their Nature and Measurement*		Osgood's semantic differential
			National Defense Education Act
	Morrison's School Mastery Tests		Frederikson's in-basket assessment technique
	Rorschach Ink Blot Test		Bloom's *Taxonomy of Educational Objectives*
	Hartshorne and May's *Character Education Inquiry*		
	Kohs's Block Design Test	1960 to 1969	National Assessment of Educational Progress
1930 to 1939	Thurstone's primary mental abilities		Flannigan's Project Talent
	Buros's *First Mental Measurements Yearbook*		Wechsler Preschool and Primary Scale of Intelligence
	Johnson's test-scoring machine		1960 revision of the Stanford-Binet

Juan Huarte (1530–1589) was probably the first author to suggest formal mental testing. His book title was translated as *The Trial of Wits: Discovering the Great Differences of Wits Among Men and What Sorts of Learning Suit Best with Each Genius.* Jean Esquirol (1772–1840), a French physician, proposed that there are several levels of mental deficiency and that language is a valid psychological criterion for differentiating among levels. Eduardo Seguin (1812–1880) also worked with individuals with mental

Table 1.1
Continued

Jensen's *How Much Can We Boost IQ and Scholastic Achievement?*	*Mental Measurements Yearbook* reviews in Bibliographic Retrieval Service
Kuder Occupational Interest Survey	*Test Critiques,* Vols. 1–7
Cattell's *Theory of Fluid and Crystallized Intelligence*	Detroit Test of Learning Aptitude IV
Kirk and McCarthy's Illinois Test of Psycholinguistic Abilities	Differential Ability Scales
	Neurobehavioral Functioning Inventory
Bayley Scales of Infant Development	Naglieri's *Nonverbal Aptitude Test: Individual Administration*

1970	Family Educational Rights and Privacy Act	Test of Nonverbal Intelligence 1–3
to	New York State Truth in Testing Act	Beta III
1979	Public Law 94-142	Bracken's *Basic Concepts Scale: Revised*
	System of Multicultural Pluralistic Assessment	Bayley *Scale of Infant Development*
	Wechsler Intelligence Scale for Children-Revised	Millon's *Index of Personality Types*
	Revised *Standards for Educational and Psychological Testing*	

	Rokeach Value Survey	1990 Sixteen Personality Factor Questionnaire V
	Peabody Picture Vocabulary Test	to *Tests in Print IV*
	Seventh and *Eighth Mental Measurements Yearbooks*	2000 Wechsler Intelligence Scale for Children IV
	Use of computers in testing	Wechsler Adult Intelligence Scale III
	McCarthy Scales of Children's Abilities	Wechsler Preschool and Primary Scale of Intelligence III
		Wechsler Individual Achievement Test
		Wechsler Abbreviated Scale of Intelligence

1980	Thorndike, Hagen, and Stattler's revision of the Stanford-Binet	*Early Reading Diagnostic Assessment: Revised*
to		*Early Mathematics Diagnostic Assessment*
1989	Kaufman Assessment Battery for Children	*Wide Range Achievement Test, 3rd Edition*
	Ninth and *Tenth Mental Measurements Yearbooks*	State Trait Anger Expression Inventory: II
	Minnesota Multiphasic Personality Inventory II	Stanford-Binet V
	Revised *Standards for Educational and Psychological Testing*	Dynamic Assessment of Test Accommodations
	Computer-adaptive and computer-assisted testing	BarOn's *Emotional Quotient Inventory*
	Wechsler Adult Intelligence Scale-Revised	First Step: Screening Test for Evaluating Preschoolers
	Nader/Nairn *The Reign of ETS*	*Tests in Print V*
	Tests in Print III	

retardation and believed that these people should be trained in sensory discrimination and in the development of motor control.

Alfred Binet (1857–1911) became the director of the first physiological-psychological laboratory in France, at the Sorbonne, and did his early work on the relationship of intelligence, palmistry, and phrenology. Binet and Henri were commissioned in 1896 by the Ministry of Public Education in Paris to recommend procedures whereby children with mental retardation might receive the benefits of an education. Binet claimed that his scale provided a crude means of differentiating between those children who could function in the regular classroom and those who could not.

The Victorian era marked the beginning of modern science and witnessed the influence of Darwinian biology on the studies of individuals. In 1879 in Leipzig, Wundt founded the first psychological laboratory. His work was largely concerned with sensitivity to visual, auditory, and other sensory stimuli and simple reaction time. He followed scientific procedures and rigorously controlled observations. He influenced the measurement movement by using methodology that required precision, accuracy, order, and reproducibility of data and findings. The interest in the exceptional individual broadened to include personality and behavior. Freud, Charcot, and Pinel were interested in individuals with personal and social judgment problems.

Many of the innovations and changes in the testing movement resulted from major crises. Both World War I and World War II stimulated major movements in testing. The armed services found that they needed a quick way of screening the level of mental functioning of recruits. They adapted the work of Otis, who developed an objective group test of intelligence and created the Army Alpha. The original purpose of the army test was to identify those recruits whose lower intelligence would create problems for the military organization. The typical recruit had only a fifth-grade education, and many candidates were illiterate. Another problem was that America had many foreign-born candidates who had little command of the English language and thereby required a nonverbal test or pictorial form with pantomime substituted for written directions. This became the Army Beta.

The first major personality assessment was also developed for use during World War I. The armed services wanted a way to screen individuals with psychosis and other emotional disabilities. Such a test was developed from the Woodworth Personal Data Sheet, a forerunner of the modern adjustment inventories.

The successful use of tests by the armed services led to widespread adoption of tests in education and industry. Other factors also contributed to the acceptance of tests. The growth in population, free public education, compulsory school attendance laws, and the increase in students going on to institutions of higher education all were factors that changed the philosophy and practice of testing. In addition, the egalitarian, political, and philosophical movements that championed integration, women's rights, rights of exceptional children and adults, and minority and ethnic group heritage influenced how people viewed testing. Tests were criticized for cultural bias, gender bias, unfairness to minority groups, and unfairness to groups with disabilities. These criticisms led to improved review procedures for the selection of test items and the selection of norming samples.

In recent years, however, the prevailing political philosophy in the United States has changed from a liberal to a more conservative orientation, which has caused a shift from open, humanistic education to back-to-basics and competency-based approaches. There are national assessment, state assessment, and minimum- and essential-level skills tests.

The testing movement has also been affected by technology. The computer has changed the scope and direction of test administration, scoring, and interpretation. Computer-based and computer-adaptive testing and myriad software packages exist to help score and interpret everything from biographical data blanks to the Rorschach test.

CURRENT ISSUES

Testing has had a history of controversy, both within the field and outside it. Some of the issues involved are recurrent and will be discussed again in other chapters. A test user, though, needs to be aware of the problem areas and learn to follow proper legal and ethical guidelines. It is best to anticipate problem areas and be proactive in communication rather than being surprised by criticism and becoming defensive. The following statements reflect some of the current issues, complaints, and controversies:

1. Testing is an invasion of privacy.
2. Tests are gender-biased and use inappropriate language, examples, and illustrations.
3. Tests are culturally biased; they are unfair and discriminate against minority groups.
4. Tests may be self-incriminating, and individuals should have the right to rebuttal.
5. Criterion-referenced tests should be used rather than norm-referenced tests.
6. Coaching will help performance of clients on scholastic aptitude tests.
7. Intelligence tests are not measuring the right constructs.
8. There are genetic differences in intelligence.
9. We cannot rely on grades and diplomas; we must have demonstration of competencies on objective tests.
10. Every school scores above the median on achievement tests. The norms are not valid; this is known as the Lake Woebegone effect.
11. Athletes should meet the same standards on the SAT as other students. Only a small percentage graduate from college.
12. Multiple-choice tests need to be replaced by authentic and performance assessment.
13. There is too much emphasis on testing and teachers teach for the tests.
14. There is too much pressure on students, teachers, and parents because of high-stakes testing, now the "in" approach in schools.
15. Psychological testing of students is intrusive meddling.

Of concern to many educators, teachers, students, and the public is the use of *high-stakes testing* in schools. These are primarily achievement tests and are used to assess student progression in three areas: reading, mathematics, and science. Some of the key data needing analysis are how well the students are performing, how well the schools are performing, and how well the students understand how much they are being taught. The tests are based on the state standards and assess student knowledge through four different kinds of questions:

1. multiple-choice items
2. guided-response items
3. short-response tasks
4. extended-response tasks

Ryan (2002), among other researcher-evaluators, feels that tests should be carefully selected and that the consequences of test results should be studied. There are a number of potentially serious consequences, such as promotion to the next grade level, certification, and award of salary. Tests can provide a critical measure of knowledge, skills, and abilities, but if used inappropriately, such measures can have negative and adverse consequences.

SUMMARY

The testing movement is about 100 years old. Some tests were developed and used in the 19th century, but the major developments have occurred in the 20th century. A number of social and political factors stimulated the movement. World War I and and World War II had an impact on how tests were scored and the content of the items on the tests. Group tests were developed in almost all fields of testing. Nonverbal tests such as the Army Beta demonstrated the utility of the format to other types of content. Test developers during the early half of the century believed "if something exists, it can be measured."

In the last half of the 20th century, psychometric procedures influenced the structure of the test and how it was administered and scored. The tools and theories of testing went through an evolution of change, and continue to do so with computer-based and computer-adaptive methods, making testing quicker and more accessible to the user.

QUESTIONS FOR DISCUSSION

1. What tests have you taken during your lifetime? For what purposes were they given? How can you organize the tests into categories? In what ways was the testing valuable to you? What type of feedback did you get about the results?

2. What types of changes have you noticed in tests and/or testing over time?

3. Should all tests be considered within a framework of cultural diversity? Are any tests culture-free, can a true culture-free test be constructed?

4. Should knowledge of the historical foundations of testing be a competency required by workers in the helping professions? Why or why not?

SUGGESTED ACTIVITIES

1. Interview individuals who are working in the helping professions to find out what tests they regularly use.

2. Secure a study guide for school counseling and mental health counseling certification and take the practice tests included in the manual.

3. Discuss the issue you think is most important for counselors to address.

ADDITIONAL READINGS

American Counseling Association. (2005). *ACA Code of ethics.* Alexandria, VA: Author.

Bringmann, W. G. (Ed.). (1997). *A pictorial history of psychology.* Chicago: Quintessence.
Brief biographies and pictures of important contributors to the history of psychology.

Clarke, M., Madaus, G., Horn, C., & Ramos, M. (2001). The marketplace for educational testing. *National Board on Educational Testing and Public Policy Statements, 2*(3), 1–11.

DuBois, P. H. (1970). *A history of psychological testing.* Boston: Allyn & Bacon.
The text has five chapters and covers early psychological testing, invention of the individual scales, invention of group tests, personality questionnaires, and the modern period in psychometrics.

Flanagan, D. P., Genshaft, J. L., & Harrison, P. L. (Eds.). (1997). *Contemporary intellectual assessment.* New York: Guilford Press.
Three chapters in Part One are valuable to readers interested in the early history of intelligence tests, the history of test development and test interpretation, and the history of intelligence.

Maxmen, J. S., & Ward, N. G. (1995). *Essential psychopathology and its treatment* (2nd ed.). New York: W. W. Norton.

Prediger, D. J. (Ed.). (1993, March). *Multicultural assessment standards.* Alexandria, VA: Association for Assessment in Counseling.

Ryan, K. (2002). Assessment validation in the context of high-stakes assessment. *Educational Measurement: Issues and Practices, 21,* 7–15.

Seligman, L. (1998). *Selecting effective treatments. A comprehensive, systematic guide to treatment of mental disorders.* San Francisco: Jossey-Bass.

Sternberg, R. J., & Berg, C. A. (Eds.) (1992). *Intellectual development.* New York: Cambridge University Press.

Suzuki, L. A., Ponterotto, J. G., & Meller, P. J. (Eds.). (2000). *Handbook of multicultural assessment: Clinical, psychological, and educational applications* (2nd ed.). San Francisco: Jossey-Bass.
Contains sections on general multicultural assessment issues, personality assessment, assessment of cognitive abilities, and daily living assessment.

2 Statistical Concepts

OVERVIEW

Workers in the helping professions collect much data on individuals or groups. Statistics provide a means to organize and interpret the data in a way that can be quantified. Statistics play a major role in assessment and measurement. They provide rules and procedures to help summarize and describe data. They pro- vide a frame of reference for interpreting and evaluating test scores. Statistics also help evaluate the psychometric properties of tests or assessment instruments. For example, correlational techniques are used to compute many of the validity and reliability coefficients discussed in Chapter 3 and 4.

OBJECTIVES

After studying this chapter, you should be able to

✔ List characteristics of the four scales of measurement

✔ Explain ways to organize and present test data

✔ Understand measures of central tendency

✔ Understand measures of the variability of scores

✔ Identify shapes and types of distributions

✔ Interpret indexes of relative position

✔ Discuss ways of comparing individual performance on two different tests

10

a score of 0 indicate an absence of a trait or characteristic, and does someone with an IQ of 100 have twice as much intelligence as a person with an IQ of 50?

Ratio Scale

Ratio measurement consists of a true or absolute zero point in addition to ranking and equal intervals. Measures such as height and weight are examples of ratio scales. Response time is often an important ratio measurement in interpreting standardized tests: 2 minutes are twice as much as 1, and there is a true zero point. Both the interval and ratio scale have interval properties and utilize the same statistical procedures.

WHAT SCORES LOOK LIKE

Often a visual picture of what the scores look like is needed. For example, a large number of tests might be organized by setting up the frequency distribution into some type of graphic presentation such as a histogram or frequency polygon.

Let's suppose we have just tested incarcerated youth who have been assigned to our cottage in a correctional facility. The scores of the Nowicki-Strickland Locus of Control Scale, Slosson Intelligence Test, and the Jesness Behavior Checklist are listed in Table 2.1. Assume we have the scores of 30 youths.

Let's look first at the scores on the Nowicki-Strickland test, given in the column headed "LOC." The scale purports to measure locus of control as defined by Rotter (1966). The test measures generalized expectancies for internal versus external control of reinforcement among children. Low scores indicate internality; high scores indicate externality. As the scores are listed, it is hard to get a picture of the characteristics of this group of offenders. To visualize the data better we could arrange the scores from high to low.

15	9, 9, 9	6, 6	3, 3, 3
14	8, 8, 8	5, 5, 5, 5	2, 2, 2
13	7, 7	4, 4, 4, 4, 4	1

Arranging the scores in order helps us to see some trends in the data more quickly. We can determine at a glance the highest score and the lowest score, and we can find the approximate middle. However, when a large number of test scores has a greater range (the spread between the high and low scores), it is not as easy to organize and record the scores and see an overall picture.

Frequency Distribution

A frequency distribution is a way of summarizing and visually presenting aspects of the test data (see Table 2.2).

These steps must be followed to complete the distribution:

1. Identify three columns to record (a) each score value, (b) a tally of the scores of each score value, and (c) a sum of each tally (frequency).

Table 2.1
Scores on the Nowicki-Strickland Locus of Control Scale (LOC), Slosson Intelligence Test (SIT), and Jesness Behavior Checklist* for Cottage 1.

Youth	LOC	SIT	AC	IS	CA	SO	CO	EN	RA	CM	IN	SC	CS	RE	FR	UN
1	1	110	12	27	24	17	23	18	22	20	13	12	28	37	18	26
2	3	120	18	27	28	23	27	16	20	24	15	18	29	33	19	34
3	5	99	15	30	20	21	28	23	19	21	12	16	31	34	18	27
4	3	95	12	22	23	16	22	18	19	21	19	15	26	33	19	33
5	8	93	12	28	18	17	25	18	22	19	12	15	30	36	18	26
6	3	112	15	24	24	20	20	17	22	22	20	12	24	35	19	29
7	9	108	13	26	16	15	23	15	19	17	19	16	18	34	15	31
8	8	82	9	21	19	16	22	16	14	16	18	11	22	30	11	24
9	2	115	11	30	21	17	23	18	19	24	20	18	25	41	21	26
10	14	70	19	20	19	22	21	18	21	14	14	15	30	40	17	30
11	9	99	20	28	22	25	27	13	25	21	13	16	23	37	21	35
12	5	83	8	24	23	15	18	22	18	18	10	9	24	34	15	17
13	5	88	17	29	19	22	26	20	23	18	16	18	24	29	16	31
14	15	75	12	21	15	15	20	15	17	18	17	11	19	34	18	26
15	6	102	15	25	21	21	29	16	19	16	16	14	28	32	16	32
16	7	76	13	28	16	17	19	13	14	19	17	16	22	32	16	27
17	3	85	16	28	15	21	25	17	16	19	17	17	32	41	19	30
18	2	112	14	29	21	19	24	20	18	21	20	18	25	40	20	32
19	13	79	13	17	20	14	27	17	12	18	15	12	25	18	16	25
20	2	117	16	24	22	22	23	17	15	15	15	15	25	32	16	28
21	4	113	15	27	16	20	23	18	22	17	15	15	29	33	22	27
22	9	91	9	27	17	11	18	14	21	16	15	12	26	32	14	18
23	6	107	9	20	18	15	29	16	18	13	18	15	22	28	14	29
24	5	105	18	28	25	23	24	16	20	20	17	15	25	35	19	26
25	4	109	15	27	22	22	22	19	15	20	17	15	26	39	15	23
26	4	107	18	25	25	22	30	17	17	18	18	19	29	38	18	33
27	7	83	17	27	23	22	21	16	23	21	18	15	27	33	17	28
28	4	111	16	16	16	20	25	8	16	13	11	18	21	34	20	32
29	4	109	9	20	13	13	20	18	14	14	16	12	23	28	13	19
30	8	101	17	27	19	21	26	13	21	10	16	16	28	33	20	27

*The Jesness scales are Anger Control (AC), Insight (IS), Calmness (CA), Sociability (SO), Conformity (CO), Enthusiasm (EN), Rapport (RA), Communication (CM), Independence (IN), Social Concern (SC), Consideration (CS), Responsibility (RE), Friendliness (FR), and Unobtrusiveness (UN).

2. Arrange the scores from high to low in the first column and complete the other two columns as indicated.

A frequency distribution helps to summarize the test data on a particular scale by arranging the scores in order of magnitude and indicating how often each score was obtained.

Sometimes there is a greater range of scores because there are more items on the test and greater variability of performance among the test takers. In such a situation it

Table 2.2
Frequency distribution of the
Nowicki-Strickland Locus of
Control Scale.

Score Value	Tally	Frequency
15	/	1
14	/	1
13	/	1
12		0
11		0
10		0
9	///	3
8	///	3
7	//	2
6	//	2
5	////	4
4	/////	5
3	////	4
2	///	3
1	/	1

is easier to group a series of score values; that grouping is called a *class interval.* We can visualize a frequency distribution if it has between 10 and 20 score intervals. The following formula can be used to determine the range of test score points that should be included in each interval:

$$\text{Class interval size} = \frac{\text{highest score} - \text{lowest score}}{\text{desired number of class intervals}}$$

If we establish 15 as the desired number of class intervals, then the difference between the highest and lowest scores is divided by 15, and the result is an estimate of the number of test score points to be included in each interval.

Let's turn back to Table 2.1 and look at the IQ scores, listed under "SIT," for the 30 youths. The Slosson Intelligence Test, an individually administered test, yields a total intelligence score measuring verbal reasoning, vocabulary knowledge, numerical reasoning, and abstract reasoning. To produce a group frequency distribution, we follow these steps:

1. Select the number of class intervals to be used.   10
2. Find the highest score.   120
3. Find the lowest score.   70
4. Subtract the lowest from the highest score.   50
5. Divide the range by the size of the class interval
   selected to determine the number of score points   5
   to be included in each interval.   10)‾50‾
6. Start the frequency distribution with the lowest score.

As we can see from Table 2.3, the grouped frequency distribution provides a good picture of the ability of the group. Because each interval consists of 5 test score points,

Table 2.3
Group frequency distribution on the Slosson Intelligence Test.

Class Interval	Tally	Frequency
120–124	/	1
115–119	//	2
110–114	/////	5
105–109	//////	6
100–104	//	2
95–99	///	3
90–94	//	2
85–89	//	2
80–84	///	3
75–79	///	3
70–74	/	1

we lose information about the individual scores. However, the grouping makes the data easier to interpret because there are fewer intervals—only 11 instead of the 51 there would be if individual scores with intervals of 1 were considered.

GRAPHIC PRESENTATIONS

Two types of graphic presentations of test data will be considered here: the histogram or bar graph and the frequency polygon, a line graph. Some people prefer a visual mode of learning, and a graph often clarifies and simplifies the presentation of the data.

A *histogram* is a type of bar graph frequently used to portray the distribution of test data. Figure 2.1 shows the histogram of the locus of control scores from Table 2.1.

Figure 2.1
Histogram of Slosson Intelligence Test scores.

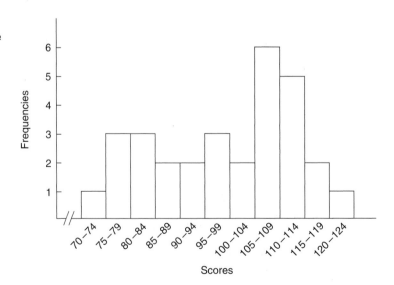

The ordinate, or *y* axis (vertical line), represents the frequencies of scores appearing at each score level. The abscissa, or *x* axis, represents the score points. The intersection of the *x* and *y* axes represents the zero point for each.

A *frequency polygon* is another type of line graph that is used to portray test data. The midpoint of each score interval is used to help plot the graph. In the group frequency distribution of scores on the Slosson Intelligence Test, a score interval of 5 was used. Thus, the midpoint of the interval 70–74 is 72. If the class interval consists of an odd number of score points, the midpoint is a whole number; if it contains an even number of points, the midpoint is expressed as a decimal number such as 1.5. Table 2.4 presents information on how the size of the class interval relates to the midpoint. A frequency polygon of the SIT scores is presented in Figure 2.2. If there were many more individuals and a greater number of intervals, the frequency polygon would reflect a smoother curve. The shape of the curve provides useful information

Table 2.4
Size of class interval, score range, and midpoint.

Size of Class Interval	Scores	Midpoint
2	70, 71	70.5
3	70, 71, 72	71
4	70, 71, 72, 73	71.5
5	70, 71, 72, 73, 74	72
6	70, 71, 72, 73, 74, 75	72.5
7	70, 71, 72, 73, 74, 75, 76	73
8	70, 71, 72, 73, 74, 75, 76, 77	73.5
9	70, 71, 72, 73, 74, 75, 76, 77, 78	74
10	70, 71, 72, 73, 74, 75, 76, 77, 78, 79	74.5

Figure 2.2
Frequency polygon of scores on the SIT.

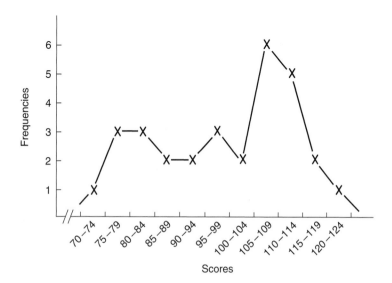

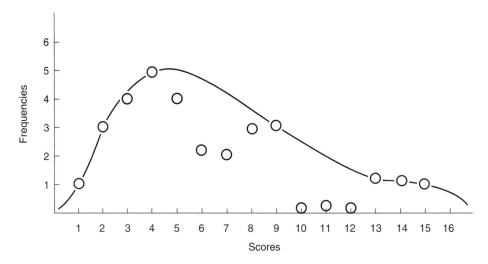

Figure 2.3
Frequency polygon of locus-of-control curves, smoothed.

for the test administrator. When the curve is smoothed out, it gives a better idea of the shape of the distribution as well as the frequency of the scores. If we made the intervals progressively smaller and increased the number of individuals tested on the Nowicki-Strickland Locus of Control Scale, the distribution might look like that shown in Figure 2.3.

Symmetry and Skewness

When we interpret the curve for a test, we evaluate two major characteristics: symmetry and skewness. There are two important types of curves: asymmetrical and symmetrical. The curve for locus-of-control scores is an asymmetrical curve. The curve for the intelligence scores, when smoothed, is more of a symmetrical curve, like that shown in Figure 2.4. In a symmetrical distribution each side is a mirror image of the other. Later, when we look at interpretation of tests, we will focus on the normal curve, which is a special type of symmetrical curve.

The distribution of locus-of-control scores is a positively skewed distribution. Most of the youths scored near the lower end of the distribution; they were internal in their orientation. A few youths had high scores and were external in their orientation.

If we smoothed the frequency polygon for the scores on the Jesness scales, we would see that most of the scores occur at the higher score levels, with very few scores at the lower levels. This distribution would be negatively skewed. Most of the youths related their social behavior very positively. The majority of the youths had low scores on the Nowicki-Strickland but high scores on the Jesness.

On criterion-referenced tests, in which students tend to get most of the items right, scores pile up at the upper end of the distribution. When tests are easy, most

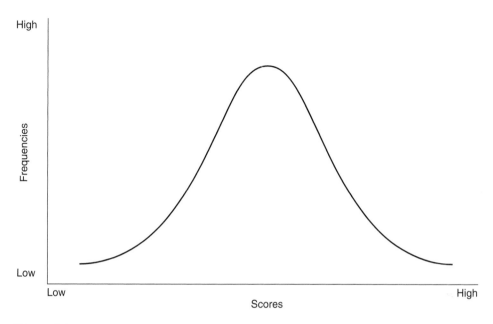

Figure 2.4
Symmetrical distribution.

individuals achieve high scores and thus the distribution will be negatively skewed. When test items are difficult, the test takers tend to make low scores on the test and thus the scores pile up at the lower end of the distribution. A few individuals will make high scores. This distribution is positively skewed. The two types of distributions are compared in Figure 2.5.

MEASURES OF CENTRAL TENDENCY

We often want to know about the typical or average performance of a group on a particular test. There are three measures of central tendency: mode, mean, and median. In part, the measure of central tendency depends on the scale of measurement used. With nominal data the only measure of central tendency is the mode. With ordinal data the median as well as the mode can be used. With the interval and ratio scale all three measures of central tendency can be used. The *mode* is the score or number that appears most frequently. The *mean* is the arithmetic average. The *median* is the middle score, or 50th percentile.

Mode

The mode is the score or numerical value that appears most frequently in a set of scores. In the ordering of the scores on the Nowicki-Strickland scale (see Table 2.2),

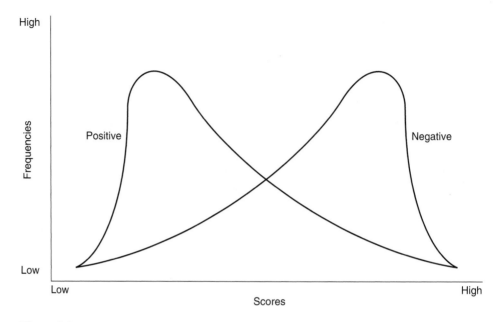

Figure 2.5
Positively skewed and negatively skewed distributions compared.

the mode is 4. For the Anger Control scale on the Jesness, try to determine the mode yourself: Is the mode 9, 12, or 15?

Sometimes there is a *bimodal* or *multimodal* distribution; in other words, two or more scores may appear most frequently in the distribution. In the distribution of scores on the Friendliness scale, the same number of people have scores of 16, 18, and 19. Certain achievement subtests produce a distribution such as the one shown in Figure 2.6. Girls tend to score higher than boys on certain scales, and vice versa, thus producing a bimodal distribution.

The mode is often used as a quick measure of central tendency, but it is affected by various factors, such as the number of people taking the test. When the group is small, the mode does not always reflect typical performance within the group. In a negatively or positively skewed distribution, the mode is often not an accurate measure of central tendency.

Mean

The mean is the arithmetic average. It is equal to the sum of the scores on a test divided by the number of individuals who took the test.

$$\overline{X} = \frac{\Sigma X}{N}$$

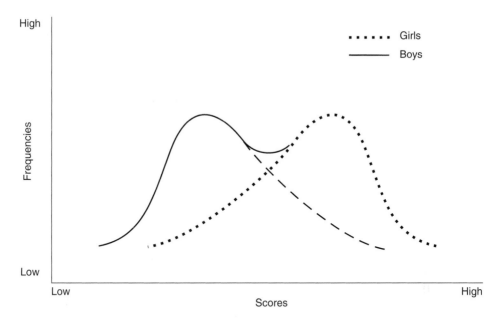

Figure 2.6
Bimodal distribution of boys' and girls' scores on reading achievement tests.

The mean ($\bar{x}$) is equal to the sum (Σ) of the scores (X) divided by the number of individuals (N). If we add together the scores of the 30 individuals taking the Nowicki-Strickland, our total is 178. To compute the mean, we divide 178 by 30. The mean is 5.93.

The mean is the most frequently used measure of central tendency. If we subtract each score from the mean and add up the sum of the differences, the sum is zero. Each score is used to compute the mean, whereas the mode considers only the score with the highest frequency. Extreme scores in the distribution affect the mean. A few extremely low scores will move the mean down; extremely high scores will move it up.

Median

The median is the middle score, or the score that divides a distribution in half; 50% of the scores will fall below the median and 50% will fall above. The median score on the Nowicki-Strickland is 5. When a set of scores consists of an odd number, the median is the middle score. For example, if the scores are 4, 6, and 8, the median is 6. With an even number of scores—such as 4, 6, 8, and 10—the sum of the two middle scores is divided by 2; the median in this case is 7. Procedures to compute the median from grouped scores in a frequency distribution can be found in most statistical texts.

The median is a better measure of central tendency in a skewed distribution. Extreme scores do not affect it. The relationship of the mean, mode, and median is shown

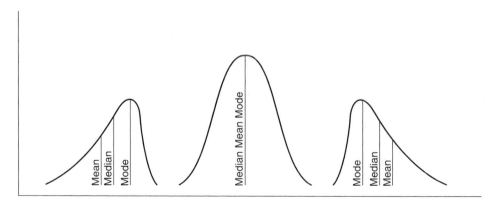

Figure 2.7
Type of distribution and measure of central tendency.

in Figure 2.7 for different types of distributions. The mean, median, and mode have the same score value only in a symmetrical distribution such as the normal curve.

Comparisons of Measures of Central Tendency

No single best measure of central tendency exists. The scale of measurement determines which measure of central tendency can be used, and the purpose of the measure needs to be kept in mind. The mode is the least stable statistic of central tendency. Test makers use the mean and median scores to portray typical or average performance. The mean is a statistic that has algebraic properties; it is used extensively in both descriptive and inferential statistics.

MEASURES OF VARIABILITY

Information about the *variability,* or spread, of the scores is necessary for proper interpretation of the data. Two measures of variability are used most often to interpret test scores: range and standard deviation.

Range

A quick measure of the spread of scores can be obtained by computing the *range.* The range is computed by subtracting the lowest score from the highest score and adding 1 to the difference. If the highest score is 3 and the lowest 1, we add 1 to the difference (2) and calculate the range of 3. The distribution would have three scores: 1, 2, and 3. In the distribution of Nowicki-Strickland scores (Table 2.1), the high score is 15 and the low score is 1, making the range 15 (15−1+1=15).

The range is easy to compute. However, an extreme score in the distribution can make the range a misleading statistic. For example, a test might produce these scores:

$$1, 2, 2, 3, 3, 3, 4, 4, 5, 5, 6, 6, 40$$

The range here would be 40 even though the other scores are grouped closely together.

The range is a valuable statistic for test interpretation, but it is most often used in conjunction with other statistics such as standard deviation and median, mode, and mean. The range helps tell us how compact or expanded the distribution is but does not always reflect the pattern of variation in the distribution of test scores.

Variance

The *variance* is a statistic that provides information on how widely spread, or scattered, the scores are from the mean. The variance is computed by subtracting the mean from each score, squaring the difference, and then computing the average squared difference between the scores and the mean. In the formula, s^2 represents the variance.

$$s^2 = \frac{\Sigma(X - \overline{X})^2}{N}$$

Standard Deviation

The *standard deviation* is the square root of the variance and the most widely used statistic of variability. It is a numerical value that describes the spread of scores away from the mean and is expressed in the same units as the original scores. The wider the spread of scores, the larger the standard deviation. Because there is a small range of scores on the Nowicki-Strickland, just 15 points rather than the 51 points of the SIT, the standard deviation on the Nowicki-Strickland Locus of Control Scale will be smaller than the standard deviation on the SIT. Figure 2.8 presents a hypothetical illustration.

To compute a sample standard deviation, let's use four scores: 3, 5, 5, and 7. First, we compute the mean.

Figure 2.8
Relationship of size of standard deviation to type of distribution.

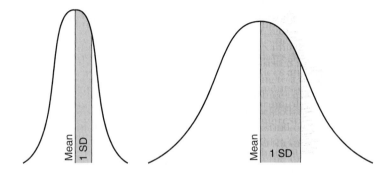

$$3 + 5 + 5 + 7 = 20 \div 4 = 5$$

Second, we subtract the mean from each score, square the difference, and then sum the squared differences.

$3 - 5 = -2$	$-2 \times -2 = +4$
$5 - 5 = 0$	$0 \times 0 = 0$
$5 - 5 = 0$	$0 \times 0 = 0$
$7 - 5 = 2$	$+2 \times +2 = \underline{+4}$
	$+8$

To find the variance, we divide that sum by the number of scores.

$$8 \div 4 = 2$$

The standard deviation is the square root of the variance; the square root of 2 is 1.414.

It is not always convenient to utilize the definitional formula just illustrated because the mean may be a decimal, making arithmetic operations more complex. A computational formula for raw scores is given here and illustrated, using the scores from the previous example and letting s represent the standard deviation.

$$s = \sqrt{\frac{\Sigma X^2}{N} - \overline{X}^2}$$

X	X^2	
3	9	$s = \sqrt{\dfrac{108}{4} - (5)^2}$
5	25	
5	25	$s = \sqrt{27 - 25}$
$\underline{7}$	$\underline{49}$	
20	108	$s = \sqrt{2} = 1.414$

When the scores tend to cluster around the mean, the standard deviation is smaller than when the scores are spread widely around the mean. The standard deviation is an important statistic for interpreting the relative position of an individual within a distribution of test scores. The statistic is stable and is one way of interpreting characteristics of the distribution of the test scores as well as providing a frame of reference for interpreting individual test scores.

MEASURES OF RELATIONSHIP

A statistical measure of *relationship* can show how two variables are related to one another. We might want to correlate the results of tests given on two different occasions or see how equivalent two forms of an intelligence or achievement test are. For tests with predictive purposes, we might want to know the relationship between intelligence and achievement or scholastic ability and grade point average. Or, we might want to correlate two tests that purport to measure the same construct, such as two intelligence tests or two self-concept tests. On other occasions we might want to see whether the scales on a particular test are independent of each other.

To obtain the desired information in these cases, we would use the statistic known as the *correlation coefficient*. Psychologists and counselors use a number of different types of correlational procedures to measure the relationship of variables. In part, the method utilized will depend on the level of measurement of the variables to be compared, the type of distribution of these variables, and the number of cases to be compared.

Pearson Product Moment Correlation

The Pearson Product Moment Correlation can be computed when we have two continuous variables and data from the interval or ratio scales. If we want to see how consistently a group performed on two different administrations of the same test, we can compute the correlation coefficient. In this case it would be the test-retest reliability coefficient. Let's assume the following scores:

Name	First (X)	Second (Y)
John	1	3
Carlo	2	2
Mary	3	4
Aziza	4	6
Heather	5	5

The formula is

$$r = \frac{N(\Sigma XY) - (\Sigma X)(\Sigma Y)}{\sqrt{[N(\Sigma X^2) - (\Sigma X)^2][N(\Sigma Y^2) - (\Sigma Y)^2]}}$$

Our first step would be to add each X value to find the sum (15). Our second step would be to add the Y values (20). We then need to square each of the X and Y scores and total those numbers. Then we must multiply each individual X and Y score. Because we have five sets of scores, $N = 5$.

X	Y	X^2	Y^2	XY
1	3	1	9	3
2	2	4	4	4
3	4	9	16	12
4	6	16	36	24
5	5	25	25	25
15	20	55	90	68

$$r = \frac{5(68) - (15)(20)}{\sqrt{[5(55) - (15)^2][5(90) - (20)^2]}}$$

$$r = \frac{340 - 300}{\sqrt{[275 - 225][450 - 400]}} = \frac{40}{50} = .80$$

Figure 2.9
Bivariate distribution.

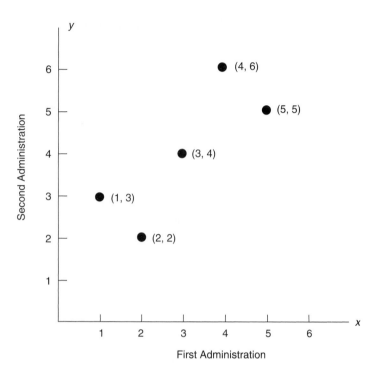

The correlation of .80 indicates a degree of association between the two testings. The correlation coefficient ranges from −1.00 to +1.00. A correlation of zero indicates no relationship. A coefficient of +1.00 indicates a perfect positive relationship.

We could plot the scores using a scatter diagram (see Figure 2.9). The x axis represents the performance on the first test; the y axis represents the performance on the second test. With a correlation of 1.00, we would have a distribution with all the points on a straight line (see Figure 2.10). If there were an inverse relationship, with students performing in reverse order on the two tests, the correlation would be −1.00, and the scores would all fall on a straight line slanted in the opposite direction.

All kinds of combinations of the two sets of scores are possible. The correlation, however, is an index number and we need to square it to find out the percentage of variance in one variable that is predictable from the other variable. The statistic is known as r^2 and is called the *coefficient of determination.* We can use Venn diagrams to illustrate the statistic (see Figure 2.11). The coefficient of determination represents the intersection of two variables and shows the proportion of variability that those variables share.

Regression

One of the major purposes of testing is prediction, and *regression* is one of the primary statistical tools for prediction. Regression analysis provides an equation that describes the relationship between two variables. If we know the correlation between an intelligence test and a reading test, for example, we can predict an individual's reading score from her IQ score. We can compute a regression line if we know the corre-

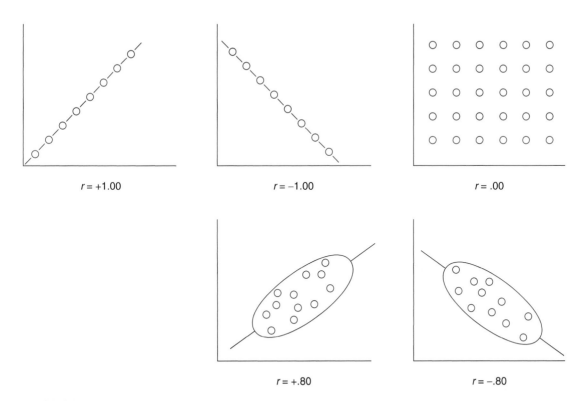

Figure 2.10
Type of distribution and magnitude of correlation coefficient.

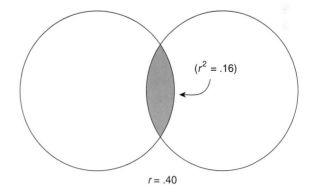

Figure 2.11
Venn diagrams as a way of
representing the coefficient of
determination.

lation between two variables and the means and standard deviations of each. The degree of accuracy of the prediction depends on the strength of the correlation between the two variables. The weaker the relationship, the smaller the error of estimate.

Regression analysis is a method for explaining or predicting the variance of a dependent variable using information about one or more independent variables. The procedure attempts to answer the question of what dependent variable values we can expect given certain independent variable values. Regression analysis can predict the value of one's variable grade point average at the end of the first semester of college by knowing the individual's SAT, level of participation in school activities, and parental education score level.

Factor Analysis

Many tests have been derived from *factor analysis,* which is a statistical technique used to identify how many factors are needed to explain or account for the intercorrelation of a set of variables. Items or scales that belong to a factor typically have moderate to high correlations with the other scales in that factor. Factor analysis is a method that can systematically summarize a large matrix of correlations. If we had 50 variables, we would have a total of 1,225 correlations. Factor analysis helps remove the duplicated information from these sets of variables; it results in a smaller set of derived factors than the original number. Kachigan (1986) identifies five major uses of this technique:

1. To identify underlying factors that make up a large set of variables
2. To screen variables for inclusion in other required statistical analyses that may need to be completed in the future
3. To reduce the number of factors necessary to explain a set of variables
4. To select a small group of representative but uncorrelated variables from among a larger set in order to solve a variety of practical problems
5. To cluster people or objects into homogeneous groups based on their intercorrelations

Johnson and Holland (1986) studied the structure of the 15 Personal Problems Inventory and found that four separate and relatively distinct factors accounted for 62% of the variance: performance anxiety problems, interpersonal problems, intrapersonal problems, and substance abuse problems.

NORMAL CURVE

The *normal curve* has many applications in the field of measurement and evaluation. It is a tool that helps us understand the nature of probability. If we obtained a distribution of most educational and psychological characteristics and graphically depicted that distribution, the scores would fall in a bell-shaped curve called the *normal curve.* The theoretical normal curve serves as an important mathematical model in test interpretation.

The normal curve is a type of symmetrical distribution (see Figure 2.12). It has the following features:

- The mean, mode, and median are the same score.
- Most distributions accumulate near the mean.
- Approximately 68% of the cases fall between −1 and +1 standard deviations.
- Approximately 95% of the cases fall between −2 and +2 standard deviations.
- Approximately 99.5% of the cases fall between −3 and +3 standard deviations.

We will find that errors of measurement and errors of prediction also have a normal distribution, and the table of the normal curve will help us understand the relative nature of those concepts.

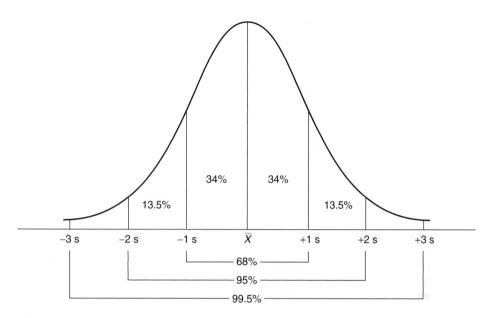

Figure 2.12
Normal curve.

INFERENTIAL STATISTICS

The table of the normal curve is utilized in some types of *inferential statistics.* We often must select samples of individuals because we are unable to test everyone in the population. In such cases, we are interested in seeing whether our sample statistics approximate the population statistics, or whether the observed differences between two groups are probably due to something other than chance. One of the major roles of statistics is to provide an inferential measuring tool, to state our degree of confidence in the accuracy of certain measurements. Another objective is to generalize conclusions beyond the actual sample of observations. Inferential statistics offer the necessary techniques to make statements of certainty that there are real as opposed to chance differences between sets of observations.

An example occurred in the 1978 edition of the Wide Range Achievement Test (WRAT), published by Jastak Assessment/Wide Range. The males and females in each age group were compared to see whether any of the differences were statistically significant, the hypothesis being that there were no significant mean differences in reading between boys and girls. The test manual presents this information (p. 45):

Grade	N	Male Mean	SD	Female Mean	SD	Significance
5.0	200	14.83	7.43	19.31	7.35	.001
5.5	200	18.32	7.65	20.21	7.56	.05

The conclusion is that there are significant differences between reading scores of boys and girls. Girls have significantly higher means than boys. At the beginning fifth-grade level the observed difference would happen only 1 time in 1,000 by chance. At grade 5.5 the observed difference would happen only 5 times out of 100 by chance.

STATISTICAL SOFTWARE

There are a number of widely used statistical software packages available for counselors and helping professionals. SPSS 13.0 is the leading statistical and data management software. This package has programs to help the researcher prepare and manage data and to compute descriptive and bivariate statistics, and is often used for the prediction and identification of groups. Graphic enhancements are available. The manufacturer's Web site is *www.spss.com*.

SUMMARY

Statistics provide test developers and users with a way to collect, organize, and interpret assessment data. Counselors use both descriptive and inferential statistics. Descriptive statistics are used to describe a set of data. There are four scales of measurement: nominal, ordinal, interval, and ratio. The type of scale of measurement and the size of the sample being tested influence what statistics are computed. Many times the counselor has to work with small samples of clients or students because the data is hard to collect. Inferential statistics are used to draw inferences on the population being studied.

There are three measures of central tendency: the mean, median, and mode. The mode is the most frequently appearing score; the mean is the arithmetic average; and the median is the middle score. Counselors also need to investigate the variability of the scores. There are several statistics that can be computed. The range is the high score minus the low score. The mean deviation involves subtracting each of the scores from the mean and then looking at the average deviation. The variance and standard deviation are two measures of variability that are most often reported in test development and interpretation. The square root of the variance is the standard deviation.

Measures of relationships are often used in determining the technical quality of tests and in prediction studies. Correlations are used to compute the reliability and validity of tests. There are a number of statistics that measure relationships, depending on what scale of measurement the correlation is. Besides being used to judge the reliability of the variables, correlation is used to predict how well the test evidences criterion validity. The coefficient of determination, or r^2, tells us how much variance is accounted for. Factor analysis is used in constructing new tests and providing evidence of the construct validity of tests.

Test makers utilize inferential statistics to answer questions like these:

1. Are there statistically significant gender differences in test scores? Recently, one study claimed that the SAT is an unfair instrument to use for assigning scholarship awards because males score significantly higher than females on the test.

2. Are there differences on the scales of the test between normally functioning individuals and those who have psychopathologies?
3. Are there statistically significant racial or cultural differences reflected in test performance?
4. Is the correlation coefficient between achievement and aptitude significantly different from chance for the sample selected?

QUESTIONS FOR DISCUSSION

1. What are the four scales of measurement, and what are the advantages and disadvantages of each? Give examples of each type of scale.
2. What are the three measures of central tendency, and what are the strengths and weaknesses of each?
3. Why is variability an important construct in testing? What are the measures of dispersion used in testing?
4. Why are measures of relationship important to measurement consumers? What is the coefficient of determination, and how is it used?
5. What are the uses of inferential statistics in measurement contexts? Discuss the uses of multivariate statistical approaches such as factor analysis.

SUGGESTED ACTIVITIES

1. Study a test manual and identify the different types of statistics reported. Make an annotated set of cards with definitions and illustrations of the statistics identified.
2. Compute the mean, mode, and median of the Anger Control and Calmness scores that are included in Table 2.1.
3. Compute the standard deviations and range of the Anger Control and Calmness scores that are included in Table 2.1.
4. Compute a Pearson correlation between anger control and calmness.
5. Construct a frequency distribution of the Sociability or Conformity scales reported in Table 2.1. Then make a histogram and frequency polygon of the scores.

ADDITIONAL READINGS

Jaeger, R. M. (1990). *Statistics: A spectator sport* (2nd ed.). Newbury Park, CA: Sage.
Describes basic statistical concepts using nontechnical terms and real-world examples. Includes measures of central tendency, variability, correlation, and some fundamentals of measurement.

Kachigan, S. K. (1986). *Statistical analysis: An interdisciplinary introduction to univariate and multivariate methods.* New York: Radius Press.

This text is designed to provide readers with an overview of univariate and multivariate methods of statistical analysis. It provides information verbally, geometrically, graphically, and by example.

Kirkpatrick, L. A., & Feeney, B. C. (2000). *A simple guide to SPSS for Windows* (Revised). Belmont, CA: Wadsworth.

Kline, P. (2000). *Handbook of psychological testing.* NY: Routledge.

Presents a comprehensive overview of psychometric theory, including chapters on factor analysis and clinical models of test errors, and lists the statistical formulae used in testing. This is one of the major statistical packages available for computing statistics using the PC. The package can be used to compute nearly all of the statistical procedures used in test construction and test interpretation.

Sheskin, D. J. (2000). *Handbook of parametric and nonparametric statistical procedures* (2nd ed.). Boca Raton, FL: CRC Press.

3 Understanding Test Scores

OVERVIEW

A clear understanding of scoring is important. Scoring errors can affect how a test score is interpreted. The test publisher has certain responsibilities in making clear to the examiner how a test is to be scored, and the examiner has the specific responsibility of ensuring that the test will be scored correctly. Then, depending on the test, some system is used to give meaning to the score.

Intrepreting test scores can involve relating the score to a performance level or comparing it to the scores of the standardizing or norming group. Scores on tests can be compared with a norming group, with content on the test, or with previous achievement of an individual or class.

OBJECTIVES

After studying this chapter, you should be able to

✔ Discuss the important components relative to scoring and interpreting tests

✔ Discuss different types of test scores

✔ Discuss frameworks used to interpret test scores

TEST SCORES

Imagine you receive a grade of 60 for a midterm exam in one of your university classes. What does the score mean, and how should we interpret it? By itself, the number has no meaning at all and cannot be interpreted. We can't determine if it's a perfect score, a failing score, or anything in between. A score has meaning only when there is some standard with which to compare it. Part of the process of understanding test scores is transforming a raw score into a transformed score. This gives meaning to the test score and allows some kind of interpretation of the score.

SCORING AND INTERPRETING TESTS

Scoring errors can affect how a score is interpreted. The test maker has certain responsibilities in making clear to the examiner how the test is to be scored. In addition, the examiner has specific responsibilities to ensure that the test is scored correctly. Most often the examiner calculates how many test answers fit a predetermined key or criterion. That number yields a raw score. Then, depending on the type of test score, some system is used to give meaning to the score. With criterion- or domain-referenced tests, such as a test measuring mastery of basic addition facts, the interpretation of scores relates to a functional performance level. With norm-referenced tests such as the Stanford Achievement Test, the interpretation of the scores is compared to the performance of the standardization or norming group. Counselors must proceed with caution when interpreting performances of minority group members or persons who are not represented in the norm group on which the instrument was standardized (National Board for Certified Counselors [NBCC], 2005).

MODELS OF SCORING

There are three primary models for scoring tests: cumulative, class, and ipsative (Hammer, 1992). *Cumulative* models assume that the number of items endorsed or responded to that match the key represent the degree of the construct or trait the test measured. The higher the score, the greater the degree of the construct present. Many achievement, aptitude, and personality tests are based on this model. These tests often involve differential weighing of items before summing the items (e.g., individual IQ tests such as the Wechsler Intelligence Scale for Children and the Wechsler Adult Intelligence Scale).

A second model is the *class* model that is used to categorize individuals for the purpose of description or prediction. Criterion-referenced and mastery tests fall within this category. Responses may be added to compute a score, but are used only to determine whether the person falls in the appropriate category. Many licensure and certification examinations use this model.

The third is an *ipsative* model. The test taker's scores on various scales within the test are compared to each other and yield a profile of the individual. Certain personality, interest, and value tests utilize this model. The individual ranks the responses internally and the ranks cannot be treated normatively.

EXAMPLES OF TEST SCORING

Some tests demand that the test scorer judge the degree of correctness of the response or compare the responses to standards provided. For example, essay questions on many college placement examinations are scored using a holistic scoring procedure. The raters have model answers that have been given certain weights, and they compare the examinee's essays to these. Such raters are asked to assess answers on a 4-point scale and make an overall rating, or holistic judgment, rather than assign a certain number of points to each possible component of the answer.

Many of the individual intelligence tests require the examiner to rate answers on a 2-point scale. For example, criterion might be the degree of abstractness or cognitive level of the answer. One child might say that orange "is a color" and receive 1 point; another child might say that an orange "is a reddish yellow citrus fruit containing vitamin C" and receive 2 points. Most test manuals have an elaborate explanation of scoring procedures and examples of typical responses of correct and incorrect answers, or 1-point and 2-point answers.

Examiners are expected to have supervised training before they use tests in which clinical judgment is necessary for scoring. In most situations dealing with individual intelligence testing, examiners are not making blind judgments and need to be alert to factors that may bias their judgment or influence the type of answers the clients give.

On most pencil-and-paper tests there is a predetermined key and a right or wrong answer for each item or a scoring key for a specific scale. These tests don't require individual judgment, but they do require accuracy in calculating the number of right or appropriate answers.

Scoring Alternate and Authentic Assessment

For certain types of tests and items the scorer has to be given a scoring rubric. Sometimes there are alternative answers that are considered "right." On writing samples, for instance, holistic scoring procedures are often used. The reader compares the writing of the student against a model. For example, the scorer might have five levels for comparison: a model of an excellent paragraph, a model of a very good paragraph, a model of a good paragraph, a model of a poor paragraph, and a model of a very poor paragraph. The examiner tries to sort the papers into these five piles.

Sometimes scorers find that there is more than one possible answer to a question. In this case, examiners need the general criteria as well as a list of alternate acceptable responses. They must also check for consistency in scoring. Many times, at least two readers score each paper; if there are discrepancies, the paper is checked by a third reviewer. Workshops for scoring and frequency consistency checks often improve reliability of the scoring, and renewal sessions for readers allow them to review responses from earlier tests. Advance placement tests and many state assessment tests use procedures similar to these to maintain scoring consistency.

CRITERION- AND NORM-REFERENCED INTERPRETATION

Raw scores have to be translated into some frame of reference to give meaning to test results. Two major approaches are criterion-referenced and norm-referenced interpretation. Overall, the examiner has to ask two questions about test scores:

1. What is the nature of the score itself: What types of scoring or scaling procedures were used to arrive at the score?
2. What type of system is going to be used to interpret the score?

The examiner must know the advantages and disadvantages of each type of score and be alert to the best way of displaying and explaining the scores on a test.

CRITERION-REFERENCED INTERPRETATION

Tests should measure how well students meet instructional objectives. In *criterion-referenced* evaluation, a student's performance is compared to established criteria rather than to the performance of other students. The criteria are the basis of evaluating student progress. Many states and school districts have set standards or competencies for students to meet, for example, mastery of essential or basic skills. Criterion-referenced evaluation should be used to evaluate student performance in classrooms. It is referenced to criteria based on learning outcomes described in the curriculum. The criteria reflect a student's performance based on specific learning activities. The individual's score is interpreted in absolute terms, such as the percentage of correct answers. The percentage of correct answers is most widely used in reporting the results of criterion-referenced tests. Table 3.1 identifies steps that may be used in criterion-referenced evaluation. Table 3.2 illustrates criterion-referenced interpretation.

Table 3.1
Steps in criterion-referenced evaluation.

Step 1	Identify the expected learning outcomes and competencies.
Step 2	Develop learning activities appropriate to each competency area.
Step 3	Provide examples of the desired levels of performance.
Step 4	Implement the learning activities.
Step 5	Assessment: Evaluate the learning activity based on the particular assignment and student.
Step 6	Review the assessment data and evaluate each student's level of performance or quality of work in relation to competency.

Table 3.2
Examples of criterion-referenced interpretation.

Writing Tasks	Right Answers	Criterion Needed	Skill Achieved
1. Identify the plural form of nouns.	4	¾	Yes
2. Use the appropriate forms of common regular verbs.	5	⅘	Yes
3. Make subjects and verbs agree.	4	⅘	Yes
4. Use the appropriate forms of common irregular verbs.	8	⁷⁄₁₀	Yes
5. Include necessary information from a phone message.	3	¾	Yes
6. Include necessary information in a written message.	5	⅘	Yes
7. Identify correct spelling of common words.	5	⁷⁄₁₀	No
8. Use commas to separate words in a series.	5	⅘	Yes
9. Use commas to separate elements in an address.	2	¾	No

NORM-REFERENCED INTERPRETATION

In *norm-referenced* interpretation, we compare an individual's test performance to that of some other, larger group. Sometimes it is important for the examiner to be able to differentiate among test takers or to discriminate among individuals on the domain being measured. The procedures used to discriminate or differentiate individual performance are based on the use of statistics of variability and central tendency. For example, T scores have a fixed mean and standard deviation and can be used to compare how high or low a score is in a distribution.

Norm-referenced test scores can be expressed in a number of different ways. In general, the interest is in the relative position of the individual within the group or in comparison to a norming group. A number of different systems can be used to express the individual's position. Two of the major methods are the use of percentiles and standard scores.

Percentiles

Percentile ranks are one of the most widely used methods to express the relative position of the test taker on a norm-referenced test. Such rankings range from 1 to 99 and tell the percentage of persons in the norming group who score at or below that particular score. A percentile rank of 50 is the median; a test taker who has a percentile rank of 15 would surpass 15% of the norming group. *Percentile rank, percentile score,* and *percentile* are used interchangeably. Table 3.3 illustrates percentile ranks.

Many standardized tests report a *percentile band* rather than a single percentile score. A percentile band is the range of percentile scores in which a test taker would be expected to score on repeated testing. The use of percentile bands takes into account measurement error as a way to avoid over-interpretation of test results and determine where the examinee's true test score may lie. The upper part of the band

Table 3.3
Simulated percentile norms from a mathematics reasoning test for grade 8.

Raw Score	Percentile Rank
45	99
44	99
43	97
42	96
41	94
40	89
39	85
38	81
//	//
31	52
30	50
29	45
//	//
15	5
14	4
13	3
12	2
0–11	1

Note: //= Omission of some scores.

Table 3.4
Use of percentile bands.

Test	Raw Score	Percentile Band
Reading	123	55%–75%
Mathematics	140	91%–99%
Listening	132	71%–89%
Social Studies	111	17%–49%

corresponds approximately to the percentile rank of a score one standard error of measurement above the obtained raw score. Likewise, the lower part of the band corresponds to the percentile rank of the score one standard error below the obtained raw score. For example, if a student had a raw score of 35, and if the standard error of measurement were 5, the percentile band would range from the 30th percentile to the 40th percentile. The Comprehensive Test of Basic Skills utilizes this format. Table 3.4 illustrates the use of percentile bands.

Standard Scores

Standard scores are a means of presenting the relative position of an individual on a test; such scores describe how many standard deviations an individual's score is from the mean. The standard deviation of the test becomes its yardstick. There are a variety of types of standard scores: z scores, T scores, deviation IQS, stanine, sten scores, and other standard score scales.

z Scores.   The z score is computed using this formula:

$$z = \frac{x - \bar{x}}{s}$$

In the formula, z = standard score, $\bar{x}$ = a given raw score on a test, $\bar{x}$ = the mean on the test, and s = the standard deviation on the test. If we know that the mean on the test was 100 and the standard deviation 20, and we know that an individual scored 125 on the test, we have the data to compute the z score.

Thus, the z score tells us that the person's score is 1.25 standard deviations above the mean. The mean for a distribution of z scores is 0, and the standard deviation is 1.0. There are two disadvantages of using z scores. First, they will be expressed in decimals; second, about half of the z scores will have a minus sign if there is a normal distribution of test scores. A test administrator would need to check carefully to see that the scores had been properly computed and recorded, each with the appropriate sign. Table 3.5 illustrates z scores. Because the scores are linear units, they can be transformed in a number of ways without having the properties of the original raw score distribution changed. For example, z scores can be converted into the T scores described in the next section.

T Scores. T scores are standard scores using a fixed mean and standard deviation in units that eliminate the need for decimals and signs. On many tests the arbitrary or fixed mean is 50 and the arbitrary or fixed standard deviation is 10. The formula is

$$T = s\,(z) + \{X\}$$

If the fixed mean in one example is 50 and the fixed standard deviation is 10, and if $z = 2.5$, then the T score is computed like this:

$$T = 10(2.50) + 50 = -5 + 50 = 45$$

The fixed mean becomes a constant that is added to each score; the fixed standard deviation becomes a constant multiplied by each z score. Negative values and decimals are eliminated through computational procedures, and whole numbers are produced. Another type of T score is known as a normalized standard score. If the distribution is skewed or deviates from a normal distribution, the percentile rank of each raw score is first computed and then the standard score value of the rank is lo-

Table 3.5
Illustration of z scores.

Test	Raw Score	Mean	Standard Deviation	z Score
Reading	100	80	10	+2.00
Mathematics	50	50	15	0.00
Science	45	55	5	−2.00
History	98	82	16	+1.00

cated in the table of the normal curve. This z unit is then used in the computation procedures.

Not all tests use the conventions of 50 as the arbitrary mean and 10 as the arbitrary standard deviation. For example, the Analysis of Learning Potential uses 50 as the mean but 20 as the standard deviation. The Army General Classification Test has 100 as the mean and 20 as the standard deviation. On the Wechsler subscales 10 is the mean on the subtests and 3 is the standard deviation. On the SAT and the Graduate Record Examinations the formula used is

$$100z + 500$$

In this case the fixed mean is 500, and the fixed standard deviation is 100.

Deviation IQs.   Most intelligence tests no longer compute intelligence quotients with a formula but use standard scores instead. The mean for a given age group becomes IQ 100, and the test utilizes a fixed standard deviation. In the past the fixed standard deviations have varied depending on the test. For example, on the 1960 revision of the Stanford-Binet the standard deviation was 16, whereas on the Wechsler scales it was 15. On the Army General Classification Test the standard deviation was 20; on the Culture-Fair Intelligence Tests scaled scores used a standard deviation of 25 as well as 15. Most of the major tests now have selected 15 as the fixed standard deviation.

It is essential for test givers to know the technical information about the test. What is the arbitrary standard deviation for the test? Scores of 116, 115, 120, and 125 may appear to reflect differences in magnitude but may reflect only that an individual is one standard deviation above the norming group. In looking at scores it is also important to determine what kind of units are being expressed or reported. Percentile ranks, for example, utilize whole numbers containing two digits.

Stanines.   Stanines (standard 9's), widely used in educational assessment, are a type of standard score ranging from 1 to 9 with a mean of 5 and a standard deviation of 2. Stanines, like percentiles, indicate a test taker's relative standing in a norm group. Stanines have a constant relationship to percentiles in that they represent a specific range of percentile scores in the normal curve. That is, a given percentile always falls within the same stanine. Because they categorize test performance into only nine broad units, stanines provide less detail about an examinee's performance than other derived scores. In general, stanines of 1 to 3 are considered below average, stanines of 4 to 6 are considered average and stanines of 7 to 9 are considered above average. A stanine to percentile rank conversion table is presented in Table 3.6.

Sten Scores.   On the personality series—the Early School Personality Questionnaire, the High School Personality Questionnaire, and the 16 Personality Factor Questionnaire—stens are used instead of stanines. Stens (standard 10's) are a normalized standard score scale utilizing 10 units. Characteristics of stens are presented in Table 3.7.

Other Standard Score Scales.   The Iowa Tests of Educational Development and the American College Testing Program use standard score scales with a mean of 15 and a standard deviation of 5. Other tests use 50 as the mean and 10 as the standard deviation.

Table 3.6
Stanine to percentile rank conversion table.

Stanine	Percentile Rank (%)
1	1–4
2	5–11
3	12–23
4	24–40
5	41–59
6	60–76
7	77–88
8	89–95
9	96–99

Table 3.7
Characteristics of stens.

Sten	Percentile Rank	Percentage of Scores in Each Category
1	1–2	2
2	3–7	5
3	8–16	9
4	17–31	15
5	32–50	19
6	51–69	19
7	70–84	15
8	85–93	9
9	94–98	5
10	99–100	2

Test users need to make sure they know the arbitrary mean and the fixed standard deviation of tests they are using.

Normal curve equivalent (NCE) scores have been used by many schools, educators, and psychologists in working with research projects for the U.S. Office of Education, especially Title 1 or Chapter 1 reading projects. NCE scores are normalized standard scores with a mean of 50 and a standard deviation of 21.06. They are computed by calibrating the baseline of a normal curve from 1 to 99 in equal units. Percentile ranks and NCE scores are identical at 1, 50, and 99.

DEVELOPMENTAL INTRAINDIVIDUAL COMPARISON

Other frames of reference can help with interpretation of test performance. Many dimensions of the cognitive, affective, and psychomotor domains develop in a systematic, chronological manner. We are often concerned about the characteristics of individuals at different age or grade levels. Two widely used developmental scales, age equivalents and grade equivalents, implicitly compare the test taker's raw score to the average raw score of people at various developmental levels.

Age Norms

Age norms have been developed for many types of behavior and performance that change with age. One of the first authors of intelligence tests, Binet, utilized a system to measure the mental age of children. Age scores can be developed for many different human characteristics, but have been used most widely in looking at educational and intellectual variables.

Most age scales are based on what the typical individual can do at a given age. Besides intelligence tests, some of the tests of cognitive and social maturity report age norms. The scores have meaning when the behaviors being measured vary systematically with age; however, for many behaviors the rate of growth varies from year to year (see Figure 3.1). Thus, an even progression is not always expressed; there may be rapid growth during some periods and a plateau or no growth during others. The scoring units are not equal units of measure because of this type of growth pattern.

Age equivalent scores are norm-referenced scores. We can compare an individual's performance with what most individuals typically do at that age. We might also

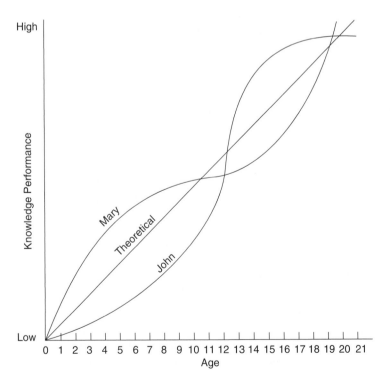

Figure 3.1
Age and learning curves.

be interested in intraindividual comparisons. We could compare an individual's mental age with her chronological age. However, we need to be cautious in our interpretation of age scores because of their psychometric properties and problems of interpretation. High age scores indicate that the individual is ahead of his or her peers developmentally but not necessarily able to perform the tasks characteristic of the higher age.

Grade Equivalent and Placement Scores

Grade equivalent scores are widely used by many of the major survey achievement batteries. These scores are based on the same assumptions that age scores are based on, but grade is the frame of reference rather than age. Grade equivalent scores are a means of comparing a student's performance with other students at a given grade level. A score of 5.0 on the reading comprehension subtest of the Stanford Achievement Test would mean that the student had a raw score equivalent to that made by a typical fifth-grade student on the test at the beginning of the school year. Test scores are compared to the average or sometimes the median performance at a given grade level.

Teachers, parents, and professionals must be cautious in their interpretation of grade placement scores. Such scores are computed by testing students across grade levels, computing the mean or median of each grade level, plotting the averages with as straight a line as possible, and extrapolating this line at the extremes to account for scores above and below the mean. The school year is divided into 10 segments based on a September-to-June school year. Thus, 5.0 would represent a period at the beginning of the fifth grade, and 5.9 would represent a period near the end of the fifth grade.

A number of problems are inherent in interpreting grade equivalent scores. A student in grade 1.9 might get all the items right on the reading comprehension test and receive a score of 4.6. Her raw score is equivalent to the mean or median raw score made by students in the middle of fourth grade. However, this does not mean the first-grade student is actually reading at the fourth-grade level. The student has perhaps gotten most of the items right on the lower-primary form of the achievement test, but there were no fourth-grade-level items on the test for the first graders.

Here are some other problems and disadvantages of grade equivalent scores:

1. The scores are not equal units of measurement but are often ordinal.
2. The scores are often used as a standard, and students are expected to be at grade level.
3. Users sometimes fail to recognize that the grade placement scores are based on the average or typical performance in the norming group. Half of the students in the norming group will have higher scores; half will have lower.
4. Standard deviations differ for the subtests within a survey achievement test. Some distributions will have small ranges; others will have large ranges. The range of grade equivalent scores will thus vary for each subtest.
5. Reading comprehension tests of different publishers usually give conflicting grade placement scores.

A summary of the various types of test scores is presented in Table 3.8.

Table 3.8
Comparison of different types of test scores.

Type of Score	Advantages	Disadvantages
Raw	Gives precise number of points scored on a test	Cannot be interpreted or compared
Percentile Rank	Easily understood by most test takers Requires no great sophistication in statistics Portrays relative position of scores in percentiles More appropriate for skewed data	Uses ordinal units of measurement Uses unequal units of measurement Does not permit averaging Cannot be compared unless groups are similar Greatly distorts score differences at upper and lower ends of distribution
Stanine	One-digit scores Can be averaged Used for simplicity and utility	May not provide enough scoring units to differentiate among scores Insensitive to sizable differences within a stanine Misleadingly sensitive to small differences on either side of the point separating adjacent stanines
Standard	Derived from properties of the normal curve Reflect absolute difference among scores Can be averaged and correlated Comparable from test to test if reference groups are equivalent	Inappropriate if data are markedly skewed Hard to explain to test takers
Grade and Age	Good if area measured is systematically related with age or grade level Compares an individual's performance with the average for that age or grade	Uses unequal units of measurement Leads to score interpretation that is too literal Can mislead in the case of scores that do not signify an ability to perform or understand at the higher grade level Has little practical meaning beyond sixth grade or age 12

NORMING GROUPS

Norming groups are a large sample of test takers who represent the population for which the test is intended. The Standards for Educational and Psychological Testing (American Educational Research Association [AERA] et al., 1999) calls for the norms that are presented to refer to clearly described groups. These groups should be those with which users of the test will ordinarily wish to compare the individuals who are tested. Norms are not standards of performance, but instead serve as a frame of reference for test score interpretation. Norming groups can range in size from a few hundred to a hundred thousand people. The more people used in a norming group, the closer the approximation to a normal distribution.

In the test manual, the test author should (1) describe who was in the norm group and (2) explain the different types of converted scores included in the tables. The test user should ask the following evaluative questions:

1. Does the norming group include the type of person with whom the test taker should be compared?

2. Do the norms include enough cases to be representative of the targeted population?
3. Do the samples include enough cases?
4. Does the manual include differentiated norms or summary information about differences among gender, ethnic, grade, or age groups?
5. Does the manual report include the year in which the normative data were collected, provide descriptive statistics, and describe the sampling design and participation rates in sufficient detail so that the norms can be evaluated?

CONVERSION TABLES

Conversion tables present every possible raw score and the derived score, such as the percentile rank or *T* score for a given norm group (e.g., 12th-grade boys, 10th-grade girls). A conversion table for hypothetical interest scores is shown in Table 3.9. Sometimes tests present multiple group norm tables. At other times a table might present the derived *T* scores for several subtests (see Table 3.10).

Some tests use abbreviated or condensed norm tables in which not every raw score value is presented (see Table 3.11).

Such tables require interpolation for scores that fall between two of the values presented in the table. Unfortunately, this procedure requires more of the test user's time, and necessary computation introduces greater chance for error.

Table 3.9
Sample conversion table for an interest test.

Scale: Technical

Group: Male	Female	*T*
36	36	80
35	32–35	78
34	30–31	75
33	28–29	72
//	//	//

Note: //= Omission of some scores.

Table 3.10
Sample norm table reporting different types of scores for several subtests.

| Stanine | Standard Score | Percentile Rank (%) | Grade | Raw Scores | | |
				ReadComp	Vocab	Total
5	50	50	11.0	30		60
5	49	48				
5	49	47			30	
5	49	46				59
5	49	45	10.9	29		

Table 3.11
Condensed norm table.

Raw Score	IQ
50	140
48	135
45	130
41	125
39	120

PROFILES

Many tests provide profile sheets to aid in interpretation of the results. These forms graphically depict the scores by providing a visual interpretation. Profiles can represent the scores on a single battery or on several tests. Figure 3.2 shows an example of a profile for an individual on the COPSystem Interest Inventory.

Guidelines for interpreting profiles include the following:

1. Small differences should not be overinterpreted.
2. Any score represents a sample of the test taker's behavior in a given domain at a given time.
3. The standard error of measurement should be used in interpretation.
4. The normal curve can be used as a frame of reference to interpret the scores on norm-referenced tests.
5. Patterns in the shape of the profile are important (are the scores all high or low?).

STANDARDS FOR SCORING AND INTERPRETATION

The standards for education and psychological tests call for test developers to specify in sufficient detail and clarity how a test should be scored (AERA et al., 1999). Accurate scoring and reporting are essential. The Code of Fair Testing Practices in Education (Joint Committee on Testing Practices, 1999) has five guidelines to help test users interpret scores correctly. The user should first obtain information about the scale used for reporting scores, the characteristics of any norms or comparison groups, and the limitations of the scores. When interpreting scores, the test user should consider any major differences between the norms or comparison groups and the actual test takers and any differences in test administration practices or familiarity with the specific questions on the tests. Counselors are cautioned against using tests for purposes not specifically recommended by the test developer unless evidence is obtained to support an alternate use. The counselor should be able to explain how any passing scores were set, demonstrate what the results of the scores reveal, and provide evidence that the test satisfies its intended purposes.

The following general guidelines are useful to keep in mind when scoring tests:

1. Routinely review a sample of the test answer sheets to verify the accuracy of the initial scoring.

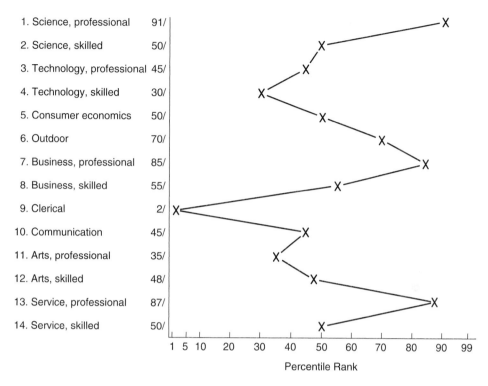

Figure 3.2
Individual profile for COPSystem Interest Inventory.

2. Employ systematic procedures to verify the accuracy and consistency of machine or computer scoring of answer sheets.
3. Obtain a separate and independent verification that appropriate scoring rules and normative conversions are used for each person tested.
4. Verify as accurate the computation and conversion of raw scores and the conversion of raw scores to normative or descriptive scales prior to release of such information to the tested person or to users of the test results.
5. Check routinely for accuracy of computer, machine, or manual reports of test results. The person performing this task must be qualified to recognize inappropriate or impossible scores.
6. Develop and use systematic and objective procedures for observing and recording the conditions and behaviors of persons being tested and make this part of the scores or test results that are reported.
7. Label clearly the scores that are reported and the date that a particular test was administered.

SUMMARY

A clear understanding of scoring is important. Three models of test scoring are the cumulative, class, and ipsative models. Intrepreting test scores can involve relating the score to a performance level (criterion-referenced) or comparing it to the scores of the standardizing or norming group (norm-referenced). Raw scores have to be translated into some frame of reference to give meaning to test results. Standard scores aid in translating raw scores by describing how many standard deviations an individual's score is from the mean. There are a variety of types of standard scores, including z scores, T scores, deviation IQS, stanines, sten scores, and other standard score scales.

QUESTIONS FOR DISCUSSION

1. How would you handle the situation if certain test results did not appear to be accurate or did not agree with the results of previous tests you had taken? If you were the examiner and found out that you had made some errors in scoring a client's test, what would you do? What steps and procedures should be taken to ensure the accuracy of test scores?

2. What are the differences in scoring and interpreting norm-referenced and criterion-referenced tests?

3. What are the different types of derived scores used in norm-referenced testing? Discuss when you would use each type of score and analyze the strengths and limitations of each type of score.

4. If you were developing a new achievement test for college-level students, how would you select your norming group? If you were developing a new personality inventory measuring psychological types, how would you select an appropriate norming group?

SUGGESTED ACTIVITIES

1. Write a position paper on one of the following topics: bias in test scoring, use of grade equivalent norms, norm-referenced versus criterion-referenced interpretation, or selecting appropriate norms.

2. Give children of various ages a short, individual vocabulary test. (If vocabulary does not appeal to you, choose some other subject area.) Analyze the answers and develop a scoring system. Try writing a set of procedures for an examiner to follow to score the test.

3. A third-grade teacher has brought you the following results of the spring testing on the Stanford Achievement Test. The teacher doesn't understand the types of

scores and the results and wants you to guide her in interpreting the results. What would you tell her?

Test	N	Mean Raw	Mean Scale	Percentile Rank	Stanine	Mean Grade Equivalent
Word Study Skills	19	40	613	52	5	4.0
Reading Comprehension	20	39	599	33	4	3.4
Vocabulary	21	19	587	9	2	2.7
Listening Comprehension	21	25	614	31	4	3.5
Spelling	21	29	642	94	8	5.1
Language	21	27	617	41	5	3.9
Concept of Numbers	21	19	574	15	3	3.4
Math Computation	21	28	603	43	5	4.4
Math Applications	21	22	580	30	4	3.5
Science	21	26	603	33	4	3.5
Using Information	21	24	613	39	4	3.5
Total Reading	18	78	602	36	4	3.6
Total Listening	21	44	601	15	3	3.1
Total Language	21	56	624	63	6	4.2
Total Mathematics	21	69	586	29	4	3.7

Content Clusters	Below Average (%)	Average (%)	Above Average (%)
Word Study Skills	5	79	16
Structural Analysis	11	68	21
Phonetic Analysis, Consonants	16	74	11
Phonetic Analysis, Vowels	11	68	21
Reading Comprehension	25	75	0
Textual Reading	20	70	10
Functional Reading	30	60	10
Recreational Reading	20	80	0
Literal Comprehension	25	65	10
Inferential Comprehension	20	60	0
Vocabulary/Listening	48	48	5
Comprehension	14	81	5
Retention	10	76	24
Organization	19	71	10
Spelling	0	71	29
Sight Words	0	43	57
Phonetic Principles	0	76	24
Structured Principles	0	48	52
Language	0	95	5
Conventions	14	81	5
Language Sensitivity	24	62	14
Reference Skills	19	62	19

ADDITIONAL READINGS

American Counseling Association (2005). *ACA Code of Ethics.* Alexanderia, VA: Author.

Anastasi, A., & Urbina, S. (1997). *Psychological testing* (7th ed.). Upper Saddle River, NJ: Prentice Hall.
    A good overview of technological and methodological principles can be found in Chapter 3, "Norms and the Meaning of Test Scores." Topics covered include developmental norms, within-group norms, relativity of norms, domain-referenced test interpretation, and minimum qualifications and cutoff scores.

Davidson, M. L. (1992). Test scores and statistics. In M. Zeidner and R. Most (Eds.), *Psychological testing: An inside view* (pp. 249–295). Palo Alto, CA: Consulting Psychologists Press.
    The chapter provides a review of different types of test scores and the statistical procedures used to produce the derived scores.

Lyman, H. B. (1998). *Test scores and what they mean* (6th ed.). Boston: Allyn & Bacon.
    Provides guidelines for interpreting tests and examples of good and bad usage of interpretations of test results.

4 Validity

OVERVIEW

Workers in the helping professions need to be able to understand and apply the fundamental concepts of measurement. Educational and psychological tests are used in a wide variety of contexts, and it is important to select and use the best possible test to obtain the desired information. Validity is a key factor in test selection. The validity of an instrument addresses the extent to which the test measures what it purports to measure.

OBJECTIVES

After studying this chapter, you should be able to

✔ Explain the meaning and importance of validity

✔ Describe the differences between content, criterion-related, and construct validity

✔ Understand the kind of evidence with which to judge the validity of a test

VALIDITY

In education and psychology, the foremost question to be asked with respect to any test is "how valid is it?" When we ask this question, we are asking whether the test measures what we want to measure, or whether the test is *valid*. According to Standards for Educational and Psychological Testing (AERA et al., 1999), validity is essential for interpretation and use of test scores. Validity is the most fundamental consideration in developing and evaluating tests.

Several types of inferences can be made from a score on a single test. Test users might, for example, be interested in the content that the test items are measuring. Or, they might be interested in how the test predicts success in a given program of study or what type of construct the test is measuring. The evidence of the validity of the test is developed through a number of different procedures. Because tests are used in a variety of ways—for description, for prediction, for measuring growth and development—there are different ways to judge the validity of the test results; yet validity remains a unitary concept.

Three major categories are used to describe test validity: content, criterion, and construct validity. Standards for Educational and Psychological Testing (AERA et al., 1999) points out that these categories are convenient, but the sum of these labels does not imply that there are distinct types of validity or that a specific strategy is best for each specific inference or test use. Rigorous distinctions between the categories are not possible. Evidence usually identified with the criterion-related or content-related categories is relevant also to the construct-related category.

Content Validity

Content validity refers to evidence that the items on a test are representative of some defined universe or content domain and that they measure the objectives they are supposed to measure. A college exam user is probably most concerned with the content validity of achievement tests (e.g., tests that assess students' knowledge and skills in a defined content area), but is also interested in the content validity of other types of tests, such as aptitude tests, interest tests, and personality tests.

A test that has validity in one situation may not have validity in a different situation. For example, a college exam on personality theories that emphasizes understanding and interpretation may have validity with one personality theories instructor . . . but may not be valid with another personality theories instructor who stresses the learning of dates and factual knowledge (Ary, Jacobs, & Razavieh, 1997). In addition, test developers may be concerned that the test format or response requirements of items on, for example, objective tests or essay tests will affect validity. Certain items may demand skills that students are not normally taught at a particular level. For instance, they may require abstract reasoning from pupils who are able to use only concrete reasoning.

Content validity requires careful and critical examination to determine if the content and objectives measured by the test represent the content domain. The content domain is often stated as objectives in curriculum guides, syllabi, and texts. Content validity is usually decided by expert judges who evaluate the test's content to determine if there is a relationship between the test and the content domain or the objectives being measured. Test developers may enlist curriculum specialists, subject matter teachers, psychologists, and college professors to assess the relationship of items to objectives being measured. These reviewers look at whether the items do in fact represent the defined universe or content domain. Another approach utilizes systematic observation of behavior. Experts or trained observers are asked to observe skills and competencies needed to perform a given task; a test or performance checklist is constructed to measure these aspects. Typical statements addressing content validity in test manuals include the following:

- The main source of words was grade placement lists developed from studies of basal readers.
- The social studies items were selected on the basis of recommendations of 40 authorities in the field.

Content validity should not be confused with *face validity,* which refers to "what it appears superficially to measure" (Anastasi & Urbina, 1997, p. 144). Face validity relates to the extent to which the test appears to be measuring what it claims to be measuring. For example, does the test "look valid" to examinees who take it, to those who administer the test, and to other technically untrained observers? Although not a measure of validity itself, face validity is a desirable feature of a test. Anastasi and Urbina described how a test designed for children and extended for adult use was initially met with resistance and criticism because of its lack of face validity. To the adult test takers, the test appeared silly, childish, and inappropriate; therefore, it lacked face validity. As a result, the adults cooperated poorly with the testing procedure, thereby affecting the outcome of the test. To help evaluate face validity on a test, Nevo (cited in Anastasi & Urbina, 1997) suggested having test takers and other nonprofessionals rate the suitability of a test for its intended use. The test user could quickly skim over the test to see whether it covers the content generally expected in such a test.

Criterion-Related Validity

Criterion-related validity is important in demonstrating that test scores are systematically related to one or more external variables (criteria). With an aptitude test, for example, test users might want evidence that the test can predict success in a training program. If the test can accurately predict success in the program, then the test has criterion-related validity. Criterion-related validity is evaluated using validity coefficients. The coefficient indicates the correlation between a test and its criterion score. Because a coefficient of 1.00 indicates a perfect positive correlation, the higher the correlation, the better the validity. Criterion-related validity is determined by calculating the correlation between the test score and the criterion measure of success. The higher the correlation, the more effective the test is as a predictor and the higher the criterion-related validity.

Criterion-related validity is broken down into two categories—concurrent validity and predictive validity. For a test to have *concurrent validity,* the test scores and criterion information should be obtained at the same time. Concurrent validity is usually appropriate for achievement, diagnostic, and certification tests. For example, a test that measures depression should have concurrent validity with the clinical diagnosis of depression. Examples of criterion-related validity from test manuals include the following:

- The scores on the Aggressiveness scale correlated .70 with the rating by teachers of students in their classes.
- The scores on the Mechanical Aptitude Test correlated significantly with supervisory ratings of the workers' performance conducted at the same time.

If test data are used to estimate criterion scores in the future, *predictive validity* is determined. For example, how well does the SAT predict a student's grade point average (GPA) at the end of the first year of college? How well does a mechanical aptitude test predict successful performance of a job requiring mechanical aptitude? Here are some examples of predictive validity:

- The SAT verbal score correlated .30 with GPA at the end of the first semester at XYZ College.
- The Spatial Relations scale correlated .70 with success in the metal fabricating training for 136 youth under the Comprehensive Employment and Training Act (CETA).

Using a personality test as an example, one of the best ways to illustrate the difference between concurrent and predictive validity is by asking, "Is Mr. Jones schizophrenic?" (concurrent validity) or "Is Mr. Jones likely to become schizophrenic?" (predictive validity).

Selecting Appropriate Criterion Measures.   Both types of criterion-related validity require relevant, bias-free, reliable, and available measures of the criterion. Choosing the appropriate criterion based upon these factors is crucial to the success of the measurement. To determine if a criterion is relevant, one must judge whether it represents successful performance on the behavior in question. For example, GPA is considered a relevant measure of success in college, therefore, it is often chosen as the criterion for validating admissions tests such as the SAT (Ary et al., 1997).

A criterion that is free from bias means that the scoring of the measure should not be influenced by any external factors other than the performance of the criterion. Assume a professor's job during the process of admitting students to a graduate program involves rating a student's interpersonal skills during an interview. If the professor allows another factor such as the student's Graduate Record Examinations (GRE) score to influence the rating, then the criterion score will be biased.

Reliable criterion measures are those in which the criterion score is both stable and reproducible. For example, for a person who shows high job performance one week then low job performance the next week, or the person who receives a high rating from one supervisor but gets a low rating from another, there is no possibility of finding a test that will predict that score (Thorndike, 1997, p. 146).

When selecting the criterion measure, one should consider the availability and convenience of the measure. What is the length of time necessary to get the criterion score for an individual? How much is the criterion measure going to cost? Is the cost prohibitive?

The selection of the criterion is also related to the context of particular types of test users. They may be students in a school system, clients in a counseling center, or employees in an industrial setting. The test user wants evidence that the test was applied in a context similar to that of the intended clients and that criterion studies were relevant. The goal is to have test scores accurately predict the criterion performance of interest.

Manuals that accompany aptitude or intelligence tests offer considerable evidence on the predictive validity of their tests. However, test users may want to check the utility of the predictor tests. Figure 4.1 presents a useful design for this purpose. A person who is predicted to pass or graduate and subsequently does pass or graduate would be tallied in the positive quadrant; someone who is predicted to pass but fails would be tallied as a false positive. The person who is predicted to fail and does so would be tallied as a negative; anyone who is predicted to fail but actually passes would be a false negative. Thus, the percentages of correct predictions can be determined and the cutoff score adjusted or a different test selected.

Theorists consider the false positive error the most important to avoid. However, these are value judgments that are partially determined by context perspective. An admissions counselor might argue that enrolling a student who subsequently fails is not all bad; at least this student is given a chance. The parent of that student, who may spend thousands of dollars for a school year with little apparent benefit, might not feel the same. A heterogeneous group tends to produce greater variability in scores and

Figure 4.1
Design for predictive validity
check.

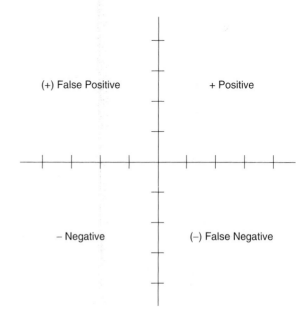

therefore higher coefficients than a homogeneous group. Moreover, concurrent validity coefficients are higher than predictive validity coefficients. The criterion used is different, and predictive validity involves time lag.

Construct Validity

The third type of validity is *construct validity.* Unlike content validity (which addresses whether a test measures what it is supposed to measure) or criterion-related validity (which determines how well a test may predict concurrent or future performance), construct validity answers the questions, "What do scores on this test mean or signify? What does the score tell us about the individual? Does it correspond with some meaningful trait or construct that will help us understand the person?" (Thorndike, 1997, p. 157). The term *construct* is used to describe a grouping of variables or behaviors that make up observed behavior patterns (such as intelligence, anxiety, motivation, self-concept). A construct itself is not measurable; only the behaviors or variables that comprise it can be tested. For example, the construct "self-concept" was developed to account for observed behavior patterns that are deemed to make up self-concept, such as a person's own view of himself or herself (Ary et al., 1997). Self-concept itself cannot be measured directly, but many of the variables that are believed to be aspects of self-concept can be described or measured. The Piers-Harris Children's Self-Concept Scale uses such variables as Physical Appearance and Attributes, Freedom from Anxiety, Intellectual and School Status, Behavioral Adjustment and Happiness, Satisfaction, and Popularity to measure the construct of self-concept.

A construct must be derived from psychological theory, prior research, or systematic observation. For example, when Doll (1935) originated the Vineland Social Maturity Scale, he defined the construct "social maturity" as a combination of interrelated elements of self-help, self-direction, locomotion, occupation, communication, and social relations through all three areas (theory, research, and observation). Tests with construct validity have items that fit the construct definitions.

Most psychological and educational tests attempt to measure one or more constructs. For example, achievement tests measure constructs such as reading comprehension; trauma symptom inventories measure the constructs of depression, dissociation, and anxiety. The authors of a test precisely define each construct and distinguish it from other constructs.

Researchers need to be able to measure constructs and find a way of validating instruments used to measure the construct. Doll (1935) was able to measure and validate his construct for social maturity by looking at relationships of constructs within the test (such as self-help, self-direction, locomotion, occupation, etc.), and externally by relationships between the scores on the test and other observations. Doll demonstrated that Vineland scores for internal constructs of social maturity correlated with one another (Ary et al., 1997, p. 263). In addition, the constructs correlated with such external measures as chronological and mental age, and with independent assessments of social maturity. Thus, Doll was able to provide evidence of both internal and external support for the construct of social maturity.

Convergent and Discriminant Validation. Convergent and discriminant validity are both considered subcategories or subtypes of construct validity. Tests should correlate positively with other data relevant to the construct. For example, a test to measure the construct "scholastic aptitude" should demonstrate correlation with grades in school, achievement test scores, or teachers' ratings of aptitude. A test to measure the construct "self-esteem" should correlate positively with perceptions, attitudes, and self-image. Positive correlation with such relevant data and other tests measuring the same construct is an example of *convergent validation.* A test user looks for a convergence of indicators of the construct by seeking out the other measures with which the construct should theoretically be correlated and then showing how they are correlated.

A test user would also look for evidence that the construct is unique and is not highly correlated with other scales and tests of other constructs. Anyone interpreting a scale for abstract reasoning would want the scale to have a low correlation with concrete reasoning. This would be an example of *discriminant validation,* a process in which a test is determined to have low correlation with instruments known to measure different constructs.

Campbell and Fiske (1959) recommend a multitrait-multimethod approach to provide evidence of the convergent and discriminant validation of a test. They advocate computing correlations between tests measuring the same trait by the same method, tests measuring different traits by the same method, tests measuring the same trait by different methods, and tests measuring different traits by different methods. For example, the Multidimensional Self-Esteem Inventory (MSEI) was correlated with the Eysenck Neuroticism and Extroversion Scales and the Guilford-Zimmerman Temperament Survey. The correlations with the Neuroticism and Extroversion Scales were seen as supporting the MSEI in that the most global scales were highly correlated with other measures of global adjustment and modestly correlated with Extroversion, a scale described by Eysenck as being independent of adjustment. Convergent validity of the NEO Personality Inventory-Revised (NEO PI-R) is demonstrated by how the scales are correlated with alternative measures of similar constructs. The Anxiety scale correlated high with the scores on the State-Trait Anxiety Scale.

Methods Used in Gathering Construct-Related Validity. Authors use many different techniques to demonstrate the construct validity of their tests. One of the simplest procedures is to show a correlation between scores on a new test and scores on an established test that is considered to be a valid measure of the construct. For example, a newly developed test for depression could be correlated with a well-established test such as the Beck Depression Inventory. If the correlation is high, one assumes that the new test is measuring the same construct as the established test—in this case, depression (Ary et al., 1997).

Test users also want to know whether a test measures a construct under conditions that have been identified as crucially related to the construct. For example, do clients score differently on a stress scale when under stress and when relaxed? If stress levels were manipulated in a controlled experiment and the resulting scores on the stress scale were found to change in the predicted way, one would have evidence that the scale does measure stress.

Another method to gather evidence for construct validity is comparing the scores of an instrument between heterogeneous groups. For example, test users would expect that scores on a depression inventory would discriminate between clients diagnosed with depression and individuals who are not depressed. The different groups used for comparison in validity studies may be age groups, gender groups, groups known to be normal or maladjusted, and so on (Ary et al., 1997). If the test scores are different between the groups, then the validity of the test has been supported.

Many authors utilize *factor analysis* to determine construct validity. Factor analysis is a statistical method for studying the intercorrelations among a set of test scores in order to determine the number of factors (constructs) needed to account for intercorrelations. The method also provides information on what factors determine performance on each test as well as the percentage of variance in the test scores accounted for by the factors. An author would start with a large number of different measures; by examining the intercorrelations among them and finding which measures seem to go together (correlate), the author may reduce the large number of measurement outcomes to a small number of factors that are actually measured. For example, the NEO-PI-R is a test that was designed to provide a general description of normal personality relevant to clinical, counseling, and educational situations. Through factor analysis, the authors found that the 240 items of the test corresponded clearly with the five-factor model of personality used in the test, including neuroticism (described as anxiety, hostility, depression, self-consciousness, impulsiveness, vulnerability), extraversion (warmth, gregariousness, assertiveness, activity, excitement-seeking, positive emotions), openness to experience (fantasy, aesthetics, feelings, actions, ideas, values), agreeableness (trust, modesty, compliance, altruism, straightforwardness, tender-mindedness), and conscientiousness (competence, self-discipline, achievement-striving, dutifulness, order, deliberation).

Threats to Construct Validity.

- *Construct Underrepresentation:* This indicates that the tasks measured in the test fail to include important dimensions or facets of the construct. Therefore, the test results are unlikely to reveal a test taker's true abilities within the construct being measured.
- *Construct-Irrelevant Variance:* The test measures too many variables, many of which are irrelevant to the construct. This type of validity threat can take two forms, *construct-irrelevant easiness* and *construct-irrelevant difficulty.* Construct-irrelevant easiness occurs when clues in the test items permit some individuals to respond correctly or appropriately in ways that are irrelevant to the construct being assessed (e.g., the way the test item was written reveals the correct answer). Construct-irrelevant difficulty occurs when extraneous aspects of the task make the task irrelevantly difficult for some individuals or groups. The first type of construct irrelevant variance causes one to score higher than one would under normal circumstances and the latter causes a notably lower score.

Consequential Validity

Consequential evidence of validity refers to examining the intended and unintended consequences of the use of test results. For example, a teacher may find that the scoring rubric used to evaluate male and female performances on a given task consistently results in lower evaluations for the male students. The interpretation of this result may be that the male students are not as proficient as the female students. Is it possible that the difference is actually a result of some other factor unrelated to the purpose of the test? Another example of consequential validity is the unintended results that high-stakes testing can have on school curriculum. When schools are judged in terms of the performance of their students in a limited range of subjects, teachers can be tempted to spend more time teaching these subjects at the expense of others (e.g., changing the curriculum to teach to the test).

Overview of Validation Concepts

Through the presentation of the various ways to determine the validity of tests, we have addressed the question, "How valid is this test?" To determine whether a test actually tests the educational content or behavioral domain to be measured, choose content validity. Criterion-related validation is used to determine if test scores can predict either concurrent or future behavior. Construct validity determines the extent to which the test measures a theoretical construct or trait. Table 4.1 summarizes the types of validity.

A validity checklist could be set up as follows:

____ Rationale is presented for each use of test

____ Procedure is presented for how scores are to be interpreted

____ Author cautions about making unsupported claims

____ Author provides evidence that supports a given test's use

____ Relation of existing validity of test is reported

____ Test is unaffected by practice or coaching

____ Theoretical or empirical evidence supports intended uses of test

____ Evidence concerning internal structure of test is provided

____ Rationale for arriving at composite scores is presented

____ Author provides rationale for selecting additional variables

____ Test scores have been subject to cross-validation

____ Regression analysis

____ Discriminant analysis

____ Factor analysis

____ Statistical adjustments have been made, for example, restriction of range, attenuation

____ Evidence of concurrent validity studies

____ Evidence of predictive validity studies

____ Control group has been described

____ Experiment groups have been described

____ Author describes relevant socioeconomic and demographic data

____ Construct validity studies are included

____ Consequential validity of study is addressed

Table 4.1
Types of validity.

Type	Purpose	Procedure	Types of Tests
Content	To compare whether the test items match the set of goals and objectives	Compare test blueprint with the school, course, program objectives Use panel of experts in content area (e.g., teachers, professors)	Survey achievement tests Criterion-referenced tests Essential skills tests Minimum-level skills tests State assessment tests Professional licensing Examinations Aptitude tests
Criterion: Concurrent	To determine whether there is a relationship between a test and an immediate criterion measure	Correlate test scores with criterion measure at or about the same time Use a rating, observation, or another test as criterion	Aptitude tests Ability tests Personality tests Employment tests
Criterion: Predictive	To determine whether there is a relationship between a test and a criterion measure to be obtained in the future	Correlate test scores with criterion measure obtained after a period of time	Scholastic aptitude tests General aptitude batteries Prognostic tests Readiness tests Personality tests Intelligence tests
Construct	To determine whether a construct exists and to understand the traits or concepts that make up the set of scores or items	Conduct multivariate statistical analysis such as factor analysis, discriminant analysis, multivariate analysis of variance	Intelligence tests Aptitude tests Personality tests

Threats to Test Validity

- *History:* Outside events occurring during the course of the test or between test-retest validation may have an influence on the results. For example, some type of environmental event may affect students' performance on a test (e.g., natural disasters like the hurricanes in Florida, Louisiana, and Mississippi in 2005). This does not make the test itself any less accurate.
- *Maturation:* Maturation refers to the natural physiological, psychological, or developmental changes that take place as we age. For example, we know diagnostically that the symptoms of major depression typically decrease significantly within a 6-month period even without psychological treatment. If we wanted to research the effectiveness of a 6-month group counseling program to treat depression, how would we know if any decrease in depressive symptoms is the result of the counseling program or is simply the result of maturation?

- *Testing Threat:* Experience of taking tests has an influence on results. For example, if a class is given a pretest in science before being taught a special science program, the students might remember some of the questions and correct answers. When they are given the test again, they may answer more questions correctly because of their familiarity with the test rather than an improvement in their overall knowledge of science.

- *Instrumentation Threat:* If you are using alternate forms of the same test (often used to avoid the testing threat), changes in scores may be related to the difference between the instruments rather than the factor being measured. Alternate forms are designed to be "equivalent" in the types of questions and level of difficulty, but what if they aren't? Changes in test scores could be attributed to the change in the instrument, not in the variable being measured. Instrumentation threats are especially likely when the "instrument" is a human observer. The observers may get tired over time or bored with the observations, or they might improve in making the observations as they practice more. Either way, it's the change in instrumentation, not the program, that leads to the outcome.

- *Statistical Regression:* This refers to the tendency of very high pretest scores to become lower and for very low pretest scores to become higher on posttesting. For example, say you are giving a fitness test to eighth-grade students. You rank the students by their test score and select the bottom half of the group. You retest the bottom half. The average score of the bottom half will probably improve somewhat on retest. Similarly, the average score of the top half will probably drop somewhat on retest. These changes in performance are called *regression to the mean,* which refers to the tendency for individuals who score below average on a test to do better next time, and for those who score above average to do worse.

- *Interaction Threat:* Two or more threats can interact. For example, a selection-maturation interaction would involve difference between ages of groups that could cause groups to change at different rates. A group of young people may show more improvement in a test than a group of older people, but that could be because their brains are developing faster relative to their age.

SUMMARY

This chapter has focused primarily on the measurement concept of validity. Validity relates to whether the test measures what it purports to measure. Content validity is established by demonstrating a similarity or relationship between what is being measured on the test and what is being taught in the targeted program. A different type of validity is established by comparing test scores with criterion measures. There are two types of criterion validity: concurrent and predictive. Concurrent validity requires that the test scores be compared to a criterion measure taken at or about the same time. In predictive validity the criterion measure is taken at some time in the future. Because most psychological variables cannot be directly measured, a third type of validity—construct validity—must be used. Construct validity is based on statistical, experimental, and judgmental information that the construct identified is actually measured by the test. Test users need to understand the different types of validity so that they can judge a test's validity for their particular purpose.

QUESTIONS FOR DISCUSSION

1. What are the different types of validity, and when would each type be important to a test user?

2. What type of validity is represented by each of these questions:

   a. Do the test items match the objectives of our school?

   b. How does the new values test compare with Super's Work Values Inventory?

   c. How well does the Algebra Prognostic Test predict success or failure in Algebra I?

   d. Is there a relationship between the score on the Minnesota Rate of Manipulation Test and workers' rate of assembly of a product?

   e. Is there a relationship between the Mechanical Ability Test and performance of individuals in a 6-week training program in mechanics?

   f. Is creativity a distinct factor measured by the test?

   g. Do the abstract thinking items cluster together?

3. Criterion-referenced validity is important in aptitude and ability testing. What are some of the problems in identifying appropriate criterion measures? How would you evaluate criterion measures?

4. You have developed a small-group guidance program in self-esteem for a group of fifth-grade students. You decide to measure the effectiveness of the program by giving an identical pretest and posttest. What potential threat to validity could you have? What could you do to reduce the threat?

SUGGESTED ACTIVITIES

1. Review several standardized tests and identify the types of validity presented in the test manuals.

2. Interview psychologists and counselors to find out how they use the standard error of measurement in their testing. See whether they have completed any studies of the validity or reliability of the tests they use.

3. Write a paper or prepare a class report on factors that affect the validity of teacher-made tests.

4. Read critical reviews of some of the tests that you have taken and see what the reviewers say about the validity of the tests.

ADDITIONAL READINGS

Anastasi, A., & Urbina, S. (1997). *Psychological testing* (7th ed.). Upper Saddle River, NJ: Prentice Hall.

Ary, D., Jacobs, L. C., & Razavieh, A. (1997). *Introduction to research in education* (5th ed.). Stamford, CT: Wadsworth.

Chase, C. (1999). *Contemporary assessment for educators.* New York: Longman.
A good discussion of validity and reliability is presented, as well as statistical procedures applied to test scores.

Doll, E. (1935). *Vineland Adaptive Behavior Scales.* Circle Pines, MN: American Guidance Services.

Educational Measurement, 17 (1998, Summer).
The issue contains five articles on consequential validity.

Embrelson, S. E., & Hershberger, S. L. (Eds.). (1999). *The new rules of measurement.* Mahwah, NJ: Erlbaum.
The authors compare the new rules for measurement with older rules.

Hood, A. B., & Johnson, R. W. (2001). *Assessment in counseling: A guide to the use of psychological assessment procedures* (3rd ed.). Alexandria, VA: American Counseling Association.

Kline, P. (1999). *Handbook of psychological testing* (2nd ed.). New York: Routledge.
Section 1 has a good presentation on psychometric theory and methods.

Nevo, B. (1985). Face validity revisited. In A. Anastasi and S. Urbina (Eds.), *Psychological testing* (7th ed.). Upper Saddle River, NJ: Merrill/Prentice Hall.

Thorndike, R. M. (2005). *Measurement and evaluation in psychology and education* (7th ed.). Upper Saddle River, NJ: Merrill/Prentice Hall.

Waltkins, C. E., & Campbell, V. L. (Eds.). (2000). *Testing and assessment in counseling practice* (2nd ed.). Mahwah, NJ: Erlbaum.
Shows readers how assessment can be used in the counseling process.

Zeidner, M., & Most, R. (Eds.). (1992). *Psychological testing: An inside view.* Palo Alto, CA: Consulting Psychologists Press.
Presents an understandable and readable discussion of the major constructs in testing.

5 Reliability

OVERVIEW

Reliability is another important factor in the evaluation of a test. Whereas validity refers to whether a test measures what it is supposed to measure, reliability refers to how *accurately* a test measures whatever it does measure. Reliability gives an indication as to whether the scores produced by particular measure are consistent and reproducible.

OBJECTIVES

After studying this chapter, you should be able to

✔ Explain the meaning of reliability, errors of measurement, and different types of reliability coefficients

✔ Describe the factors that influence the reliability of a test and the types of evidence by which to judge the reliability of a test

RELIABILITY

Reliability is defined as the degree to which test scores are consistent, dependable, and repeatable. We are not asking what a test measures; rather, we want to know how accurately a test measures what it is supposed to measure. If we were to measure an individual again, how accurately will the score be reproduced? We recognize that neither educational nor psychological instruments measure perfectly. Therefore, reliability refers to how consistently a test measures and the extent to which it eliminates change and other extraneous factors in the results (Hood & Johnson, 2001).

A client tested on two different occasions would score differently, even on the same test. The difference is caused in part by errors of measurement. For example, the test taker may guess better one time than another, know more of the content on one test form than another, or be less fatigued or less anxious at one time. These are all factors that cause errors of measurement, or changes in an individual's scores, from one occasion to the next. Changes also can be due to maturation or intervention between testing periods.

Measurement errors reduce the reliability and generalizability of the scores obtained on a given test; the higher the error of measurement, the lower the reliability. However, the intended use of the test results influences the final judgment of the reliability of the test. A test might have sufficient reliability for appraising the achievement level of a school district but may not have sufficient reliability to screen individuals for specific placement decisions. The test developer bears the major responsibility for providing evidence of a test's reliability and error measurement in each of its intended uses.

A test provides a sample of behavior at a given moment in time; it can sample only the domain being tested. *Error of measurement* is defined as the difference between a person's observed, or obtained, score and his or her true score. Thus, the obtained score partly represents a true level of ability, skills, or knowledge and partly an error component that may raise or lower the score. The true score and error score are both theoretical; we can only hypothesize what a true score might be. The standard error of measurement, which is discussed in more detail later in this chapter, is used to estimate a score range in which a true score may fall. It is important to know that a test can be reliable without being valid, but in order to have good validity, high reliability is necessary.

Reliability Coefficients

A measure is reliable to the extent that an individual's score remains nearly the same on repeated measures, indicated by a low standard error of measurement. *Correlation coefficients* provide a statistical index of the extent to which two measurements are reliable—designated as *reliability coefficients*. These correlation coefficients are used in computing different measures of reliability: test-retest reliability, alternative forms, split-half reliability, and other internal consistency methods. The coefficient is a positive index number ranging from .00 to 1.00, with .00 indicating a lack of reliability and 1.00 indicating perfect reliability.

Methods of Assessing Reliability

Test-Retest.   When the same test is given twice, the two sets of scores can be correlated and a test-retest coefficient obtained. In other words, the first set of scores is correlated with the second set of scores. This method provides a coefficient of stability. Correlations range between 0 (low reliability) and 1 (high reliability).

Because there are two administrations of the test, a number of variables can influence an individual's performance. The amount of time allowed between measures is critical. The shorter the time gap, the higher the correlation because people may remember some of the questions and their responses. The longer the time gap, the lower the correlation since the results may be confounded with learning and maturation, that is, changes in the persons themselves.

Another variable might be the way the test was administered. The examiner may have made errors in timing, or an interruption may have occurred. Such errors in test administration reduce reliability. Furthermore, the test taker may vary in performance; motivation, mood, and health may fluctuate.

Finally, exposure to any intervention such as educational training or counseling affects performance on a second testing. Consequently, the coefficient obtained after such intervention would not be a proper indicator of the stability of the constructs measured.

Examples of test-retest reliability include the following:

- On the MSEI, the test-retest coefficient on the Global Self-Esteem scale was .87 over a 1-month interval.
- The subset of 208 college students in a 3-month retest on the five domains of the NEO-PI-R resulted in coefficients of .79, .79, .80, .75, and .83 for N, E, O, A, and C, respectively.
- The test-retest coefficients on the Vocational Preference Inventory (VPI) for a group of 100 females on the Realistic scale were .79 over 2 weeks, .57 over 2 months, .86 over 1 year, and .58 over 4 years.

Alternative Forms.   Two equivalent forms of a test permit correlation of scores on the two measures to provide an estimate of reliability. This method gives a coefficient of stability because an individual's behavior is being measured at two different times. It also provides a coefficient of equivalence that tells how closely the two tests measure the same constructs. Sources of measurement error occur in both the two forms and the two testings.

Alternate, or parallel, forms of a test present the same type of format and have almost equal difficulty. They are based on the same blueprint, have the same number of items, and include the same directions for administering, scoring, and interpreting the test. They do not use the same specific items, but a sample of different items forms the same domain. This method eliminates the problem of memory and practice, which affects test-retest reliability. Most survey achievement tests, scholastic aptitude tests, and general aptitude batteries have two or more forms. Alternate forms are especially helpful when pretest and posttest comparisons are needed and high correlation is thus required. For example, on the Primary 1 Battery, Form F Reading correlated .95 with Form G Reading for 1,326 second-grade students.

Split-Half Reliability.   Split-half reliability requires only one administration of a given test. However, the test is divided into two comparable halves—for example, the odd items and even items. The scores on the two subtests are then computed and correlated, and the resulting coefficient provides an estimate of the equivalence of the two forms. Because we are comparing the relationship of two halves rather than full-length tests, we adjust the coefficient, using the Spearman-Brown prophecy formula, to get an estimate of what the coefficient would be if the test halves were full length.

$$\text{total test reliability} = \left(\frac{2r}{1 + r} \right)$$

In the formula, r represents the correlation between the two halves. If the correlation is .60, we can substitute the coefficient in the formula and calculate a reliability estimate for the full test.

$$\text{total} = \frac{2(.60)}{1 + (.60)} = \frac{1.20}{1.60} = .75$$

The estimated reliability of the full test is .75. In general this method tends to give a higher estimate of reliability than do the methods previously discussed. As an example, on the reading portion of the Metropolitan Achievement Test Primary 1 Battery, the split-half coefficient corrected by the Spearman-Brown formula was .96 for a group of second graders.

Internal Consistency Methods.   *Internal consistency* refers to how well each item relates independently to other items on a test, as well as how they relate to the overall test. The Kuder-Richardson formulas (K-R 20 and K-R 21) are the standard for estimating reliability for single administration of a single form and measuring inter-item consistency. It is tantamount to doing a split-half reliability on all combinations of items resulting from different splittings of the test. The K-R 20 formula is

$$r = \frac{n}{n - 1} \left(1 - \frac{\Sigma pq}{s^2} \right)$$

In the formula, r = reliability, n = number of items on the test, Σ = sum of, p = proportion of examinees getting each item correct, q = proportion of examinees getting each item incorrect, and s^2 = variance of the test. The following example illustrates the K-R 20 formula.

Item	1	2	3	4	5
p	.5	.4	.8	.6	.7
q	.5	.6	.2	.4	.3
pq	.25	.24	.16	.24	.21

$(\Sigma pq = 1.10)$
$(s^2 = 2.00)$

$$\frac{5}{4} \left(1 - \frac{1.10}{2.00} \right) = \frac{5}{4}(.45) = .56$$

The K-R 21 formula is easier to compute. The procedure is based on the assumption that the difficulty levels are similar for all items on the test. K-R 21 tends to underestimate the reliability of a test if the items vary in difficulty.

$$r = \frac{n}{n-1}\left[1 - \frac{\overline{X}(n-\overline{X})}{ns^2}\right]$$

In this formula, r = reliability, n = number of items, $\overline{X}$ = mean, and s^2 = variance of the test. If $n = 80$, $\overline{X} = 50$, and $s^2 = 100$, then the K-R 21 reliability is computed as follows:

$$r = \frac{80}{79}\left[1 - \frac{50(80-50)}{80(100)}\right]$$

$$r = \frac{80}{79}\left[1 - \frac{1500}{8000}\right]$$

$$r = 1.01[1 - .19]$$

$$r = 1.01[.81] = .82$$

Another internal consistency method of computing reliability is Cronbach's Alpha (Cronbach, 1951), which is a method of computing the reliability of a test through using interclass correlation. It can be used when two or more scoring weights are assigned to answers and does not require the right-wrong scoring as does K-R 20.

A number of problems are associated with using or interpreting estimates of internal consistency reliability. First, this method works best with a test measuring a single construct, domain, or subject area. The magnitude of the relationship is affected by the degree of homogeneity of the items on a test. If the test items measure heterogeneous dimensions, the coefficients are lower. Second, the method is not appropriate for speeded tests that consist of a series of relatively easy items or tasks, or problems that have to be completed in a strict time period (e.g., the Clerical Speed and Accuracy test from the Differential Aptitude Test Battery). The estimates of these speeded tests are inflated. The Salience Inventory, for instance, reports Cronbach's alpha coefficients on the Participation scale of .88 for studying, .85 for working, .93 for community service, .87 for home and family, and .88 for leisure activities.

Table 5.1 summarizes the methods for assessing reliability.

Standard Error of Measurement

To apply the reliability information to the interpretation of individual scores, information is needed on the standard error of measurement. *Standard error of measurement* is a measure of the "spread" of a person's scores had the person been tested repeatedly. If an individual were to take the same test repeatedly (with no new learning taking place between testings and no memory of test items/answers), the standard deviation of his or her repeated test scores is denoted as the standard error of measurement.

There is often confusion between standard error of measurement and standard deviation. The standard deviation of scores on a test refers to the standard deviation of the test scores obtained by a *group* of persons on a single test. It is a measure of the "spread" of scores between students. In contrast, the standard error of measurement

Table 5.1
Methods of assessing reliability.

Method	Procedure	Coefficient	Problems
Test-retest	Same test given twice with time interval between testings	Stability	• Memory effect • Practice effect • Change over time
Alternate forms	Equivalent tests given with time between testings	Equivalence and stability	• Hard to develop two equivalent tests • May reflect change in behavior over time
Split-half	One test is divided into two comparable halves (e.g., odd items and even items)	Internal consistency	• Uses shortened forms
Internal consistency	One test given at one time (items compared to other items or to the whole test)	Equivalence and internal consistency	• Only good if test content is homogeneous • Gives high-reliability estimate on a speeded test

refers to the standard deviation of test scores that would have been obtained from a *single* person had that person been tested multiple times. The standard error of measurement is computed by using this formula:

$$SEM = s\sqrt{1 - r}$$

In the formula, SEM = standard error of measurement, s = standard deviation of the test, and r = reliability coefficient of the test. If, for example, the standard deviation on the Erewhon IQ test is 15 and the reliability coefficient is .91, the standard error of measurement is computed as follows:

$$SEM = 15\sqrt{1 - .91}$$
$$SEM = 15\sqrt{.09}$$
$$SEM = 15 \times .3 = 4.5$$

If the reliability of the test is .64 instead, the standard error of measurement is computed as follows:

$$SEM = 15\sqrt{1 - .64}$$
$$SEM = 15\sqrt{.36}$$
$$SEM = 15 \times .6 = 9.0$$

The standard error of measurement tells the range within which a person's true score may fall. The range variability of an individual's score is a function of the reliability of the test. If the reliability is 1.00, the standard error is 0. The individual's obtained score would be her or his true score. Standard errors of measurement are distributed normally and form a normal curve. On the Metropolitan Achievement Test the standard errors are presented for the raw scores, standard scores, and grade equivalent scores: Reading K-R 20 5 .93, Split-half = .95, SEM RS = 2.3, SEM SS = 2.7, and SEM GE = .3.

We can look at the confidence band of the range in which the true score might fall.

$$\pm\ 1\ \text{SEM} = 68 \text{ times out of } 100$$
$$\pm\ 2\ \text{SEM} = 95 \text{ times out of } 100$$
$$\pm\ 3\ \text{SEM} = 995 \text{ times out of } 1000$$

In other words, 68 times out of 100 a person's true score will fall within the range formed by that person's obtained score plus or minus one standard error of measurement. If John scored 100 on the IQ test and the standard error of measurement was 4.5, we can say that 68 chances out of 100, or 68% of the time, John's true score will fall between 95.5 and 104.5. Ninety-five times out of 100, or 95% of the time, his true score will fall between 91 and 109.

Factors Influencing Reliability

Length of Test.   One of the factors influencing reliability is the length of the test. There is a trend to develop quick methods of assessing individual aptitude, as with CAPS, the Career Ability Placement Survey (see Chapters 7 and 9). However, one of the major ways of increasing the reliability of a test is to increase its length. This works, up to a point, because more items can cover the test domain more completely and can assess a larger sample of behavior. A revision of the Spearman-Brown prophecy formula indicates the reliability of the test with increased length.

$$r = \frac{(nr)}{1 + (n - 1)r}$$

In the formula, r = reliability of the test and n = number of times the test length is increased. If the reliability of a 10-minute spatial aptitude test is .50, increasing the test length can increase the reliability.

$$\frac{2(.50)}{1 + (2 - 1)(.50)} \quad \frac{3(.50)}{1 + (3 - 1)(.50)} \quad \frac{4(.50)}{1 + (4 - 1)(.50)}$$

Theoretically, if we can increase the length of the test two, three, or four times, the reliability increases to .67, .75, or .80. There may be a point at which the test is too long, making it hard to get the test taker to attend to the tasks at hand. Fatigue and frustration may also have an effect on test performance.

Reliability of Scoring.   Certain types of scoring are more reliable than others. Some types of tests such as multiple-choice and true-false are objective, and the accuracy of the scoring can be checked readily. However, this condition is not true of some of the projective personality tests or essay tests. When ratings are used as scores, rater bias can be a major source of unreliability.

Group Variability.   A third factor that affects the reliability coefficient is the variability of the group. For instance, the reliability coefficients for individual grades or age groups will be lower than for the coefficients for an age span or grade span.

Grade 4	.82
Grade 5	.83
Grade 6	.85
Grades 4–6	.92

If the group is more homogeneous, the reliability will be lower than it is for a heterogeneous group. There is less variability of scores in a homogeneous group and more variability in a heterogeneous group.

Difficulty of Test Items.   Reliability coefficients are lower when the test is either too easy or too difficult; the distributions of scores become more homogeneous under such circumstances. On difficult tests, test takers decrease reliability of the test by guessing.

SUMMARY

This chapter focused primarily on the reliability of tests. Reliability relates to the precision or accuracy of measurement. Different types of procedures are used to establish the reliability of a test: test-retest, alternate forms, split-half, and internal consistency methods. Reliability coefficients range from .00 to +1.0; the higher the coefficient, the more reliable the test. Errors of measurement interfere with the consistency and accuracy of measurement. Therefore, we use the standard error of measurement as a way of looking at the confidence we can have in interpreting a score.

QUESTIONS FOR DISCUSSION

1. What are the different methods of estimating the reliability of a test? What are the advantages and disadvantages of each method?

2. Which factor do you believe is more important in selecting a test: validity or reliability? Under what conditions would validity be the most important factor? Reliability?

SUGGESTED ACTIVITIES

1. Review several standardized tests and identify the types of reliability presented in the test manuals.

2. Construct an achievement test on the concepts introduced in this chapter and administer it to a number of students in your class. Then compute the reliability of the test using split-half and K-R 20 or K-R 21.

3. Write a paper or prepare a class report on one of the following topics: factors that affect test reliability, reliability, reliability of teacher-made tests.

4. Read the critical reviews of some of the tests that you have taken and see how the reviewers rate the reliability of the test.

5. Study the following descriptions of two tests and answer the questions that follow the descriptions.

Test A: 40 items
  Subscales: General Self-Esteem, Social Self-Esteem, Personal Self-Esteem, Lie.
  Administration: Self-administering.
  Item format: Items in form of questions and test taker checks "yes" or "no" (example: Do you enjoy taking tests? Y N).
  Scoring: Hand scoring; one template with the targeted answers and scales identified.
  Interpretability: Norm tables provided; illustrative case studies presented.
  Reliability: Test-retest for adult sample .81.
  Alpha coefficients: General .78, Social .57, Personal .72, Lie .54.
  Validity: Content-developed construct definitions for self-esteem and test items cover all areas of the construct; concurrent-correlated scale with Coopersmith's Self-Esteem Inventory $r = .80$; correlation with Beck Depression Inventory and the MMPI also presented; construct-factor analysis completed on the scale revealed five subtests for the children's version and four for the adult version; correlations between the scales indicate General correlated .89 with Total, .67 with Social, and .79 with Personal.

Test B: 116 Items
  Scales: Global Self-Esteem, Competence, Lovability, Likeability, Self-Control, Personal Power, Moral Self-Approval, Body Appearance, Body Functioning, Identity Integration, and Defensive Self-Enhancement.
  Administration: Self-administering.
  Item format: Client responds to each item on a 5-point scale ranging from "completely true" to "completely false" and on section 2, from "almost never" to "very often" (example: People tend to like to include me in their plans).
  Scoring: The answer sheet is designed so that it can be scored immediately by ripping the answer booklet to reveal the scoring sheet and counting the numerical weights of the options chosen. There are separate profile sheets for males and females on which the *T* scores and percentile ranks can be identified by circling the computed raw score for each scale.
  Interpretability: The manual does not have any case studies illustrating test interpretation. The manual does provide a description of what low scores and high scores mean on each scale.
  Reliability: Test-retest coefficients are reported for the test and range from a high of .89 on the Body Functioning scale to a low of .78 on the Identity Integration scale. The alpha coefficients range from a low of .78 on Defensive Self-Enhancement to .90 on Global Self-Esteem and Body Functioning.
  Validity: The test is a hierarchical model with the first level measuring global self-esteem and the second level corresponding to self-evaluations at an intermediate level of generality.

Convergent and Discriminant Validity: The scale was correlated with the Guilford-Zimmerman Temperament Survey, the Eysenck Personality Inventory, and the Body Cathexis Scale, among others. The average convergent correlation was .58 and the discriminant coefficient was .31. Factor analysis was also conducted on the scaled scores on the test. Factor analysis is used as a means of exploring the underlying factor structure of a set of test scores. Eigenvalue is a mathematical property of a matrix. It provides a criterion both as a method of determining the number of factors to be extracted and as a measure of variance accounted for in a given dimension. Three factors were extracted with eigenvalues greater than 1.

a. Given this descriptive and technical information, which of the two tests would you select?

b. What additional information would you want in order to make your decision?

ADDITIONAL READINGS

Anastasi, A., & Urbina, S. (1997). *Psychological testing* (7th ed.). Upper Saddle River, NJ: Prentice Hall.

Ary, D., Jacobs, L. C., & Razavieh, A. (1997). *Introduction to research in education* (5th ed.). Stamford, CT: Wadsworth.

Chase, C. (1999). *Contemporary assessment for educators.* New York: Longman.
A good discussion of validity and reliability is presented, as well as statistical procedures applied to test scores.

Doll, E. (1935). *Vineland Adaptive Behavior Scales.* Circle Pines, MN: American Guidance Services.

Embrelson, S. E., & Hershberger, S. L. (Eds.). (1999). *The new rules of measurement.* Mahwah, NJ: Erlbaum.
The authors compare the new rules for measurement with older rules.

Hood, A. B., & Johnson, R. W. (2001). *Assessment in counseling: A guide to the use of psychological assessment procedures* (3rd ed.). Alexandria, VA: American Counseling Association.

Kline, P. (1999). *Handbook of psychological testing* (2nd ed.). New York: Routledge.
Section 1 has a good presentation on psychometric theory and methods.

Nevo, B. (1985). Face validity revisited. In A. Anastasi and S. Urbina (Eds.), *Psychological testing* (7th ed.). Upper Saddle River, NJ: Prentice Hall.

Thorndike, R. M. (2005). *Measurement and evaluation in psychology and education* (7th ed.). Upper Saddle River, NJ: Merrill/Prentice Hall.

Waltkins, C. E., & Campbell, V. L. (Eds.). (2000). *Testing and assessment in counseling practice* (2nd ed.). Mahwah, NJ: Erlbaum.
Shows readers how assessment can be used in the counseling process.

Zeidner, M., & Most, R. (Eds.). (1992). *Psychological testing: An inside view.* Palo Alto, CA: Consulting Psychologists Press.
Presents an understandable and readable discussion of the major constructs in testing.

6 Process and Procedures of Testing

OVERVIEW

Because workers in the helping professions are often responsible for locating and selecting tests, they need to be familiar with the different sources of test information that are available to them. They need to know the particular strengths and weaknesses of each source and be familiar with the criteria for evaluating educational and psychological tests.

In addition, there are issues related to administration of the test that need to be considered. The professional needs to practice administering and scoring the test so that he or she can be fluent in giving the test. To produce reliable and valid test results, a test has to be administered under standardized or controlled conditions. If not administered as directed, the test results may be different from those obtained under standard procedures, and nonstandardized results may affect the accuracy of the interpretation. Major competencies needed by test administrators include adequate training, knowledge of the content being measured, knowledge of test construction, awareness of measurement concepts, and knowledge of good assessment practices.

OBJECTIVES

After studying this chapter, you should be able to

✔ Describe the sources of test information

✔ Describe the decision theory model used to help make judgments and test selection decisions

✔ Explain the criteria that should be used to evaluate a test

✔ Discuss the standards for test administration

✔ Explain the procedures that an examiner should follow

✔ Discuss the major issues in administering tests

DECISION THEORY MODEL

A decision theory model provides professionals with a frame of reference to guide them in deciding whether to test and how to locate and select a test. The following represent the various steps in a decision theory model:

1. Making judgments and decisions. (What kinds of judgments or decisions have to be made?)
2. Identifying the type of information needed.
3. Identifying available information.
4. Strategies to obtain additional information.
5. Locating appropriate tests.
6. Evaluating and selecting tests.

Making Decisions and Judgments

Workers in the helping professions are often asked to provide information to help counselors, teachers, and other professionals decide the best type of psychological or educational program to use with a client or clients, or the best type of intervention. Helping professionals are often asked to diagnose the strengths and weaknesses of a student with problems in reading or mathematics. Or they may be asked to predict the success of a student in a given educational or vocational program or a client in a treatment program. A school system may want to have a description of the basic skill competencies students have mastered. Or a client may want guidance in what career to consider.

These are only a few examples of the decisions and judgments that must be made. Sometimes the judgments focus on one individual, sometimes on a group. Sometimes their purpose is to predict behavior, sometimes to understand behavior, and sometimes to describe behavior. The key concept is that counselors need to be able to identify clearly the kind of decision or judgment that has to be made. The more specific the problem is, the easier it is to proceed to the next step in the model. The more abstract or vague the issue is, the more difficult it is to ask the right questions.

Identifying the Type of Information Needed

The second step in the decision-making process is to identify the type of information needed, carefully considering the scope and range of information required. Sometimes, for a particular job a checklist can be developed of the types of information normally needed and the types of questions that should be asked. A career counselor with a client suffering from midcareer crisis might be interested in the individual's employment history as well as current and future job desires. The counselor might also want information about the client's educational background, aptitudes, values, interests, and level of achievement. Cultural and environmental factors, marital status, socioeconomic class, and age are other dimensions that might be relevant. Of course, not all of the information would be gained through testing. It is valuable to discuss a case with colleagues or other professionals to be sure all types of necessary information have been identified. Even though problems may often appear to be unique, a thorough analysis helps develop a systematic approach to identifying needed information.

Identifying Available Information

The next step is to identify what part of the necessary information is already available. In clinical settings intake questionnaires, biographical data banks, and preliminary diagnoses by clinicians and physicians are available. School settings provide access to cumulative folders containing family information, educational history, grades, assessment and test results, anecdotal records, and attendance and health information. Unfortunately, overtesting may sometimes occur—that is, a client may be asked to repeat a recent test or take a similar one. One school district gave all of its students in grades 9 and 10 the Otis-Lennon School Ability Test, the Differential Aptitude Test Battery, the School and College Ability Tests, and the California Test of Mental Maturity. These tests repeatedly assessed the same factors. On an individual basis it is sometimes valuable to have more than one measure of scholastic aptitude or ability. However, when clients are asked to repeat the same test in a short time frame, they may lose motivation or even become hostile. It may be helpful to develop a checklist of information typically available on clients in a particular context. Figure 6.1 presents a sample checklist for a counselor or psychologist in a school setting.

Strategies to Obtain Additional Information

After identifying the type of information needed and the information already available, the professional needs to decide how and when to obtain additional information. If the information needed is to aid in curriculum and instructional decisions for a school system, a schoolwide testing program might be desirable. If the goal is to see whether a student has some type of learning disability, an individual battery of tests would be appropriate.

The time of day, the day of the week, the physical or emotional condition of the client, and the newness of the client to the environment are some of the factors to be considered. In addition, age, grade, level of anxiety and stress, and other issues can be important. Legal aspects need attention in many contexts, especially in testing students with exceptionalities, when parental as well as student approval is sought. Some legal requirements can be quite time consuming. Because of the total time required to identify and review tests that would be appropriate in a given context and to have the booklets and answer sheets available when needed, many schools and agencies develop an approved list of tests to use for different types of decisions or judgments.

Testing also has to be coordinated with the school schedule, student schedule, or treatment schedule so that the program is not disruptive or traumatic for the client. The examiner wants cooperative and motivated test takers in order to get valid information from the testing. Students tend to perform better in the morning and poorly right before a holiday.

Practices in Education, Ethics in Assessment, Standards for Multicultural Assessment, and more. Its Web site is *aac.ncat.edu.*

Divisions of professional organizations that focus on testing publish a number of newsletters that emphasize current trends, issues, and news in the field such as *SCORE,* a quarterly published by the Evaluation, Measurement, and Statistics division of the American Psychological Association. The National Council on Measurement in Education also publishes a quarterly newsletter. The Association for Assessment in Counseling of the American Counseling Association publishes *Newsnotes.*

Journal Articles.   An excellent source to locate information about tests is refereed journal articles. Articles that focus specifically on the area being tested or researched can provide professionals with information about widely used assessment instruments. For example, if a professional has interest in identifying the most accepted and widely used instrument to measure behavior problems in children, he or she could conduct a review of refereed journal articles focusing on research studies on child behavior problems. From the studies, the professional could identify assessment instruments already used by researchers in that field. In this example, the professional would find that the Child Behavior Checklist (CBCL) is one of the most commonly used instruments in that field.

Another source of information is journals that focus specifically on measurement. The following are such journals:

Applied Measurement in Education

Applied Psychological Measurement

Assessment and Evaluation in Higher Education Assessment

College Board Review

Educational Assessment

Educational Measurement: Issues and Practices

Educational and Psychological Measurement

Journal of Educational Measurement

Measurement and Evaluation in Counseling and Development

A number of other journals publish occasional articles on tests and testing issues, such as the *American Psychologist,* the *Journal of Counseling and Development,* and the *Educational Researcher.*

Compendia of Nonstandardized Instruments.   Many compendia are now available, including the following:

Encyclopedia of Psychological Assessment

PsycINFO

Cumulative Index to Tests in Microfiche

Tests: A Comprehensive Reference for Assessments in Psychology, Education, and Business

Measures for Psychological Assessment: A Guide to 3,000 Original Sources and Their Applications

Measures of Personality and Social Psychological Attitudes

Directory of Unpublished Experimental Mental Measures

The ETS Collection Catalog, Vol. 1: Achievement Tests and Measurement Devices

Tests and Measurements in Child Development: Handbooks I and II

The Experience of Work: A Compendium and Review of 249 Measures and Their Use

Measures for Clinical Practice: A Sourcebook

Measures of Occupational Attitudes and Occupational Characteristics

Measures of Political Attitudes

Measures of Social Psychological Attitudes (Rev. ed.)

Scales for the Measurement of Attitudes

Mirrors for Behavior II: An Anthology of Observation Instruments

Publishers' Catalogs.   After locating a list of tests, the potential user might want more specific information before ordering a specimen set to review. Publishers' catalogs (available online) provide a brief description about the test; information about norms, validity, reliability, scoring, and interpretation; and cost of the complete testing program, manual, test booklets, and/or answer sheets.

Professionals can order a specimen set of the test and review the test booklet as well as available manuals, answer sheets, and scoring services. The goal is to assess whether the test has validity for the intended purpose or purposes. A list of test publishers is located in Appendix B.

EVALUATING AND SELECTING TESTS

In order to select the most appropriate test, it is always important to have appropriate components—test booklets, answer sheets, technical manual, administrator's manual, and any manual for evaluating the test. This section discusses questions that can guide helping professionals in selecting a test.

1. *Was the test designed to measure the behavior under consideration? Does the test manual describe the purposes of the test? Does the intended purpose correspond to one that the test was designed to accomplish? Does the test manual adequately describe the behaviors that it measures?* A good test manual provides a statement of the purpose or purposes of the test and a description of the behaviors it measures. Sometimes the descriptions are brief; at other times the authors provide a complex matrix of objectives as well as levels measured.

2. *Do the test items appear to be measuring the traits, objectives, or behaviors that are to be assessed?* The next step is to review the test booklet. A survey achievement battery might have only one item measuring a specific objective in mathematics or only 4 or 5 items measuring a specific aptitude. To measure a specific

competency in mathematics, a criterion-referenced test with 5 to 10 items on a given objective might be preferable. However, to gain a picture of overall achievement in a school system, the survey achievement test might be sufficient. In addition, it is important to look at how test items are phrased. An item could be measuring simple recall of factual information or assessing higher-level cognitive skills, such as analysis or evaluation. Items on a personality test may be direct (e.g., "Do you like to take tests?") or less direct (e.g., "In a classroom choose the situation you most prefer: taking a test, giving an oral report, doing a workbook page."). A test reviewer must sometimes make subjective judgments about items.

3. *Does the test have validity information?* As noted, validity is the concept that deals with whether a test measures what it was designed to measure. The test reviewer must determine whether the test is valid for the intended purpose. If the test results will be used to describe competencies in a certain subject or in content fields, the reviewer should check the content validity of the test. Because a test includes only a limited sample of items representing the objectives or behavior to be measured, it is important that those items be as representative as possible. In addition, because tests use hypothetical constructs that have been operationally defined by the test authors, the reviewer should check the authors' evidence to support the construct validity of the tests.

4. *Is the test reliable?* It is important to know how stable or consistent a test is over time, sample of items, or occasions; how precisely the test results can be interpreted; and how the score is affected by measurement errors. The reviewer should check the reliability information in the test manual, inspecting not only the types of reliability cited but also the magnitude of the coefficients reported. Coefficients will be higher for achievement tests than for personality tests, and higher for high school students than for preschool students. The acceptability of the coefficient depends on the intended use of the test results. If test results will be interpreted for individuals, the reviewer should be sure the manual gives information on the standard error of measurement. A test with a large standard error of measurement might not be appropriate for individual diagnosis, placement, or prediction.

5. *Does the test provide sufficient information for the psychologist or counselor to interpret the results?* A test should provide the necessary information to make a proper interpretation. In norm-referenced tests such as survey achievement tests and scholastic ability tests, an individual's score is compared with the scores of other individuals in a selected reference or norm group. The client being tested should be represented in that norming group. Is there information on how the norming group was formulated? The examiner may want to know about the geographic areas, ages, gender composition, school locations (e.g., urban, rural, suburban), cultural groups, and educational levels included in the norms. The author should explain the procedures to translate raw scores into derived scores and should provide appropriate tables for different types of scores. The author should also describe techniques for interpreting the test and should adequately explain the meaning of the various scales.

A counselor or psychologist might be interested in more than just a total score and might want specific item information. Some tests do have computerized reports that give information by objective or by item. The test reviewer should study the types of scoring services available and should have sample copies of the printout of results and interpretation.

6. *Does the test provide interpretive feedback for the examinee?* It is important to provide information to clients about their performance on a given test. With achievement tests and school testing programs the information needs to be shared not only with students but also with parents or guardians. In adaptive testing, clients taking tests on a personal computer can get immediate feedback on the screen as well as a hard copy from the printer. Many tests have self-interpretive leaflets or booklets that examinees can use to interpret and understand their results. However, examiners should never allow self-interpretive booklets to take the place of a counselor's communication and explanation of results. Such tools are an excellent supplement, but the counselor must be sure that all information is understood.

7. *Is the test appropriate for the examinee?* A test may measure appropriate behaviors and have excellent reliability and validity but be inappropriate for the client. One important dimension to be considered is the reading level of the items on the test. If the reading level is too difficult, the client may not be able to understand the vocabulary or sentence structure used. A second important dimension is the physical format of the test. The print size, visual layout of questions, and use of color and white space need to be considered. A third dimension is the manner of responding to questions. Are answers to be recorded on a separate answer sheet or in the test booklet, or are they to be spoken, written, marked, or performed?

   Examiners must also consider whether the tasks on the test are age- or grade-appropriate; whether the test is appropriate; whether the test is appropriate for clients of different social backgrounds; whether it is appropriate for individuals with various physical, mental, or academic disabilities; and whether special equipment or facilities are needed to administer the test.

8. *Is the test free from bias?* Lately, attention has focused on cultural and gender bias in test items. Test authors should give evidence in their manuals of the procedures used to eliminate bias. The goal is to have items that are relevant and understandable for the individuals being tested. Some older tests do contain biased language.

9. *What level of competency is needed to administer the test?* Some tests can be administered to large or small groups and have easy directions for the examiner. Other tests demand careful monitoring and can be administered only individually. In most testing programs the counselor or psychologist trains examiners and teachers to administer the less complicated group achievement and ability tests. But certain individual intelligence tests and personality tests require specialized training for the examiner. Different levels of psychological tests can be purchased and used only by qualified individuals. Sometimes tapes are available to guide test administration, and there may be separate directions for administering the test to special populations. The proper administration of a test is necessary if results are to be valid. Procedures for administering tests are discussed in more detail in the next section.

PRACTICAL ISSUES IN TESTING

A number of practical features need to be considered in the evaluation of a test. Validity and reliability may hold more importance, but other factors also merit attention.

Time of Testing

The time it takes to give a test may be a factor. Can the test be administered during the regular class period, or does the examiner need more time? How many individually administered tests can an examiner reasonably schedule during a day? Time is a factor that is important in decision making. The purpose of the testing can determine how important that factor may be. For example, time constraints may be a critical variable when the concern is with getting information quickly to facilitate decision making. We know that the longer the test, the more reliable the results; but the question might concern how much reliability is necessary for a particular purpose.

Cost of Testing

Cost is an important feature because most schools and agencies have limited budgets. Some test companies now lease tests, especially achievement batteries, rather than requiring the user to purchase them. Also, some test booklets are reusable, requiring the examiner to purchase only answer sheets for another testing. If computer software is available, evaluation of total cost should consider not only the purchase of test materials but also the time needed to administer, score, and interpret the tests. There are many scoring services to which most of the major tests and test batteries can be sent for scoring and interpretation—at an additional cost, of course.

Format of Test

Just as in the evaluation of other printed material, test users should consider factors such as size of print, attractiveness of format, and clarity of illustrations. Some tests are attractively designed and utilize a variety of colors and print sizes. Some, however, have print that is too small or dark paper that is hard to read. Some tests may use double columns to cut down on necessary eye movements; others spread the items across the whole page. The test user should think of the test taker. An attractive format may provide more valid results.

Readability

The readability of the test is an important factor. In general, unless the intent is to test the reading level or verbal facility of the test taker, the reading level should be kept simple so that the construct is measured rather than a reading comprehension factor. Even a test presented on a cassette should use an appropriate reading level and vocabulary.

Ease of Administration

Administration of tests is discussed in more detail later in the chapter, but it should be noted here that there are different levels of tests. Some require extensive training to administer and score; others do not. Some tests are more difficult to administer because they have a number of individually timed subtests and elaborate instructions for the test taker. The test users should read through the test manual and evaluate the difficulty of test administration.

Ease of Scoring

Some tests have scoring templates and are easy to score by hand or by computer. Other tests require considerable judgment and experience on the part of the examiner. Behavioral observations may require specialized training to score. It is possible for scoring to take more time than administering a test. Even when a test is objective and has a predetermined scoring key, the test user should double-check the accuracy of the scoring.

Ease of Interpretation

Results are not useful unless they are interpretable, and both test makers and examiners are expected to provide explanation. Many tests do provide manuals of interpretation for the examiner or detailed sections in the test manual. The better tests have sample or illustrative case studies. Test users should also check to see whether there are special profile sheets or materials to guide the test takers in understanding the results.

Available Aids for Test Administrators

A number of tests now exist on audiotape, some on videotape. All kinds of software packages are available for users, and many tests and questionnaires are now administered on personal computers. Available aids may make a test easier to administer. For example, a videotape of directions given in sign language might facilitate a test given to an individual who is deaf.

Usefulness of the Test Manual

A test manual should be understandable and thorough. Standards for Educational and Psychological Testing (AERA et al., 1999) lists specific standards for manuals. Some of the major components are as follows:

1. The manual should provide evidence to support any use of a single item as a basis of assessment and should caution the user about errors of that approach.
2. The manual should include evidence of the distinctiveness of the constructs being measured. The authors need to discuss how the test was developed and revised.
3. The manual should provide scientific evidence on the test.
4. The manual should provide adequate description of the domains assessed and the types of items included in the domain.

5. The manual should include a description of the course or training program for which the test was designed and the year the materials were prepared.
6. On interest inventories, the authors should provide the extent to which average patterns of interests or abilities for an occupation are compatible with the major specialties within that occupation.
7. For adaptive tests the developers need to provide the procedures for selecting items, stopping the test, and scoring the test.
8. The manual should present the implications of the research for test design, interpretation, and use.
9. The manual should summarize evidence derived from research studies to indicate the degree to which improvement can be expected from practice or coaching.
10. The manual should explain in sufficient detail and clarity the procedures for scoring tests to maximize the accuracy of scoring.

Section 5 of the standards is devoted to standards specifically for test publications: technical manuals and user guides. Figure 6.2 shows a checklist summary of those standards.

STEPS IN TEST DEVELOPMENT

Professional standards and ethics of psychologists and counselors focus on test development. Test authors and developers are advised to provide evidence of the reliability and validity of their tests in meeting the purposes for which they were developed. Authors and developers should also provide manuals and norms to help users administer, score, and interpret the tests; they should anticipate how their tests will be used and misused and design materials to foster proper use. Authors and developers have the responsibility to present information in a readily accessible form and to include summaries and interpretations to aid users in reviewing and evaluating the tests.

The test development process may vary somewhat depending upon the type of test being constructed. The following steps are involved in developing an achievement test or aptitude test.

Phase 1:   Establishing the Need
　　　　　　1. Consider informal and formal requests for such a test.
　　　　　　2. Conduct surveys to see if a need exists.
　　　　　　3. Review and critique other similar tests.
　　　　　　4. Be knowledgeable of tests that have computer-assisted and computer-adaptive forms.
Phase 2:   Defining the Objectives and Test Parameters
　　　　　　1. Establish the purpose of the test—who is to be tested and why.
　　　　　　2. Define what objectives will be required of the test takers.
　　　　　　3. Discuss how the test information will be useful to the users as well as the test takers.
　　　　　　4. Consider the type of question format and the number of questions to be included.

	Yes	No
1. Technical manual available at time of publication of test	_____	_____
2. Rationale and uses of test discussed	_____	_____
3. User cautioned about possible misuses	_____	_____
4. Studies presented on general uses	_____	_____
5. Studies presented on specific uses	_____	_____
6. Special qualifications of users stated	_____	_____
7. Bibliography of research and studies on test presented	_____	_____
8. Test manual updated and revised when new edition of test was published	_____	_____
9. Inquiries invited from potential users	_____	_____
10. Relationships between test scores and criteria reported	_____	_____
11. Test administration conditions and modes explained	_____	_____
12. Interpretive aids provided for test takers	_____	_____
13. Promotional materials accurately supported by research base	_____	_____
14. Test interpretation easy to understand	_____	_____
15. Automated test interpretation service available	_____	_____
16. Rationale presented and conceptualized if cutoff scores are given	_____	_____
17. Validity of interpretation discussed	_____	_____
18. Evidence presented on whether construct being measured corresponds to nature of assessment intended	_____	_____
19. Rationale for specific combination of subtests and justification of interpretive relationships among scores included	_____	_____
20. Gender and relevant racial or ethnic group information presented	_____	_____
21. Method of recommended linguistic modification described in detail	_____	_____

Figure 6.2
Checklist for evaluating a test manual.

Phase 3: Involving Advisory Committee Input
1. Select a focus group of experts in the field (e.g., teachers, administrators, subject area specialists, consumers).
2. Review the objectives, purposes, and parameters of the test.
3. Determine the table of specifications (blueprint) for the test.

Phase 4: Writing the Questions (Test Items)
1. Use subject matter specialists or experts in the test domain to write test items.
2. Have a measurement specialist review test items prior to the field test; have the review panel see whether the test measures the intended domain and whether the items match the specifications in the test blueprint.

Phase 5: Conducting a Field Test of the Items
    1. Use a test sample similar to the targeted group for which the test is being developed.
    2. Compute item difficulty and discrimination indices.

Phase 6: Reviewing the Items
    1. Check for gender bias, cultural bias, and disability bias.
    2. Eliminate items that might be unfair or offensive to any group.

Phase 7: Assembling the Final Copy
    1. Be sure the type and number of items meet the coverage specified in the blueprint.
    2. Check the validity of the scoring key with independent judges. Remember that there have been occasions when the student had the correct answer but was told the answer was incorrect.
    3. Have the test reviewed by external as well as internal committees.

Phase 8: Securing Necessary Technical Data
    1. Determine sampling procedures.
    2. Administer and score the test.
    3. Compute reliability and validity.
    4. Develop appropriate norms.

TEST ADMINISTRATION GUIDELINES AND PROCEDURES

A test has to be administered under standardized or controlled conditions. If the examiner does not administer the test as directed, the results may be different from those obtained under standard procedures, and nonstandard results may affect the accuracy of the interpretation.

Saklofske, Kowalchuk, and Schwean (1992) identify five major competencies needed by test administrators: adequate training, knowledge of the content being measured, knowledge of test construction, awareness of measurement concepts, and knowledge of good assessment practices. These competencies will be discussed in more detail in the following sections.

Standards for Test Administration

Professional standards such as the Standards for Educational and Psychological Testing (AERA et al., 1999) call for proper procedures in administering tests. The test administrator is cautioned to carefully follow the standardized procedures for administration and scoring specified by the test publishers. Both the test administration skills and the interpersonal style of the examiner may influence the test takers' performance. If the test administrator can build a dynamic relationship with the test takers, more valid results will be achieved.

The administrator needs to accept responsibility for the competent use and administration of the test and should be trained and qualified to use appropriate tests and to understand the content that the test measures. The National Board for Certified

Counselors' Code of Ethics (1989) reminds counselors that there are many types of assessment techniques. Certified counselors must recognize the limits of their competence and perform only those functions for which they have adequate training.

The various standards call for the administrator to establish a comfortable testing environment with minimal distractions. Test materials need to be carefully selected to meet the developmental level of the client; that is, the test should be readable and understandable. Screens for computer-administered tests should be legible and free from glare.

In addition to being responsible for quality control, the test administrator needs to ensure the validity of the test results by eliminating opportunities for the test takers to attain scores fraudulently. The test giver needs to monitor the testing situation and must refrain from helping any favored person with answers or coaching individuals on the test items.

Any modification of standard administration procedures or scoring should be described in the test report so the reader is alert to the modifications. Users should be cautioned regarding the possible effects of such modifications on the validity of the test results. Test administrators are cautioned not to modify prescribed administration procedures to adapt to particular individuals such as reading test items to an individual, defining specific words in an item, or encouraging an individual to reconsider answers (Test Users Training Work Group, 1993).

Pretesting Procedures

Responsibilities of Users of Standardized Tests (ACA, 2003) includes under test administration all the procedures to ensure that a test is presented consistently in a manner specified by the test developers and used in the standardization, and that the individuals being tested have orientation and conditions that maximize their opportunity for optimum performance. The Code of Ethics of the NBCC (1998) also states that counselors must provide specific orientation of information to an examinee before and after administration of an assessment instrument or technique so that the results may be put in the proper perspective with other relevant factors. The examiner must carry out a number of important duties even before the test date. When conducting a psychoeducational evaluation or counseling consultation, the National Association of School Psychologists' Principles for Professional Ethics (2000) calls for psychologists to consider individual differences such as age, gender, and socioeconomic and ethnic backgrounds and to strive to select and use appropriate procedures, techniques, and strategies relevant to such differences.

In many situations the approval of the examinee is needed before testing can be scheduled. If the client is a minor, it is necessary to get parental approval. Most agencies and school systems have set procedures that must be followed prior to testing. The examiner needs to know the ethical and legal procedures and guidelines. In addition to securing the appropriate permission, test administrators need to consider the privacy of the client and any ethical or legal problems that testing might raise. They also need to review the items on the test prior to administering it and explain why the test will be given and who will get the results.

Examiner Knowledge

The first major responsibility of the examiner prior to testing is to know all about the test. The examiner needs to review the test booklet, test manuals, and answer sheet. The test administrator needs to be familiar with the content of the test, the type of test items, and the directions for administering the test. One of the best ways to become familiar with the test is to follow the procedures and actually take the test. Many tests require the examiner to read directions to the examinees; other tests also require the examiner to read the test items. Responsibilities of Users of Standardized Tests (ACA, 2003) states that effective administration of tests requires that the administrator have knowledge of and training in the actual instruments and processes of presentation. Some individual and group tests require extensive training, and only qualified, experienced persons should administer standardized tests. Saklofske et al. (1992) suggest that administrators also need to understand test construction, measurement concepts, and good assessment practices.

Management Details

Test companies require purchasers to furnish evidence of their qualifications to use tests. Forms request information on the training level of the purchasers, their professional credentials and educational background, the updating of their professional knowledge and skills, and any other special competencies. They are also questioned about the purposes of the testing. On the Riverside Publishing Company's form, test purchasers are asked to read five principles of effective test use and then sign the form stipulating that they will follow these guidelines:

1. Maintain the security of testing materials before and after the testing.
2. Avoid labeling students based on a single test score.
3. Adhere strictly to the copyright law and under no circumstances photocopy or otherwise reproduce answer forms, test booklets, or other materials.
4. Administer, score, interpret, and use tests exactly as specified in the manual.
5. Release results only to authorized persons in a form consistent with the accepted principles of test interpretation.

Many management tasks have to be done prior to testing. For example, it is necessary to secure the appropriate number of tests as well as answer sheets and scoring keys. Any order should be double-checked before it is sent and when it is received. Here are some of the other tasks that need to be accomplished:

1. Schedule the date for the test.
2. Schedule the room or facilities.
3. Count the number of booklets, answer sheets, pencils, and any other needed materials.
4. Secure a stopwatch, if needed, and a do-not-disturb sign.
5. Arrange materials for distribution.
6. Determine the order in which tests or subtests will be administered.
7. Decide on the procedures for collecting test materials.

The client must agree on the date and time of testing, and it is helpful to issue a reminder. It is usually wise to avoid testing the day before a holiday, and it is always important to schedule enough time. Time should be added for giving directions, answering questions, distributing test materials, and collecting test booklets and answer sheets. In school contexts it is important to avoid conflicts with other school activities.

Training Test Administrators

When testing a large number of clients or students, the examiner will need help from other individuals such as teachers, administrators, or counselors. The training of these assistants needs to be specific to the test being administered. They will need a general overview of the test and preferably some practice giving and taking it. Hands-on experience helps in identifying some of the types of problems that might arise—for example, what to do with clients or students who finish early. All test administrators need to know the guidelines for answering questions about the test and the importance of following standardized procedures in administering the test. Each examiner might benefit from a checklist like the one illustrated in Figure 6.3.

Awareness and Orientation

A test administrator often must be responsible for awareness and orientation. Codes of test standards remind test administrators that they have responsibility for orientation of the test takers. They recommend that the candidates for testing as well as the relevant institutions or agencies and the community be informed about testing programs. Orientation should describe the purposes of the tests, content areas measured, method of administration, and reporting and utilization of scores. In school contexts students and parents need to be made aware of the testing. If the test is part of the system's overall testing program, the examiner should provide news releases not only for the school paper but also for local news media sources. Sometimes agencies or schools publish newsletters that include information on tests and testing programs scheduled in the near future.

Many test publishers provide information sheets and brochures about a test or testing program. These sources usually describe the type of tests, the purpose(s) of the test, the types of test items used, type of scoring, and the method of reporting the results. In some cases the cost of the testing is given, along with the time schedule for the testing and the mode of administration (see Table 6.2).

The examiner must be sure that orientation makes a test relevant to the test taker(s). Seven general topics should be covered in orientation sessions:

1. Purpose of the test
2. Criteria used for selecting the test
3. Conditions under which the test is to be taken
4. Range of skills or domains to be measured
5. Administrative procedures and concerns (e.g., group or individual administration, time involved, cost)
6. Types of questions on the test and an overview
7. Type of scoring, method, and schedule for reporting results to the test taker

Pretesting Procedures

_____ Send out notice to remind client(s) of testing time.

_____ Send out information on testing program to public and/or parents.

_____ Get informed consent if needed.

_____ Have testing materials on hand.

_____ Check schedule to see whether there is adequate time for testing.

_____ Check date of testing to avoid conflicts.

_____ Arrange for distribution of test materials.

_____ Decide on order of administration of tests.

_____ Decide on procedures for collection of test materials.

Test Knowledge

_____ Review test manuals and test booklets.

_____ Know the makeup of the test.

_____ Read and practice the directions for administering the test.

_____ Check time limits for the test.

_____ Know the directions for recording answers.

_____ Take the test.

_____ Be familiar with scoring procedures.

_____ Prepare answers for specific questions clients might ask.

Management Details

_____ Schedule room and facilities.

_____ Make and check seating arrangements.

_____ Check lighting and ventilation.

_____ Arrange clear and adequate work space.

_____ Organize materials and arrange for distribution.

_____ Highlight directions in the manual.

_____ Develop agenda for the day.

Information for Examinees

_____ Provide sample copies, study guides, and an overview.

_____ Explain purpose of testing.

_____ Communicate the conditions under which the test is to be taken.

_____ Identify any cost of testing.

_____ Identify any special materials or tools needed.

_____ Explain what will happen with the results.

_____ Discuss test scoring procedures.

Figure 6.3
Checklist for test administrators.

Many standardized tests provide sample items and an overview of the test. The examiner should be sure that all who are going to take a given test have had specific practice with sample problems or have worked on test-taking skills prior to the test. This requirement is especially appropriate for aptitude, achievement, and ability testing.

Table 6.2
Modes of test administration.

Mode	Description	Advantages	Disadvantages
Self-administered	Examinees read the instructions themselves and take the test.	The examiner does not need to be present.	The motivation or attitudes of test takers are not known. They may be confused or unclear about tasks.
Group-administered	Examiner reads the directions to small or large group, answers any questions, and follows the standardized procedures outlined in the manual.	This is the most cost-effective method.	The motivation and attitude of the test takers are unknown.
Individually administered	Examiner administers test to one individual at a time, following the procedures found in the examiner's manual.	The examiner can assess the motivation and attitudes of the test taker as well as thought processes and cognitive level. The examiner can probe to gain more information.	This method is expensive, and only a few individuals can be tested each day. The examiner needs special training and experience in administering individual tests.
Computer-based/ Computer-adaptive	The directions for taking the test and the test itself are presented on the screen.	The test taker often can get immediate feedback. The examiner does not necessarily have to be present. This method allows for flexibility in scheduling. The computer can score, analyze, and interpret the tests of a large group of individuals. Computer-adaptive tests usually take less time to complete.	Some individuals may not perform well because of certain disabilities or because of their attitude toward computers. This method may not be practical if many individuals are to be tested.

Administering the Test

Test administration begins with a final check to see that all is in order—lighting, ventilation, seating arrangements, clear work space for examinees, sharpened pencils, a do-not-disturb sign, and provisions for the toilet needs of examinees. The test itself presents further administrative tasks. One of the most important tasks on a standardized test is to deliver verbatim instructions given in the test manual and to follow the stated sequence and timing. Any deviation may change the nature of the tasks on the test and may negate any comparison of test results with those of the norming group.

The examiner also needs to establish rapport with the examinees. For some the test may be a new and frightening experience; they may feel fear, frustration, hostility, or anxiety. In individual testing the examiner can assess these emotional and mo-

Table 6.2

Continued

Mode	Description	Advantages	Disadvantages
Videotape-administered	Directions for taking the test and actual test items are presented on the screen.	This method allows for both audio and visual stimuli to be combined. Simulated or real situations can be presented. A wider variety of behaviors can be assessed.	The method may be inappropriate for individuals with certain disabilities.
Audiotape-administered	The test is presented on audiotape.	The examiner can circulate to see whether there are any problems. Testing time can be controlled. The quality of the recording and the type of voice can be uniformly controlled. This method is good to use with individuals with reading problems.	This method is inappropriate for individuals with hearing, listening, or attention deficits.
American Sign Language	The examiner gives directions and presents the test items using sign language.	American Sign Language is the first language of many individuals with hearing impairments.	The examiner needs to be experienced in signing and working with individuals with hearing impairments. Some of these individuals might have learned a different system.
Pantomime	The examiner avoids oral or written directions and relies on pantomime to administer the test.	This method is appropriate for certain individuals with disabilities, such as those with speech disabilities.	The examiner must be trained in administering such tests and experienced in working with the various special populations.

tivational factors and positively support the test taker. In group testing it is harder to establish rapport, but the examiner can be warm, friendly, and enthusiastic. The goal is for the results to give a valid picture of the attributes measured, so the examiner should encourage the examinees to do their best on each task. Saklofske et al. (1992) indicate that the test administrator should demonstrate clear verbal articulation, calmness, and positive anticipation, and also have empathy for and social identification with the examinees. Positive reinforcement may help in establishing rapport and reducing anxiety. It should not be artificial and should not be overused. Helping professionals recognize that the examiner needs to be genuine and both understand and recognize personal biases in order to be both positive and objective. One way this is done is by listening carefully and observing nonverbal cues. Impartial treatment of all those being testing is essential.

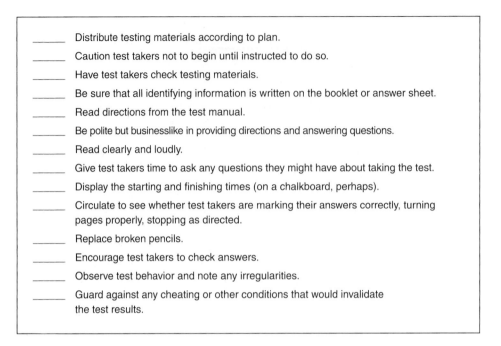

_____ Distribute testing materials according to plan.

_____ Caution test takers not to begin until instructed to do so.

_____ Have test takers check testing materials.

_____ Be sure that all identifying information is written on the booklet or answer sheet.

_____ Read directions from the test manual.

_____ Be polite but businesslike in providing directions and answering questions.

_____ Read clearly and loudly.

_____ Give test takers time to ask any questions they might have about taking the test.

_____ Display the starting and finishing times (on a chalkboard, perhaps).

_____ Circulate to see whether test takers are marking their answers correctly, turning pages properly, stopping as directed.

_____ Replace broken pencils.

_____ Encourage test takers to check answers.

_____ Observe test behavior and note any irregularities.

_____ Guard against any cheating or other conditions that would invalidate the test results.

Figure 6.4
Checklist of activities during testing.

A list of activities for test administrators during testing is included in Figure 6.4. The examiner must be alert to what is going on in the testing situation. In addition, the examiner must be alert to the unique problems of special populations. Young children and individuals with disabilities may need shorter test periods and perhaps smaller numbers in the testing group. The examiner may have to administer tests individually or make special provisions for visual, auditory, or perceptual-motor impairments, being sure to record any deviation from standardized administrative procedures. Many tests and assessment inventories are designed to test people with disabilities or give suggested procedures to accommodate various disabilities.

The test administrator must be a keen observer of what is going on in the testing situation. Most individual intelligence tests have observation forms on which an examiner can record test-taking behavior. Independent scales are also available, focusing attention on both normal and abnormal aspects. The examiner should record any critical incidents that may increase or reduce an individual's opportunity to perform to capacity. If a test administrator has no direct responsibility during a test, he or she should circulate among the examiners and offer assistance if needed.

Posttesting Procedures

A routine saves time. The administrator needs to collect materials according to a predetermined order, counting the test booklets and answer sheets and arranging them all face up. In addition, everything should be put back in the testing kit in the proper way so that it is ready for future use. With individual testing the examiner should take time immediately to record any incident that might invalidate scores.

Recording Test Behavior. Test behavior can be recorded on some of the standardized checklists designed to accompany various individual tests or on examiner-made scales. The examiner should determine whether any unusual behaviors might give insight into examinee performance or personality. Different rating forms usually rate examinees on physical reactions, test behavior, social behavior, and observable verbal characteristics. Sometimes it is just as important to know how the individual arrived at an answer as to know whether the answer is right or wrong. Careful observation gives clues to typical behavior as well as to methods of problem solving and reaction to different domains.

The test administrator may want to write a short anecdotal record of an individual or an incident and file it with the test. For example, the examiner might note that John marked all the answers on his answer sheet in about 2 minutes and put his head down on the desk. When asked what he had done, he said, "I just put marks down on the paper to see how many items I can get right by guessing." Recording brief accounts can be enlightening.

MAJOR ISSUES AND PROBLEMS IN TEST ADMINISTRATION

Problems in test administration are often the result of inadequate preparation for test taking. The awareness or orientation phase is an important element in helping to alleviate response set problems, anxiety, and tension. However, certain problems present themselves only during the testing situation. Some of these, with possible solutions, are detailed in Table 6.3.

Examiner Bias

A number of factors can bias test results. Rapport (or lack thereof) is one factor. An effective interpersonal relationship must be established between the test administrator and test takers. Partly it involves encouraging test takers to do their best, to be cooperative, and to show responsiveness. Warm interpersonal relationships during testing may improve test results.

The gender, race, or ethnic heritage of the test administrator and test takers may also affect test scores (Skiba, Knesting, & Bush, 2002), Administrators need to recognize that race, gender, socioeconomic class, and cultural and educational background can significantly influence test results. The use of reinforcement and encouragement is likewise complex because its effectiveness depends on the aforementioned factors (Saklofske et al., 1992). Other factors, such as a lack of sensitivity to the psychological, emotional, and intellectual needs of the test takers, may also bias the test results. One biasing dimension that should not be overlooked is the examiner's beliefs and attitudes. Both verbal and nonverbal cues can demonstrate bias.

In general, examiner bias takes six forms: race, communication skills, attitudes and expectations, gender, competence, and test ethics. Oakland and Parmelee (1985)

Table 6.3
Problems encountered in test administration.

Problem	Possible Solution
Cheating	Create an environment in which cheating is impossible because of spacing of desks, work areas, and so on.
Client asks question that is not addressed in manual	Respond with good judgment based on experience with similar tests.
Guessing	Encourage examinees to work on known items first, leaving unknown items until the latter part of the testing time. Advise clients to guess if they wish if the test does not penalize guessing.
Lack of effort	Be positive and businesslike in explaining the purpose and importance of the test and exhorting the test taker to do well.
Questions during testing	Explain in the beginning that questions will not be answered during the test session. While circulating around the test room, quietly answer only questions resulting from confusion.
Distractions	Eliminate the distraction if possible. Apologize to test takers and explain as much as possible. Allow extra time.
Refusal to answer	In individual testing repeat the questions and ask whether the test taker understands it. After testing, inquire further if the test taker should have been able to answer.
Examiner indecision in the use of praise and encouragement	Positive reinforcement may help in establishing rapport and reducing anxiety. It should not be artificial and should not be overused.
Examiner effects	Recognize personal biases and be positive but objective. Listen carefully and observe nonverbal cues.

indicate there is a popular belief that attributes the lower test scores of minority individuals to the test administration of a White examiner. Although there is not strong support in the literature for their premise, Oakland and Parmelee suggest, "White examiners may contribute to anxiety, fears and suspicion, verbal constriction, strained and unnatural reactions, insecurity, latent prejudice, and other such reactions as a result of racial differences" (p. 719). On the other hand, some examiners exhibit paternalism, overidentification, and exaggerated concerns or fear of negative client reactions. In general, a test administrator might consider assigning a minority examiner to test minority clients if those clients have a strong preference to work with a minority professional.

In their meta-analysis of the effects of examiner familiarity on children's test performance, Fuchs and Fuchs (1986) found that examiner familiarity raised test performance an average of .28 standard deviations. Study results indicated that differential performance favoring the familiar examiner was greater when subjects were of low socioeconomic status, were assessed on comparatively difficult tests, and knew the examiner for a relatively long duration. The authors concluded that the effects of examiner familiarity demonstrate the importance of contextual factors in testing. They see these factors as intervening between the test's sampling of skills or abilities and client performance, bringing into question the view of the test instrument as the most important, if not the exclusive, variable in test performance (p. 257).

A second factor in testing bias is the language and dialect of the examiner and test taker. Communication between the two may be impeded, and verbal and nonverbal cues may be misunderstood. Bilingual and non-English-speaking examinees often score higher on performance and nonlanguage tests than on verbal tests.

The third factor in testing is the attitudes and expectations of the examiner. The examiner who has warmth, empathy, or genuine concern for the examinee may behave quite differently from the examiner who rejects or is indifferent toward the examinee. Bias and prejudice may prevent an examiner from objectively understanding the characteristics of those being tested.

The fourth factor in testing bias is the gender of the examiner. Sattler (1988) concludes that female examiners tend to elicit slightly better performance than do male examiners. The competence of the examiner is another factor. Some test administrators are poorly prepared to do a clinical, behavioral, and psychoeducational assessment of certain age or cultural groups. Others may conduct the assessment mechanically and superficially.

A final factor is the ethical standards of the examiner. The APA's (2002) Ethical Principles of Psychologists and Code of Conduct calls for the psychologist to believe in the dignity and worth of the individual and to commit to freedom of inquiry, communication, and concern for the best interests of clients, colleagues, and society in general. The psychologist is responsible for protecting the welfare of all clients.

FEEDBACK ON THE TEST AND TEST ADMINISTRATION

In *Educational and Psychological Testing: The Test Taker's Outlook,* Nevo and Jaeger (1993) emphasize the need to get evaluative feedback from the test takers on their attitudes not only toward the test but also toward the test administration, testing environment, and test orientation. Here are a few possible questions that could be included in such an evaluation:

1. How would you rate the physical environment for this testing?
2. How would you rate the performance or competencies of the test administrator?
3. Was the time allotted adequate to finish the test?
4. Was the orientation to the test helpful?
5. Do you feel that the test was fair?

SUMMARY

This chapter walks through the process of locating and selecting tests, evaluating tests, and test administration. As the first step, a worker in the helping professions needs to know how and where to locate sources of test information. A number of databases as well as reference sources are readily available. Other traditional sources of test information include specimen sets, publishers' catalogs, test review collections, ERIC professional journals, and newsletters. Peers and colleagues may also be a good source of information.

It is important to secure a specimen set of a test from the publisher and to check the face validity of the test. If the test looks promising, its validity, reliability, usability, and practicality should be checked carefully as well as various reviews by experts in the field.

The next step, how a test is administered, can affect the accuracy and validity of the test results. The test administrator must have important competencies. One key component is knowledge of and training with the test being administered. The attitude of the examiner toward testing and toward clients is crucial, and variables such as environmental conditions can interfere with proper results.

Many tasks, such as orientation, must be completed prior to testing. Other tasks, such as circulating around the room, are accomplished during testing. The administrator must be a keen observer of what is taking place during testing and should record any factors that might be important in test interpretation. The examiner should try to maintain a positive attitude, maximize achievement and motivation, and equalize advantages.

QUESTIONS FOR DISCUSSION

1. What are the major steps that an examiner should follow in determining what test to use?
2. What are the different sources of test information that can be used in selecting a test? What are the advantages and disadvantages of each?
3. What practical issues need to be considered in selecting a test?
4. How would you compare the procedures to be followed in administering both group and individual tests?
5. What techniques should the examiner use to establish rapport with test takers?
6. What types of behavior should an examiner avoid during test administration? Why?

SUGGESTED ACTIVITIES

1. Devise a checklist to use to evaluate tests.
2. Critically review a test in your field. Use the guidelines in this chapter to organize your evaluation.
3. Compare reviews of the same test found in different editions of *Mental Measurements Yearbooks,* in *Test Critiques,* and professional journals. What themes did they agree on, and what were some of the sources of disagreement? What parts of the reviews were helpful to you? Write a composite evaluation of the test from these different reviews.
4. Read the manual for test administration for a major controlled testing program such as the Scholastic Aptitude Test or the Graduate Record Examinations. Interview

the person who is responsible for the administration of the test in your area. What kinds of problems has the person encountered in administering the test? How adequate were the directions in the manual for handling those problem situations?

5. Review the literature on test bias and write an analysis of what the literature has to say about good and poor test administration practices.

6. Design a program to train a group of counselors or teachers to administer a specific test.

7. Locate several test manuals and read the sections on test scoring and interpretation. Compare the presentation. How clear and understandable are the procedures? Are possible problems addressed? Are models of correct answers given? Are case studies presented?

ADDITIONAL READINGS

Anastasi, A., & Urbina, S. (1997). *Psychological testing* (7th ed.). Upper Saddle River, NJ: Prentice Hall.

Clemans, W. V. (1971). Test administration. In R. L. Thorndike (Ed.), *Educational measurement* (2nd ed.). Washington, DC: American Council on Education.
This chapter gives a good overview of the many details involved in administering tests.

Educational Testing Service (ETS). (1987). *Directory of selected national testing programs*. Phoenix: Oryx.

ETS Test Collection Catalogs. (1986). *Vol. 1: Achievement tests and measurement devices*. (1988). *Vol. 2: Vocational tests and measurement*. (1989). *Vol. 3: Tests for special populations*. (1990). *Vol. 4: Cognitive, aptitude and intelligence tests*. (1991). *Vol. 5: Attitude tests*. Phoenix: Oryx.

Fabriano, E. (1989). *Index to tests used in educational dissertations*. Phoenix: Oryx.
The author lists the tests used in dissertations.

Impara, J. C., & Plake, B. S. (Eds.). (2001). *The fourteenth mental measurements yearbook*. Lincoln: University of Nebraska Press, Buros Institute.
Reviews widely used tests.

Murphy, L. L., Conoley, J., & Impara, J. C. (2002). *Tests in print VI*. Lincoln: University of Nebraska Press, Buros Institute.
Contains a brief description of the instruments. It considers intended purpose; information on the test's population, administration, and scoring; and a reference list of professional literature, citing articles relevant to the instruments.

Popham, W. J. (1993). Educational testing in America: What's right, what's wrong? *Education: Measurement Issues & Practice, 12*(1), 11–14.

Science Directorate of the American Psychological Association. (1993). *Finding information about psychological tests: A guide for locating and using both published and unpublished tests*. Washington, DC: Author.
This is a good guide for helping individuals locate the many test sources and information.

Test Users Training Work Group of the Joint Committee on Testing Practices. (1993). *Responsible test use*. Washington, DC: American Psychological Association.

7 Legal and Ethical Concerns and Issues in Testing

OVERVIEW

Codes of ethics express the values on which helping professionals build their practice. They provide a framework for responsible test use. There are probably as many codes of ethics as there are professional societies; but to become dynamic helping professionals, individuals must be committed to the ethical standards of their profession and follow them in their practice. In addition, a number of laws at both the state and national level affect testing and testing practices. Professionals need to be familiar with the laws as well as with the court decisions that interpret them.

OBJECTIVES

After studying this chapter, you should be able to

✔ List and discuss the major codes of professional ethics as they apply to tests and testing practices

✔ Compare and contrast the commonalities and differences among the different codes

✔ Identify the important federal and state legislation that affects tests and testing practices

✔ Discuss relevant court decisions and their impact on tests and testing practices

✔ Demonstrate knowledge of legal and ethical issues in evaluation and assessment

PROFESSIONAL STANDARDS AND CODES OF ETHICS

Because of the impact of testing on society and lives, professional standards and ethics have been developed to promote responsible professional practice in psychological testing and assessment. Ethics can be viewed as moral principles adopted by an individual or group that provide the basis for right conduct. Most professional organizations have established codes of ethics for their members to follow. In addition, state and national laws regulate ethical behavior. The primary purpose for laws and ethical codes is to protect the welfare of the client. Laws and ethical codes provide guidelines for professionals; however, neither provides exact answers to all ethical dilemmas. Thus, it is up to individual professionals in the field to reflect on their behavior and assess whether what they're doing is in the best interest of their clients.

Although a number of professional organizations related to testing and assessment have ethical codes, the discussion will be organized around several of the general ethical principles put forth by the National Board of Certified Counselors (2005), the American Counseling Association (2005), the American Psychological Association (APA; 2002), the Standards for Educational and Psychological Testing (American Educational Research Association, American Psychological Association, National Council on Measurement in Education, 1999), and the National Council on Measurement in Education (NCME; 1995).

NBCC Code of Ethics

The National Board for Certified Counselors (NBCC, 2005) identifies 15 standards dealing with measurement and evaluation located in section D of its Code of Ethics. The first deals with counselor competence. Counselors must recognize their limitations and perform only techniques or administer assessment instruments for which they have received appropriate training.

Counselors utilizing tests or making decisions based on test results need appropriate training and skills in educational and psychological measurement, validation criteria, test research, and guidelines for test development and use.

The counselor must provide orientation to the examinee prior to and following administration of assessment instruments. In the orientation, the counselors must inform the client of the explicit use of the test results.

The counselor is responsible for the appropriate selection of the assessment instruments to be used, and must ensure the validity and reliability of the instrument. Instruments that are biased or otherwise inappropriate will provide invalid information for decision making.

The counselor must be guarded when making statements to the public about specific instruments and techniques. False claims and unwarranted connotations often result from misunderstanding or poor communication.

Counselors must record when tests are not administered under standard conditions or when irregularities or unusual behavior arise during testing. The behavior might invalidate the results. The NBCC code deems unsupervised or inadequately supervised tests as not meeting ethical standards. The exception to this are tests such as interest inventories, which are often designed to be self-administered and self-scored.

Counselors must maintain test security. Coaching and dissemination of test items and materials can invalidate the test results. Counselors, however, must discuss the conditions that might provide more favorable results, such as telling test takers that they can guess without any penalty.

Counselors must understand the technical limitations of an instrument when interpreting the results. Counselors need to schedule periodic review and/or retesting of the client to help prevent stereotyping.

The counselor must be concerned about the welfare of the test takers. Who receives the results and how they will be used are important considerations. Interpretations must be made in light of any limitations in the instruments or norming group.

Computer-generated test administration and scoring programs may be utilized if the counselor is sure that this type of testing will provide the client with accurate results. Computer-based interpretations must be checked for validity by developers before being marketed.

If the tests report insufficient technical data, counselors must explicitly state to examinees the specific purposes for the use of such instruments.

Counselors need to be cautious when evaluating or interpreting the performance of minority group members or other individuals not represented in the standardized sample. Counselors need to recognize that test results give a picture of the test taker at only one moment in time and may become obsolete.

APA Standards

The *Ethical Principles of Psychologists and Code of Conduct* (APA, 2002) lists 11 standards for assessment. The first is that psychologists should base recommendations on information and techniques sufficient enough to substantiate their findings. They are to have conducted adequate assessment of an individual in or to support their statements or conclusions.

The second standard relates to the use of assessment techniques, interviews, tests, or instruments. Psychologists must use valid and reliable assessment techniques in an appropriate manner as evidenced by research. Psychologists must consider the various characteristics of the individual being assessed that might affect their judgments or reduce the accuracy of their interpretation.

The next standard relates to informed consent in assessment. Psychologists must obtain informed consent when using assessment techniques; this includes explaining the nature and purpose of the assessment, fees, involvement of third parties, and limits of confidentiality.

Psychologists must not release *test data* (clients' test results) unless the client gives permission to release such data. In the absence of client permission, psychologists provide test data only as required by law or court order.

The fifth standard refers to test construction. If psychologists are involved in test development, they are responsible for conducting research with tests and other assessment techniques using scientific procedures and current professional knowledge for test design, standardization, validation, reduction of bias, and recommendations for use.

In interpreting test data, psychologists need to explain results in the language that can be understood by the individual being assessed. The psychologists must give appropriate explanations of results.

Psychologists have a responsibility of not promoting the use of psychological assessment techniques by unqualified examiners.

The freshness of results also is a factor. Psychologists refrain from basing their assessment, intervention decisions, or recommendations on outdated test results and measures that are not useful for the current purpose.

Individuals offering assessment or scoring services to other professionals have the obligation to make sure their procedures are appropriate, valid, and reliable.

In explaining assessment results, psychologists must ensure that explanations are given by appropriate individuals or services.

The last standard holds the psychologist responsible for making reasonable efforts to maintain the integrity and security of tests and other assessment techniques consistent with the law, contractual obligations, and the code of ethics.

ACA Code of Ethics

The American Counseling Association (ACA, 2005) has a code of ethics that has a specific section on Evaluation, Assessment, and Interpretation—Section E. This section begins with a general introductory subsection describing (1) the crucial importance of assessments being reliable and vaild and (2) the counselor's responsibilities to not misuse assessment information and to share with clients their assessment results, the counselor's interpretation of those results, and how the assessment will be used to inform the counselor's work with the client. Section E of the ACA Code of Ethics then goes on to discuss counselor competence to use and interpret assessment, informed consent, release of data to qualified professionals, the diagnosis of mental disorders, instrument selection, conditions of assessment administration, multicultural and diversity issues in assessment, scoring and interpretation of assessments, assessment security, obsolete assessments and outdated results, and, finally, assessment construction.

Standards for Educational and Psychological Testing

One of the most comprehensive documents on ethics is the 1999 *Standards for Educational and Psychological Testing.* Three professional organizations took the lead in developing this position statement: the American Educational Research Association (AERA), the American Psychological Association (APA), and the National Council on Measurement in Education (NCME). This document, which we will refer to as the *Standards* represents the sixth in a series of publications that originated in 1954 to provide developers and users of tests with assistance in evaluating the technical adequacy of their instruments for educational and psychological assessment. The intent of the Standards is to promote the sound and ethical use of tests and to provide criteria for the evaluation of tests, testing practices, and the effects of test use.

The current revision of the Standards is organized into three parts. Additionally, it contains more extensive introductory text material than its predecessor. We recommend that anyone who routinely engages in any form of testing—from test design and implementation to assessment and evaluation—obtain a copy of the Standards and become familiar with the guidelines.

Test Construction, Evaluation, and Documentation.   This section contains standards for validity; reliability and errors of measurement; test development and revision; scaling, norming, and score comparability; test administration, scoring, and reporting; and supporting documentation for tests. According to the Standards, "validity is the most fundamental consideration in developing and evaluating tests" (AERA et al., 1999, p. 9). As such, the Standards addresses the different types of validity evidence needed to support test use. In addition, standards on reliability and errors of measurement address the issue of consistency of test scores. Although the Standards supports standardized procedures, it recognizes special situations that arise in which modifications of the procedures may be advisable or legally mandated; for example, "persons of different backgrounds, ages, or familiarity with testing may need nonstandard modes of test administration or a more comprehensive orientation to the testing process" (AERA et al., 1999, p. 61). Standards for the development and revision of formal, published instruments, an often overlooked area of importance, describe criteria important for scale construction.

Fairness in Testing.   This section contains standards on fairness and bias, the rights and responsibilities of test takers, testing individuals of diverse linguistic backgrounds, and testing individuals with disabilities. This section emphasizes the importance of fairness in all aspects of testing and assessment. "The fair treatment of test takers is not only a matter of equity, but also promotes validity and reliability of the inferences made from the test performance" (AERA et al., 1999, p. 85). Special attention to issues related to individuals of diverse linguistic backgrounds or with disabilities may be needed when developing, administering, scoring, interpreting, and making decisions based on test scores.

Testing Applications.   This final section includes standards involving general responsibilities of test users, psychological testing and assessment, educational testing and assessment, testing in employment and credentialing, and testing in program evaluation and public policy. In addition to emphasizing the ethical obligations of test users, the Standards addresses specific issues related to psychological, educational, employment, program evaluation, and other specific applications of test results.

National Council on Measurement in Education

The National Council on Measurement in Education (NCME; 1995) published its *Code of Professional Responsibilities in Educational Measurement* (CPR). The council

    a. What are the testing issues in the situation?

    b. What factors or testing practices are involved?

    c. If you were a consultant invited by the college to help the admissions committee in the selection and retention of students, what would you advise?

To remain competitive, Memorial Hospital has decided it needs to cut its budget by downsizing semiskilled workers such as orderlies, custodians, cafeteria personnel, stockroom clerks, fileroom clerks, and so on. The hospital would like to help these workers qualify for higher-level jobs so that they can remain with the organization. From the attrition rate, the hospital administrators know they will need workers with advanced technical skills and will have to recruit from the outside to fill these positions if they have no one qualified internally. The personnel department has decided to give all the targeted workers who will lose their positions the Wide Range Achievement Test and the Wonderlic Personnel Test and select those with the highest scores to be retrained. Of the workers, 80% are women and minority group members.

    a. What are the ethical and legal issues related to this case?

    b. What testing factors are involved?

    c. If you were a consultant hired by the hospital to help identify workers to be retrained and do outplacement counseling for those who are to be let go, what would you advise Memorial to do?

ADDITIONAL READINGS

American Psychological Association. (1993). *Responsible test use: Case studies for assessing human behavior.* Washington, DC: Test User Training Work Group of the Joint Committee on Testing Practices.

    Contains 78 cases to train professionals to use tests wisely. Cases are from seven different settings, ranging from counseling to speech-language-hearing contexts, and cover 86 elements of proper test use.

American Psychological Association. (2001). *Rights and responsibilities of test takers: Guidelines.* Washington, DC: Author.

    Topics related to test construction, test selection, test administration, and test administration are illustrated.

American Psychological Association. (2002). *Ethics code.* Available at *http://www.apa.org/ethics/*.

Bond, T. (2000). *Standards and ethics for counselling in action* (2nd ed.). Thousand Oaks, CA: Sage.

    Part 2 of the book covers topics related to the client such as counseling competency and avoiding exploitation of clients.

Cronbach, L. J. (1994). *Essentials for psychological testing* (3rd ed.). New York: Harper & Row.

National Board for Certified Counselors. (1998). *NBCC code of ethics.* (Approved 1997). Greensboro, NC: Author.

National Council on Measurement in Education. (1995). *Code of professional responsibilities in educational measurement.* Washington, DC: Author.

Paniagua, F. A. (1998). *Assessing and treating culturally diverse clients* (2nd ed.). Thousand Oaks, CA: Sage.
Contains chapters on guidelines for and treatment of African Americans, Hispanics, Asians, and American Indians. There is a chapter on using culturally biased instruments.

Remley, T. P., & Herlihy, B. (2005). *Ethical, legal, and professional issues in counseling* (2nd ed.). Upper Saddle River, NJ: Merrill/Prentice Hall.

Sue, D. W. (Ed.). (1998). *Multicultural counseling competencies.* Thousand Oaks, CA: Sage.
Addresses topics such as multicultural evaluation and multicultural counseling.

8 Ability and Intelligence Testing

OVERVIEW

One of the most controversial areas in testing is the measuring of ability and intelligence. Issues include the nature-nurture controversy, cultural bias, and the construct validity of intelligence tests. Many types of intelligence tests are widely used in educational and clinical settings with all age groups and all types of individuals. Currently, the most influential development in our view of intelligence has come from educational and psychological research on cognitive psychology, especially the conceptualizations of Robert Sternberg, Howard Gardner, and John Horn.

OBJECTIVES

After studying this chapter, you should be able to

✔ Define intelligence

✔ Discuss some of the major theories of intelligence

✔ List the major types of tests used to measure intelligence

✔ Identify what types of intelligence tests should be used and why

✔ Explain how the results of intelligence tests should be reported

✔ Identify the kinds of factors that should be considered in interpreting intelligence test results

DEFINITIONS OF INTELLIGENCE

The authors of intelligence tests have given many different definitions of intelligence. Aiken (1985) indicated that the word *intelligence* was almost unknown in popular speech until the Victorian era. Francis Galton and Herbert Spencer used the Latin word for intelligence to refer to individual differences in mental ability. These individuals as well as other psychologists such as Cattell were influenced by Darwin to look at dimensions of individual differences. They felt that intelligence was a genetic factor, separate from special abilities. Binet and Simon (1916) conceptualized intelligence as the capacity of the individual to judge well, to reason well, and to comprehend well, and postulated that intelligence was a general ability. Wechsler (1958), on the other hand, defined intelligence as the "aggregate or global ability of the individual to act purposefully, to think rationally, and to deal effectively with his environment" (p. 7). It is extremely important to check a test's manual to determine how the test authors define intelligence.

In general, most intelligence tests measure the individual's cognitive ability to think abstractly or use verbal, numerical, or abstract symbols. The subjects taking these tests must substitute symbols for actions and manipulate ideas that represent not only current happenings but also events remote in time and space (Stoddard, 1943). Wechsler's definition also includes the dimension of adapting to the environment and adjusting to problems and changing conditions. We must remember that the scores on an intelligence test measure how well an individual performs the set of tasks assessed by the test, rather than intelligence in general. Table 8.1 shows a comparison of a number of definitions of intelligence.

Table 8.1
Definitions of intelligence.

Author/Researcher	Definition
Boring	Intelligence is what intelligence tests test
E. L. Thorndike	The power of good responses from the point of view of truth or facts
Thurstone	The ability to carry out abstract thinking
Pinter	The ability to adapt oneself adequately to relatively new situations in life
Henmon	The capacity for knowledge and knowledge possessed
Colvin	The ability to learn or having learned to adjust oneself to the environment
Binet	Contained in the meaning of four terms: comprehension, inventiveness, direction, and criticism
Berg	The mental abilities of processes involved in providing an optimal fit between one's self and one's environment

Source: Adapted from Sternberg et al., 2000.

MODELS OF INTELLIGENCE

Many attempts have been made over the past century to develop models that conceptualize the facets of intelligence. Whether one agrees or disagrees with a particular model depends partly on the individual's theoretical orientation and partly on the type of statistical analysis used with test results. Potential test users should be concerned with the purpose of an intelligence scale and the theories and approaches that will provide the most valid information.

Spearman's *g*

One of the first theories was that of Charles Spearman, who postulated a two-factor theory of intelligence. In interpreting his statistical analysis of test performance, Spearman (1927) identified two factors—a *g*, or *general intelligence*, factor that each individual possesses and an *s*, or *specific*, factor that varies for each task undertaken.

Thurstone's Multifactor Theory

Thurstone (1938), on the other hand, proposed a multifactor theory. He analyzed 57 different tests taken by a high school group and concluded that there was a small group of primary factors rather than a single *g* factor. Thurstone termed these factors *primary mental abilities* and constructed a test called the Primary Mental Abilities Test. These are the seven primary mental abilities he identified:

1. Number ability—ability to perform basic mathematic processes accurately and rapidly.
2. Verbal ability—ability to understand ideas expressed in word form.
3. Word fluency—ability to speak and write fluently.
4. Memory—ability to recognize and recall information such as numbers, letters, and words.
5. Reasoning—ability to derive rules and solve problems inductively.
6. Spatial ability—ability to visualize form relationships in three dimensions.
7. Perception—ability to perceive things quickly, such as visual details and similarities and differences among pictured objects.

E. L. Thorndike

One of the major issues during the 1920s concerned controversy over the nature of intelligence; the debate still continues in psychological circles today. E. L. Thorndike (1927) believed that this type of debate is not productive. He disagreed with the concept of a singular and relatively independent mental process, or *g* factor, and concluded that there were many special or grouped abilities, such as mathematical and mechanical skills. He postulated that there were three major types of intelligence: *abstract, practical,* and *social*.

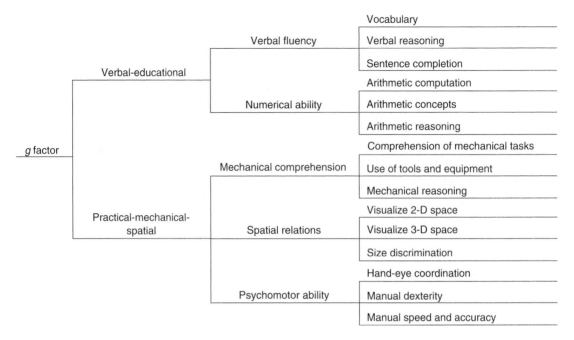

		Vocabulary
	Verbal fluency	Verbal reasoning
Verbal-educational		Sentence completion
		Arithmetic computation
	Numerical ability	Arithmetic concepts
		Arithmetic reasoning

(diagram: Vernon's hierarchical model of intelligence)

Figure 8.1
Adaptation of Vernon's hierarchical model of intelligence.

Hierarchical Theory

Vernon (1960) proposed a hierarchical model of intelligence that identified four levels of factors (see Figure 8.1). The trunk, or first level, includes the *g* factor, which is a general or cognitive factor. The two main branches of the second level are verbal-educational and practical-mechanical-spatial factors. The third level identifies component factors of these two main branches. The verbal-educational area comprises abilities such as verbal fluency and numerical ability. The practical-mechanical-spatial area includes factors such as mechanical ability, psychomotor ability, and spatial relations. The fourth level of the hierarchy consists of more special and specific factors peculiar to tests in each of the domains above it. Vernon's model presents a conceptual way of including the general intelligence dimension of Spearman's work and the multifactor approach identified by Thorndike, Thurstone, and Guilford.

Guilford's Model of Intelligence

Guilford (1967) developed a multifactor approach to intelligence. He proposed a three-dimensional model that includes five types of operations, four types of content, and six types of products. The model contains 120 cells. Operations include cognition, memory, divergent thinking, convergent thinking, and evaluation. The four types of content are figural, symbolic, semantic, and behavioral. The six products are units, classes, relations, systems, transformations, and implications. A number of tests have been developed to measure the cells of Guilford's model. His approach is an extension of the multifactor approach advocated by Thurstone.

Cattell's Fluid and Crystallized Intelligence

Cattell (1963) used factor analytic studies to identify a two-factor theory of intelligence based on fluid and crystallized intelligence. Fluid intelligence is general to many different fields and is used in tasks requiring adaptation to new situations. Heredity is an important factor in fluid intelligence. Crystallized intelligence is more specific to a given field, such as education. This type of ability depends more on the environment. The Culture-Fair Intelligence Tests were designed to measure fluid intelligence.

Carroll (1998) also has a factorial model of intelligence that measures fluid and crystallized intelligence. In his factor analytic study of 460 data sets he identified three strata of cognitive abilities. The highest stratum is a general factor often designated by g for *general intelligence.* The second stratum consists of broad factors that include fluid intelligence, crystallized intelligence, general memory and learning, broad visual perception, broad auditory perception, broad retrieval ability, broad cognitive speediness, and processing speed. The third stratum consists of narrow abilities related to the broad areas previously listed. For example, under fluid intelligence falls general sequential reasoning, induction, and qualitative reasoning. Under crystallized intelligence falls reading comprehension, reading decoding, spelling ability, writing ability, foreign language proficiency, foreign language aptitude, language development, lexical knowledge, listening ability, phonetic coding, communication ability, oral production and fluency, grammatical sensitivity, and verbal language comprehension.

Horn (1989), a student of Cattell, concluded that the theory can be thought of as a theory of multiple intelligences. These intelligences are "outcroppings of distinct influences operating through development, brain functioning, genetic determination, and the adjustment, adaptation, and achievement of school and work" (p. 76).

Sternberg's Cognitive Approaches to Intelligence

Sternberg's (1980, 1985) theory utilizes the information-processing components of intelligence. He identified three different types of information-processing components as important to consider: metacomponents, performance components, and knowledge acquisition components. First, *metacomponents* are the higher-order control processes used to oversee the planning, monitoring, and evaluating of task performance. Sternberg identified 10 metacomponents as the most important in intelligent functioning (1985, p. 62):

1. Recognition that a problem of some kind exists.
2. Recognition of the nature of the problem.
3. Selection of a set of lower-order, non-executable components.
4. Selection of a strategy for task performance, combining the lower-order components.
5. Selection of one or more mental representation for information.
6. Decisions on how to allocate additional resources.

7. Monitoring one's place in the task performance—what has been done and what needs to be done.
8. Monitoring one's understanding of internal and external feedback concerning the quality of the task performance.
9. Knowing how to act on the feedback that is received.
10. Implementing action as a result of the feedback.

Sternberg identified *performance components* as lower-order processes used in the execution of strategies needed to perform a task: encoding the nature of the stimulus, inferring the relations between two stimulus terms that are similar in some ways but different in others, and applying a previously inferred relation to a new situation. *Knowledge acquisition components* are processes involved in learning new information and storing it in memory. Sternberg considers the three most important of these components to be selective encoding, selective combination, and selective comparison. Selective encoding requires sorting out relevant from irrelevant information. Selective combination refers to the combining of information in a way that maximizes its internal coherence or connectedness. Selective comparison relates new information to information already stored in memory to maximize the connectedness of the new knowledge.

Sternberg (1985) postulated six primary sources of individual differences in information processing (pp. 64–65):

1. Components—an individual may use more or fewer components or even different components than those another individual uses.
2. Combination rule for components—different individuals may use different rules to combine.
3. Mode of component processing—different persons prefer to process particular components in different modes.
4. Order of component processing—different persons may use different sequences to order components.
5. Component time and accuracy—one person may be able to process a particular component more quickly or accurately than another person.
6. Mental representations on which components act—different individuals may use different representations of information.

Sternberg (1990) argued that memory and analytical reasoning are the operations necessary for success in school and that tacit, informational knowledge rather than explicit, formal knowledge is required to be successful at work. Most traditional tests are contextualized with respect to the school; the problems are relatively short, have single correct answers, and contain no "real-world" content.

Sternberg (1990) has a research form of test that includes both academic and work contexts called the Sternberg Triarchic Abilities Test. The test has overlapping grade and age levels and can be administered from kindergarten through adulthood. Included on the test are these types of items (pp. 216–219):

| Componential | Verbal | Measures test taker's ability to learn from context and pick up information from relevant context. |
| | Quantitative | Measures inductive reasoning ability in the numerical domain such as extrapolation of a sequence of numbers. |

Coping with Novelty	Verbal	Assesses the ability to think in novel ways and requires hypothetical thinking with counterfactuals or novel verbal analogies which require counterfactual reasoning.
	Quantitative	Assesses coping with novelty skills in the context of the quantitative domain and utilizes a numerical matrix format in which the test taker has to substitute a number in place of a given symbol.
	Figural	Requires test takers to complete the series in a newly mapped domain and includes items similar to the figural completion type.
Atomization	Verbal	Requires test takers to make rapid decisions as to whether two letters are in the same category (vowel or consonant) or are different (vowel consonant or consonant vowel).
	Quantitative	Requires the test taker to make rapid judgments as to whether two numbers have the same or different properties, such as being odd or even.
	Figural	Measures the test taker's ability to judge whether two figures have the same or different properties such as the number of sides.
Practical	Verbal	Measures the test taker's ability to respond to everyday inferential reasoning problems.
	Quantitative	Measures the test taker's ability to reason quantitatively with practical, everyday problems.
	Figural	Measures the test taker's ability to perform route planning from information given on a map or diagram.

Sternberg (1986) utilized three subtheories to account for intelligence. The components subtheory relates to the internal world of the individual, the experiential subtheory relates intelligence to the experiences of the individual with tasks and situations, and the contextual subtheory relates intelligence to the external world of the individual. Sternberg states that the components of intelligence are manifested at different levels of experience with tasks and with situations of varying degrees of contextual relevance to a person's life (p. 102).

Piaget's Theory of Cognitive Development

Piaget (1970) conceptualized a theory of intellectual development by observing and interviewing children. His task was to discover the basic psychological structures that underlie the formation of concepts fundamental to philosophy and science. He was intrigued by the errors of young children on a test of reasoning and found that older children were not only quantitatively more intelligent but also qualitatively different from younger children. Piaget focused on the qualitative differences, concluding that learning is fundamentally an internal process of construction, and identified organization and adaptation as two invariant functional properties of all living organisms. Organization is the general tendency to arrange both the physical and psychological

Figure 8.2
Piaget's stages of cognitive
development.

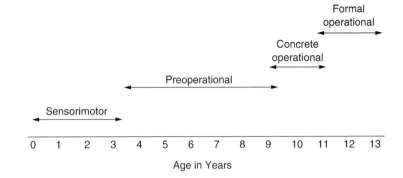

processes in a coherent system. Two important dimensions of adaptation are assimilation and accommodation. *Assimilation* is the process by which a child relates new objects and ideas to familiar objects and ideas. *Accommodation* is the process by which a child changes behavior and psychological structures in response to environmental events.

Piaget divided intellectual development into four major stages, which are presented in Figure 8.2. These four stages are the sensorimotor period, the preoperational period, the concrete operational period, and the formal operational period. Piaget further identified four factors that affect development and the transition from one stage to another: maturation, experience, transmission, and equilibration. *Equilibration* can be described as the relative balance that exists between the individual's psychological structures and perceived events in the environment. Developing structures continually move toward greater and greater equilibrium. Piaget's theories have been the basis of the design of curriculum materials and educational programs, and a number of scales have been published to assess an individual's stage of intellectual development.

Gardner's Theory of Multiple Intelligences

Gardner (1983) postulated a theory of intelligence that focuses on a symbol-system approach and combines both factor-analytical and information-processing models. He identified seven forms of intelligence: verbal/linguistic, logical/mathematical, visual/spatial, bodily/kinesthetic, musical/rhythmic, interpersonal, intrapersonal, and environmental. ("Naturalistic" was added by Holland as an eighth intelligence in 1998.)

Verbal/linguistic intelligence involves word meaning and understanding, reading, grammar, and humor. Logical/mathematical intelligence involves inductive and deductive reasoning, scientific reasoning, mathematical understanding, mathematical operations, and critical and abstract thinking. Visual/spatial intelligence entails understanding relationships of objects in space, mental images, graphic representation, and perception from different angles. Bodily/kinesthetic intelligence involves complex motor coordination, awareness and control of body movements and functions, and mind and body integration. Musical/rhythmic intelligence requires sensitivity to sounds and recognition, creation, and reproduction of both melody and rhythm; and appreciation and enjoyment of the structure of music. Interpersonal intelligence requires effective verbal and nonverbal communication, sensitivity to the feelings of others, and ability to understand

and work with others. Intrapersonal intelligence is dependent on metacognition, higher-order thinking, concentration, self-awareness, and other types of self-improvement skills.

Gardner (1993) states "intelligences work together to solve problems to yield various kinds of end states—vocations, avocations, and the like" (p. 9). Interpersonal intelligence describes one's ability to understand the moods of other people as well as their own. Intrapersonal intelligence depends on an understanding of one's own feelings and an ability to use self-knowledge productively.

Krechevsky (1994) devised an observational schedule to assess students' skills based on Gardner's model of multiple intelligences. The subject areas on the rating form include visual arts, mechanical sciences, movement, music, social understanding, mathematics, science, and language. The tasks measure specific abilities that can be observed in a one-to-one situation. For example, in mathematics the scale requires observations in three areas: numerical reasoning, spatial reasoning, and logical problem solving. Can the student use estimation, find spatial patterns, and make logical inferences? Interpersonal and intrapersonal intelligences are also assessed. This scale has three components: understanding of self, understanding of others, and assumption of distinctive social roles. For example, can the student reflect on her own feelings, experiences, and accomplishments? Does the individual demonstrate knowledge of peers and their activities? Does the student share ideas with other children? A summary of some of the major models of intelligence is presented in Table 8.2.

Table 8.2
Models of intelligence.

Type	Characteristics
Neural Efficiency	Provides an uncomplicated, reductionistic view of intelligence as a biological phenomenon.
Hierarchical (Horn, Cattell)	Structure of intelligence can be discovered by analyzing the interrelationship of scores on mental ability tests.
Three Strata Theory (Carroll)	g underlies all intellectual activity and has a high degree of heritabilities that are classified as broad abilities and enduring characteristics of the individual.
Triarchic Theory (Sternberg)	There are three interacting aspects: 1. Internal information-processing guides to intelligence 2. Three knowledge-acquisition components appear to be central in intellectual functioning: selective encoding, selective combination, and selective comparison. 3. Ability to capitalize on one's experiences to process novel and unfamiliar information
Multiple Intelligences (Gardner, Holland)	The focus is more on domains and less on mental processes. Individuals develop one or more through genetic inheritance, training, and socialization of cultural values. There are eight types.
Bioecological Model (McArdle, Goldsmith)	Postulated that intelligence is a function of the interaction between innate potential abilities, environmental context, and internal motivation.

MULTICULTURAL ISSUES

One of the most controversial issues in the area of assessment is intelligence testing of racial or ethnic minorities. Significant differences between racial or ethnic groups continue to be reflected in intelligence test scores. Suzuki, Short, Pieterse, and Kugler (2001) identified the following factors that influence test performance (p. 368):

1. Higher socioeconomic status (SES) has been related to higher intelligence scores.
2. Certain populations at higher risk for health impairment tend to score lower.
3. Children living in isolated communities may score lower because of lack of familiarity with test stimuli.
4. The level of knowledge of English affects verbal test scores.
5. The degree of familiarity with the dominant culture upon which the test is based has an impact on test performance.
6. Family background, parenting style, and parental education level may affect test scores.

TYPES OF TESTS

A number of methods to classify the various types of intelligence assessments and related tests are used by counselors and psychologists. Individual or group tests, verbal and nonverbal or performance tests, culture-fair tests, and developmental scales are examples. Procedures exist to measure intelligence in every age range from infant to senior citizen. Some tests can be classified into more than one category, and not all tests specify an IQ.

Individual Scales

The Wechsler Scales.   In 1939, David Wechsler, a psychologist at Bellevue hospital in New York, published an individual intelligence scale designed specifically for adults. Since then, Wechsler intelligence tests for various age groups been developed. The Wechsler intelligence scales are individually administered tests with appropriate forms for different age spans. There are three scales: the Wechsler Adult Intelligence Scale III (WAIS-III), the Wechsler Intelligence Scale for Children-IV (WISC-IV), and the Wechsler Preschool and Primary Scale of Intelligence-Revised (WPPSI-III).

Wechsler Adult Intelligence Scale III (WAIS-III).   The WAIS-III was constructed and standardized in the mid-1990s and published by the Psychological Corporation in 1997. The WAIS-III scales have 14 subtests, half belonging to the Verbal Scale and the other half to the Performance Scale. The tests yield a Verbal, Performance, and Full Scale (total) IQ score.

The Verbal Scale was designed by Wechsler to measure the examinee's ability to work with abstract symbols, the benefit the examinee received from his or her background, his or her verbal memory abilities, and his or her verbal fluency. The six areas included are information, digit span, arithmetic, comprehension, similarities, and vocabulary.

The *information subtest* focuses on knowledge and information acquired through educational experiences. Individuals with high scores have a wide variety of experiences, cultural opportunities, and outside interests. Low scores may show a lack of intellectual curiosity or a poor cultural environment.

The *digit span subtest* measures short-term or immediate memory. The task is to repeat digits in order as well as backwards. The test demands concentration and attention; examinees with high scores have good short-term memory and can focus their attention well. This ability may relate to low anxiety or stress levels. Low scores may indicate poor attention or an inability to concentrate, perhaps resulting from anxiety or stress.

The *arithmetic subtest* focuses on items that require basic mathematical skills such as addition, subtraction, multiplication, and division, and the ability to apply these skills. High scores are an indication of alertness, ability to concentrate and focus on tasks, and good arithmetic reasoning. Low scores may indicate a poor background in mathematical skills and/or reasoning and an inability to concentrate.

The *comprehension subtest* focuses on the individual's ability to make social judgments and requires information and knowledge of moral codes, social rules, and regulations. High scores are an indication of reality awareness, capacity for social compliance, and good judgment. Low scores may indicate poor judgment and possibly impulsiveness, antisocial tendencies, or some type of personality disturbance.

The *similarities subtest* measures reasoning and conceptual thinking ability. The test taker is presented with word pairs and must explain their similarities. The tasks demand inductive reasoning; the individuals must take specific facts and see how they fit a general rule or principle. Individuals with high scores have good verbal fluency and concept formation. Those with low scores have poor ability to think abstractly and see things flexibly.

The *vocabulary subtest* contains words from easy to difficult and from concrete to abstract. The test taker is asked to give meanings. The test measures general word knowledge and language development. This subtest is found on almost all general intelligence and scholastic aptitude tests. The performance of the individuals is influenced by cultural experiences and educational backgrounds. Those with high scores on this subtest usually have a wide range of interests, good recall, and high general intelligence. Those with low scores may have had a limited educational background or may be poorly motivated.

The *performance scale* includes a number of subtests: picture completion, picture arrangement, block design, coding, and matrix reasoning.

The *picture completion subtest* requires the test taker to identify the missing part of a drawing. The subtest measures long-term visual alertness and memory as well as visual acuity. The test taker must be able to differentiate important details from minor details. The tasks require perceptual alertness and concentration and an ability to organize visual material. Those with high scores on this subtest have the ability to recognize essential visual information and reveal alertness and good visual acuity. Those with low scores often have poor ability in visual organization and poor ability to concentrate. Impulsive examinees make quick responses without carefully analyzing the whole picture.

The *picture arrangement subtest* requires the examinee to put scrambled comic strip pictures in the correct order to tell a story. The test requires temporal visual sequencing, social awareness, planning ability, and nonverbal reasoning. It also requires knowledge of American subcultural values and may be inappropriate for individuals from other cultures. Those with high scores on this test have social intelligence and the ability to anticipate the consequences of initial acts. Those with low scores usually have problems in interpersonal relationships, few ideas, and poor ability to plan ahead.

The *block design subtest* requires the examinee to copy a set of designs utilizing colored blocks. The test requires visual-spatial organization, the ability to analyze a whole into parts, and the use of nonverbal problem-solving skills. Those with high scores have good visual-motor-spatial skills and are able to concentrate. Those who score low have poor visual-motor-spatial and perceptual skills and poor visual integration. They may also have problems in concentration.

The *object assembly subtest* is a set of jigsaw puzzles that require visual-motor speed and coordination as well as the ability to configure and organize the parts to the puzzle. Those with high scores on this test have excellent visual organizational abilities and demonstrate perceptual-motor coordination. Those with low scores have problems in visual-perceptual-motor areas and in visual concept formation. This subtest is optional in the third edition.

The *coding,* or *digit symbol, subtest* requires quick and accurate coding of symbols that are paired with numbers of geometric shapes. The scale measures visual-motor speed and accuracy as well as short-term visual memory and the ability to follow directions. It demands an ability to learn an unfamiliar task. Those with high scores have effective visual-motor skills (e.g., good eye-hand coordination) and are mentally efficient. They have the ability to memorize by rote new visual material. Those with low scores have poor visual-motor skills and an inadequate capacity for visual associative learning. They may have poor mental alertness.

The *matrix reasoning subtest* measures nonverbal analytical reasoning; in other words, the ability to quickly perceive visual details. The examinee is presented with a series of designs (e.g., a pattern of triangles, squares, and circles) with one part missing. The examinee would then be asked to find the missing element that would complete the design.

A comparison of the dimensions measured in the Wechsler Verbal and Performance Scales is given in Table 8.3.

Interpreting the WAIS.   The first step in interpretation of WAIS-III results is to analyze the three global estimates of the client's ability—Verbal, Performance, and Full Scale. The examiner can compare the individual's full IQ score with the appropriate ability classification listed in Table 8.4.

The second step is to analyze the Verbal and Performance scores to see whether they are significantly different; a 12-point difference is significant at the .05 level, and

Table 8.3

Comparison of verbal and performance scales of the WAIS-III.

Verbal	Performance
General	*General*
Work with abstract symbols	Nonverbal contact with the environment
Utilization of school or educational background	Work with perceptual-motor tasks
Verbal memory abilities	Work with concrete tasks and problems
Verbal fluency	
Specific	*Specific*
Computational skills	Long-term visual memory
Numerical reasoning	Visual alertness
Logical thinking	Ability to differentiate among details
Abstract thinking	Temporal visual sequencing
Ability to form verbal concepts	Social awareness
Word knowledge	Nonverbal reasoning
Language development	Planning ability
Awareness of social rules	Verbal concept formation
and mores	Whole/part analysis
Common sense	Visual-spatial ability
Use of past experience	Sensory-motor feedback
Short-term auditory memory	Visual-motor speed, coordination, and accuracy
Recall of information	Short-term visual memory
	Ability to follow directions
	Visual planning
	Ability to follow a visual pattern

Table 8.4

Classification of range of intelligence scores.

IQ Range	Classification	Percentile Range %
130 and above	Very Superior	98–99
120–129	Superior	91–97
110–119	High Average	75–90
90–109	Average	25–74
80–89	Low Average	9–24
70–79	Borderline	3–8
69 and below	Below Average	1–2

a 15-point difference is significant at the .01 level (Kaufman, 1976, 1990). In summarizing the research findings on significant differences between the Verbal and Performance Scales, Groth-Marnat (1997) identified the following possible hypotheses:

1. If the Verbal IQ is 15 or more points above the Performance IQ, it might show that the individual (a) has a high level of academic achievement, (b) comes from an urban environment, (c) has some type of neurosis (anxiety and tension state, obsessive-compulsive, or depression), (d) has learning problems of a perceptual nature, or (e) has a right-hemisphere cerebral impairment.
2. If the Performance IQ is significantly higher than the Verbal IQ, it might show that the individual (a) is an underachiever or has not made use of educational opportunities, (b) comes from a lower socioeconomic level or a different cultural or language background, (c) is a delinquent or a sociopath, (d) has severe reading difficulties, or (e) has a left-hemisphere impairment.

The next step is to analyze and interpret the subtests. The examiner might look at the scatter or scores on the subtests and identify the highest and lowest scaled scores on the subtests.

Each subtest has a standard score with a mean of 10 and a standard deviation of 3 for that subtest. The examiner might determine the number of subtests that deviate by 3 points or more from the fixed means. The subtests that are 3 points or more above the mean are identified as strengths, and those 3 points or more below the mean are identified as weaknesses. Subtest patterns are then analyzed for commonalities. Bannatyne (1971, 1974), for instance, organizes the subtests into the following categories: (a) verbal conceptual ability—comprehension, similarities, vocabulary; (b) spatial ability—block design, object assembly, picture completion; (c) sequencing ability—arithmetic, coding, digit span; and (d) acquired knowledge—arithmetic, information, vocabulary. The examiner might look at the scatter of the items within a subtest. Is there any pattern of how the individual responds to the items within the tests? This is a more qualitative analysis.

The last step is to analyze the content of the responses on the various subtests. The examiner may be able to assess the client's level of thinking and identify any unusual associations as well as certain dimensions of personality and learning style.

In addition to the three basic scales, the WAIS-III allows for computing *Index Scores* derived from factor analysis of the subtests. These include Verbal Comprehension, Working Memory, Perceptual Organization, and Processing Speed. These four index scores are comprised of eleven subtests. The *verbal comprehension* subtests measure verbal comprehension and expression. *Working memory* subtests measure attentional abilities and the degree to which an individual can efficiently perform mental operations. *Perceptual organization* consists of those subtests that best measure an individual's ability to process complex visual information and solve problems. *Processing speed* consists of the subtests that best measure speeded visual information processing—these tests involve scanning of visual information and the rapid writing of responses on a page. Table 8.5 shows the subtests that comprise each index. The index scores from the WAIS-III provide a second look at verbal and nonverbal abilities.

Table 8.5
Subtests of index scores.

Verbal Comprehension	Working Memory
Vocabulary	Arithmetic
Similarities	Digit Span
Information	Letter Number Sequencing
Perceptual Organization	*Processing Speed*
Picture Completion	Digit Symbol-Coding
Block Design	Symbol Search
Matrix Reasoning	

Note: *Picture Arrangement, Comprehension,* and *Object Assembly* do not contribute to index scores.

Extensive reliability testing was done, and internal consistency reliability is outstanding for the Full Scale IQ (.97), the Verbal Scale (.97) and Performance Scale (.93). In terms of validity, it is correlated highly with other IQ tests (e.g. the Stanford-Binet), it correlates highly with empirical judgments of intelligence, and it is significantly correlated with a number of criteria of academic and life success (e.g., college grades, measures of work performance and occupational level).

Typically, Caucasian individuals score higher than African Americans and Hispanic Americans on the WAIS-III scales. Hispanic Americans tend to have somewhat higher Performance Scale IQs than Verbal Scale IQs-likely related to their Spanish-language background (Sattler, 2001). Spanish versions of the WAIS-III scales are available.

CASE STUDY

Ms. Johnson is a 23-year-old Caucasian female who was self-referred for evaluation. She is having difficulty deciding what direction to take concerning vocational plans. She was administered the WAIS-III.

On the Wechsler Adult Intelligence Scale (WAIS-III), Ms. Johnson achieved a Full Scale IQ of 80, which is at the 9th percentile and in the Low Average range of intellectual functioning. Ms. Johnson scored as follows:

IQ/Index	Scores	Percentile
Verbal IQ	80	9
Performance IQ	84	14
Full Scale IQ	80	9
Verbal Comprehension Index	88	21
Perceptual Organization Index	82	12
Working Memory Index	71	3
Processing Speed Index	99	47

Verbal Subtests		*Performance Subtests*	
Vocabulary	8	Picture Completion	7
Similarities	7	Digit Symbol-Coding	11
Arithmetic	4	Block Design	6
Digit Span	5	Matrix Reasoning	8
Information	8	Picture Arrangement	6
Comprehension	8	Symbol Search	9
Letter Number Sequencing	7		

Ms. Johnson's Full Scale IQ score is in the Low Average range of intelligence. As indicated by the Verbal Comprehension Index and Perceptual Organization Index, Ms. Johnson's verbal comprehension skills and perceptual organization skills appear to be relatively equally developed, in the Low Average range. Ms. Johnson did demonstrate a weakness in working memory as evidenced by her percentile score on the Working Memory Index. Among subtests, Ms. Johnson demonstrated a significant weakness on arithmetic (basic math skills, mental concentration) and a significant relative strength on coding (psychomotor speed, visual short-term memory, visual-motor coordination, concentration). Overall, these assessment results generally indicate Low Average ability with strength in clerical speed and weaknesses in short-term memory and especially in long-term retrieval and retention.

Wechsler Intelligence Scale for Children-IV (WISC-IV). The WISC-IV is the fourth generation of the most widely used children's intellectual ability assessment. It is an individually administered clinical instrument for assessing the cognitive ability of children age 6 years through 16 years and 11 months. The WISC-IV has 15 subtests that make up four Index Scores that produce the Full Scale IQ score. The four Index Scores include the following:

- *Verbal Comprehension Index (VCI):* Indicates how well the child did on tasks that require listening to questions and verbalizing answers to them. These tasks evaluate skills in understanding verbal information, thinking and reasoning with words, and expressing thoughts as words.
- *Perceptual Reasoning Index (PRI):* Measures ability to examine and think about things such as designs and pictures, and to solve problems without using words. These tasks evaluate skills in solving nonverbal problems, sometimes using eye-hand coordination, and working quickly and efficiently with visual information.
- *Working Memory Index (WMI):* Measures ability to learn and retain information in memory while using the learned information to complete a task. These tasks measure skills in attention, concentration, and mental reasoning. Such skills are closely related to learning and achievement.
- *Processing Speed Index (PSI):* Measures ability to quickly scan symbols and make judgments about them. These tasks measure skills in speed of mental problem solving, attention, and eye-hand coordination.

The four Index Scores and 15 subtests of the WISC-IV are outlined in Table 8.6. A description of each of the subtests follows.

Table 8.6
WISC-IV scales and subtests.

Indexes	Subtests
Verbal Comprehension Index (VCI)	Similarities
	Vocabulary
	Comprehension
	Information
	*Word Reasoning**
	Block Design
Perceptual Reasoning Index (PRI)	*Picture Concepts**
	*Matrix Reasoning**
	Picture Completion
	Digit Span
	*Letter-Number Sequencing**
Working Memory Index (WMI)	Arithmetic
	Coding
	Symbol Search
Processing Speed Index (PSI)	*Cancellation**

* *Italics* indicates new subtest.

Verbal Comprehension Subtests:

- *Similarities:* measures verbal reasoning and concept formation. This test requires the child to identify the similarity between two dissimilar items (words presented to the child)
- *Vocabulary:* measures the child's word knowledge and verbal concept formation. For the picture items, the child is required to name the pictures in the book. For the verbal items, the child is required to give definitions for words the examiner reads aloud.
- *Comprehension:* measures the child's verbal reasoning and conceptualization, verbal comprehension, and verbal expression. This test requires the child to answer questions based on his or her understanding of general principles and social situations.
- *Information:* measures the child's ability to acquire, retain, and retrieve general factual knowledge. The test requires the child to answer questions that address a broad range of general knowledge topics.
- *Word Reasoning:* measures verbal comprehension, analogical and general reasoning ability, verbal abstraction, domain knowledge, the ability to integrate and synthesize different types of information, and the ability to generate alternative concepts. This test requires the child to identify the common concept being described in a series of clues.

Perceptual Reasoning Subtests

- *Block Design:* measures the child's ability to analyze and synthesize abstract visual stimuli. The child views a constructed model or a picture in the stimulus book, and uses red-and-white blocks to re-create the design within a specified time limit.
- *Picture Concepts:* measures abstract, categorical reasoning ability. The child sees rows with pictures of various objects and selects those objects that are similar and should be grouped together. For example, the similar items might be trees or animals.
- *Matrix Reasoning:* measures fluid intelligence and provides a reliable estimate of general nonverbal intelligence. In this exercise, a child sees a grid partially filled with certain shapes (e.g., stars, pentagons). The child then selects an item from five choices that completes the grid.
- *Picture Completion:* measures visual perception and organization, concentration, and visual recognition of essential details of objects. This test requires the child to view a picture and then point to or name the important part missing within a specified time limit.

Working Memory Subtests

- *Digit Span:* measures auditory short-term memory, sequencing skills, attention, and concentration. The Digit Span Forward task requires the child to repeat numbers in the same order as read aloud by the examiner. Digit Span Backward requires the child to repeat the numbers in the reverse order of that presented by the examiner.
- *Letter-Number Sequencing:* measures sequencing, mental manipulation, attention, short-term auditory memory, visuospatial imaging, and processing speed. It requires the child to read a sequence of letters and numbers and recall the numbers in ascending order and the letters in alphabetical order.
- *Arithmetic:* measures mental manipulation, concentration, attention, short- and long-term memory, numerical reasoning ability, and mental alertness. It requires the child to mentally solve a series of orally presented arithmetic problems within a specified time limit.

Processing Speed Subtests

- *Coding:* measures the child's short-term memory, learning ability, visual perception, visual-motor coordination, visual scanning ability, cognitive flexibility, attention, and motivation. It requires the child to copy symbols that are paired with simple geometric shapes or numbers.
- *Symbol Search:* measures processing speed, short-term visual memory, visual-motor coordination, cognitive flexibility, visual discrimination, and concentration. This test requires the child to scan a search group and indicate whether the target symbol(s) matches any of the symbols in the search group within a specified time limit.

- *Cancellation:* measures processing speed, visual selective attention, vigilance, and visual neglect. It requires the child to scan both a random and structured arrangement of pictures and mark target pictures within a specified time limit.

Variability between subtest scores is common. It does not necessarily indicate a learning disability or other cognitive problem. However, some differences among Index scores and Subtest scores may indicate children with learning disorders. The following is a description of the typical composite scores on the WISC-IV for some learning disorders and Attention Deficit Hyperactivity Disorder. Composite scores consist of all four indexes and the full scale IQ score.

- *Reading Disorders:* When compared to a matched control group, children with reading disorders have significantly lower scores for all composites, with the largest difference on the Working Memory Index. Children with reading disorders also tend to score lower on the Vocabulary and Information subtests, which may reflect a deficiency in the "general fund of information" typically acquired through reading. Scores on the Arithmetic subtest is also lower which supports the possible role of working memory in reading disorders.
- *Math Disorders:* When compared with a matched control group, the scores for children with math disorders were significantly lower on all composites except the Processing Speed Index. The difference in the Perceptual Reasoning Index score was the largest of all index scores. This is primarily due to the performance on the Picture Concepts subtest, which requires fluid reasoning with abstract verbal concepts. At the subtest level, a large difference was observed for solving word problems mentally on the Arithmetic subtest, which may suggest deficits in numerical skill and working memory. Children with math disorders also tend to score lower on the Picture Concepts, Information, and Arithmetic subtests.
- *Attention-Deficit/Hyperactivity Disorder (ADHD):* For children with ADHD, the largest difference in scores occurred on the Coding and Arithmetic subtests. This is consistent with research indicating that children with ADHD typically achieve scores near the normal range of intellectual functioning, but may perform worse on measures of processing speed and working memory.

The WISC-IV has outstanding reliability, with all scales having internal consistency reliability coefficients and test-retest reliability coefficients exceeding .89. Clinicians are required to be at C-level to be qualified to administer the Wechsler test.

Wechsler Preschool and Primary Scale of Intelligence—Third Edition (WPPSI-III). The WPPSI-III is designed for children age 4 to 6 ½ years. The test is divided into six verbal and five performance subtests. The 11 subtests are presented in the following order: information, animal house and animal house retest, vocabulary, picture completion, arithmetic, mazes, geometric design, similarities, block design, comprehension, and sentences.

The WPPSI-III is an individual test that does not require reading or writing. Verbal subtests are oral questions without time limits. Performance subtests are nonverbal (both spatial and fluid reasoning) problems, several of which are timed. Subtest scores,

IQ scores, Processing Speed Quotients, and General Language Composite scores were normed on 1,700 children, ages 2 years and 2 months to 7 years and 3 months.

Kaufman Assessment Battery for Children-II.   The KABC-II is a measure of the processing and cognitive abilities of children and adolescents between the ages of 3 years and 18 years and 11 months. Five cognitive abilities (corresponding to five KABC-II scales) are measured by the KABC-II: Short-Term Acquisition and Retrieval (Gsm), Long-Term Storage and Retrieval (Glr), Visual Processing (Gv), Speed of Processing (Gs), and Quantitative Knowledge (Gq).

The KABC-II is organized into three levels (age 3, ages 4–6, ages 7–18). It has one to five scales depending on the age of the child and the interpretive approach that the clinician chooses to take. At age 3, there is only one scale, a global measure of ability composed of either five or seven subtests. For ages 4 to 6, subtests are organized into either three or four scales: Sequential/Gsm, Simultaneous/Gv, Learning/ Glr, and Knowledge/Gc. For ages 7 to 18, four or five scales are available, with the Planning/Gf scale joining the aforementioned scales. The scales and subtests are described in Table 8.7.

The KABC-II is based on the theory of intelligence that distinguishes between sequential and simultaneous mental processes. *Sequential processing* (Kaufman, Kamphaus, & Kaufman, 1985) relates to the ability to solve problems by mentally arranging input in a sequential or serial order. *Simultaneous processing* refers to the ability to synthesize information from mental wholes to solve the problem. Simultaneous processing is used in such tasks as learning the shapes of letters, deriving meaning from pictorial stimuli, and determining the main idea from a paragraph of text. Sequential processing is used in learning grammatical relationships and rules, understanding the chronology of events, and making associations between sounds and letters.

Internal consistency reliabilities and test-retest reliabilities are excellent: all exceed .86. The KABC-II was standardized on variables that match 1980 U.S. Census Data including age, sex, geographic region, social economic status, race or ethnicity, and community size. However, Hispanic Americans were underrepresented by 24%.

The following case study of George shows how individual testing can be used.

Table 8.7
Description of KABC-II subtests.

Scale/Subtests	Description
Sequential/*Gsm*	
Word Order	The child touches a series of silhouettes of common objects in the same order as the examiner said the names of the objects.
Number Recall	The child repeats a series of numbers in the same sequence as the examiner said them, with series ranging in length from two to nine numbers.
Hand Movements	The child copies the examiner's precise sequence of taps on the table with the fist, palm, or side of the hand.

Table 8.7
Continued

Simultaneous/*Gv*

Rover | The child moves a toy dog to a bone on a checkerboard-like grid that contains obstacles (rocks and weeds) and tries to find the "quickest" path (e.g., the one that takes the fewest moves).

Triangles | For most items, the child assembles several identical rubber triangles (blue on one side, yellow on the other) to match a picture of an abstract design.

Conceptual Thinking | The child views a set of four or five pictures and identifies the one picture that does not belong with the others.

Face Recognition | The child attends closely to photographs of one or two faces that are exposed briefly and then selects the correct face or faces, shown in a different pose, from a group photograph.

Gestalt Closure | The child mentally fills in the gaps in a partially completed inkblot drawing and names or describes the object or action depicted in the drawing.

Block Counting | The child counts the exact number of blocks in various pictures of stacks of blocks.

Planning/*Gf*

Pattern Reasoning | The child is shown a series of stimuli that form a logical, linear pattern, but one stimulus is missing; the child completes the pattern by selecting the correct stimulus from an array of four to six options at the bottom of the page (most stimuli are abstract, geometric shapes).

Story Completion | The child is shown a row of pictures that tell a story, but some of the pictures are missing. The child is given a set of pictures, selects only the ones that are needed to complete the story, and places the missing pictures in their correct location.

Learning/*Glr*

Atlantis | The examiner teaches the child nonsense names for fanciful pictures of fish, plants, and shells; the child demonstrates learning by pointing to each picture (out of an array of pictures) when it is named.

Atlantis Delayed | The child demonstrates delayed recall of paired associations learned about 15–25 minutes earlier during Atlantis by pointing to the picture of the fish, plant, or shell that is named by the examiner.

Rebus Learning | The examiner teaches the child the word or concept associated with each particular rebus (drawing), and the child then "reads" aloud phrases and sentences composed of these rebuses.

Rebus Learning Delayed | The child demonstrates delayed recall of paired associations learned about 15–25 minutes earlier during Rebus by reading phrases and sentences composed of those same rebuses.

Knowledge/*Gc*

Riddles | The examiner provides several characteristics of a concrete or abstract verbal concept, and the child has to point to it or name it.

Expressive Vocabulary | The child provides the name of a pictured object.

Verbal Knowledge | The child selects from an array of six pictures the one that corresponds to a vocabulary word or answers a general information question.

Note: Descriptions are adapted from the *KABC-II Manual* (Kaufman & Kaufman, 2004).

CASE OF GEORGE

George Gray
Middletown Elementary School: Grade K
Date of birth: 3/22/96
Chronological age: 7.03
Date of examination: 7/8/03

Tests Used

Kaufman Assessment Battery for Children (K-ABC), Peabody Picture Vocabulary Test-Revised, Developmental Test of Visual-Motor Integration, Goodenough-Harris Draw-a-Woman Test

Reason for Referral

George Gray was referred for possible program change. He is currently participating in the language-impaired program at Middletown Elementary School.

Background Information

George was previously tested on 7/31/02. He was given the Stanford-Binet Intelligence Scale, Leiter International Performance Scale, Peabody Picture Vocabulary Test, and the Developmental Test of Visual-Motor Integration. The Stanford-Binet Intelligence Scale yielded an IQ of 48. The Leiter International Performance Scale was administered because of George's delayed language development, and an IQ score of 77 was obtained. The Peabody Picture Vocabulary Test-Revised revealed a standard score below 40, an age-equivalent score of 3 years, 6 months, and a significant deficit in the receptive vocabulary area. A communication evaluation was completed on 11/7/02, indicating that George had an articulation disorder and was severely delayed in language skills. The Vineland Adaptive Behavior Scale was completed on 6/19/03 with these results:

Scale	Age Equivalent
Receptive language	3.11
Expressive language	3.3
Written language	1.6

George's adaptive behavior composite on that evaluation equated to 60.

Another communication evaluation was conducted on 4/24/03. The speech and language pathologist reported that the two communication evaluations were consistent. George was functioning at approximately a 3-year-old level during both evaluations. Vision and hearing were found to be within acceptable limits at the school level.

Examiner Observations

George is a 7-year-old male of average stature for his chronological age. He was somewhat uncooperative by being continually out of his seat and exhibited poor listening skills. His work habits were somewhat slow, but his behavior could be described as extremely active. He was aware of his failures, and he typically gave up on a task at the very beginning if he believed he could not accomplish it. He appeared agitated after his failures. His speech was poor and his language inarticulate. At times his responses were vague, and the examiner had to encourage him to continue responding. He usually spoke only when he was spoken to. On the visual-motor tasks his reaction time was slow; he used a trial-and-error method of problem solving.

Results

The Kaufman Assessment Battery for Children (Kaufman & Kaufman, 1983) gave these Global Scale standard scores:

Sequential Processing	56 ± 10
Simultaneous Processing	71 ± 9
Mental Processing Composite	63 ± 8
Achievement	Below 40
Nonverbal	67 ± 8

These were the Achievement standard scores:

Space and Places	65 ± 13
Arithmetic	62 ± 13
Riddles	59 ± 11
Reading/Decoding	67 ± 7
Reading/Understanding	0

The Mental Processing Scale scores included these scores for Sequential Processing:

Hand Movement	3
Number Recall	1
Word Order	4

These were the scores for Simultaneous Processing:

Gestalt Closure	7
Triangles	10
Matrix Analogies	6
Spatial Memory	2
Photo Series	3

These were the Nonverbal scores:

Hand Movement	3
Triangles	10
Matrix Analogies	6
Spatial Memory	2
Photo Series	3

Significant differences and overall scores were as follows:

Sequential < Simultaneous	.05
Sequential > Achievement	.05
Simultaneous > Achievement	.01
MPC > Achievement	.01
Mean Achievement	
Standard Score	50.6
Mean Scaled Score	4.5

Scores on the Peabody Picture Vocabulary Test were as follows:

Raw Score	27
Standard Score	< 40
Age Equivalent	3.2

Cognitive Development and Interpretation

George was administered the K-ABC to assess his current mental processing abilities and level of achievement. The K-ABC measures one's style of problem solving. Two types of mental functioning are identified: sequential processing, which involves processing stimuli bit by bit or in serial order, and simultaneous processing, which incorporates a holistic and frequently spatial integration of stimuli.

George's Sequential Processing standard score of 56 ± 10 (95% confidence level) is in the educable mentally handicapped range of functioning. His Simultaneous Processing score of 71 ± 9 is in the borderline range. Thus, there is a significant difference (15 points) between his sequential processing and his simultaneous processing. This difference suggests that George has greater abilities in solving problems holistically or processing many stimuli at one time, rather than stimulus by stimulus.

George's Achievement standard score of below 40 represents a significant discrepancy between his school achievement and mental processing abilities. His Simultaneous Processing standard score of 71 is significantly greater than his Achievement standard score. This difference is found in less than 1% of the individuals within George's age group and may be associated with school-related learning tasks on the test, which are usually more sequentially oriented.

George's Mental Processing Composite (MPC) of 63 ± 8 is in the educable mentally handicapped range. His true score has a 95% chance of being between 55 and 71. Thus, his MPC score is significantly higher than the Achievement standard score and indicates that he has greater processing potential than is being exemplified in school-related achievement.

Internal analysis of the K-ABC reveals a mean score of 4.5, which is considered in the handicapped range of functioning. A relative strength is noted on the Triangles subtest, which measures abstract concept formation. A significant weakness is noted in short-term recall via simultaneous processing (Spatial Memory). All his scores on the Mental Processing subtests, except for Triangles, are considered below the average for children within George's age group.

The Nonverbal standard score of 67 was compiled from the subtests Hand Movements, Triangles, Matrix Analogies, Spatial Memory, and Photo Series. George's Nonverbal standard score was not significantly higher than his Mental Processing score, suggesting that his abilities, as measured by the K-ABC, are not significantly different. Language impairment is the major influence, but other factors also appear to be contributing to George's low-functioning intellect.

Receptive Language

On the Peabody Picture Vocabulary Test—Revised, which requires the subject to point to one of four pictures corresponding to a word presented orally by the examiner, George received a standard score below 40. This score is greater than one standard deviation below the mean when considering chronological age and current cognitive functioning, and it represents a process deficit in the receptive language area.

Perceptual-Motor

On the Developmental Test of Visual-Motor Integration, which requires the subject to reproduce geometric designs with pencil and paper, George received a standard score of 4 and an age equivalent of 5.1. This score is within one standard deviation of the mean, when considering chronological age and current cognitive func-

tioning, and represents adequate development in the perceptual-motor area. The Goodenough-Harris Draw-a-Woman Test revealed a mental age of 5.9 and an estimated IQ of 79.

Diagnostic Impressions

George is functioning in the educable mentally handicapped range. He demonstrates significantly greater abilities in simultaneous processing, as compared with sequential processing. He also demonstrates a relative strength in his nonverbal concept formation and his word recognition and letter naming. A significant weakness is noted in his short-term memory recall.

George's Achievement scores are significantly lower than his potential indicates. His nonverbal abilities are not demonstrated as being significantly higher than his total Mental Processing Composite. A process deficit is noted in receptive language, consistent with his history of poor language development. Perceptual-motor abilities appear to be adequately developed. Just how much George's poor language development has affected his intellectual functioning is not known. Presently his intellectual functioning, as measured by the K-ABC, is somewhere between the educable mentally handicapped and borderline range of functioning. Current remediation strategies should address his language delay as well as his current estimated intellectual functioning.

The K-ABC-II has an interpretative manual, which suggests these five steps:

- Obtain the derived scores and describe them with bands of error, descriptive categories, national and sociocultural percentile ranks, age equivalents, and grade equivalents.
- Compare standard scores on the Sequential Processing and Simultaneous Processing scales.
- Compare standard scores on the Mental Processing and Achievement scales.
- Determine strengths and weaknesses on the Mental Processing subtests.
- Determine strengths and weaknesses on the Achievement subtests.

The K-ABC-II lists these primary goals: to measure intelligence from a strong theoretical and research basis, to separate acquired factual knowledge from the ability to solve unfamiliar problems, to yield scores that translate into educational interventions, to include novel tasks, to be easy to administer and objective to score, and to be sensitive to diverse needs of preschool, minority groups, and children with exceptionalities (Kaufman & Kaufman, 1983, p. 5).

In a review of the K-ABC, Merz (1984) concludes that the authors have met the goals and that the test will fairly assess minority group members and individuals with language impairments.

Kaufman Adolescent and Adult Intelligence Test.   The Kaufman Adolescent and Adult Intelligence Test (KAIT) was designed for individuals ages 11 to 85+ years. The core battery consists of six subtests within two scales. The KAIT measures fluid intelligence, adaptability, and flexibility in problem solving through three subtests. The crystallized scale measures ability to solve problems and make decisions based on acquired knowledge, verbal conceptualization, formal and informal education, life experience, and acculturation through subtests on auditory comprehension, double meaning, and definitions. A composite score provides a measure of overall intellectual functioning. The examiner can also add one to four additional subtests to the battery: memory for block designs, famous faces, rebus recall, and auditory recall. A rebus is a picture that stands for a word. Individuals are asked to read phrases or sentences composed of rebuses on the fluid scale, then read the phrases or sentences on the added recall test that were learned earlier during the rebus learning subtest. The KAIT can measure immediate and delayed recall. The construct validity of the KAIT is shown through studies correlating the KAIT with the WISC-IV, the WAIS-III, and the K-ABC-II. Internal consistency reliability coefficients in the .90s were reported, and concurrent validity with other tests of intelligence are in the .55 to .85 range.

Stanford-Binet Intelligence Scale, Fifth Edition.   The Stanford-Binet is an individually administered assessment of intelligence and cognitive abilities. Lewis Terman made the American revision in 1916. The fifth edition (SB5), developed in 2001, was normed on a stratified random sample of 4,800 individuals matching the data from the 2000 U.S. Census. The test can be administered to individuals age 2 to 90 and takes, on the average, 45 to 60 minutes. The SB5 measures five factors: fluid reasoning, knowledge, quantitative reasoning, visual spatial processing, and working memory. The test yields a full IQ and verbal and nonverbal scores with a standard score of 100 and a standard deviation of 15. The author conducted studies on the test items to assess whether gender, ethnic, or socioeconomic status affected the validity of the test. Subtest scores have a mean of 10 and a standard deviation of 3. Many of the test items were adapted from previous editions of the Binet. Extensive low-end and high-end items were included to enhance the assessment of both the gifted and children with mental disabilities. Nonverbal performance items make up half of the test items. The test can be scored by computer or by hand.

Studies compare the SB5 with the fourth edition, Form L-M, the Woodcock-Johnson, and the Wechsler scales. Concurrent as well as construct validity was collected and found high correlation between the composite IQ scores of the SB5 and the composite scores of previous editions of the Stanford-Binet and all of the major IQ batteries used for all populations.

The SB5 adequately describes individuals who have problems in learning, ADHD, and the like. The following are some of the features of the test:

- variety of items requiring nonverbal performance
- assessment of individuals with limited English skills and communication problems
- evaluation of individual's performance in five domains: fluid reasoning, knowledge, working memory, visual, and quantitative reasoning
- results can be used to compare verbal and nonverbal assessment of working memory
- extensive high-end items; improved low-end items

The Stanford-Binet consists of four factors. The Verbal Reasoning factor includes four subtests: vocabulary, comprehension, absurdities, and verbal relations. The Abstract/ Visual Reasoning component also includes four subtests: pattern analysis, copying, matrices, and paper folding and cutting. The Quantitative Reasoning factor has three subtests: quantitative, number series, and equation building. The Short-Term Memory factor includes four scales: bead memory, memory of sentences, memory of digits, and memory of objects. The overall composite scores and scaled scores have a fixed mean of 100 and a fixed standard deviation of 15. The subtests have a mean of 10 and a standard deviation of 3.

The items on the test are arranged in levels designated by the letters A through Y. Some tests contain 20 or more levels and cover the entire range from 2 to adulthood; others contain 10 levels and cover a narrower range of chronological age. The purpose of this format is to facilitate adaptive testing. Chronological age and performance on the vocabulary test are used to identify the level at which testing should begin. As in previous editions of the Stanford-Binet, basal and ceiling levels are established.

Intelligence Tests for Special Populations

A number of assessment instruments have been developed recently for special groups such as children with attention-deficit hyperactivity disorder (ADHD), neuropsychological impairments, those for whom English is a second language, children with hearing and visual impairments, and so on. Table 8.8 shows a brief description of some of these instruments.

The Leiter Performance Scale-Revised (LIPS-R) has two domains, attention and memory, and can accurately identify children with ADHD or neuropsychological impairments. The authors have included a complete profile of cognitive strengths and weaknesses. Scores are presented for each subtest and skill area. The Leiter was found to correlate with the WISC-II (r = .85). There are four rating scales to assess the social, emotional behavior of the student: Examiner, Teacher, Parent, and Self-Rating. The LIPS-R has been used to test a wide variety of individuals, including those

Table 8.8
Intellectual assessment tests for special populations.

Test	Type	Features
Leiter International Performance Scale-Revised (LIPS-R)	Fluid Nonverbal New attention domain New memory domain	Free from cultural and language bias Game-like administration Correlated .85 with WISC
Stoelting Brief Intelligence Test (S-BIT)	Four subtests Figure ground Form completion Repeated patterns Sequential order	Can be used with special populations Effective diagnostic instrument
Merrill-Palmer Scale-Revised	Nineteen scales	For children aged 18 months Individually administered
Slosson Intelligence Test-Revised-Third Edition (SIT-R3)	Assesses information comprehension, math similarities and differences Vocabulary Auditory memory	For individuals aged 4–65 For use with individuals who are blind Ten to twenty minutes to administer
Slosson Intelligence Test-Primary Memory memory (SIT-P)	Vocabulary Similarities Block design Digit sequence Perceptual-motor Visual-motor	For children aged 2–8 Measures cognitive and noncognitive Performance screening
Universal Nonverbal Intelligence Test (UNIT)	General IQ 100% nonverbal	For individuals aged 5.0–17.11 Fairness for all students irrespective of race, culture, gender, etc.
Cognitive Assessment System (CAS)	Measures four core processes Planning, attention, processing, etc.	One level for individuals aged 2.6–17.11; another level for children aged 3.6–6.11 Twelve subtests Forty minutes to administer
Test of Memory and Learning (TOMAL)	Verbal memory Nonverbal Delayed recall Sequential memory Attention Free recall Composite memory	For children aged 4.0–19.11 Forty-five minutes to administer

continued

Table 8.8

Continued

Test	Type	Features
Wechsler Abbreviated Scale of Intelligence (WASI)	Two forms Developed in 1999 Quick, reliable test Vocabulary similarities Matrices Block design	Two or four subtests For individuals aged 6–89 Four subtests
Beta III	Quick measurement of nonverbal IQ	For individuals aged 16–89 Useful for working with low-functioning test takers
Comprehensive Test of Nonverbal Intelligence (CTONI)	Computer administered	For individuals aged 6.0–90.11 About 1 hour to administer
Wide Range Intelligence Test (WRIT)	Fluid IQ Crystalized IQ Verbal crystallized Nonverbal fluid	For individuals aged 4–85 Twenty to thirty minutes to administer

with hearing and language disabilities, mental disabilities, cultural disadvantages, or non-English-speaking backgrounds. The LIPS-R measures dimensions of perceptual and conceptual abilities. The perceptual items present tasks involving shapes, colors, block design, and visual closure. The conceptual items require clients to deduce underlying relationships, categories, and classes; demonstrate an understanding of visual-spatial relationships; and understand numerical processes. The categories are symbolic transformation, quantitative discriminations, spatial imagery, genus matching, progression discriminations, and immediate recall. Matey (1984) rates the LIPS-R as valuable for psychologists engaged in the assessment of the mental abilities of children with hearing impairments, children with severe expressive or receptive language disabilities, and adults with severe or profound mental retardation. The LIPS-R is also considered an appropriate instrument for those who have motor and manipulative difficulties in addition to impaired communication skills.

The Authur Point Scale of Performance Tests-Revised Form II is an individual scale that measures the mental abilities of individuals with reading, hearing, speech, emotional, or cultural disabilities. The Authur Point Scale contains five tests: Knox Cube Test, Sequin Form Board, Arthur Stencil Design, Healy Picture Completion, and Porteus Maze Test.

The Peabody Picture Vocabulary Test-III measures receptive vocabulary knowledge for standard American English and provides an estimate of the verbal ability and scholastic aptitude of the test taker. The examinee is shown a plate containing four pictures and is asked to point to the picture that corresponds to the stimulus word. A Spanish version is available.

The Slosson Intelligence Test-Revised-Third Edition (SIT-R3) provides a quick assessment of mental abilities of children and adults age 4 to 65. The SIT-R is a 187-item oral screening instrument with questions arranged on a scale by chronological age. The test contains 33 vocabulary items, 29 general information items, 30 similarities and differences items, 33 comprehension items, 34 quantitative items, and 28 auditory memory items. The SIT-R correlates .892 with the WISC-R Verbal IQ (VIQ) and .863 with the WISC-III FSIQ (Full Scale IQ). The K-R 20 reliability coefficients are .90 or higher for all age groups. An item analysis identifies the strengths and weaknesses of an individual in eight learning areas.

The Test of Nonverbal Intelligence-3 (TONI-3) provides a language-free measure of cognitive ability. The TONI-3 is used with clients having speech, language, or learning disabilities, who are deaf or hearing impaired, or who have suffered some form of brain injury. It can also be used with clients who do not speak English or for whom English is not their first language. A 50-item, point-to-the-response test can be given by pantomime to the examinee, who responds by pointing to the selected answer. The test can be given to individuals aged 6 to 89 and takes 15 to 20 minutes.

The Raven's Progressive Matrices (RPM) consist of a series of three nonverbal tests for different ability levels. In measuring the nonverbal component of Spearman's *G* factor, the items are designed to assess clients' ability to make sense of complex situations, derive meaning from events, and perceive and think clearly. It can be group administered and has been utilized with clients with mental impairments. The Coloured Progressive Matrices (CPM) are used to spread the scores for the bottom 20% of the general population. Norms are available for children and adolescents aged 6.5 to 16.5. The Standard Progressive Matrices (SPM) measure the performance in the average range and consist of five sets of 12 problems each. The Advanced Progressive Matrices (APM) are designed to spread the scores of the top 20% of the population.

The Das Naglieri Cognitive Assessment System (CAS) provides information on the strengths and weaknesses of four major cognitive processes and yields useful information about the intellectual strengths and weaknesses of children with mental disabilities. It can be administered to individuals age 2.6 to 17.11. There are two levels. The upper preschool level is used with children age 3.6 to 6.11 and yields two scores: Verbal Ability and Nonverbal Ability. The school level also provides a composite score in Spatial Ability. Both core and diagnostic subtests are part of the assessment.

The following subsections will help the reader compare the components and assumptions of some of the widely used conceptualizations of intelligence.

The Universal Nonverbal Intelligence Test (UNIT) is a language-free test that requires no receptive or expressive language from the examiner or examinee. UNIT measures a number of types of intelligence and cognitive abilities. The test is made up of six subtests designed to measure the functioning of the client according to a two-tier model of intelligence, memory, and reasoning. The memory subtests are object memory, spatial memory, and symbolic memory. Also, three subtests assess reasoning, design, mazes, and analogic reasoning. Although five of the subtests require motoric manipulation, they can be adapted for a pointing response. On the Spatial Memory subtest, the examinee must remember and re-create the placement of colored chips. On the Object Memory scale the examinee is shown a visual array of common objects such as a pan, computer, and rose for 5 seconds and then has to identify the objects shown from a larger array of objects in pictures. The internal consistency coefficient for 5- to 7-year-olds ranged from .83 in analogic reasoning to .89 in design.

Culture-Fair Intelligence Tests are a series of tests developed by R. B. Cattell and A. K. S. Cattell. Scale 1 is used for ages 4 to 8; scale 2 for preadolescents, adolescents, and adults with average abilities; and scale 3 with college students and adults with above-average ability. Scales 2 and 3 are group-administered nonverbal tests measuring perceptual tasks such as completing a series, classifying, solving incomplete designs, and evaluating conditions. The tests measure the fluid dimension of Cattell's theory mentioned earlier in this chapter.

The Cognitive Abilities Test (CogAT) was originally developed by R. L. Thorndike and E. P. Hagen and is a multilevel battery used to test children from kindergarten to grade 12. Verbal, quantitative, and nonverbal batteries are utilized. The verbal battery measures vocabulary, sentence completion, classification, and analogies. The quantitative battery measures relations, number series, and equation building. The nonverbal battery utilizes figure classification, analogies, and synthesis. The test can be group administered to classes and hand- or computer-scored. Levels 1 and 2 are designed for kindergarten through grade 3; level A, for grades 3 to 12. Testing time is about 90 minutes. A CogAT Interpretive Guide for Teachers and a manual, "Preparing for Testing with the CogAT," are available to facilitate proper use and interpretation of the test. The current edition of the test is Form 6 (Lohman & Hagen, 2001).

The Otis-Lennon School Ability Test (OLSAT) was developed by A. S. Otis and later revised by R. T. Lennon. The OLSAT is currently in its eighth edition. The OLSAT has seven levels. The primary batteries are read to the students by the examiner. Verbal, figural, and numerical items are rotated. The test yields a *g* score. The OLSAT is used for predicting success in cognitive, school-related areas. It yields a school ability index, national percentile rank, stanine, and national NCE by age and grade. Local norms can also be included in the report. The computer report provides a narrative explaining the student's performance in easy-to-understand language. That performance is analyzed by clusters, including verbal comprehension, verbal reasoning, figural reasoning, and quantitative reasoning.

The School and College Ability Tests (SCAT) are a series of group tests measuring verbal and quantitative ability from grade 3.5 to grade 14.0. The verbal section measures students' understanding of words and analogies, and the quantitative section measures students' understanding of fundamental number concepts. The SCAT reports scores in both verbal and quantitative areas in percentile bands.

The Test of Cognitive Skills Second Edition (TCS-2) is a group test used to assess four areas of the cognitive skills of students in grades 2 to 12: analogies, sequences, memory, and verbal reasoning. The analogies test assesses students' ability to see abstract or concrete relationships and to classify objects or concepts according to common attributes. The memory test assesses students' abilities to recall information presented at the beginning of the test. The sequences test assesses students' ability to comprehend a principle or a rule implicit in a pattern or sequence of figures, letters, or numbers. The verbal reasoning test assesses students' ability to discern relationships and reason logically. The TCS-2 yields scores in each of the four areas and provides a verbal, nonverbal, and total IQ.

The Primary Test of Cognitive Skills (PTCS) was developed by Huttenlocher and Levine to measure the cognitive skills of children in kindergarten and first grade and has four subscales: verbal, spatial, memory, and concepts. These four subscales are combined to yield a Cognitive Skills Index, utilizing a mean of 100 and a standard deviation of 10.

TRENDS AND ISSUES

Intelligence testing is still an issue of controversy. Many definitions of the construct of intelligence have led to the development of many different models, theories, and tests. There is no shared agreement as to what intelligence is and how it should be measured. We are not even sure of what words we should use to describe the construct— *ability, aptitude, cognitive abilities, intelligence,* or *potential.* The cognitive and information-processing movements in psychology have had an impact on the theories and have influenced how we interpret and title our tests. Instead of using "intelligence" in the title, many tests now refer to cognitive abilities.

Many models have been developed to help us conceptualize intelligence, such as those by Spearman, Thurstone, E. L. Thorndike, Guilford, Gardner, Horn, Piaget, Sternberg, Wagner, Vernon, and Jensen. The controversy still centers around the issue of whether intelligence is a general attribute or has many specific attributes.

The heredity and environment issue is also still debated. Historically, social scientists have been divided over the relative importance of heredity and environment in relation to intelligence. In their book *The Bell Curve* (1994), Herrnstein and Murray conclude that heredity plays an important role in intelligence. Among other evidence, they note that IQ scores are highly correlated with academic success, job performance, and infant mortality. Current studies are exploring how the interaction between heredity and environment affects intelligence.

Psychologists also do not agree as to the purposes of intelligence testing. Sternberg and Wagner believe the tests should be used to help provide useful information for understanding and improving the learning process of individuals tested.

Much concern is still focused on the biased nature of IQ tests. White, middle-class test takers score better than individuals from different racial and cultural groups. Loehlin, Lindzey, and Spohler (1975) concluded that such distinctions reflect biases in the tests themselves, differences in the environments of the groups, and differences in the genetic makeup of the individuals studied. The three factors are viewed as interactive but not necessarily independent. Attempts were made, for example, on the Wechsler Intelligence Scale for Children to minimize bias. Statistics were computed to identify and eliminate items preferential to certain age, ethnic, or gender groups in the current fourth edition.

Another question often debated deals with the stability of intelligence over time. Research has indicated that IQ scores are very unstable in early childhood. Later, scores may decline with age on some types of items and increase on others. IQ is not viewed as a fixed attribute. Some dimensions may be influenced by genetic makeup, but typically one develops greater general knowledge, problem-solving ability, and comprehension with age. On the other hand, the psychomotor performance of an individual might decrease with age.

SUMMARY

This chapter focused on the individual and group intelligence tests that are most widely used today. The tests cited illustrate that there are many definitions and models of intelligence. Such tests help teachers make instructional decisions about what methods and materials would be best for their students. They help workers in the helping professions to develop realistic expectations for their clients and students. The information from intelligence tests is also valuable in guiding individuals to make educational and vocational decisions. The tests provide a frame of reference for looking at cognitive abilities and making placement and classification decisions on the basis of such scores. Intelligence tests are also used for descriptive and predictive purposes.

Kamphaus, Petoskey, and Morgan (1997) point out that there have been four major approaches to intelligence test interpretation. The first was to design a system to classify individuals according to their abilities. Recall that the early work of Binet and others was to classify individuals into specific groups based upon the scores they achieved on intelligence tests.

The second approach was to use profile analysis to help achieve a more complete understanding of an individual's cognitive skills. Rapaport and Wechsler led this second wave of test interpretation.

The third wave was the use of psychometric profile analysis stimulated by the availability of computer and statistical software packages. Scales on the Wechsler tests were factor analyzed. Cohen was the leader in this movement and helped clinicians understand the necessity of considering subtest score interpretation. Kaufman extended our understanding of the problems associated with profile analysis.

The fourth wave was applying theory to intelligence test interpretation. Integrative approaches emphasized that results can be interpreted meaningfully only in the context of other test results such as clinical findings, background information, and the like. Findings were seen as meaningful if supported by research evidence. Knowledge of theory is a key element in helping the examiner conceptualize a client's score.

QUESTIONS FOR DISCUSSION

1. Compare the different theories of intelligence. What theory do you find most acceptable and why? Why are theories important?

2. What are the advantages and disadvantages of group intelligence tests? Of individual tests? When would you use each?

3. E. L. Thorndike said there were three types of intelligence: abstract, social, and practical. Do you agree with his view? How do they compare with Sternberg's and Gardner's types?

4. Turn back to the "Case of George." He was given the Stanford-Binet Intelligence Scale, Leiter International Performance Scale, Peabody Picture Vocabulary Test,

Goodenough-Harris Draw-a-Woman Test, and Developmental Test of Visual-Motor Integration. Why was each test given? Why are there differences in the scores on these tests? Would you have given George any other test? Why or why not?

5. Do you feel that most tests are biased in favor of the White, middle-class examinee? Do you believe that we should use only culture-fair tests? Defend your beliefs.

6. What factors influence how an individual performs on an IQ test? Do you believe that items on the intelligence tests should be radically changed so the test can be of more use? Why or why not?

SUGGESTED ACTIVITIES

1. Critique a group or an individual intelligence test discussed in this chapter.

2. Interview psychologists and counselors who use intelligence tests. Find out which tests they use and why and when they test. Report your results to the class.

3. Make an annotated bibliography of the intelligence and scholastic aptitude tests you would use in your field.

4. Write a review of the literature or a position paper on one of the following topics: bias in intelligence testing, history of intelligence testing, socioeconomic class and intelligence, genetic studies of intelligence, computer-adaptive intelligence testing.

5. Take a group IQ test, score it, and write a report of the results.

6. Read *The Bell Curve* and be prepared to discuss the book in class.

7. Read the following case and answer the questions at the end.

Case of Roberta

Roberta is a ninth-grade student who was referred to the school psychologist for psycho-educational evaluation to assess possible causes of her unacceptable behavior and poor peer and adult relationships.

School personnel are concerned about Roberta's inability to function in a school setting. She is frequently off task, asks inappropriate questions, comes unprepared, wanders around the classroom, and seeks to make herself the center of attention. Roberta is making fair grades in average group classes. She appears to be preoccupied and also seems to fear her parents, not wanting them to know what happens in school.

Examiner observations:

Roberta is a thin, pale girl with unkempt hair. She has an excellent vocabulary and a good sense of humor. However, she does not know how to respond to teasing or correction and seems to enjoy telling stories about how she gets back at people who offend her. Her speech is affected, leaning toward the theatrical, and she appears to enjoy the attention testing afforded.

She was observed in the class and in the halls. She was unprepared for class, not having paper. This seemed to be a common occurrence. She gave responses to questions in a mumble. When asked to speak louder, she became quite dramatic. In the halls she keeps to herself. She leaves class late and hurries to her next class. She stands out in the crowd. Her mannerisms and dress set her apart.

Results:

Stanford-Binet (full scale)=132

Wide Range Achievement Test

Subject (%)	Grade Equivalent	Standard Score	Percentile
1. Reading	12.7	139	99.1
2. Spelling	11.7	127	96
3. Arithmetic	10.0	114	82
4. Arithmetic (untimed)	12.8	133	99

WISC-IV

Index Scale	Score
1. Verbal Comprehension:	131.7
2. Perceptual Reasoning:	126.4
3. Working Memory:	117.7
4. Processing Speed:	104.3
5. Full Scale IQ:	127.2

    a. Describe Roberta's intellectual abilities.

    b. Are the results similar for the different tests?

    c. What additional information would you like to have about Roberta?

ADDITIONAL READINGS

Berg, C. A., & Sternberg, R. J. (1985). A triarchic theory of intellectual development during adulthood. *Developmental Review, 5,* 334–370.

Binet, A. E., & Simon, T. (1905). Methodes nouvelles pour le diagnostic du niveau intellectuel des anormaux. *L'annee Psychologique, 11,* 191–244.

Boring, E. G. (1923). Intelligence as the tests see it. *New Republic, 35,* 35–36.

Carroll, J. B. (1998). *Human cognitive abilities: A survey of factor analysis studies.* New York: Cambridge.

Flanagan, D. P., Genshaft, J. L., & Harrison, P. L. (1997). *Contemporary intellectual assessment: Theories, tests, and issues.* New York: Guilford Press.
Covers the origins of intellectual assessment, contemporary and emerging theories, new tests, and alternate techniques for assessing intelligence, and integration and synthesis of current theories and trends.

French, J., et al. (1974). *The Henman-Nelson test of mental ability.* Chicago: Riverside.

Gardner, H. (1983). *Frames of mind: The theory of multiple intelligences.* New York: Basic Books.

Gardner, H. (1993). *Multiple intelligences: The theory in practice.* New York: Basic Books.
The two Gardner books present a detailed description of Holland's theory.

Jensen, A. R. (1980). *Bias in mental testing.* New York: Free Press.

Jensen, A. R. (1981). *Straight talk about mental tests.* New York: Free Press.
Jensen's writings have been influential and enlightening but also quite controversial.

Kamphaus, R. W. (1993). *Clinical assessment of children's intelligence: A handbook for professional practice.* Boston: Allyn & Bacon.
Provides examples and cases to facilitate understanding and interpretation of the WISC-III, Stanford-Binet, K-ABC, and Woodcock-Johnson. Information on use of tests for infant and preschool assessment is presented.

Kaufman, A. S. (1990). *Assessing adolescent and adult intelligence.* Boston: Allyn & Bacon.
Discusses the clinical and neuropsychological assessment of the intelligence of adolescents and adults, with special attention given to the Wechsler Adult Intelligence Scale-Revised.

McGrew, K. S. (1994). *Clinical interpretation of the Woodcock-Johnson Tests of Cognitive Abilities—Revised.* Boston: Allyn & Bacon.
Presents a detailed, step-by-step analysis of the 21 WJTCA tests and includes a special strengths and weaknesses worksheet as well as diagrams and figures to help examiners understand and interpret the test.

Pintner, R. (1931). *Intelligence testing* (2nd ed.). New York: Holt.

Roid, G. (2003). *Stanford-Binet Intelligence Scale* (5th ed.). Chicago: Riverside Publishing.

Sternberg, R. J. (1985). *Beyond IQ: A triarchic theory of human intelligence.* Cambridge, MA: Cambridge University Press.
Sternberg is one of the leading writers on the role and function of intelligence.

Sternberg, R. J., & Detterman, D. K. (Eds). (1986). *What is intelligence? Contemporary viewpoints on its nature and definition.* Norwood, NJ: Ablex.

Thorndike, E. L. (1921). On the organization of intellect. *Psychological Review, 28,* 141–151.

Thurstone, L. L. (1938). Primary mental abilities. *Psychometric Monographs,* No. 1.

Wagner, R. K., & Sternberg, R. J. (1984). Alternative conceptions of intelligence and their implication for education. *Review of Educational Research, 54* (2), 179–223.

9 Aptitude Testing

OVERVIEW

Aptitude testing has been used in education and psychology since the 1920s. Aptitude was considered by some early theorists to be innate but now is viewed as the result of learning experiences. The current operational definition of the construct addresses an individual's ability to learn certain skills or tasks if given the opportunity. Aptitude tests measure an individual's capacity, or potential, for performing a given skill or task and are used to predict behavior—will the individual be successful in a given educational program, vocational program, or occupational situation?

OBJECTIVES

After studying this chapter, you should be able to identify and discuss the

✔ Uses of major multiaptitude test batteries

✔ Uses of special abilities tests

✔ Uses of work-sample aptitude tests

✔ Problems and issues related to aptitude testing

✔ Uses of scholastic aptitude tests

APTITUDE TESTS

Aptitude tests measure a person's performance on selected tasks to predict how that person will perform sometime in the future or in a different situation (Thorndike, 2004). The aptitude could involve school performance, job performance, or some other task or situation. There is no widely accepted definition of "aptitude" and "ability," and the terms are often used interchangeably.

Aptitude tests include tests of general ability and tests of special abilities (e.g., verbal, clerical, mechanical). Aptitude tests are often used as part of selecting individuals for occupational training or job placement. Aptitude tests help counselors advise individuals about appropriate academic programs and training or suitable occupations. The aptitude test results can be compared with the requirements of many areas of work so that a realistic vocational plan can be developed.

The content of aptitude, intelligence, and achievement tests overlaps. For example, vocabulary items are part of all three types, as are numerical computations and reasoning items. One of the primary differences among these tests is how the tests are used. Scholastic aptitude, general aptitude, intelligence, and special abilities tests are often used for predictive purposes, whereas achievement tests measure what has been learned and are most often used for descriptive purposes and assessment of growth and change.

MULTIAPTITUDE BATTERIES

Multiaptitude batteries are tests that measure a number of relatively broad ability areas, such as verbal reasoning, numerical reasoning, mechanical reasoning, and abstract reasoning. The most widely used and highly rated multiaptitude batteries are the Armed Services Vocational Aptitude Battery (ASVAB), Differential Aptitude Test (DAT), and the General Aptitude Test Battery (GATB).

Such tests are used primarily for educational and vocational counseling. They permit intraindividual comparisons, showing the highs and lows of an individual's performance on the various subtests. Studies are made of the construct and criterion-referenced validity of these tests. The potential test user wants a battery with subtests that are relatively independent of one another (i.e., measuring different abilities and having low intercorrelations) and have a high correlation of success in various educational and vocational programs. Unfortunately, the factors on most aptitude batteries have moderate to high intercorrelations.

Armed Services Vocational Aptitude Battery

The Armed Services Vocational Aptitude Battery (ASVAB) was first developed in 1966 and has gone through a number of revisions since then: Forms 18 and 19 are the current versions. Multiaptitude batteries are a fundamental component of a comprehensive counseling program. Results from these batteries help students assess their aptitudes, predict performance in academic and occupational areas, select career exploration activities, and make tentative career choices. The ASVAB measures aptitudes for general academic areas and career areas that encompass most civilian and military

Table 9.1
Subtests of the Armed Services Vocational Aptitude Battery.

Scale	Time (min)	Items	Description
General Science	11	25	Measures knowledge of the physical and biological sciences
Arithmetic Reasoning	36	30	Measures ability to solve arithmetic word problems
Word Knowledge	11	35	Measures ability to select correct meaning of words through synonyms
Paragraph Comprehension	13	15	Measures ability to obtain information from written material
Mathematics Knowledge	24	25	Measures knowledge of mechanical concepts and applications
Electronics Information	9	20	Measures knowledge of electricity and electronics
Auto and Shop	11	25	Measures knowledge of automobiles, tools, and shop terminology and practices
Mechanical Comprehension	19	25	Measures knowledge principles of mechanical devices, structural support, and properties of materials.

Source: From the ASVAB Career Exploration Program Counselor Manual, 2002. Washington DC: U.S. Department of Defense.

work. The test is used with individuals in grade 11 and higher. The authors claim the test is valuable for military and nonmilitary purposes because it can be used for academic and career counseling. The ASVAB consists of eight subtests, which are described in Table 9.1. Three special career exploration scores—Verbal Skills, Math Skills, and Science and Technical Skills—are derived from these subtests, which test takers use to explore the world-of-work. The Verbal Skills score combines the word knowledge and paragraph comprehension subtests; the Math Skills score combines the arithmetic reasoning and mathematics knowledge subtests; Science and Technical Skills combines general science, mechanical comprehension, and electronics information. The test takes 3 hours to complete—144 minutes of testing and 36 minutes of administrative time.

The test was normed on a national representative sample of 12,000 men and women aged 16 to 23. Alternate forms reliability is greater than .84 for the three career exploration scores. Internal consistency reliabilities for each ASVAB test are also high, exceeding .71. There are guides for both the counselor and test takers, and a computerized profile is given to the test takers. Figure 9.1 shows an example of a profile. The validity of the ASVAB as an aptitude or achievement test is substantial and has been correlated with other widely used achievement and aptitude tests. The ASVAB mathematics and verbal subtests correlate at least .68 with the corresponding math and verbal

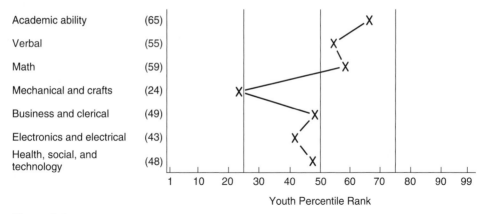

Figure 9.1
Individual profile of performance on the Armed Services Vocational Aptitude Battery.

tests of the California Achievement Test. Large correlations have also been reported between corresponding tests on the ASVAB and the Differential Aptitude Test (DAT).

All test takers receive the ASVAB summary results, an individualized report that shows scores of the eight ASVAB tests and the three Career Exploration scores. Standard scores are converted to percentile scores. To indicate how well the test taker did in relation to others, the report also provides percentile scores of others of the same gender, opposite gender, and grade level. Narrative information is included that helps test takers understand the results. Once test takers receive the results of their exploration scores, they can look up potential occupations in the OCCU-FIND, a manual that lists over 400 occupations. The OCCU-FIND organizes occupations by interest codes (based on Holland's RIASEC model), the ASVAB Career Exploration scores, and the Military Career score (also found on the ASVAB summary results report).

Differential Aptitude Test Battery, Fifth Edition

The Differential Aptitude Test, Fifth Edition (DAT) is a battery of eight subtests used for vocational and educational guidance purposes with students in grades 7 through 9 (level 1) and grades 10 through 12 and adults (level 2). The test was originally developed in 1947 by Bennett, Seashore, and Wesman and published by the Psychological Corporation. The current revision is the fifth edition (1990). The test takes about 2½ hours. The eight subtests are verbal reasoning, numerical reasoning, abstract reasoning, perceptual speed and accuracy, mechanical reasoning, space relations, spelling, and language usage. The verbal reasoning and numerical ability scores are combined to make a composite index of scholastic aptitude.

The authors claim the results help students plan their futures soundly. The test is also viewed as a tool for the early identification of students with superior intellectual promise. Available with the DAT is a Career Interest Inventory and a computerized report form that provides a combined assessment of interests and aptitudes that may then be linked to potential occupations (Kapes & Whitfield, 2001).

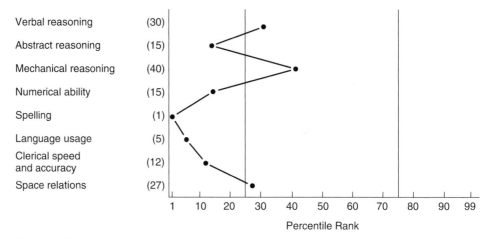

Figure 9.2
Individual profile of performance on the Differential Aptitude Test battery.

The DAT is useful in exploring a student's academic and vocational possibilities. Test limitations relate to the lack of independence of some of the scales and the separate gender norms. Both computerized-scoring services and hand-scoring stencils are available for the test. A computer-adaptive edition of the DAT is available. The form is parallel to the printed test but results in reduced testing time, and immediate scoring reports are available on the completion of the tests. Figure 9.2 presents an example of a profile from the DAT.

General Aptitude Test Battery

The United States Employment Service (USES) General Aptitude Test Battery (GATB) is one of the most widely used batteries for assessment in vocational counseling. It is used primarily by the employment services but administered in some secondary schools and in employment projects. The test takes 150 minutes, but only 48 minutes of actual testing time. The GATB is a pencil-and-paper test that measures nine dimensions: verbal, numerical, spatial, form perception, clerical perception, motor coordination, finger dexterity, manual dexterity, and general learning ability. Support systems for the counselor include the Guide for Occupational Exploration, Dictionary of Occupational Titles, and the Bridge of the World of Work. Keesling and Healy (1988) conclude that the GATB, despite its psychometric limitations, may help clients to make reasonable estimates of their standings on the aptitudes relative to working adults.

Career Ability Placement Survey

The Career Ability Placement Survey (CAPS) is a quick, 50-minute battery used to assess abilities for a majority of jobs in 14 occupational clusters. The CAPS contains eight tests:

1. Mechanical reasoning (MR) measures understanding of mechanical principals.
2. Spatial relations (SR) measure the ability to think and visualize in three dimensions.
3. Verbal reasoning (VR) measures the ability to reason with words.
4. Numerical ability (NA) measures the ability to reason with and use numbers.
5. Language usage (LU) measures recognition and use of proper grammar and punctuation.
6. Word knowledge (WK) measures understanding of the meaning and precise use of words.
7. Perceptual speed and accuracy (PSA) measures rapid and accurate perception of small details.
8. Manual speed and dexterity (MSD) measures rapid and accurate hand movement.

There are both self-scoring and machine-scoring forms of the test, and Integrated Reporting and Interpretation System (IRIS) provides computerized scoring and reporting for CAPS.

The test authors, L. F. Kapp and R. R. Kapp, say that the test has five major uses:

1. Classroom career exploration units, matching individual students' ability with occupational requirements
2. School course or training program selection
3. Curriculum evaluation
4. Career development in conjunction with the COPSystem Interest Inventory and COPES, a value profile
5. Employee evaluation

All types of supportive materials are available for the counselor and client: a self-interpretation profile sheet and guide, occupational cluster charts, COPSystem Career Briefs Kit, and COPSystem Career Cluster Booklet Kits, in addition to an examiner's manual, tapes for administration, and visuals for orientation. Table 9.2 shows a comparison of the ASVAB, the DAT, the GATB, and the CAPS.

Table 9.2
Comparison of subtests on multiaptitude scales.

ASVAB	DAT	GATB	CAPS
Arithmetic reasoning	Abstract reasoning	Clerical perception	Manual speed and dexterity
Auto and shop	Perceptual speed and accuracy	Finger dexterity	Language usage
Coding speed		Form perception	
General science	Mechanical reasoning	General learning ability	Mechanical reasoning
Electronics information	Numerical reasoning	Manual dexterity	Perceptual speed and accuracy
Mathematics knowledge	Language usage	Motor coordination	
Numerical operations	Space relations	Numerical	Spatial relations
Paragraph comprehension	Verbal reasoning	Spatial	Verbal reasoning
Word knowledge		Verbal	Word knowledge
			Numerical ability

ADMISSIONS TESTS

American College Testing Program (ACT).   The ACT is a comprehensive system for collecting and reporting information about students planning to enter postsecondary education. It consists of four major components: the Tests of Educational Development, the Course/Grade Information Section, the Student Profile Section, and the ACT Interest Inventory. A description of each test follows.

- The Tests of Educational Development are designed to assess students' general educational development and their ability to complete college-level work. The multiple-choice tests cover four skill areas: English, mathematics, reading, and science. The optional Writing Test is a 30-minute essay test that measures students' writing skills in English. The tests emphasize reasoning, analysis, problem solving, and the integration of learning from various sources, as well as the application of these proficiencies to the kinds of tasks college students are expected to perform.
- The Course/Grade Information Section provides 30 self-reported high school grades in the areas of English, mathematics, natural sciences, social studies, language, and the arts. The courses include those that customarily form the core of a college preparatory curriculum and are frequently required for admission to college.
- The Student Profile Section contains nearly 200 pieces of information reported by students when they register for the ACT. This information includes the following categories: admissions/enrollment information; educational plans, interests, and needs; special educational needs, interests, and goals; college extracurricular plans; financial aid; demographic background information; factors influencing college choice; characteristics of high school; high school extracurricular activities; and out-of-class accomplishments.
- The ACT Interest Inventory is a 90-item survey, called the UNIACT, that reports six scores that parallel John Holland's six interest and occupational types. The main purpose of the interest inventory is to help students identify majors congruent with their interests.

The SAT.   Nearly every college in America accepts the SAT or Subject Tests as a part of its admissions process. That's why more than two million students take the SAT every year. The College Board's SAT Program consists of the SAT Reasoning Test and SAT Subject Tests. The SAT is 3 hours and 45 minutes, including an unscored 25-minute variable section (which helps in the development of future test questions). The SAT is typically taken by high school juniors and seniors. Although most questions are multiple-choice, students are also required to write a 25-minute essay. Each section of the SAT is scored on a scale of 200–800.

The SAT Reasoning Test is a measure of the critical thinking skills needed for academic success in college. The SAT has three sections: Math, Critical Reading (previously known as the Verbal section), and Writing (new section).

- Math: The math section has a testing time of 70 minutes and includes two 25-minute sections and one 20-minute section. It measures Number and Operations, Algebra I and II, Functions Geometry, Statistics, Probability, and Data Analysis.

- Critical Reading: The critical reading section takes 70 minutes with two 25-minute sections and one 20-minute section. It's content includes Extended Reasoning, Literal Comprehension, and Vocabulary in Context.
- Writing: The writing section takes 60 minutes to complete with a 35-minute multiple choice section and 25-minute essay. The content of the Multiple-Choice section includes Identifying Errors and Improving Sentences and Paragraphs. The Student-Written Essay measures Effectively Communicate a Viewpoint and Defining and Supporting a Position.

The SAT Subject Tests are one-hour, mostly multiple-choice tests in specific subjects. These tests measure knowledge of particular subjects and the ability to apply that knowledge. Many colleges require or recommend one or more of these tests for admission or placement purposes. The 20 Subject Tests fall into five general subject areas: English, history and social studies, mathematics, science and languages.

Preliminary SAT/National Merit Scholarship Qualifying Test (PSAT/NMSQT). The PSAT/NMSQT is a standardized test that provides high school students firsthand practice for the SAT Reasoning Test. It also gives students a chance to enter National Merit Scholarship Corporation (NMSC) scholarship programs. The PSAT/NMSQT measures critical reading skills, math problem-solving skills, and writing skills. It provides students with feedback on their strengths and weaknesses on skills necessary for college study, helps students prepare for the SAT, and enables students to enter the competition for scholarships from the National Merit Scholarship Corporation.

Graduate Records Examinations (GRE). The GRE is taken by individuals applying to graduate schools. Graduate program admissions are usually based on the GRE score, college GPA, and other requirements specific to that graduate program. There are two tests: the General test and Subject tests.

The GRE General Test measures skills that are acquired over a long period of time and are not related to any specific field of study. The test consists of four sections: the Quantitative Section, the Verbal Section, the Analytical Writing Assessment, and the Unscored Section. The total time for the test is approximately 3 hours.

- The *Quantitative Section* consists of 28 questions and measures the test takers ability to understand basic concepts of arithmetic, algebra, geometry, and data analysis; reason quantitatively; and solve problems in a quantitative setting.
- The *Verbal Section* consists of 30 questions and measures the ability to analyze and evaluate written material and synthesize information obtained from it; analyze relationships among component parts of sentences; and recognize relationships between words and concepts.
- The *Analytical Writing Assessment* was developed to provide graduate schools with an assessment of critical thinking and analytical writing skills. It consists of two analytical writing tasks: a 45 minute "Perspective on an Issue" task, and a 30 minute "Analysis of an Argument" task. The test measures the ability articulate complex ideas clearly and effectively; examine claims and

accompanying evidence; support ideas with relevant reasons and examples; sustain a well-focused, coherent discussion; and control the elements of standard written English.

- The *Unscored Section* is used by the test maker to try out questions for future use.

The GRE Subject Tests gauge undergraduate achievement in specific fields of study. The tests assess knowledge of subject matter emphasized in many undergraduate programs as preparation for graduate study. Each Subject Test is intended for students who have majored in or have extensive background in that specific area, including biochemistry, cell and molecular biology; biology; chemistry; computer science; literature in English; mathematics; physics; and psychology.

The GRE has paper-and-pencil and computer versions. The computer version is a Computer Adaptive Test; that is, it is tailored to the test taker's performance level. The test begins with questions of middle difficulty. As you answer each question, the computer scores that question and uses that information to determine which question is presented next. As long as you respond correctly to each question, questions of increased difficulty typically will be presented. When you respond incorrectly, the computer typically will present you with questions of lesser difficulty. This means that different test takers will be given different questions.

The reliability of the GRE test has been computed using the Kuder-Richardson 20 formula. This coefficient provides an estimate of the internal consistency of the test and alternate form reliability. The test bulletin reports that the reliabilities on the General Tests and Subject Tests range from .88 to .96. The content validity of the subject examination is extremely critical and is evaluated by a committee of professors working with Educational Testing Service (ETS) test development specialists. The main type of validity for the test is its predictive validity—to predict success in graduate school.

Miller's Analogies Test (MAT).   The MAT is another test taken by individuals applying to graduate schools. The MAT is an objective, group-administered test of mental ability, consisting of 100 multiple-choice analogy items. The content for the analogies comes from literature, social sciences, chemistry, physics, mathematics, and general information. The test is given only at controlled testing centers and requires 50 minutes of testing time.

In each MAT analogy item, one term is missing and has been replaced with four answer options, only one of which correctly completes the analogy. The terms in most of the MAT analogy items are words, but in some cases they may be numbers, symbols, or word parts. For example:

PLANE : AIR :: CAR : (a. submarine, b. fish, c. land, d. pilot)

The first step in solving a MAT analogy is to decide which two of the three given terms form a complete pair. In the example, this could either be "PLANE is related to AIR" (the first term is related to the second term) or "PLANE is related to CAR" (the first term is related to the third term). On the MAT, it will never be "PLANE is related to (a. submarine, b. fish, c. water, d. pilot)"; the first term is never related to the fourth term.

Other Admissions Tests.   Other widely used admission tests in higher education include the Medical College Admissions Test (MCAT), Law School Admissions Test

(LSAT), and the Graduate Management Admissions Test (GMAT). The most important consideration in the use of these tests is whether the validity of the test for a particular program has been established, especially through studies at a local college or university.

SPECIALIZED APTITUDE TESTS

Specialized aptitude tests assess an individual's capacity to perform specific skills. These tests help individuals determine their strengths and weaknesses in a particular subject or job-related area. Common aptitude test categories include, among many others, clerical ability, mechanical ability, psychomotor ability, artistic ability, musical ability, and computer ability.

Clerical Ability

Clerical ability refers to the abilities required in satisfactorily carrying out office duties. Although the number and types of abilities measured may vary from test to test, a clerical test usually assesses such abilities as filing, coding, verbal, arithmetic, and checking. Ability to follow directions and short- and long-term memory are also included on some of the tests.

- The General Clerical Test (GCT) was developed to assess clerical speed and accuracy, numerical skills, and language related skills. The GCT takes approximately one hour and includes three subtests: clerical, numerical, and verbal.
- The Hay Aptitude Test Battery is a general battery that measures number perception, name finding, and number series completion and predicts aptitude for a variety of positions. It is designed for selecting tellers, data entry personnel, order pickers and customer service representatives.
- Minnesota Clerical Test, Revised (MCT-R) consists of two parts: number comparison and name comparison. There are 200 pairs of numbers and 200 pairs of names. The test taker is to check each pair in which the items are identical. The test is speeded, and the examinee has 8 minutes for the number section and 7 minutes for the name section.
- The Office Skills Test assesses an individual's ability to perform essential clerical tasks quickly and accurately. The skills assessed are filing, performing arithmetic calculations, checking, vocabulary, and understanding and following directions.
- The PSI Basic Skills Tests consist of 15 individual tests that measure fundamental skills such as reasoning, numerical ability, perceptual ability, and verbal ability. The tests assess skills necessary for customer service, administrative, and clerical job tasks.

The descriptions of these tests reveal that some of the subtests are similar to those on some of the group intelligence and scholastic aptitude tests as well as some of the scales on the DAT, ASVAB, and GATB.

Mechanical Ability

Mechanical aptitude is the ability to learn about and use tools, machines and equipment. Some believe individuals have a natural ability that makes them capable of understanding how things work. Mechanical ability tests typically measure a person's ability to use various tools and materials as well as spatial reasoning (the ability to visualize a three-dimensional object from a two-dimensional pattern).

- Bennett Mechanical Comprehension Test (BMCT) measures an individual's understanding of basic mechanical operations and the application of physical laws. The test is used to screen job applicants for positions requiring complex machine operation and repair and other types of positions requiring practical application of mechanical principles. Norms are available for industrial job applicants, industrial employees, and students. The test requires 30 minutes of testing time.
- The Mechanical Aptitude Test is a 45-minute test for high school students and adults that measures comprehension of mechanical tasks, use of tools and materials, and matching tools with operations.
- The Ramsay Corporation's Mechanical Aptitude Test was developed to measure a person's mechanical aptitude in the following areas: household objects, work (production and maintenance), school (science and physics), and hand and power tools.
- The SRA Mechanical Aptitude Test is a 35-minute test for high school students and adults that measures mechanical knowledge, space relations, and shop arithmetic.
- The SRA Test of Mechanical Concepts is a 35–40-minute test for adults measuring the individual's ability to visualize and understand basic mechanical and spatial interrelationships. It contains three subtests: mechanical interrelationships, mechanical tools and devices, and spatial relations.
- The Wiesen Test of Mechanical Aptitude (WTMA) is designed for use in selecting entry-level personnel for jobs involving the operation, maintenance, and repair of mechanical equipment of various types. The WTMA measures basic ability rather than formal schooling or job experience. The test asks questions about everyday objects and situations.

Psychomotor Ability

Psychomotor ability is the ability to perform body motor movements (e.g., movement of fingers, hands, legs, body) with precision, coordination, or strength. It can include multi-limb coordination (ability to make quick specific or discrete motor movements of the arms or legs), arm-hand steadiness (ability to precisely and skillfully coordinate arm-hand positioning in space), manual dexterity (ability to make precisely coordinated movements of a hand, or a hand and the attached arm), finger dexterity (ability to make precisely coordinated movements of the fingers), visual-motor skills (eye-hand coordination) and static strength (ability to exert muscular force to move, push, lift, or pull a heavy or immobile object). Psychomotor ability tests include the following:

- The Crawford Small Parts Dexterity Test (CSPDT) is designed to measure fine, eye-hand coordination and is used in job selection for occupational areas such as instrument mechanic, engraver, etcher, precision electronics assembler or watch repairman. Part one requires use of tweezers to assemble pin and collar assemblies; part two requires putting small screws into threaded holes in a plate and screwing them down.

- The Hand-Tool Dexterity Test assesses whether an individual has the basic skills necessary for any job requiring hand tools, such as aircraft or automobile mechanics, machine adjusters, maintenance mechanics and assembly line workers. The test requires the examinee to take apart 12 assemblies of nuts, bolts, and washers from a wooden frame and then reassemble them.

- The Minnesota Manual Dexterity Test measures capacity for rapid simple eye-hand coordination needed for semiskilled shop and clerical operations such as wrapping, sorting, and packing. The test taker is given a long board containing four rows of holes. In the placing test, pegs are to be transferred to the empty board just as they were presented, using only one hand. In the turning test, the pegs are to be removed with one hand one at a time, turned over, transferred to the other hand, and replaced in the same position on the board.

- The Minnesota Rate of Manipulation Test measures finger-hand-arm dexterity and is used to select employees for jobs that require manual dexterity and in vocational and rehabilitation training programs. There are five subtests in the battery: placing, turning, displacing, one-hand turning and placing, and two-hand turning and placing. The test also uses a test board with round holes arranged in four rows and round blocks painted orange and yellow.

- The O'Connor Finger Dexterity Test measures finger dexterity and is useful in determining aptitude for assembly line jobs requiring rapid handwork. This test uses a smaller board containing a shallow well and many holes arranged in 10 rows. The test taker is given a set of 300 pins and is required to place three in each hole. The test has been useful in predicting success in machine and lathe work, watch and clock repair, and assembly of small parts.

- The O'Connor Tweezer Dexterity Test measures fine hand-eye coordination and the ability to use small hand tools. The test uses the same smaller board with the same small holes in it. However, the test taker is given 100 pins and is required to put one in each hole, using only a small tweezer. This type of skill is required of laboratory workers, medical personnel, and watch repairers.

- The Purdue Pegboard Test has been used to aid in the selection of employees for jobs that require fine and gross motor dexterity and coordination. It measures gross movements of hands, fingers and arms, and fingertip dexterity as necessary in assembly tasks. The test taker works with pegs, washers, and collars — putting in the pegs, placing washers over them, and then putting on the collars.

- The Stromberg Dexterity Test is a fast, objective means of measuring basic manual dexterity for positions such as punch press operator, machine molder, assembler, or welder. Applicants must discriminate among and sort 54 biscuit shaped discs and insert them into a form board as quickly as possible.

- Valpar's Component Work Samples are a series of tests that involve generalized work-like tasks that are administered under specific instructions. Valpar produces over 20 tests that measure such psychomotor ability as finger dexterity, upper extremity range of motion, whole body range of motion, multi-limb co-ordination, spatial reasoning and a variety of other skills needed for assembly, machine operating, shipping and receiving, sorting, and other mechanical/manual tasks.

Artistic Aptitude

Three classic tests measure dimensions of art aptitude:

- The Graves Design Judgment Test presents 90 sets of two- or three-dimensional designs that vary in unity, balance, symmetry, or other aspects of aesthetic order. The test taker is asked to select the best in each set.
- The Meier Art Test: Aesthetic Perception presents four versions of the same work, each differing in terms of proportion, unity, form, or design. The test taker is asked to rank each set in order of merit.
- The Meier Art Test: Art Judgment consists of 100 pairs of pictures of famous works of art. One of the pair has been altered, and the test taker is asked to choose the better of the two pictures.

Musical Aptitude

A number of tests have been developed to measure musical aptitude. The classic test in this field is Seashore Measures of Musical Talents. The test takes about 1 hour of testing time and can be administered to students in grade 4 and above and adults. The test presents on tape six subtests measuring dimensions of auditory discrimination: pitch, loudness, time, timbre, rhythm, and tonal memory. Unfortunately, the test lacks sufficient documentation of validity and reliability.

Other tests also purport to measure musical aptitude:

- The Kwalwasser Music Talent Test is a 50-item orally administered pencil-and-paper test to assess musical aptitude of fourth graders to college students. It presents three-tone patterns that are repeated with variations in pitch, tone, rhythm, or loudness.
- The Musical Aptitude Profile (MAP) is a comprehensive test of music aptitude with seven components: tonal imagery (melody and harmony), rhythm imagery (tempo and meter), and musical sensitivity (phrasing, balance, and style). The test takes about 3.5 hours to administer. Revised in 1995, the MAP includes re-mastered recordings and an updated manual.

Unfortunately, research has been limited on the value of these tests. Music teachers tend to rely more on their own clinical judgment and look for individual performance of music as it is written.

Computer Aptitude

Computer aptitude has become an important skill. Computer literacy is now being taught in kindergarten and technology is infused throughout the K-12 curriculum.

Computers have become inexpensive and readily available, and a number of instruments have been developed to assess aptitude in this field.

- The Aptitude Assessment Battery Programming (AABP) is used to evaluate the aptitude of individuals, at all experience levels, for their suitability for all aspects of applications programming. It can be used for individuals with or without prior programming training and evaluates abilities to draw deductions with the aid of simple calculations; understand the kind of complicated instructions that are found in programming reference manuals; understand complicated specifications, statements written succinctly, without further explanation; reason with symbols according to their specific definitions; annotate and document their work so that other programmers can follow their reasoning easily; and desk-check and debug their work.
- The Computer Aptitude Test assesses an individual's potential to learn computer programming. Each of the three sub-tests measures abstract reasoning abilities required by computer programming. It can be used to assist managers in making selection decisions for appointment or for placement into training programs, identifying training and development needs, and counseling for career transitions.
- The Computer Programmer Aptitude Battery (CPAB) can help determine an individual's aptitude for success as a computer programmer or system analyst. Five subtests help assess applicants' abilities in the following areas: verbal meaning, reasoning, letter series (ability to use abstract reasoning to find patterns in given series of letters), number ability, and diagramming (ability to analyze problems and figure solutions in a logical sequence).
- The Computer Operator Aptitude Battery (COAB) can help determine an individual's ability to perform the job of computer operator and potential for learning computer programming. The three subtests help measure the following critical aptitudes: sequence recognition, format checking, and logical thinking.

TRENDS

The last century was marked by dazzling changes in many areas of ability testing, such as technology and communications. Predictions into the second century of ability testing are difficult; however, several trends are anticipated.

Although the classic test theory is that longer tests are more reliable, it is predicted that shorter and more reliable tests will soon become commonplace in the second century of testing (Embretson, 2004). Shorter and more reliable tests depend on the use and ongoing development of *adaptive* testing.

During the first century of testing, objective test items were primarily limited to the multiple-choice format. Other formats, such as essays, completions, and worked problems, required human raters, which led to greater expense, unreliability, and delay of test scores. However, Embretson (2004) predicts a far greater use of essays, completions, and worked problems beginning in 21st century through the use of such computer programs as E-Rater. E-Rater is a computer program that scans essays. The program scores essays on a large number of linguistic variables, such as syntactic structure, vocabulary level, and word content. The results on E-Rater have been quite promising; for example, the correlation of E-Rater scores with human raters has been found greater than the correlation of the raters with each other. In fact, E-Rater is now one of the two raters (the other rater is human) used operationally in scoring the essays on the Graduate Management Admissions Test (GMAT).

Embretson (2004) predicts that test development procedures will evolve more quickly in the technologically sophisticated society of the second century of testing. She forecasts that continuous test revision, automated validity studies, and item development by artificial intelligence, will be major developments early in the second century of testing. In fact, the research foundations and technology required for these developments are currently in progress.

SUMMARY

Multifactor aptitude batteries are used in educational and business contexts. Many aptitude batteries are a part of career guidance systems. The most widely used batteries are the Armed Services Vocational Aptitude Battery (ASVAB), the General Aptitude Test Battery (GATB), and the Differential Aptitude Test (DAT) battery.

Specialized aptitude tests are designed to measure the ability to acquire proficiency in a specific area of activity, such as art or music. Mechanical and clerical aptitude tests have been used by vocational education and business and industry personnel to counsel, evaluate, classify, and place test takers. Both multifactor and special aptitude tests are designed to help the test takers gain a better understanding of their own special abilities.

QUESTIONS FOR DISCUSSION

1. What are the major multifactor aptitude batteries? When should they be used and why? What are the advantages and disadvantages of this type of test?

2. When would you use special aptitude batteries and why? What are the advantages and disadvantages of such tests?

3. Critics have said that multiaptitude tests provide little differential predictions and are of little value. Do you agree with their evaluation? If you have taken aptitude tests, what value did the results have for you? Did the scores provide a useful framework for looking at your aptitudes and abilities?

4. Some school districts require that all students be given an aptitude battery at some time during their 4 years of high school. Do you agree or disagree with this requirement? Why?

5. Do you feel that there can be pencil-and-paper aptitude tests to measure aptitudes in art, music, and mechanics? Why or why not?

SUGGESTED ACTIVITIES

1. Write a critique of a widely used multiaptitude or special aptitude test.

2. Interview workers in the helping professions who use aptitude tests—employment counselors, career counselors, and school counselors—and find out what tests they use and why. Report your findings to the class.

3. Take a multifactor or specialized aptitude test and write a report detailing the results and your reaction to the test.

4. Make an annotated bibliography of aptitude tests you would use in your field.

5. Write a critical review of the literature on one of the following topics: validity of aptitude tests, new directions in aptitude testing, computer-adaptive aptitude testing, and performance aptitude tests.

6. Study the case that follows and answer the questions at the end.

Case of Albert

Albert is a 23-year-old White male who dropped out of school in the 10th grade. He is enrolled in a high school equivalency program at a local community college sponsored by the Private Industry Council. He has had numerous jobs in the food services industry but has not been able to hold on to them. He has a wife and three children and now realizes he needs further training and education to support his family.

The Private Industry Council arranged for some vocational testing. He was administered the DAT with the following results:

Verbal reasoning 40%

Numerical reasoning 55%

Abstract reasoning 20%

Mechanical reasoning 55%

Space relations 30%

Spelling 3%

Language usage 5%

Perceptual speed and accuracy 45%

a. How would you characterize Albert's aptitudes?
b. What additional information about Albert would you like to have?
c. If you were a counselor, what educational and vocational directions would you encourage him to explore?

ADDITIONAL READINGS

Chase, C. (1999). *Contemporary assessment for educators.* New York: Addison-Wesley. Includes broad coverage of educational, aptitude, multiaptitude, special aptitude, and other tests.

Hunter, J. E. (1983). *Test validation for 12,000 jobs: An application of job classification and validity generalization analysis to the General Aptitude Battery* (USES Test Research Report No. 45). Washington, DC: U.S. Department of Labor, Employment and Training Administration, Division of Counseling and Test Development.

Kapes, J. T., & Whitfield, E. A. (2001). *A counselor's guide to vocational guidance instruments* (4th ed.). Falls Church, VA: National Vocational Guidance Association.
Reviews multiaptitude batteries as well as other aptitude batteries used with special populations.

Loch, C., Kass, C., & Kass, J. (2001). *PESCO.* Pleasantville, NY: Authors. Available online at *www.pesco.org.*

Lowman, R. L. (1991). *The clinical practice of career assessment: Interest, abilities, and personality.* Washington, DC: American Psychological Association.
Provides guidelines and examples in the use of tests of the affect domain in career counseling.

Walsh, W., & Betz, N. (2000). *Tests and assessments* (4th ed.). Upper Saddle River, NJ: Prentice Hall.

10 The Assessment of Achievement

Achievement testing is the primary type of testing used in educational programs at all levels. Achievement tests measure acquired knowledge and skills, whereas aptitude tests measure potential, or the ability to learn new tasks. The main distinctions between achievement and aptitude testing relate to the type of learning being measured and the intended use of the test results. Achievement tests come in a variety of types: survey achievement batteries, single-subject-area tests, criterion-referenced tests, minimum-level skills tests, individual tests, and diagnostic tests.

Observation is another primary data-gathering tool of workers in the helping professions. The main purpose of observation is to collect information that will be useful in de-scribing, interpreting, and explaining client behavior. Sometimes an individual is observed in a natural situation such as on the job, in the classroom, or at home. At other times the individual can be observed in a contrived or simulated situation. Observation of test behavior is sometimes as important as the actual answers given by the individual.

There has been a growing dissatisfaction with traditional testing procedures and a movement toward alternative and authentic assessment techniques. These procedures have primarily been used in assessing achievement, but are currently being used in other areas. The second part of the chapter focuses on these three different assessment approaches.

OBJECTIVES

After studying this chapter, you should be able to

✔ List and discuss the different types of achievement tests

✔ Identify situations in which each type of test would be used

✔ Explain the problems and issues in achievement testing

✔ Interpret the results of an achievement test

✔ Identify the different methods of observation and the procedures and techniques used

✔ Identify the methods, procedures, and techniques of alternate and authentic assessment

✔ Identify the use of rating scales, interview schedules, and checklists

✔ Identify the use of observation in analyzing test behavior

✔ Identify the problems that arise in the use of interview schedules and rating scales

TYPES OF ACHIEVEMENT TESTS

Achievement tests are found in many forms. The following section describes the basic types of achievement tests and the function of each.

Survey Achievement Batteries

The survey battery, the most widely used achievement test, is part of most school testing programs. It usually has a number of subtests—such as reading, mathematics, social studies, and science—and measures the objectives that are typically addressed in grades K-12. A number of different levels or separate tests are in the achievement battery, which is most often given at the beginning or end of the school year. The test provides teachers and administrators with a picture of what the student has learned or achieved.

The survey achievement battery subtests are all coordinated with standardized administration and scoring procedures, have a common format, and have little content overlap. In addition, all of the subtests are normed on the same sampling group. Comparisons between the tests are thus more valid than when each subtest is normed on a different sample. Some widely used achievement batteries are described here.

- The Basic Achievement Skills Inventory (BASI) consists of four different levels spanning grades 3–12. The BASI assessment provides grade equivalency and standard scores for six areas of academic achievement: vocabulary, reading comprehension, spelling, language mechanics, math computation, and math application.
- The California Achievement Test, sixth edition, (CAT/6) is administered to students in grades K through 12. The CAT measures achievement in traditional school areas—reading, language, mathematics, reference skills, and spelling.
- The Comprehensive Test of Basic Skills, Fifth Edition (CTBS/5) is a multilevel achievement battery consisting of 10 levels and measuring three to seven areas, such as reading, language, mathematics, science, social studies, spelling, and reference skills. The CTBS was standardized along with the Short Form Test of Academic Aptitude (California Test of Mental Maturity). The test has forms for students in grades K through 12.
- The Iowa Tests of Basic Skills (ITBS) assesses the skills of students in grades K through 8. It has a separate test for primary grades and test for grades 3 to 8. Some of the test areas include vocabulary, word analysis, reading comprehension, listening, language, mathematics, social studies, science, sources of information, spelling,

capitalization, punctuation, usage and expression, maps and diagrams, reference materials, word analysis, and listening.

- The Metropolitan Achievement Test, Eighth Edition (MAT-8) is designed to provide assessment of K–12 students' achievement in reading, mathematics, language arts, science, and social studies at appropriate levels.
- The National Achievement Test (NAT) is a standardized achievement test designed to be used with K–12 school children. It is recommended for use with two other tests, the Developing Cognitive Abilities Test and the School Attitude Measure, in order to assemble student profiles of how ability, attitude, and achievement are interacting, although it can be used alone.
- The Sequential Tests of Educational Progress (STEP) assess English, reading, and mathematical skills. The preschool and primary test diagnoses the instructional needs of students and measures their interests, problem-solving and reading skills, mathematics concepts, and psychomotor skills. The upper-grade test measures achievement levels in English expression, reading, mechanics of writing, mathematics computation, mathematics basic concepts, science, and social studies.
- The Stanford Achievement Test, Tenth Edition (SAT10) is designed for K–12 students. Every item on SAT10 is classified into one of the two following major cognitive categories: (1) Basic Understanding, the ability to recall or recognize factual information; and (2) Thinking Skills, the ability to analyze and synthesize information; to classify and sequence information; to compare and contrast information; to evaluate information in order to determine cause and effect, fact and opinion, and relevance and irrelevance; and to interpolate and/or extrapolate in order to draw conclusions, make predictions, and hypothesize. The SAT10 results can be compared to results from the Otis-Lennon School Ability Test, Eighth Edition, to see if students are achieving at or above their tested ability level.

Criterion-Referenced Tests

Criterion-referenced tests, sometimes called domain-referenced tests, measure specific objectives and skills. They differ from norm-referenced tests and survey achievement tests in that they focus on mastery of a given objective or skill. Norm-referenced tests usually include only one or two items to measure a given objective, whereas criterion-referenced tests include many items on a specific objective. The criterion-referenced test is scored to an absolute standard, usually the percentage of correct answers. The teacher may be required to assign grades to the test takers, or students may be required to meet a certain score, say 70%, as evidence of mastery. In systems requiring mastery of objectives, the test taker is not allowed to go on to the next unit until passing the one being studied.

Criterion-referenced tests can be used for other purposes also:

1. To evaluate the curriculum
2. To identify topics that should be remediated or enriched
3. To provide information for the counselor to use in educational and vocational planning with students
4. To help students select courses
5. To document student mastery of objectives

6. To provide systematic evidence of student attainment of objectives across levels and fields over time
7. To help the counselor mark the progress of the child over time

Here are a few examples of criterion-referenced tests and testing systems:

- College Basic Academic Subjects Examination (College BASE) is a criterion-referenced achievement test focusing on the degree to which college students have mastered particular skills and competencies consistent with the completion of general education coursework. It assesses achievement in four subject areas: English, mathematics, science, and social studies. As of 2001, the exam was used by approximately 150 institutions nationwide. The users included both community colleges and four-year institutions whose Carnegie designations range from baccalaureate college to research university.
- Criterion Test of Basic Skills, 2002 edition (CTOBS-2) is a criterion-referenced assessment of reading and arithmetic skills. The Reading subtest assesses basic word attack skills in the following areas: letter recognition, letter sounds, blending, sequencing, decoding of common spelling patterns and multi-syllable words, and sight word recognition. The Arithmetic subtest assesses skills in these areas: counting, number concepts and numerical recognition, addition, subtraction, multiplication, and division, measurement concepts, fractions, decimals, and percents, geometric concepts, pre-algebra, and rounding and estimation. It is for students from grades 6 through 11.
- The Instructional Objectives Exchange has a series of tests available for teachers to use to assess specific skills and objectives in reading, mathematics, and writing.
- Multiscore is a criterion-referenced testing instrument used to evaluate and report performance in terms of reading and language arts objectives for students from grades 1–8.

Item Banks

Commercial and public domain test item banks are available for educational purposes. Item banks allow school districts to custom-design achievement tests for specific objectives. Aiken (2000) points out that these item banks have several disadvantages, such as the problem of deciding on an acceptable passing score or mastery level for each test, the limited reliability of the many subtests used to measure given instructional goals or objectives, and the questionable validity of the items as representative of the objective being measured.

Westinghouse Learning Corporation, Science Research Associates, and Houghton Mifflin, among other publishers, provide item banks. Publishers who market survey achievement batteries have a large pool of items from old editions not included in current editions. Many states and consortiums have also developed item banks that come from tests developed under federal or state grants; these should be screened for local applicability.

Minimum-Level Skills Tests

Many districts establish minimum-level skills tests in each subject area that require mastery for a student to pass to the next grade level. Absolute standards are often set, for example, at a score above 75%. These essential-skills tests are criterion-referenced and are designed to measure the reading and mathematics skills of students from kindergarten to college. Although commercial tests are available, theses tests are often locally constructed. For example, the College-Level Academic Skills Test (CLAST) is an achievement test that measures students' attainment of the college-level communication and mathematics skills that were identified by the faculties of Florida community colleges and state universities. The CLAST consists of four subtests: essay, English language skills, reading, and mathematics. Since August 1, 1984, students in public postsecondary institutions in Florida have been required to pass the CLAST in order to receive an associate of arts degree and for admission to upper-division status in a state university in Florida.

State Assessment Tests

A number of states require school districts to administer assessment tests in selected grades. Sometimes these tests focus only on essential skills. Other times they survey student knowledge, skills, and understanding in a given subject area such as science, social studies, reading, mathematics, health and nutrition, career education, citizenship, music, and fine arts. The purpose is to help school districts identify problem areas and evaluate their curriculum. For example, the Florida Comprehensive Assessment Test (FCAT), is administered to all students in Florida public schools. Every year all students in grades 3 through 10 take the FCAT reading and math tests. Students in grades 4, 8, and 10 also take the FCAT writing test. And students in grades 5, 8, and 10 take the FCAT science test as well. The tests are based on the Sunshine State Standards and contain items that are challenging for students at all levels of academic achievement. For example, the mathematics test for grade 10 contains some Sunshine State Standards that are currently taught in Geometry and Algebra II classes.

Exams contain computational items, multiple-choice items, essay-type items, and short-response and extended-response performance tasks. For example, a short-response task may require a student to explain the main idea of a reading passage in three or four sentences, or write an equation that will solve a mathematical problem. The mathematics test contains gridded response items. These items require students to write and grid numerical solutions on the answer grid. Here is a typical goal statement based on the FCAT reading test:

Goal: Students will be able to construct meaning from informational text

Content: Nonfictional articles, textbooks, reference materials, and primary sources

Objectives:

- To recognize or explain the main idea, the author's point of view, and cause-and-effect relationships

- To differentiate between fact and opinion

- To compare similarities and differences within and across text
- To demonstrate knowledge of vocabulary
- To retell or summarize the meaning of a passage
- To select and use information from a passage to perform a task

A central testing concern is accountability. President Bush developed his plan for testing in the No Child Left Behind Act of 2001, which allows individual states to develop their own tests. However, NAEP standards will be used in future years as a check on the present system.

National Assessment of Educational Progress

The National Assessment of Educational Progress (NAEP), also known as "the Nation's Report Card," is the only nationally representative and continuing assessment of what America's students know and can do in various subject areas. Since 1969, assessments have been conducted periodically in reading, mathematics, science, writing, U.S. history, civics, geography, and the arts.

NAEP reports information for the nation and specific geographic regions of the country. It includes students drawn from both public and nonpublic schools and reports results for student achievement at grades 4, 8, and 12. It does not provide scores for individual students or schools; instead, it offers results regarding subject-matter achievement; instructional experiences, and school environment for populations of students (e.g., fourth-graders) and groups within those populations (e.g., female students, Hispanic students). NAEP results are based on a sample of student populations of interest.

NAEP long-term trend (LTT) assessments are designed to give information on the changes in academic performance of America's youth. They are administered nationally every four years (but are not reported at state or district level) and report student performance at ages 9, 13, and 17 in mathematics and reading. In 2004, NAEP administered the latest long-term trend assessment to approximately 75,000 students at ages 9, 13, and 17 in public and nonpublic schools throughout the nation. It found that the average reading scores of students at ages 9 and 13 were higher in 2004 than in 1971, and the average mathematics scores of students at ages 9 and 13 were higher in 2004 than in 1973.

Subject-Area Tests

Subject-area tests differ from subtests on a survey achievement battery. The survey subtests cover the general curriculum areas of an educational program—reading, mathematics, science, spelling, language, and social studies. These fundamental concepts and skills become competencies upon which more advanced study is based. Survey achievement batteries may provide some measure of students' basic skills but little information on achievement in a given subject. Subject-area achievement tests provide more reliable and valid information.

Subject-area tests have somewhat the same use as achievement batteries in that student performance can be compared against national norms. A number of subject-area tests are available to high schools. Test questions are often derived from instruction across many school districts and states. Some states require students to pass subject-area examinations or minimum-level skills tests in all high school subject areas in order to graduate. Subject-area tests are also part of major national testing programs used by colleges and universities to determine advanced placement, credit, or as one of the criteria for admission. Many states and professional organizations also require licensing examinations, which are really specialized types of subject-area achievement tests.

An example of subject-area tests comes from the Graduate Record Examinations (GRE). The GRE has eight subject tests in biochemistry, biology, chemistry, computer science, literature in English, mathematics, physics, and psychology. The scores provide common measures for comparing the qualifications of applicants and aid in the evaluation of grades and recommendations. Some subject tests yield subscores that can indicate the strengths and weaknesses of individual students' preparation and may be useful for guidance and placement purposes.

Many professional societies have developed achievement tests. The American Chemical Society, for example, offers achievement tests in general organic-biological chemistry, inorganic chemistry, instrumental determination analysis, general chemistry, and so on.

Individual Achievement Tests

Workers in the helping professions often use individual achievement tests to assess a client's achievement and cognitive processes. The tests provide useful information on the attitudes and motivation of the test takers and may be a single-subject or a survey-achievement type of test:

- The Basic Achievement Skills Individual Screener (BASIS), published by the Psychological Corporation, is designed for pupils from grades 1 through 8. It includes three subtests—reading, spelling, and mathematics—and an optional writing exercise. Both criterion-referenced and norm-referenced, the test provides beginning-of-the-grade and end-of-the-grade norms as well as age and adult norms. It takes about 1 hour to administer and is designed to help examiners formulate individual educational plans for exceptional and special populations.
- The Keymath Diagnostic Arithmetic Test-Revised (KMDAT), published by the American Guidance Service, is a single-subject individual test used to diagnose children's strengths and weaknesses in mathematics. It measures the test taker's knowledge of operations—addition, subtraction, multiplication, division, mental computation, and numerical reasoning; mathematical applications—word problems, missing elements, money, measurement, and time; and also content areas such as numeration, fractions, geometry, and symbols. The examiner uses test plates and records the test taker's performance on an individual record form.
- The Peabody Individual Achievement Test-Revised/Normative Update (PIAT-R/NU), published by the American Guidance Service, can be a survey battery and is given to clients age 5 to adulthood. The PIAT-R/NU takes about 60 minutes to

administer and provides information on not only achievement in reading, mathematics, spelling, and general knowledge (science, social studies, fine arts, and sports) but also diagnostic information. The examiner uses easel kits and test plates. The PIAT-R/NU yields grade equivalents, age percentile ranks, and standard scores by age or grade.

- The Wechsler Individual Achievement Test, Second Edition (WIAT-II) was developed for use in conjunction with the Wechsler Intelligence Scale for Children-IV (WISC-IV) and was co-normed. Subtests include basic reading, mathematical reasoning, spelling, reading comprehension, listening comprehension, mathematics computation, oral expression, and written expression. The test can be given to students age 4 through 85.
- The Wide Range Achievement Test, Third Edition (WRAT-3) is usually administered individually, although the spelling and arithmetic subtests are suitable for group administration. The reading subtest calls for the test taker to recognize and name letters and pronounce printed words; the examiner is encouraged to analyze error patterns. The test is given to both children and adults between the ages of 5 and 75.
- The Woodcock–Johnson III (WJ-III) has two forms that measure achievement in reading, mathematics, written language, and knowledge the way they are typically taught in schools. The WJ-III can be given to individuals age 2 to 90.

Some examiners individually administer other survey and subject-area achievement tests, especially if a student has a disability. Individually administered tests do not rely as heavily on reading speed and accuracy. Individual oral administration of a test can be used as a validity check of the scores on a group-administered test.

Adult Achievement Tests

Many tests that can be used to measure the achievement of adults have already been listed and discussed—for example, the WRAT-3 and the PIAT-R-NU. Most major testing programs, such as the Graduate Record and College Board tests, have achievement tests in subject areas that are used with adults. In 2001, the General Educational Development Test (GED), a high school equivalence examination, was administered to approximately 1,016,000 people in the United States, Canada, and U.S. territories. More than 648,000 of these test takers earned diplomas.

Certain tests are designed specifically for use with adult populations:

- The Adult Language Assessment Scale (ALAS), is designed to assess how well nonnative English speakers can function. It can be used as a screening test for the English as a second language (ESL) population to plan individual instruction, to measure growth in English proficiency, and to help employers design appropriate training.
- The Test of Adult Basic Education (TABE) measures adult proficiency in reading, mathematics, and language. The TABE is used as a diagnostic tool and has five forms: TABE 7 & 8, TABE 9 & 10, TABE Advanced Level Tests, TABE Work-related Foundation Skills, and TABE Español. The reading test assesses vocabulary and comprehension; the language test measures mechanics, expression, and spelling; and the

mathematics test evaluates computation skills, knowledge of concepts, and problem solving. A locator test is used first to determine which is the most appropriate form and then a practice exercise is available to reduce the test taker's anxiety. Depending on the form, the test requires 1½ to 2½ hours of testing time. TABE-PC Assessments are also available.

Diagnostic Tests

One of the major purposes of achievement testing is to diagnose strengths and weaknesses. Diagnostic tests are based on the essential skills and competencies needed for success in a given subject area or educational program, and they use numerous items to measure a skill or objective. The tests can be given individually or in groups, and the information provides a profile of strengths and weaknesses in a particular area of concern. Many of the tests already discussed are utilized for diagnostic purposes—for example, the PIAT-R/NU, the WRAT-3, and the KMDAT. In addition, some tests are used specifically for diagnostic purposes. One of the most widely used tests, the Woodcock-Johnson III Complete Battery (WJ-III), provides tests for measuring general intellectual ability, specific cognitive abilities, scholastic aptitude, oral language, and academic achievement. Together, these batteries comprise a wide age-range, comprehensive system for measuring general intellectual ability, specific cognitive abilities, scholastic aptitude, oral language, and achievement. The test battery is recommended for use in individual assessment, screening, and diagnosis of strengths and weaknesses in cognitive, achievement, and interest areas. It is also used for evaluation of individual growth and program effectiveness, research purposes, and teaching purposes (e.g., training in individual test administration).

Some special diagnostic tests concern only reading. The Gates-McKillop-Horowitz Reading Diagnostic Test, Second Edition, has 15 individually administered subtests to provide a profile of a student's ability to recognize words and their component sounds. The test enables the teacher to diagnose weaknesses in such areas as coding skills, sight word recognition, auditory blending, auditory discrimination, spelling, and written expression.

USING ACHIEVEMENT TEST RESULTS

Workers in the helping professions can use the results from standardized achievement tests in a variety of ways. One of the primary uses is instructional. Test results can help teachers evaluate individual and group progress as well as materials and methods of instruction. An achievement test is just one source of information, but it is a systematic approach using standardized methods and items that are carefully screened. Achievement test information can be useful in selection and placement decisions; it can be used to help place students and to check on the validity of such placements. Achievement data may show growth in content areas or specific subject areas over time and can serve as one of the criteria to evaluate a school's curriculum.

FACTORS AFFECTING TEST SCORES

A variety of factors can effect students' test scores and need to be taken into consideration:

1. Grade level—The test measures what has been taught in this and preceding grades.
2. Number of years at current school—Students who move often and change schools may be at a disadvantage.
3. Age—Students who are in the age range typically served by a grade level tend to achieve higher scores than younger students or students who have been retained a year or more.
4. Out-of-school experience—Students who travel and read independently and have peers at home who are interested in learning tend to achieve at a higher level.
5. Health and nutrition—Healthier individuals who eat a balanced diet tend to score higher than those who do not.
6. Self-concept—Students with positive academic and general self-concepts tend to achieve higher scores than those with negative self-concepts.
7. Socioeconomic level—Students from lower socioeconomic levels may not have an equal opportunity to learn.
8. School environment—The quality of the classroom environment and the attitude of the teacher(s) toward the students can influence performance.
9. Test content—The test content may not reflect completely what is taught in a particular district. Also, certain questions may be biased and unfair to certain students, and not all students have the same opportunity to experience and learn certain material.
10. Test administration—Proper administrative procedures, time limits, and monitoring of student test-taking behavior are all important.

CASE OF JAMES

The case of James illustrates steps in interpreting achievement test data from a survey achievement test. James is in fifth grade and is having some academic difficulties in school. He is 10.3 years old, weighs 80 pounds, and is 4 feet 9 inches tall. His profile on the Stanford Achievement Test is shown in Figure 10.1. The derived scores plotted in the profile are percentile ranks and represent how the student performed in relation to students in the national sample.

A profile often has peaks and valleys, representing the learner's relative strengths and weaknesses. The median is the 50th percentile and represents typical or average performance. Some tests use different systems to classify superior or poor performance. Workers in the helping professions need to be familiar not only with what scores mean but also with what is measured by each subtest and which scores are combined to give total scores. In this case the test user needs to be familiar with the Teacher's Guide for Interpretation of the Intermediate Level I battery of the SAT.

A total listening score is based on the combination of the vocabulary and listening comprehension scores, which provide data on the

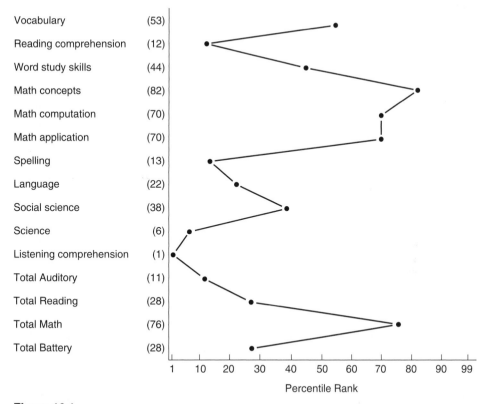

Figure 10.1
Profile of James's scores on the Stanford Achievement Test.

learner's ability to understand and remember information presented orally. A total reading score helps test users identify students who might have deficiencies in reading comprehension as well as overall scholastic achievement.

Additional Information Needed for the Case of James

One of the first questions to consider is how James's test performance compares to his performance in class. His teacher reports that he is an average student in mathematics but has problems in reading comprehension and following directions. He does not seem to listen at times and cannot remember what he is supposed to do. His problems in reading comprehension also create problems in understanding his science and social studies materials.

A second question is how his current test profile compares with other test results. On a local essential skills test (a minimum-level or basic skills criterion-referenced test), James failed the following areas (i.e., he had fewer than 75% of the items correct): vocabulary, listening comprehension, synonyms, antonyms, sequencing, facts and opinions, recalling details, main ideas, and sentence completion. The problem of comprehension is very real; James scored at the 12th percentile on the SAT Reading Comprehension, 82 out of a possible 133 right. In mathematics he failed only word problems and association of numbers with words. James scored 111 out of 125 on this test, with a passing score being 94. His reading comprehension problem did not seem to affect his performance on the SAT section on mathematics word problems: he scored at the 70th percentile. Test results are inconsistent in this dimension. Previous standardized achievement scores were low average in reading, average in mathematics, and average in social studies.

A third question is how James performs in relation to his ability. Many school districts no longer include scholastic aptitude testing as part of the school testing program. If the student is referred to a child study team, the counselor may give the student an individual test such as the Peabody Picture Vocabulary Test, the Slosson Intelligence Test, or even a group IQ test such as the Otis-Lennon School Ability Test. The psychologist may administer the Stanford-Binet or the Wechsler Intelligence Scale for Children. Scholastic aptitude or intelligence testing would help in developing an individually prescribed learning program for James, but no scholastic aptitude or intelligence data were available in his cumulative folder.

A fourth question is whether there are other factors that should be taken into consideration in interpreting the test results. James has progressed normally in school; he was never retained at a grade level and has been at the same school since the beginning of the third grade. He did attend two schools in other states prior to that time. James has had all the normal childhood diseases, but is healthy and has not missed many days of school.

James is the oldest child of three siblings; he has an 8-year-old brother and a 3-year-old sister. He lives with his mother and stepfather, who works as a carpenter for a construction company. His mother works part time as a checkout clerk in a supermarket. His father is in the Navy, and his parents were divorced when James was in kindergarten.

James's mother is concerned about his progress and is open to any suggestions the teacher or counselor may have to improve his academic performance. James relates fairly well with his classmates but gets easily frustrated when he cannot understand his lessons or recite correctly for the teacher. He likes to perform duties around the classroom and has become strongly attached to his teacher.

Two other questions relate to an analysis of the data. How does James perform in relation to the national norms? How is he mastering the objectives required for the fifth grade? The scores on the SAT profile show that he scored high in relation to other fifth graders in math concepts and just slightly lower in math computation and application. Clearly, his strongest area of achievement is mathematics. In the two listening tests, he scored average in vocabulary and poor in listening comprehension. His total listening performance is below average compared to his peers. He is also below average in spelling, language, science, and reading comprehension. His word study skills are average, as are his scores in social science. James is in danger of being retained in the fifth grade because his reading scores are below the criterion for promotion. He has a second chance to pass the essential skills test, but needs help to accomplish that task.

Although each item on the survey achievement test relates to a specific behavioral objective, often only one or two items measure a specific objective. An item analysis on such a test may provide good information for the teacher who has a total class profile, but it is of limited value in diagnosing James's educational problem. The essential-skills test is based specifically on the behavioral objectives taught in James's class, whereas the SAT is based on a wide sampling of objectives and textbooks from schools across the nation. Teachers and counselors should check the face validity and content validity of a norm-

Attitudes Toward the Test	Low			Moderate			High
Interest in the test	1	2	3	4	5	6	7
Motivation to perform well	1	2	3	4	5	6	7
Attitudes Toward the Examiner							
Degree of rapport	1	2	3	4	5	6	7
Degree of cooperation	1	2	3	4	5	6	7
Degree of comfort	1	2	3	4	5	6	7
Degree of openness	1	2	3	4	5	6	7
General Behavior							
Degree of anxiety	1	2	3	4	5	6	7
Degree of self-confidence	1	2	3	4	5	6	7
Praise or reinforcement needed	1	2	3	4	5	6	7
Frustration tolerance	1	2	3	4	5	6	7
Work Style							
Attention span	1	2	3	4	5	6	7
Impulsivity	1	2	3	4	5	6	7
Persistence	1	2	3	4	5	6	7
Methodical thinking	1	2	3	4	5	6	7
Interest in being challenged	1	2	3	4	5	6	7
Response time	1	2	3	4	5	6	7
Personality Style							
Introversion	1	2	3	4	5	6	7
Reality orientation	1	2	3	4	5	6	7
Mood swing	1	2	3	4	5	6	7
Seriousness	1	2	3	4	5	6	7
Degree of spontaneity	1	2	3	4	5	6	7
Internality	1	2	3	4	5	6	7

Figure 10.3
Test observation form.

Slosson and Callisto (1984) designed a scale called Observational Analysis to aid the examiner in the observational process. The behavioral profile calls for the examiner to check categories such as outward behavior, relationship with examiner, recall, affective tone, attitude, work habits, and expression. The authors also have a visual scanning form to be used for physical observations of the client, including observations of the head and face; arms, torso, and hands; legs and gait; and miscellaneous other categories. A posttest questionnaire requests verbal answers from the client in response to questions such as "Did you feel comfortable or uneasy about taking the test?" The system involves observation of the client in the total communication process.

Clinical Observations

The examiner may also want to observe the client in learning, performing, or social situations. Observations may be focused on a specific observable behavior, such as time on task, or may cover a wide variety of behaviors, such as affective, cognitive, psychomotor, and social. The examiner might use a checklist of whether a behavior was present or record anecdotal records of typical behavior. Clinical observation is an extremely valuable tool in working with very young children or with clients who have mental or emotional disabilities.

The examiner might be concerned with dimensions of psychomotor performance. Observation of fine motor coordination might focus on hand-eye coordination; use of fingers; angle of paper to body; reversals or rotations in copying, drawing, or writing; and handedness (Hargrove & Poteet, 1984). Observation of gross motor behavior might look at balance, activity level, body shifts, body positioning, and coordination.

Observation of social behavior can also be helpful, focusing on the relationships the client has with peers, teachers, authority figures, siblings, and parents. Dimensions of cognitive behavior might also be interesting—not only learning styles but also approaches to reasoning and ways of memorizing. Many affective components are related to learning, such as frustration and fatigue, motivation and effort, attention to task, and distractibility.

Self-Observations

On many occasions self-observations are important. A variety of types of data may be collected. Shapiro and Cole (1993) state that the simplest and most common method for collecting self-monitored data is to have the client record the occurrences of the targeted behavior. The data can be summarized over time and frequency rates complied. Sometimes the client is asked to tally the number of incidences of the targeted behavior in time units. There are mechanical devices to help the client tally such as golf counters and wrist counters.

A counselor is often helped in interpreting a case study by an autobiography, diary, journal, letters, themes, stories, and poems. Aiken (1985) states that most people spend quite a bit of time observing themselves. He cautions that self-observations are likely to be more biased than the observations made by others (p. 325). However, individuals can be trained to be more objective and systematic in self-observation. They can be trained to keep records of their thinking, actions, and feelings. Because data are recorded by the individual, periodic checks for accuracy might be necessary. Often the data is checked against ratings by others.

Autobiographies are used to provide insight into individual behavior, attitudes, and personality dimensions. Counselors can specify a certain format or allow individuals to arrange their thoughts however they want. Autobiographies include the facts the clients think are important about their environments. This form of expression also reveals self-concept, but it does rely on trust, and individuals may be concerned about confidentiality. Although autobiographies may give insight into personality dynamics and conflicts, counselors should interpret the data in light of other available information.

One of the problems with this method is that many clients tend to overlook their limitations and weaknesses.

The two major autobiography formats are structured and unstructured. The counselor may specify the format or allow the individuals to arrange their thoughts any way they want. The counselor must study the autobiography and then interpret the data along with other types of information collected. Autobiographies may give some insight into the personality dynamics and conflicts of the clients.

Logs, journals, and diaries are other approaches. These sources help counselors discern individual interests and activities, but it is difficult to get people to keep logs and diaries on a daily basis. Themes, poems, letters, and stories authored by the client may also provide valuable information about the individual or at least stimulate discussion in a counseling situation. Content analysis is used in looking at this data; the methodology is described in most textbooks on research methods in the social sciences.

Unstructured versus Structured Observation

One way of looking at observation is by classifying it into structured and unstructured categories. Unstructured observation is open-ended. The helping professional observes the behavior of the client, recording as much as possible of whatever appears to be useful or important. After the data are collected, the observer attempts to analyze and evaluate the behavior. A different approach is the use of structured observation, in which the helping professional has already determined why the observation is to take place, what is to be observed, and how the data will be recorded. This approach is deliberately systematic. The different purposes of observation lead to different approaches.

Problems in Observation

Sometimes breakdowns happen in the tracking and recording of observations. Barrios (1993) identified four such problems. The first is lack of a clear definition of the construct to be observed. To prevent this, the definition needs to be more precise, concrete, and observable. A second problem is the demands of the scale. Sometimes the observer has to record too many behaviors. The validity and reliability of the observations can be increased if the number of behaviors, complexity of the coding, or duration of the observation is decreased. The third breakdown is caused by distractions. Occasionally some external or internal event diverts the observer's attention and focus. This could be eliminated or reduced by imposing greater structure on the observation, changing the milieu of the observation, or, in some cases, changing the observer. Mistreatment is the last type of breakdown. Sometimes observers are not treated with dignity and respect. This breakdown can be avoided by ensuring dignity, respect, and greater appreciation for the observers. They should be praised when they do a good job.

Critical Incident Approach

Flanagan (1954) proposed using another form of uncontrolled and naturalistic observation called the critical incident technique. Supervisors are asked to identify specific

			a	b	c	d		e		
0	5	10	15	20	25	30	35	40	45	50

a = Work experience in community agency during high school
b = Graduated from college with degree in psychology, got married, did not work
c = Divorced, took job as secretary, went part time to the university to become certified as an elementary teacher
d = Began teaching second grade
e = Felt burnt out, decided to change careers and become a guidance counselor, went back to the university for master's

Figure 10.4
Critical events exercise.

behaviors that are critical to job performance or that distinguish good or poor work behavior. Analysis of their input provides valuable information on the requirements for effective performance. This technique has been applied to a number of contexts. Shertzer and Linden (1979) point out that having an individual clarify critical events in his or her life provides insight into the personal and social factors that have affected that person's behavior.

Some career planning exercises call for individuals to make a time line and record the 10 most critical events in their lives (see Figure 10.4).

Situation Tests

Situation tests are a form of controlled observation. In one classic example of the technique, Hartshorne and May (1928) studied character traits by observing children in a variety of structured situations, some of which permitted them to cheat and win at a game, copy test answers, or steal coins. The researchers found that children's honesty was highly dependent on the situation in which they were observed. For example, no child tended to be totally honest or totally dishonest. A boy who was an excellent student but a poor athlete would not cheat if asked to correct his own paper, but would inflate his score in a sports situation. A girl who excelled in physical performance but was a poor speller would record her physical performance correctly but cheat on scoring her spelling.

Another example occurred during World War II when the U.S. Office of Strategic Services (OSS) had to select special agents to carry out espionage or other special intelligence assignments. The candidates were observed and participated in a wide variety of assessment techniques, including pencil-and-paper tests, stress interviews, problem-solving exercises, and various situational tests (OSS Assessment Staff, 1948). The candidates were rated by the assessment staff and by their own peers, but the validity of these procedures was never established because per-formance on the tasks was never correlated with success on assignments carried out by those selected.

Situational testing has been utilized in a variety of settings, including the selec-tion of clinical psychologists (Kelly & Fiske, 1951). One variation of this technique is a leaderless group discussion in which group process becomes the means of observ-ing individual behavior. Candidates for a position might all be invited to a session in which they are given a problem situation to solve, a controversial topic to discuss, or a plan of operation to devise. Observers focus on certain salient traits that they are looking for, such as leadership or problem-solving ability.

A simulated work experience assessment is the In-Basket Test (Frederiksen, Saun-ders, & Wand, 1957), in which the examinee is given a variety of materials that provide background information from memoranda to technical reports. The examinee is then presented with a series of problems in the "in" basket and is asked to take action— for example, hiring or firing personnel or handling production problems. A number of versions of this approach have been developed for different groups, such as school administrators and military officers. Candidates demonstrate how they would handle each problem and are evaluated not only on their solutions but also on the processes used. Simulated tests are becoming more popular with the availability of varied soft-ware programs for the microcomputer.

Brown (1983) identifies problems that arise in the scoring and interpreting of sit-uational tests. He concludes that the data generated with this technique often have un-desirable statistical properties, are based on ratings using ordinal scales, have a limited range of values, and in general are unreliable.

Unobtrusive versus Participant Observation

Often it is possible to observe an examinee through a two-way mirror. Because the observer in this situation is not seen by the examinee, ethical guidelines call for the examinee to be informed and give approval. Unfortunately, when an examinee real-izes he or she is being observed, performance may not be typical. However, when vis-itors come by regularly, targeted individuals may not be aware of being observed. When there is no interaction between the observer and those being observed, and when the individual's behavior is not affected by the situation, observations are said to be unobtrusive.

Participation observation, a tool of the cultural anthropologist, involves the ob-server as part of the observational situation. The observer evaluates the group or in-dividuals while participating in the interaction. Aiken (1985) states that the observer's own behavior affects the reactions of other people in the situation (p. 32), but the technique can aid the observer to understand the dynamics of the situation.

Training Observers

Barrios (1993) points out that a key factor in getting valid and reliable data from ob-servation is the training of observers. The first step is orientation, explaining the pur-pose and importance of observation. The second step is education, instruction in the

definitions and recording schemes. The third step is evaluation, which involves assessing the observer's knowledge of the definitions, coding, and tracking procedures.
The fourth step is application, in which observers obtain experience in a number of
different situations. The fifth step, recalibration, involves checking the accuracy and
agreement of observers and correcting any deviation. The last step is termination, or
seeking the observers' feedback and evaluation of the process. Their contribution to
the project needs to be acknowledged. Observers should be reminded of the need to
maintain confidentiality.

METHODS OF DATA COLLECTION

The observer may want to focus on a single incident or on all client behavior in a given
period. The records needed depend on the purpose of the observations. The observer
might take notes, dictate observations into a tape recorder, or use a checklist, rating
scale, or behavior tallying or charting procedure.

Decisions beforehand include the following:

1. Who will be observed
2. What will be observed
3. Where the observation will take place
4. When the observation will take place
5. How the observation will be recorded

Anecdotal Records

One method of recording is the anecdotal record, which is a good way to gather information about a client's social adjustment. Anecdotal records are brief accounts of
behavior that are recorded in a log or on index cards. An anecdote is a written description of an observed event. The following information should be included:

1. Name of individual observed
2. Name of observer
3. Date and time of the observation
4. Location of the observation
5. Anecdote
6. Context
7. Interpretation

The following are procedural suggestions for recording behavioral anecdotes:

1. Focus on a single specific incident.
2. Be brief but complete.
3. Use objective behavioral descriptions.
4. Use phrases rather than sentences as long as the phrases are understandable.
5. List the behaviors in the sequence in which they occurred.
6. Evaluate what you have written. Is it a good snapshot of behavior?

7. Include direct quotations whenever possible and significant.
8. Record both positive and negative statements.

An advantage of the anecdotal record is that it does not depend upon the individual's capacity to communicate with the observer. In addition, this approach uses natural settings to observe behavior, and the systematic collection of such information can help in the understanding of a client's behavior. The major disadvantages are the time and expense of observation, the time it takes to write down the verbal description, and the questionable objectivity and reliability of the records.

Behavior Tallying and Charting

Many times the easiest way to record certain behaviors is to tally their occurrences. Sometimes concern centers around the number of times a behavior occurs, as is the case in educational environments where precision teaching or behavior modification efforts are taking place. At other times concern focuses not only on the frequency of behavior but also on the duration of a behavior. A teacher might be interested in how much time a student spends in her own seat or what percentage of time a preschooler spends crying. Time sampling might be used for behaviors that occur at high rates; that approach involves the recording of behaviors at certain times rather than continuously. Figure 10.5 illustrates a record used to assess the frequency of behavior, and

---

Date   2/1 to 2/5

Name _____

Observer _____

Description of Behavior   Physically aggressive - any deliberate body
                           contact made with any part of the body,
                           hands, legs, etc.

Days	Tallies	Total
Monday	////////	8
Tuesday	//////////	10
Wednesday	///////	7
Thursday	////////////	12
Friday	///////////////	15
Average = 10.4		

Figure 10.5
Record of the frequency of behavior.

Name _____

Observer _____

Description of Behavior   *Out of seat, wandering around classroom.*
                           Cannot state why when away from the desk.

Day	Time	Total minutes
Monday	9:10 – 9:30	20
	10:07 – 10:15	8
	11:00 – 11:07	7
	2:00 – 2:22	22
Tuesday	9:05 – 9:27	22
	9:50 – 10:03	13
	1:15 – 1:38	23
Wednesday		
Thursday		
Friday		

Average _____

Figure 10.6
Record of the duration of behavior.

Figure 10.6 shows a figure used to record the duration of behavior. Before any intervention is tried, it is important to establish the base rate of the behavior to be modified in order to determine later whether the behavior has been strengthened or eliminated.

Name_____

Observer_____

Date_____

Time observed_____

Yes	No	
_____	_____	Interrupted others when they were talking.
_____	_____	Gave compliments or encouragement when talking to others.
_____	_____	Argued or quarreled with others.
_____	_____	Swore and used vulgar language.
_____	_____	Took kidding without getting upset.
_____	_____	Looked at people directly when talking to them.
_____	_____	Had a short temper and got angry quickly.
_____	_____	Was blunt and direct and got to the point.
_____	_____	Expressed his/her opinion freely.
_____	_____	Got loud and noisy in conversation.
_____	_____	Disagreed and took opposite point of view.
_____	_____	Was nervous and tense when talking with others.
_____	_____	Was positive about self and others.
_____	_____	Spoke slowly and softly.
_____	_____	Made grammatical errors often.
_____	_____	Had difficulty pronouncing certain words.

Figure 10.7
Checklist of social behavior.

Checklists

Checklists are a way to record the presence or absence of specific behaviors in a given situation. A checklist normally consists of statements about expected behaviors. The observer checks yes or no to indicate whether the behavior occurred. A sample checklist is shown in Figure 10.7. Piacentini (1993) suggests that they can be used to assess a broad band or can be global in design to assess specific disorders or problem areas.

Rating Scales

Rating scales are devices that can be used to record impressions of behaviors that have been selected in advance. Such scales can help focus attention on specific behaviors. Rating scales most often consist of behaviors to be observed and require the rater to indicate the degree or frequency of behavior occurrences. Sometimes the rater is asked to rate the characteristics of the observed behavior or performance. A number of different rating scales are commonly used. Some of the formats are illustrated in Figure 10.8.

Rating scales provide a standardized format for the collection of data, ensuring systematic and comprehensive coverage of the behavior in question (Piacentini, 1993). The structured format reduces subjectivity and increases reliability. Dependence on the rater's experience and day-to-day variability are minimized.

Semantic Differential Type
Behavior with examiner
    Reserved ____ ____ ____ ____ ____ ____ ____   Open
                1   2   3   4   5   6   7

Response to testing process
    Leery ____ ____ ____ ____ ____ ____ ____   Confident
            1   2   3   4   5   6   7

Graphic Type
Reaction to test environment
Comfortable   Somewhat comfortable   Uncomfortable   Ill at ease
    1   2   3   4

Necessity to repeat questions
            Never   Occasionally   Often
                1   2   3   4   5   6   7

Numerical Type
Rapport with examinee
                1   2   3   4   5   6   7
            Low   High
Examples needed by test taker
                    1   2   3   4
            Only 1   5 or more

Figure 10.8
Sample formats showing semantic differential, graphic, and numerical types of rating scales.

Table 10.2
Rating scale errors.

Error	Description
Leniency or generosity	Ratings tend to always be at the top of the range.
Severity	Ratings tend to always be at the lower end of the scale.
Central tendency	Ratings tend to fall consistently in the middle or average range.
Halo effect	Ratings tend to be influenced by good impressions. High ratings on some traits are generalized to others.
Negative halo	Bad ratings on some items are generalized to others.
Logical error	Ratings are similar on characteristics rater feels are logically related.
Contrast error	Ratings on current candidate are influenced by the previous candidate.
Proximity error	Ratings made on items that are printed close together tend to be rated the same.
Most recent performance error	Ratings are influenced by the person's most recent performance rather than his or her usual level of performance.

Raters need to be trained to increase the reliability of the ratings. The scales need to be well constructed and have the proper format (Aiken, 2000). Raters need to be aware of the various rating errors (see Table 10.2).

GUIDELINES FOR OBSERVATION

Certain guidelines should be considered for observation:

1. Be objective. Be aware of personal biases and prejudices.
2. Be aware of the halo error—the tendency to be influenced by your first impression of an individual or by an exceptional trait. Such influence can be a source of bias.
3. Recognize personal response tendencies—perhaps rating everyone high (generosity error) or low (severity error), or in the middle (central tendency error). Be alert to only positive or only negative observations.
4. Focus on relevant behaviors. Attend to only the assigned behaviors on the checklist or rating scale.
5. Be as unobtrusive as possible.
6. Observe more than once; the more observations, the better the chance of getting a complete and accurate picture.
7. Have more than one person observe to permit comparison of results.
8. Train observers so all focus on and record the same behavior in the same way.
9. Instruct observers and have practice sessions in what behaviors are to be observed and how they are to be recorded.

AUTHENTIC ASSESSMENT

The major testing movement of the 1990s has been authentic assessment. *Authentic assessment* is one form of alternate assessment in which students are asked to perform real-world tasks that demonstrate meaningful application of essential knowledge and skills. Often used synonymously with *performance assessment,* it is a way of evaluating activities that are essential, genuine, and meaningful in themselves. These tasks can include essays, projects, portfolios, performance tasks, and open-ended exercises. These assessment procedures are not entirely new—the National Assessment of Educational Progress initiated similar formats in 1969.

Authentic assessment focuses on the development of assessment exercises that will not be biased against any group of students and can be reliably scored and validly interpreted. Raters are needed in many cases to score the assessments. Current research on a pilot project in Vermont indicates low reliability of the scoring procedures. Miller and Seraphine (1993) conclude that authentic assessment will probably be useful in low-stake assessments such as in classroom situations. Further, they note that multiple assessments will have value but will take more time from instructors and learning and will increase the anxiety level of students, teachers, and administrators.

Authentic assessment, according to Meyer and Davis (1992), involves real-life experiences. Students may be asked to write a speech that could be delivered to the county commissioners (performance assessment). If they presented it, the assessment used for evaluating this assignment would be authentic assessment.

Guidelines for Authentic Assessment Systems

The National Council on Measurement in Education (1994) provided criteria for evaluating alternative assessment procedures. The purpose of the assessment needs to be identified. Multiple measures should be used and the process should have technical rigor. The process must be cost effective, of educational value, and equitable to all students. The information should be useful to decision makers.

Gooding (1994) has seven criteria that should be reflected in a good evaluation system. It needs to be longitudinal and assess student learning over time. It should be authentic and focus on knowledge and skills the learner would need for success outside of school. The objectives of the assessment should be communicated effectively so that they are known by teachers, parents, and students. It should be nonbiased and fair to individuals of different learning backgrounds and cultures. It should be process oriented and require students to produce a product or performance. It should be student oriented and involve them in self-assessment and evaluation. Learners should be required to produce knowledge and apply it when solving problems.

The National Council of Teachers of Mathematics (1993) listed six standards for alternative or authentic assessment in mathematics; the principles also apply to other content areas:

1. Assessment should reflect the mathematics skills that are most important for students.
2. Assessment should enhance mathematics learning.
3. Assessment should promote equity by giving each student optional opportunities to demonstrate mathematical power and by helping each student meet the profession's high expectations.
4. All aspects of the mathematics assessment process should be open to review and scrutiny.
5. Evidence from assessment activities should yield valid inferences about students' mathematics learning.
6. Every aspect of an assessment process should be consistent with the purpose of the assessment.

Scoring Rubrics

As opposed to most traditional forms of testing, performance assessments don't have clear-cut right or wrong answers. Rather, there are degrees to which a student is successful or unsuccessful. A rubric is a rating system that determines at what level a student is successful or not successful.

Scoring rubrics have become a common method for evaluating student work in both the K–12 and the college classrooms. Rubrics provide explicit criteria for the individual to demonstrate in order to meet educational objectives of a particular assignment/project. To develop a rubric, you need to define the elements (or criteria) of the project to be evaluated to determine student success. Each element is then evaluated using terms such as "below expections," "meets expectations," or "exceeds expectations." Table 10.3 is an example of a scoring rubric for a graduate paper.

Issues and Problems

One of the big challenges for helping professionals in the authentic assessment movement is helping teachers link assessment to ongoing instruction. Teachers need a better understanding of their classroom practices and the ethical aspects, reasoning, and consequences of good or poor instruction. Teacher training institutions need to help preservice interns improve their assessment skills.

Math teachers, for example, need to consider that mathematics assessment may demand substantial linguistic ability, and thus be unfair to those who are lacking in such skills. Because performance-based assessment uses only a small number of tasks, these may favor one group over another. Students must be provided with assessment alternatives that are appropriate to their ethnicity, gender, disability, or language. The use of portfolio assessment requires teachers to adapt to ever-changing curricular and instructional demands (CRESST, 1994).

Portfolio Assessment

Portfolio assessment appears to be one of the most widely used types of alternative or authentic assessment. Many teachers keep portfolios of student work. The purposes of the portfolio are as follows:

1. To help document the growth and development of the student
2. To serve as a vehicle for communication among teacher, student, and parents
3. To guide instructional planning for the student
4. To maintain a standard assessment procedure throughout the program.

Portfolios include the assessment record of the child, checklists, teacher communications, writing activities, and reading assignments. Additional information such as reading logs, writing logs, goal sheets, journals, teacher's notes, learning logs, teacher-student conference logs, and screening data might be used.

Portfolios can help show students' growth over time, the process by which work was done as well as the final product, their favorite or personally important work, and the evolution of one or more projects or products. The portfolio can also be used to prepare a sample of the best work for employment or college admissions. It can be used for student placement decisions or to achieve alternative credit for a course. It is a helpful tool in curriculum and program evaluation.

Johnson (1996) calls the portfolio the "multiple choice" of performance assessment. Schools and teachers differ on the type of entries to be included as well as how they are going to be evaluated. Sometimes that criteria is very structured; other times a minimum of structure is required.

Table 10.3

Rubric for a Graduate Paper

	Below Expectations	Meets Expectations	Exceeds Expectations
Reasoning	1. Presentation is illogical. 2. Ideas from different sources are presented without synthesis.	1. Logical, orderly presentation. 2. Effort is made to synthesize ideas from different sources.	1. The writing is logical, orderly, and well developed. 2. Ideas are well synthesized, following an established outline.
Communication	1. Incoherent organization. 2. Writing is choppy, with many awkward passages. 3. Heavy reliance on quotations or paraphrasing.	1. Organization is acceptable. 2. Sentences and paragraphs relate to each other. 3. Original writing supported with occasional quotations, paraphrasing.	1. Organization is excellent. 2. Writing is flowing and easy to follow. 3. Limited quotations and paraphrasing.
Grammar	Substantial grammatical errors.	Grammatical errors are minimal.	The document is free of grammatical errors.
APA Style	Several APA errors.	Few errors in APA style.	APA style is employed perfectly.
Mechanics	Spelling, punctuation, or format errors are noticeable.	Minimal spelling, punctuation, or format errors.	No spelling, punctuation, or format errors.
Content/Focus	1. Unclear main idea. 2. No evidence of purpose or direction. 3. Content does not support main idea.	1. Clear main idea. 2. Purpose and direction discernable. 3. Content provides some support for the main idea.	1. Very clear and effectively limited and manageable topic. 2. Clear purpose and direction. 3. Content clearly supports main idea.
References	1. Inappropriate references. 2. Many errors in the citations in either the body or the reference section. 3. Many references in the body are not cited in the reference section and vice versa.	1. References are appropriate. 2. A few incorrect citations are in either the body or the reference section. 3. A few citations in the body do not match those in the reference section.	1. References are appropriate and exceed the minimum number of sources. 2. Citations are correctly cited in both the body and the reference section. 3. Citations match in the body and in the reference section.

Student_____Date_____
Class_____Teacher_____

Mechanics
_____Correct spelling
_____Correct grammar
_____Appropriate word usage
_____Subject-verb agreement
_____Correct punctuation
_____Other_____

Structure
_____Well organized
_____Coherent
_____Paragraph unity
_____Appropriate topic sentences
_____Logical conclusions

Style
_____Style appropriate for purposes
_____Tone fits topic

Teacher action
_____Rewrite and resubmit
_____Correct errors noted and resubmit
_____Correct errors and place in portfolio
_____Read comments and place in portfolio

Outside rater
_____Meets school criteria

Figure 10.9
Evaluation checklist for portfolios.

Figure 10.9 shows an evaluation checklist for portfolios created in a middle school English class.

Johnson (1996) states that the key design elements to consider when developing portfolios are the following:

1. Specify the desired outcomes and expectations.
2. Create rubrics and criteria that define quality of work.
3. Involve students in the decisions of how the portfolio is to be structured and evaluated.

The portfolio approach helps demonstrate both the learning process and the product. The process gives the counselor a portrait of the problem-solving techniques used by the student. The individual also has the opportunity to demonstrate what he or she knows and can do. In any field portfolios encourage self-reflection and metacognitive strategies. Although the portfolio process has a high degree of realism and creativity, the validity and reliability of the process are often questioned.

SUMMARY

Achievement tests are used at all age and grade levels to measure what individuals have learned. They are used for a wide variety of purposes, such as diagnosis, placement, growth, and description. A variety of achievement tests include individual and group; norm- and criterion-referenced; survey batteries and single-subject; and diagnostic, prognostic, and readiness tests.

Local school districts, states, and the federal government are involved in assessing achievement. Local school districts develop a series of criterion tests to measure how well students are achieving the minimum-level skills and essential-level skills being taught. The tests are valuable for educational and vocational guidance purposes, evaluation of curriculum and teaching methods, and demonstration of growth from grade to grade.

Achievement tests are not free from controversy. Critics are concerned that certain tests and test items may be biased against certain groups.

Observational techniques are widely used in assessing and evaluating clients. Counselors and psychologists use observational techniques in assessing the client's behavior in play therapy, sociodrama, psychodrama, simulated experiences, role-playing, test performance, discussion groups, conferences, interviews, and in job, home, or school situations. Sometimes observation is a secondary part of a testing situation. On most individual tests the examiner rates the test taker's behavior as well as his or her answers. Observational techniques show promise but do have psychometric problems that interfere with their validity and reliability.

QUESTIONS FOR DISCUSSION

1. Compare survey achievement and criterion-referenced tests. In what situations would each be the best measure to use?

2. Is it necessary to give both survey achievement tests and minimum-level and essential-level skills tests within one district? Defend your position.

3. How would you go about developing a minimum-level skills test in a content field in junior or senior high school?

4. For what purposes should survey achievement tests be used? For what purposes should we avoid using the tests?

5. Look at the scores found in Table 10.2 and answer these questions: (a) How are class members achieving in relation to their ability? (b) How is the class achieving in each subject area? (c) Are there any students who need help or who are having problems in one or more achievement areas?

6. State your position on one of the following issues: (a) Testing controls what is taught in schools. (b) The best predictor of future success is past achievement, not aptitude. (c) Achievement tests should be banned from use.

7. What are the major types and sources of errors likely to arise in observational situations? How can you eliminate or reduce these sources of error?

8. Some individuals advocate the use of unobtrusive observation, claiming that clients will tend to perform in more natural and typical ways. Think of situations in which unobtrusive observation is not possible. How can you enhance the validity of your observations when it is impossible for you to be unobtrusive? Should contrived situations be used?

9. Interview some counselors and psychologists. Ask them how much time they spend using observational techniques and find out whether they use structured or unstructured observation. What instruments or schedules do they use? How valid and reliable do they feel the observations are?

10. When would you make use of self-observational techniques? What training or instructions would you give a client before assigning self-observation? What psychometric problems do you see with these techniques?

SUGGESTED ACTIVITIES

1. Select one of the major achievement tests and write a critique of it.

2. Assemble an annotated bibliography of achievement tests related to your field of interest.

3. Interview workers in the helping professions who use achievement tests in their work. Find out what tests they use and why, and how they use the results. Report your findings to the class.

4. Administer an individual achievement test or diagnostic test and write a report of the results.

5. Review the research and write a paper on one of the following topics: bias in achievement testing, gender differences in achievement testing, the national assessment program, current trends and issues in achievement testing, criterion-referenced testing.

6. Choose a type of behavior that is of interest to you and prepare an operational definition of the behavior. Construct a checklist to record the number of times that the behavior occurs in a given situation.

7. Review the different observational checklists that are part of many individual tests. What commonalities exist among these scales? What differences? How observable are the behaviors or constructs to be rated by the examiner?

8. Review some of the standardized rating scales that are widely used in your field. What scales have higher reliability—structured or unstructured, self-rating or rating by other scales, categorical or summary-type? Report your findings to the class.

9. Study the case of Alicia that follows and answer the questions at the end.

Case of Alicia

Alicia is in a community college outreach program and is participating in a 2-week session designed to help students develop skills and see the importance of staying in school and going on to postsecondary education. The program is for rural, underachieving minority students.

The following are entries in Alicia's journal:

Monday: Yesterday when I first got their we went to the dorms got our name log then we went and put our clothes in the dorms. Then I went outside to mess with the boys and we had fun with one of the counselors. We played basket in the gym and I had lots of fun. I also like this boy name Rod but me and him both can't talk to each other because he has a girlfriend and I have a boyfriend. I guess I have to put that in the closet. Well get back to real business I think this program so far have done me some good because sometimes other people can learn things better than others. I ihig over her I catch on easy so you know how that is. Because I really want to learn more because up their in life it's gonabe hard down that long road and because we are black you know they think black people can't be or do anything and tha's why am going to pay atton and make something out of my self. Also I think this program is good for us because it keeps you off the streets Keeps you away from drugs it keeps you from lots of things think about. They alway told me my 15 years I been on this earth can't do a thing when you just sit around doing nothing. Also I want to go to college and be in a marching band and major in mathematics. Because me an person that likes to need losts of people and fun things like that you know. Well kind of ran out of words to say But I will always remember to stay in school BECAUSE IF YOU BELIEVE YOU WILL ACHIEVE.

Tuesday: Today's Tuesday, so far so good I got up this moing thank God for waking me up. Well let me get on withit took me a shower put on some clothes and went to breakfast. Well breakfast was pretty good this morning. I got full and started on my way to go back to my room and got my books fo my class we went to reading class we was learning about verbs and good stuff like that then we came to Study Hall and did the homework our english teach gave us it was not much but it was rough. Well sitting her in Study Hall listen to thes boys trip on each other one boy told this other boy that he looked like a snaping turtule that mess was funny to. also Miss Pam told one of my friends that she write to big and told one boy he write to bad She coud not read nothing he say. they she asked one boy how to spell it was that he was not using his studing time all they do is paly stand and tell jokes so I don't pay them no mind. Oh when we was comming to Study Hall we was so sorry we did not want to take the stairs so we took the elavater now tell me is that sorry or what. Well I am running out of words to say gotta go See YA

Wednesday: Today is Wednesday I got up this moing went to the bathroom and brush my teeth. Then I went to my room and put some clothes on then went to brakfast and got full. Then I went to Reading class and learned a little bit then we went to Study Hall then we started triping you know we started tell jokes and stuff like that we tried to tell Miss Pam that we did not have any work to do but she fooded us She made us work asnway. Then she made us take a test and some of us did not study and probely flunk the test you know. Also I think Shon is very nice because he is always smiling and that's the way I like to see pople smiling all the time. Also when I was going to Study hall I touch rod on his arm I like that you know how that is to touch someone you really want to get to. Well we know some flunk Because he told everybody that he miss eight and he told Miss Pam that he want to take the test over becausse she could not read it with his bad handwriting. Of I flunk the test too. I miss five I think I need to study. Know let me get to yesterday we had so much fund we was in the gym and the boys was playing basketball and Chad and Rod and all of them I was cheering for all of the exspecally Rod I like him as you can see. Oh By the way our team did not win because they say we cheated but we didn't we won fare and squar. After we got finished with the relay we ate snacks then we went to take a shower then went to bed well got to go. See YA when I see YA Peace

  a. What are the major themes in Alicia's journal?
  b. What kind of system would you develop to analyze these journals?
  c. What kind of impact do you think the program had on Alicia? Why?

10. Read the case that follows and answer the questions at the end.

Case of Danny

A teacher noticed Danny's constant battle with fellow classmates in class. Danny doesn't seem to have any friends. When his other teachers were asked about him, a mystery seemed to exist.

Elementary School Record:

First Grade		*Second Grade*		*Third Grade*		*Third Grade (This year)*	
Reading	D	Reading	D	Reading	D	Reading	C
Spelling	C	Spelling	D	Spelling	D	Spelling	C
Writing	C	Writing	D	Writing	C	Writing	C
Math	D	Math	D	Math	F	Math	C
				Lang. Arts	F	Lang. Arts	D
				Soc. St.	D	Soc. St.	D
				Science	F	Science	C

Current Test Record
Grade 3 (current)

Minibattery of Achievement

Subject	*Score*
1. Reading	2.7
2. Math	2.6
3. Writing	2.0
4. Factual	2.2

WISC-IV

	Composite Score	*Percentile Rank*
Full Scale IQ	101	53
Verbal Comprehension	102	55
Perceptual Reasoning	106	66
Working Memory	102	55
Processing Speed	85	16

Health Record:

Danny's physical condition is good. He has had the normal childhood diseases.

Family Background:

Danny's father is a heating and air-conditioning technician and a high school graduate; his mother is a housewife and has an eighth-grade education. The parents are separated and Danny lives with his grandparents. He has lived with his grandparents since he was 4 years of age, when he was taken out of St. John's Orphanage. Home conditions are average considering his grandparents are older. They lack interest in how he is doing at school.

Social Life:

Danny belongs to no organizations or clubs and he does not have any close friends. He frequently starts arguments in class and on the playground. He is very outspoken.

Interests and Abilities:

Danny has a lot of interest in making things; this is evident in his science projects and art. He has special skills in making things with his hands. He does little reading but watches lots of TV. He fails to do his homework most of the time.

Other Teachers' Assessment of Danny:

They comment on his family environment and say that the continual moving of his grandparents has deprived Danny of companions. They say that he acts out to gain attention.

a. Provide a capsule summary of Danny's achievement and aptitude.
b. What additional information about Danny would you like to have?
c. Do his test results correlate with his grades?

ADDITIONAL READINGS

Read current issues of the *Journal of Behavioral Assessment, Behavioral Assessment,* and *Journal of Abnormal Child Psychology.* These journals publish research on observational techniques and instruments.

Aiken, L. R. (1996). *Rating scales and checklists.* New York: Wiley.
 Provides information on how to design, construct, administer, and score rating scales.

Cronbach, L. J. (1990). *Essentials of psychological testing* (5th ed.). New York: HarperCollins.

Farr, R. (1994). *Portfolio and performance assessment.* San Antonio, TX: Psychological Corporation.
 Provides specific procedures and techniques for using portfolios and integrating them into the instructional program and school assessment practices.

Glatthorn, A. (1998). *Performance assessment and standards based curricula: The achievement cycle.* Larchmont, NY: Eye on Education.

Goldstein, G., & Hersen, M. (1990). *Handbook of psychological assessment* (2nd ed.). New York: Pergamon.
 Three chapters on interviewing and two on behavioral assessment provide good information.

Johnson, B. (1996). *The performance assessment handbook. Vol. 1: Portfolios and Socratic seminars. Vol. 2: Performances and exhibitions.* Princeton, NJ: Eye on Education.
 Gives examples of the use of portfolios, performances, exhibitions, and Socratic seminars in education.

Millman, J., & Greene, J. (1989). The specification and development of tests of achievement and ability. In R. Linn (Ed.), *Educational measurement* (3rd ed.). New York: Collier Macmillan.

4. identify shared interests with people successfully employed in an occupation
5. identify careers to explore for possible midcareer change
6. help identify an interest in management
7. help counselors understand an employee's job satisfaction or dissatisfaction
8. aid in retirement planning

The following updated and enhanced reports and support materials make up the product suite for the revised Strong assessment at this time: *Strong Interest Inventory Manual; Profile; Profile, College Edition; Profile, High School Edition; Interpretive Report; Skills Confidence Inventory;* and *Career Exploration: A Journey of Discovery.*

Career Occupational Preference System

The Career Occupational Preference System (COPS) has three components. The first section, the COPS interest inventory, is a 20–30 minute test designed to measure interests in 14 "career clusters":

Science Professional	Business Skilled
Science Skilled	Clerical
Technology Professional	Communication
Technology Skilled	Arts Professional
Consumer Economics	Arts Skilled
Outdoor	Service Professional
Business Professional	Service Skilled

The second part of the test battery is an aptitude test, the Career Ability Placement Survey (CAPS). It is a comprehensive, multi-dimensional battery designed to measure vocationally relevant abilities. Its scales include mechanical reasoning, spatial relations, verbal reasoning, numerical ability, language usage, word knowledge, perceptual speed and accuracy, and manual speed and dexterity. The CAPS takes approximately 50 minutes to complete.

The third part of the battery measures work values, the Career Orientation Placement and Evaluation Survey (COPES). It provides a measure of values to supplement programs in educational and industrial career counseling. It, too, has eight scales: investigative/accepting, practical/carefree, independence/conformity, leadership/supportive, orderliness/flexibility, recognition/privacy, aesthetic/realistic, and social/reserved. The COPES takes approximately 30 to 40 minutes to complete.

The COPSystem Career Measurement Package includes all of the materials you need to administer, score, and interpret the COPS Interest Inventory, CAPS ability battery, and the COPES work values survey.

Other Interest Inventories

Many other interest tests are available. Critical reviews can be found in the *Buros Mental Measurement Yearbooks, Tests in Print*, and *A Counselor's Guide to Career Assessment Instruments* (Kapes & Whitfield, 2001). A special annotated bibliography on personality and vocational assessment instruments is part of the ETS Test Collection.

Some of the other widely used inventories are identified here:

- The Campbell Interest and Skills Survey (CISS) focuses on careers that require a postsecondary education and is most appropriate for use with individuals who have completed college or plan to attend. The CISS adds a parallel skill scale that reports the estimate of the individual's confidence in his or her ability to perform various occupational activities.
- The Career Assessment Inventory-Vocational Version compares an individual's vocational interests to those of individuals in 91 specific careers that reflect a range of positions in today's workforce—including skilled trades and technical and service professions—requiring 2 years or less of post-secondary training. The Career Assessment Inventory-Enhanced Version compares an individual's occupational interests to those of individuals in 111 specific careers that reflect a broad range of technical and professional positions in today's workforce.
- The Harrington-O'Shea Career Decision-Making System-Revised, 2005 Update (CDM-R) is designed for use with seventh graders to adults and provides scale scores in six interest areas (e.g., crafts, arts, scientific, social). It assesses abilities, interests, and work values in one instrument. The CDM Level 1 is for middle school students. The CDM Level 2 is for high school and college students and adults.
- The Interest Determination, Exploration, and Assessment System (IDEAS) provides scores on such scales as mechanical, electronics, nature/outdoor, science, numbers, writing, arts/crafts, social service, child care, medical service, business, sales, office practice, and food service. The test is designed for use in grades 6 through 12.
- The Jackson Vocational Interest Survey (JVIS) is used with high school students, college students, and adults and has 34 basic interest scales such as creative arts, performing arts, mathematics, skilled trades, dominant leadership, business, sales, law, human relations, management, and professional advising. It also has 10 occupational themes such as assertive, enterprising, helping, and logical.
- The Judgment of Occupational Behavior-Orientation, Third Edition, (JOB-O) is designed to work best with 4th through 6th grade populations. This assessment allows students to consider their pre-existing interests, and then helps relate them to careers.
- The Kuder Career Search with Person Match is an interest assessment for ages from middle school to adult. It reports on the test-taker's similarity with groups of employed people in six career clusters: Outdoor/Mechanical, Science/Technical, Arts/Communication, Social/Personal Services, Sales/Management, and Business Operations. The test is available in three formats: (1) a pencil and paper version which is scored and profiled by the user; (2) a pencil and paper version which is mailed back to the publisher for scoring; and (3) an Internet-based inventory.

The helping professional may want to check the validity of test or inventory results by asking clients about their interests and activities, inquiring about their preferences, and finding out why areas are liked and disliked. Individuals may have had no experience or opportunity in certain areas, and some likes and dislikes may be influenced by parent, spouse, or family attitudes. Interests cannot be determined by how clients spend their time. Time may be spent doing things under pressures from parents, spouse, family, or peers. Or individuals simply may not have time to do the things they most enjoy.

Client performance should be considered on more than just interest tests. In many situations, aptitude and achievement data also help in the decision-making process. Clients may learn and like what they do best, but not necessarily. A number of other factors may be involved, such as opportunity and experience.

VALUES

Values are an important dimension of personality, and value assessment is an important component of career guidance testing. There are two types of values: intrinsic and extrinsic. *Intrinsic values* are related to the work itself and what it contributes to society. *Extrinsic values* include external features, such as physical setting and earning potential. Value inventories will ask questions like the following:

- Is a high salary important to you?
- Is it important for your work to involve interacting with people?
- Is it important for your work to make a contribution to society?
- Is having a prestigious job important for you?

The following are a list of common values inventories:

- The Hall Occupational Orientation Inventory Fourth Edition is based on the humanistic theory of personality (Maslow) emphasizing dynamic, changing, developing nature of one's work motivation/behavior. The inventory is designed to help individuals understand their values, needs, interests, and preferred lifestyles, and how these relate to career goals and future educational plans. Three forms are available: Intermediate (grades 3–7), Young Adult/College, and Adult Basic (used for adults with GED and below).
- The Minnesota Importance Questionnaire (MIQ) measures 20 vocational needs and 6 underlying values related to those needs. The values assessed are achievement, altruism, autonomy, comfort, safety, and status. The instrument is for individuals ages 15 and up and takes about 20–35 minutes to complete.
- Rokeach Values Survey is a rank order instrument where the test-taker is presented with 18 instrumental and 18 terminal values and asked to rank them. Terminal values are the end-state we hope to achieve in life, such as freedom, a world of peace, family security, pleasure, health, excitement, or a comfortable economic life. Instrumental values are the means by which we achieve terminal values, such as being polite, ambitious, caring, self-controlled, obedient, or helpful.
- The Salience Inventory (Research Edition) measures the importance of five major life roles—student, worker, homemaker, leisurite, and citizen. The inventory consists of 170 items resulting in 15 scales that examine the relative importance of these five roles in participation, commitment, and value expectations. The inventory can be administered to adults and high school students.
- Super's Work Values Inventory-revised is an online inventory that can be completed in less than 15 minutes. The inventory assesses 12 work-related values

including income, creativity, mental challenge, prestige, variety, achievement, independence, co-workers, work environment, supervision, security, and lifestyle.

- The Values Scale was developed to measure intrinsic and extrinsic life and career values. The test has some scales similar to the Work Values Inventory (for example, achievement, aesthetics, altruism, economic returns, prestige, and variety) but it also has scales such as ability utilization, advancement, authority, creativity, lifestyle, personal development, physical activity, risk, social interaction, social relations, working conditions, cultural identity, physical prowess, and economic security.

GUIDELINES FOR INTERPRETING TESTS

Consider these general guidelines when interpreting interest and values tests:

1. Scale titles should be translated into terms clients can understand. Clients may be confused by scale titles such as "altruism" and "aesthetics."
2. Clients may be encouraged to plot their own scores and make profiles, identifying their own high and low scores. This is a type of ipsative interpretation, with clients making their own intraindividual comparisons.
3. Client profiles can be compared with norming groups and available vocational and educational groups.
4. If key items are identified by research, specific responses may be considered and discussed with the client.
5. The meaning of values and interests in work and career fields should be discussed.

CAREER DEVELOPMENT INSTRUMENTS

Career development and maturity instruments were developed to help counselors assess career awareness and knowledge. These instruments can provide counselors with valuable information about the career development and educational needs of individual clients and can provide survey information to help in planning career guidance programs.

- The Career Development Inventory has forms for both middle and high school and college and university students. The test contains five scales: career planning, career exploration, decision making, world-of-work information, and knowledge of preferred occupational group. The scales are combined to give scores in career development attitudes, career development knowledge and skills, and career orientation.
- The Career Factors Inventory (CFI) is designed to help people determine whether they are ready to engage in the career decision-making process. The CFI can be used for individuals age 13 and above; its 21-item self-scorable booklet takes 10 minutes to complete. It explores an individual's perceived issues of

lack of self-awareness, lack of career information, career anxiety, and generalized indecisiveness.

- The Career Maturity Inventory is an instrument for grades 6 through 12 that measures the attitudes and competencies related to variables in the career-choice process. The test has two parts: an attitude test and a competence test. The attitude test measures attitudes toward decisiveness, involvement, independence, orientation, and compromise dimensions of career maturity. The competence test has five subtests: knowing yourself (self-appraisal), knowing about jobs (occupational information), choosing a job (goal selection), looking ahead (planning), and what should they do? (problem solving).

One problem with many instruments is that they do not require students to apply these skills to themselves. It is not enough for clients to gain some understanding of the process; they must also see how this information can be transferred to their own real world.

COMBINED PROGRAMS

The trend in career guidance is for assessment to include interest, values, and other dimensions such as aptitude, career development, and maturity. The COPSystem previously discussed in this chapter includes interest, values, and aptitude assessment. Here are some other examples of combined programs:

- The Career Planning Program (CPP) of ACT is designed to help students from grade 8 to adults identify and explore personally relevant occupations and educational programs. The assessment stresses career exploration and helps individuals relate information about their interests, experiences, and abilities to the work world.
- Choices Explorer is an online education and career exploration system that provides education, career and recreation articles in an interactive magazine-style format for high school students. Through the Internet, students have access to over 900 career profiles, 330 post-secondary programs, 200 career videos and more. Students can create their own career library and store meaningful information for future use. Students can also use Choices Planner, an online career information delivery system that helps students build career plans in a personal portfolio. Assessments instruments are used to identify skills, interests and values to increase self-awareness. Comprehensive school, program and career reports show students school-to-major-to-career connections.
- DISCOVER is a computerized comprehensive career planning program available online through the American College Testing Program (ACT). The DISCOVER program collects information about individuals including interests, abilities, and values through self-assessment tools. The results are then matched to world of work information that can suggest specific majors needed for a particular career. DISCOVER provides guidance on choosing a major, information on schools that offer specific areas of study, resources for financing the cost of higher education, and job search tools. The DISCOVER

program also provides a World-of-Work Map that illustrates how interests, abilities, and work values relate to each other. The World-of-Work Map organizes occupations into six clusters (parallel to John Holland's six occupational types), 12 regions, and 26 career areas (groups of similar jobs). It graphically shows how occupations relate to each other according to primary work tasks.

- The World of Work Inventory (WOWI) is a comprehensive career assessment instrument designed to provide an assessment of three major considerations in vocational counseling, planning, and career decision making: interests (Career Interest Indicators), aptitudes-abilities (Vocational Training Potentials), and temperaments (Job Satisfaction Indicators). The WOWI can be administered online and can be completed in approximately 50–65 minutes. It has applications in business, vocational rehabilitation, high schools, colleges and universities, career counseling, and job training programs.

PROBLEMS OF INTEREST MEASUREMENT

Counselors need to be aware of a number of problem areas when using interest tests:

1. Even though there is much evidence of the stability of interests, especially from the late teens on, some clients change their interests dramatically in their adult years.
2. Tests given before grade 10 or 11 may not be accurate measures of interests. Students may not have had the background of experiences, real or vicarious.
3. Job success is usually correlated more to abilities than interests.
4. Many interest inventories are susceptible to faking, either intentional or unintentional.
5. Response set may affect the validity of an individual's profile. Clients may choose options they consider more socially desirable or acquiescence may prevail.
6. High scores are not the only valuable scores on an interest inventory. Low scores, showing what people dislike or want to avoid, are often more predictive than high scores.
7. Societal expectations and traditions may prove more important than interest in determining vocational selection. Gender bias was a major concern in interest measurement during the past several decades and needs to be considered when selecting instruments and interpreting profiles.
8. Socioeconomic class may affect the pattern of scores on an interest test.
9. The inventories may be geared to the professions rather than to skilled and semi-skilled areas. Many inventories were criticized because they were geared exclusively to college-bound students.
10. A profile may be flat and hard to interpret. In such a situation a counselor should use other tests and techniques to determine interests.
11. Tests use different types of psychometric scoring procedures. Some interest tests use forced-choice items, in which individuals are asked to choose from a set of options. Examinees may like or dislike all of the choices but still must choose. Scoring procedures will have an impact on interpretation of results.

EMPLOYMENT TESTING

Tests are used in employment contexts for placement decisions, assignment to training programs, promotion, retention, licensing, and certification. Tests can be used, for example, to select individuals for entry-level positions, make differential job assignments, select individuals for advanced and specialized positions, decide who will be promoted within an organization, decide who is eligible for training, and provide diagnostic and career development information for individuals. To be effective, tests must be valid for the intended purpose and should be the least discriminating tool for the decisions that need to be made. Tests can help ensure fair treatment of workers in an employment context.

Employees in the private sector work primarily in manufacturing, retail trades, and service occupations. Clerical workers constitute the largest group, numbering approximately 20 million people. Tests are used in the private sector to help make decisions in selection, placement, training, and promotion of personnel. Tests are also used to provide credentials or certification.

Types of Tests

Many employers use tests as part of the assessment process to develop work-related information and recommendations or decisions about people who work for them or are seeking employment with them. Common employment tests include general aptitude, cognitive ability, clerical achievement, spatial and mechanical abilities, perceptual accuracy, and motor ability tests for selection and promotion.

Personality tests are used in some employment contexts. In general, the most widely used personality tests discussed in the text are used in industrial contexts also, such as the Myers-Briggs Type Indicator, the California Psychological Inventory, the Edwards Personal Preference Inventory, and the Guilford-Zimmerman Temperament Scale. Assessment of attitudes, stress, organizational commitment, and work environment are used to diagnose strengths and weaknesses in the organization and to monitor changes in the workforce. Scales of job satisfaction measure dimensions such as attitude toward supervision, the company, the coworkers, pay, working conditions, promotion, security, subordinates, autonomy, and esteem needs.

Some of the standardized tests that are used in business and industry are described here:

- The Career Attitudes and Strategies Inventory (CASI) helps to identify career problems requiring further discussion and exploration. It includes a career checkup; a self-assessment of the client's career or situation; and a survey of the beliefs, events, and forces that affect the client's career.
- The Comprehensive Ability Battery (CAB) contains 20 pencil-and-paper subtests that measure a single primary-ability factor related to performance in an industrial setting. The subtests are verbal ability, numerical ability, spatial ability, perceptual completion, clerical speed and accuracy, reasoning, hidden shapes, rote memory, mechanical ability, meaningful memory, memory span,

spelling, auditory ability, esthetics judgment, organizing ideas, production of ideas, verbal fluency, originality, tracking, and drawing.

- The Comprehensive Personality Profile (CPP) is a personality test for positions requiring significant client interaction such as customer service, telemarketing and sales. The primary traits assessed are emotional intensity, intuition, recognition, motivation, sensitivity, assertiveness, trust, and good impression.
- The Employee Aptitude Survey Test Series (EAS) consists of 10 tests that measure cognitive, perceptual, and psychomotor abilities required for successful job performance in a wide variety of occupations. Tests include verbal comprehension, visual pursuit, visual speed and accuracy, space utilization, numerical reasoning, verbal reasoning, word fluency, mechanical speed and accuracy, and symbolic reasoning.
- The Employment Barrier Identification Scale assesses the ability of an unemployed client to gain and retain employment. It looks at job skills, education, environmental support, and personal survival skills.
- The Employee Reliability Inventory is an 81-item, pre-interview questionnaire designed to help employers identify reliable and productive individuals prior to making a hiring decision. It measures emotional maturity, conscientiousness, trustworthiness, long-term commitment, safe job performance, and courteous behavior with customers.
- The Job Effectiveness Prediction System is a selection system for entry-level employees in clerical positions (e.g., administrative assistant, customer service representative, etc.) and technical/professional positions (e.g., underwriter, annuity analyst, etc.). It includes tests such as coding and converting, comparing and checking, filing, language usage, mathematical skill, numerical ability, reading comprehension, spelling, and verbal comprehension.
- The Office of Personnel Management (OPM) is the Federal government's human resource agency that works to build a high quality and diverse Federal workforce. The agency provides tests designed to evaluate candidates' job-related competencies for employee selection, promotion, and development. Occupational areas for which tests are currently available include: Administrative Support/Clerical, Aide/Technician, Air Traffic Control, Apprenticeships, Benefits Review, Tax & Legal, Computer Operations, Finance & Management, Food Inspection, Health, Safety & Environment, Law Enforcement, and Writing & Public Information.
- The Wesman Personnel Classification Test assesses general verbal and numerical abilities and is used for selection of employees for clerical, sales, supervisory, and managerial positions.
- The Wonderlic Personnel Test measures general verbal, spatial, and numerical reasoning and is used for selection and placement purposes. It measures a candidate's ability to learn a specific job, solve problems, understand instructions, apply knowledge to new situations, benefit from specific job training, and be satisfied with a particular job. It can be administered using paper/pencil, computer or Internet.

Since the start of the Internet, companies delivering employment assessment products online have come into being. These companies offer a complete range of online employment testing for pre-screening, skill assessment, employee evaluations and career assessments. The companies include Brainbench, CraftSystems, Ergometrics, Assessments.Biz, SkillCheck, and more.

CASE OF NORMA

Norma is a 32-year-old single parent with a 10-year-old son and an 8-year-old daughter. She is a high school graduate and currently works as a clerk in a law office. She feels she is being discriminated against and passed over for promotions. She claims she needs more money to live on, and more time to spend with her children.

Norma was asked to take the Career Attitudes and Strategies Inventory (CASI). The session also included a series of self-report questions related to her career situation.

1. How would you describe Norma's CASI profile?

	T score
Job satisfaction	30
Work involvement	35
Skill development	25
Dominant style	30
Career worries	70
Interpersonal abuse	54
Family commitment	74
Risk-taking style	60
Geographic barriers	50

2. What other types of information would help the counselor in working with Norma?

Certification

Job applicants are often required to complete competency testing before they submit their applications. In addition, there are the statutory-based licensing examinations and certification programs. Shorthand reporters, automobile mechanics, respiratory therapists, and mental health counselors all take licensing or certification examinations.

Merely passing the test is not enough; the public is concerned about continued competence and has pressed for continuing education and recertification programs.

TEST USE IN GOVERNMENT

The federal government became involved in employment testing in 1883, when Congress created the U.S. Civil Service Commission. In 1979 the Office of Personnel Management (OPM) became involved in the testing process and established standards for job classification and competitive examinations for more than 1,000 types of jobs. The OPM has responsibility for two-thirds of the federal civilian workforce, and a large percentage of these workers are selected by one of the testing programs.

Other government agencies develop and administer their own tests. The U.S. Department of State, for example, uses its own tests to select foreign service officers. The U.S. Employment Service (USES) has developed tests for use in the local and state employment offices. The General Aptitude Test Battery (GATB) is widely used; it compares examinee scores with workers in more than 600 jobs. USES has also developed interest inventories and tests of proficiency in dictation, typing, and spelling.

State and local government agencies often require tests for selection purposes. Tests are frequently required of police officers and firefighters, as well as clerical workers. Local governmental agencies tend to use tests less than state agencies. However, both state and local agencies use oral and performance examinations more than federal agencies do (Friedman & Williams, 1982). Skilled workers tend to be given tests more than unskilled workers, and tests are not used as a sole criterion. Education, experience, character, and residence requirements are other important factors considered in hiring.

Occupational and Professional Licensing

States often mandate occupational and professional licensing for which some type of examination is required. This is true even in education in many states, with teachers and principals required to pass licensing examinations. States often establish a licensing board for a specific occupation. Occupations requiring licensing examinations include the following: architects, acupuncturists, audiologists, chiropractors, dentists, dental hygienists, engineers, funeral directors, landscape architects, land surveyors, occupational therapists, psychologists, speech pathologists, hearing aid counselors, optometrists, registered nurses, practical nurses, pharmacists, physical therapists, physicians, physician's assistants, podiatrists, and social workers.

TEST USE IN THE MILITARY SECTOR

The military sector makes extensive use of tests for selection and classification purposes. The Armed Services Vocational Aptitude Battery (ASVAB) was developed in 1976 by combining the validated subtests from the various test batteries used by each of the services. One form has been developed to be used in high schools as a guidance tool for counselors and as a recruiting tool. ASVAB helps identify the proper technical training or education needed for various types of occupational areas in the armed forces. In addition, there are specific tests that are used to select candidates for admission to the service academies, reserve officer training programs, officer candidate schools, and specialized programs such as flight training. The Cadet Evaluation Battery, the Air Force Officer Qualifying Test, the Flight Aptitude Selection Test, and the Defense Language Aptitude Test are examples.

PERSONNEL SELECTION AND CLASSIFICATION TECHNIQUES

A number of procedures and devices other than psychological tests are used in personnel selection and classification.

Biographical Data

Almost all employers require prospective employees to complete an application blank, a biographical information blank, or a life history. Employers believe that these forms provide information on what the candidate has done in the past and can be used to predict future behavior. Gatewood and Feild (1990) identify three assumptions for the use of biographical data. The best predictor of applicants future behavior is what they have done in the past. Applicants' life experiences provide an indirect measure of their motivational characteristics. Applicants are less defensive in describing their previous behaviors on the form than discussing their motivations for these behaviors. Research does indicate that biographical information has been a useful predictor of turnover and job success (Perloff, Craft, & Perloff, 1984). Biographical data also have been valuable in assessing individuals and classifying them into subgroups for purposes of better placement and utilization. Personnel directors sometimes divide large groups of current and former employees into categories of successful and unsuccessful workers and determine which items differentiate the two groups. Cook and Cook (1988) state that biodata instruments are less expensive than other custom-made tests, but are not as valid as cognitive tests.

Interviews

The selection interview is one of the basic tools of the personnel director. The purpose of the interview is to gain information about candidates' qualifications and experiences relevant to the available job. Perloff and colleagues (1984) conclude that limited evidence indicates the procedure is valid and reliable. More systematic, structured, job-related interviews tend to have higher validity. The situational interview, with specific questions based on job-related critical incidents, has also proven to be a valid assessment tool. Studies of the interview show that interviewers tend to make decisions about candidates early in the interview. Negative information tends to be weighed more heavily than positive information, and visual cues tend to be more important than verbal cues. In addition, ratings are affected by how many others are being rated at the same time; clients who share similarities with the interviewer—the same race, gender, and so on—tend to be more favorably rated. Often applicants are rated the same in evaluations, either superior (leniency error), average (central tendency error), or poor (stringency error). Sometimes one or two either good or bad characteristics of an applicant tend to influence the ratings of all the other characteristics (halo error). Sometimes the interviewer allows the quality of the applicants who preceded the present applicant to influence the ratings of the present applicant (contrast effect). Interviewers at times are overconfident in their ability to evaluate applicants; as a result, they make hasty decisions.

Interviewers need training and instruction in these skills (Gatewood & Feild, 1990, p. 481):

1. Creating an open-communication atmosphere
2. Delivering questions consistently
3. Maintaining control of the interview
4. Developing good speech behavior

5. Learning listening skills
6. Taking appropriate notes
7. Keeping the conversation flowing and avoiding leading or intimidating the interviewee
8. Interpreting, ignoring, or controlling the nonverbal cues of the interview

The selection interview can be valuable if the interviewers are trained in the process, panels are used whenever possible, job-related questions are used, and multiple questions are designed for the requirements of the job.

Assessment Center

The most widely used multiple assessment procedure in industry is the assessment center. Primarily, the center has been used to evaluate the potential of candidates for promotion to managerial positions. The center usually analyzes a candidate's performance on several standardized assessment exercises. These are usually selected and/or constructed from a thorough job analysis of the positions for which the assessment is to be made. Perloff et al. (1984) conclude that the overall evidence suggests that assessment center evaluations are valid and promising predictors for all groups, regardless of gender or minority status. Cook and Cook (1988) state that the assessment center is referred to as the "Rolls-Royce" of selection methods because it is expensive and uses a wide range of assessment methods and trained assessors. On the other hand, the range of assessors and assessment methods reduces bias and gives candidates a chance to show their strengths and weaknesses. Byham and Thornton (1986) indicate that the three most widely used techniques are the in-basket exercises, assigned leaderless group discussions, and interview simulations. They emphasize that the assessment center exercises mirror the majority of day-to-day activities of individuals performing the target jobs.

To evaluate and select the exercises, the observer needs to ask the following questions:

1. Is the exercise appropriate for the targeted job?
2. Does the exercise represent an important component of the job?
3. Have most of the important dimensions of the job been included in the exercises?
4. Are the exercises efficient and cost effective?
5. Are the exercises valid?
6. Do the exercises accomplish their purpose?

Thornton and Byham (1982) identify nine dimensions frequently measured in assessment centers: (1) the use of oral communication in individual or group situations; (2) planning and organizing strategies (setting goals, making proper assignments, and allocating resources); (3) delegating of responsibilities and use of subordinates effectively; (4) control (monitoring and regulating activities and responsibilities); (5) decisiveness (readiness in making decisions, rendering judgments, and taking action); (6) initiative (influencing events to achieve goals); (7) tolerance for stress; (8) adaptability (maintaining effectiveness with various tasks, responsibilities, or people); and

(9) tenacity. The administrator of an assessment center should keep in mind the following guidelines:

1. Assessment should be based on clearly defined dimensions of the position or behavior in question.
2. Multiple assessment techniques should be used.
3. A variety of job-sampling techniques should be used.
4. Familiarity with the job and the organization is needed; experience in the job or role is desirable.
5. Thorough training in assessment center procedures is necessary for all observers and raters.
6. All pertinent behavior should be observed, recorded, and communicated to other raters and observers.
7. Group discussion and decision-making procedures are used to integrate observations, rate dimensions, and make predictions.
8. Clients should be assessed against clearly understood external norms, not against each other.
9. Observers should guard against first impressions and other errors commonly made in rating and observation.

Job Analysis

One of the key elements in employee assessment is job analysis. Gatewood and Feild (1990) define job analysis as a purposeful, systematic process for collecting information on the important work-related aspects of a job (p. 251). Familiar terms such as knowledge, skills, ability, effort, responsibilities, and working conditions must all be put together so that they describe the quantity and quality of the work performed. Task analysis of the worker's functions is required, including the instruction and training that are part of the job. Variables will relate to both job content and job context. Effort, responsibility, and working conditions are contextual factors; knowledge, skill, and ability are job content factors. Both how-to aspects of the job and level of performance are important. A job analysis should follow these steps:

1. Read and review existing materials and data on the job to be analyzed.
2. Have supervisors and experienced workers in the field meet and discuss the job requirements, producing a list of tasks and roles that are performed.
3. Write the tasks and job characteristics on a flip chart so those involved in the position can react to what you have written.
4. List outputs, knowledge, skills, and abilities, including use of machines, tools, equipment, and work aids needed to get the job done. Get agreement on the tasks performed.
5. Have the workers determine the percentage of time spent on each task or skill.
6. Group common tasks together.
7. Have the workers tell how they know or recognize excellent, satisfactory, or poor performance of the tasks and the job.

What is your job title?
Where do you work?
Of what department or division are you a member?

Job Tasks
What do you do? How do you do it? Do you use special equipment?
What are the major tasks you perform on your job? What percentage of time do you spend on
    each task?

Knowledge Requirements
For each task you perform, what type of knowledge is necessary?
What types of formal and informal knowledge do you need to perform these tasks?
Do you need formal coursework, on-the-job training, etc.?
What level of knowledge is required?

Skill Requirements
What types of manual, mechanical, or intellectual skills are necessary to perform your job?
What types of tasks require these skills?

Ability Requirements
What types of communication skills, oral or written, are required for your job?
Do you have to prepare reports or complete records as part of your job?
What types of thinking, reasoning, or problem-solving skills are required?
What types of quantitative and mathematical abilities are required for your job?
What types of interpersonal abilities are required?
Are you responsible for supervision of other employees?
What types of physical abilities are required?

Physical Activities
What types of physical activities are required to perform your job?
How often are you engaged in physical activities?

Environmental Conditions
What types of environmental conditions do you encounter on your job?

Other
Describe a typical day.
Are there any other facets of your job that need to be described?

Figure 11.1
Schedule for a job analysis interview.

8. Construct an instrument to assess job performance and have supervisors and
   workers react to the tasks and performance standards identified.

An example of a job analysis interview is shown in Figure 11.1.

A number of task inventories are available to counselors. They contain three major sections: background information on the respondents, job tasks, and other miscellaneous information. The Position Analysis Questionnaire (PAQ) is one of the leading commercial measures available. It has six sections:

1. Information input—where and how the worker receives information about how to perform the job.
2. Mental processes—the cognitive skills necessary for job performance.
3. Work output—tools, equipment, and physical activities needed to perform the job.
4. Relationships with other persons—how other people are related to and interact with the job.
5. Job context—the physical and social environment in which the work is performed.
6. Other characteristics—characteristics and activities not covered by previous questions.

The respondent is asked to rate 194 items on the extent of use, amount of time, importance to the job, possibility of occurrence, and applicability to the job in question.

WorkKeys

WorkKeys is a system developed by American College Testing (ACT) that gives students and workers reliable, relevant information about their workplace skill levels. Combined with information about skill levels required for jobs, assessments information can help users make better career and educational decisions. WorkKeys assessments are available in paper-and-pencil and computer-based formats. Table 11.1 lists the available WorkKeys assessments.

Guidelines for Employee Selection

A number of guidelines should be followed by personnel workers who are developing an employee selection process:

1. Know the legal and ethical considerations thoroughly.
2. Know basic measurement concepts.
3. Know the steps in collecting evidence of criterion-referenced validity.
4. Be able to analyze the skills, competencies, and personal qualities that relate to successful performance on the job.
5. Consider practical factors, such as cost, number of employees involved, and time.
6. Locate tests that purport to measure the characteristics identified for the job.
7. Administer the tests to workers on the job as well as to new applicants.
8. Observe the workers tested and have supervisors report on the performance of these workers.
9. Analyze how the test scores and ratings relate to success on the job.
10. If evidence is favorable, formulate an operational plan to utilize the data for selection purposes. If evidence is not favorable, select other instruments and get additional ratings.
11. Systematically monitor and evaluate the system.

Cronbach (1984) advocates more persistent and analytical research, starting with the development of limited and measurable criteria. If the criteria are diverse and dependable, he concludes that it is far more instructive to find out what factors predict each of the criteria rather than combining the criteria into one index.

Table 11.1
WorkKeys Assessments

Reading Information	Measures the skill people use when they read and use written text in order to do a job. The written texts include memos, letters, directions, signs, notices, bulletins, policies, and regulations.
Applied Mathematics	Measures the skill people use when they apply mathematical reasoning, critical thinking, and problem-solving techniques to work-related problems.
Business Writing	Measures the skill individuals use when they write an original response to a work-related situation. Components of the Business Writing skill include sentence structure, mechanics, grammar, word usage, tone and word choice, organization and focus, and development of ideas.
Writing	Measures the skill individuals use when they write messages that relay workplace information between people.
Locating Information	Measures the skill people use when they work with workplace graphics.
Teamwork	Measures the skill people use for choosing behaviors that both lead toward the accomplishment of work tasks and support the relationships between team members.
Observation	Measures the skill people use when they pay attention to and remember work-related instructions, demonstrations, and procedures.
Listening	Measures the skill that people use when they receive verbal information in the workplace and relay it to another person.
Applied Technology	Focuses on reasoning and problem solving.
Readiness	Designed for those working with low literacy populations and others who may be uncertain about the appropriateness of using the operational WorkKeys assessments for their clientele or employees.

Using the MBTI in Organizations

The Myers-Briggs Type Indicator (MBTI) can be used in most business or industrial organizations as a tool to help individuals understand themselves and others and approach problems in different ways. The test can help organizations with career planning and development, improving teamwork, conflict resolution, and improving individual communication with supervisors, peers, and employers. There are 16 profiles possible on the MBTI. Consider the following example:

Individuals classified as ESTJ (Extroversion, Sensing, Thinking, Judgment) by the MBTI tend to be analytical, decisive, logical, and tough-minded and are adept at planning and organization. According to Hirsh and Kummerow (1990), such people contribute an ability to see flaws in advance, to critique problems logically, and to organize people, processes, and products.

ESTJs are take-charge leaders who are able to use past experiences to solve problems. They tend to make decisions quickly. They like to work in environments that are task oriented, organized, and structured and where meeting goals are rewarded. They like their associates to be hard-working people who

ences. The career and vocational counselor needs to have a comprehensive knowledge of the world of work as well as extensive knowledge of assessment techniques and counseling procedures.

There are 17 specific standards for testing in employment and credentialing detailed in the *Standards for Educational and Psychological Testing*. Employment testing has been a center of controversy. Laws and court decisions have had an impact on employment testing. Testing is more widely used in federal and state agencies than in business and industry. In addition, many skilled and professional workers must take certification or licensing examinations, such as certification as a school counselor or a mental health counselor, which then become the prerequisite for hiring. Tests in business and industry are primarily used for selection purposes, most often for clerical personnel. The decline in testing has led to a movement away from objective selection procedures. Analysis of research has indicated that testing does not discriminate against minority groups and women and saves the organization money. Nevertheless, currently there is more reliance on clinical judgment and consideration of the applicant's experience and education. Personnel psychologists need to be guided by the nine specific standards for the use of tests in employment contexts.

QUESTIONS FOR DISCUSSION

1. Do you believe that interest tests are not necessary, that the best way to find out about a person's interests is to ask, "What are you interested in, or what would you like to do or be?" Defend your position.

2. Interests tests have been criticized as having gender and cultural biases. What procedures can ensure that tests are developed and used properly by workers in the field?

3. The format and mode of presentation of career guidance tests are changing. Some tests are presented by videotape and on the computer screen. The test taker can see video pictures of individuals performing a job. Do you believe that these modes of test administration will prove to be more valid than the traditional pencil-and-paper approach? Which type of inventory would you prefer to take, and why?

4. What career guidance tests have you taken? What impact have these tests had on your career development? When did you take these tests? How were the results presented to you? Did you agree with the results? If you were displaced from a current job, would you seek testing to help you identify other possible jobs or career fields?

5. Batteries of tests often include aptitude, values, and interest tests rather than just interest tests alone. The computerized career guidance systems often include short tests of values and aptitudes rather than just asking individuals to rate their aptitudes and values. What factors do you think an individual needs to consider in making a career choice? Are there other areas you would include in the bat-

tery? What specific tests would you use? What types of nontest information would you find important? What type of assessment program would you use with high school students? With young adults with disabilities? With clients experiencing midcareer crises? With older adults?

6. Many employment test experts believe that the guidelines from the courts and government are outdated and make costly demands on employers that are not justified by the latest research. Do you agree or disagree with this position? Why?

7. If you were being considered for promotion on your job, what type of assessment procedures would you consider most valid: pencil-and-paper instruments, behavioral assessments, observation, or some other approach? Why?

8. How would you go about the task of setting up a licensing examination for workers in your field? What things would you do to ensure that you met all of the legal guidelines?

9. The use of tests by business and industry has decreased, yet we are hearing more about the need for accountability, worker efficiency, and competence to be competitive in the global marketplace. What do you predict the future of employment testing will be? What trends do you predict for the next 10 years?

SUGGESTED ACTIVITIES

1. Evaluate an instrument listed or discussed in this chapter and write a critical review of it. Be sure to read the evaluations of the test in the *Mental Measurement Yearbooks, Test Critiques*, and *A Counselor's Guide to Vocational Guidance Instruments*.

2. Administer several career guidance tests and write an interpretation. Tape or role-play the results for the client.

3. Write a position paper on one of the following topics: the role of assessment in career guidance, gender and cultural bias in interest measurement, computer-assisted career guidance testing, or the history of career guidance testing.

4. Develop a career guidance and testing program for one of the following: an elementary school, a middle school, a high school, an employment agency, a counseling and testing service, a mental health agency.

5. Design some nontest techniques to assess individual interests and values. Try out your assessment techniques on a sample of individuals and write a report of your findings.

6. Study the following hypothetical case and answer the questions that follow it.

Case of Mary

Mary is 35 years old and has gotten tired of working at the same job. She has experienced some job burnout and has decided to see what other types of careers she might be able to pursue. She agreed with the counselor that an interest inventory might be a good starting point for discussion. The counselor administered the COPSystem Interest

Inventory and the Career Ability Placement Survey (CAPS). Mary had the following profile on the COPSystem:

Cluster	Raw Score	Percentile
1. Science, Professional	26	91
2. Science, Skilled	11	50
3. Technology, Professional	9	45
4. Technology, Skilled	4	30
5. Consumer Economics	11	50
6. Outdoor	18	70
7. Business, Professional	26	85
8. Business, Skilled	14	55
9. Clerical	1	2
10. Communication	15	45
11. Arts, Professional	17	35
12. Arts, Skilled	21	48
13. Service, Professional	30	87
14. Service, Skilled	17	50

These are Mary's CAPS scores:

1. Mechanical Reasoning	13	83
2. Spatial Relations	15	92
3. Verbal Reasoning	24	98
4. Numerical Ability	18	92
5. Language Usage	22	83
6. Word Knowledge	41	68
7. Perceptual Speed and Accuracy	116	83
8. Manual Speed and Dexterity	230	32

   a. How would you describe Mary's pattern of interests?
   b. How would you describe Mary's pattern of aptitudes?
   c. What further information would you want to have about Mary?
   d. What further information would you want to have about the tests?
   e. The CAPS has a self-interpretive profile and guide. How would you use this with Mary?

7. Interview an individual who is working in the personnel field in business and industry. Find out what types of assessment procedures that person's company uses to hire workers and to promote workers. Report your findings to the class.

8. Conduct a task or job analysis of your current job Get the reactions of others— that is, your coworkers and your supervisors. See if they agree. Then design assessment instruments to rate individuals in your field. Identify standardized instruments and procedures that might already be available.

9. Design an assessment program to hire workers in your field, to identify professional development needs, and to identify those who should be promoted to managerial levels.

10. Write a critical review of the literature on one of the following topics: assessment centers, job analysis, legal aspects of employment testing, leaderless group discussion, internet-based employment testing.

11. Critically analyze one of the widely used tests listed in this chapter.

ADDITIONAL READINGS

Farr, J. M., & Ludden, L. (2000). *Enhanced occupational outlook handbook* (3rd ed.). Indianapolis, IN: Jist.

Based on data from the U.S. Department of Labor, the book gives complete descriptions of 253 jobs that are listed in the *Occupational Outlook Handbook,* including earnings, job growth, education and skills required, and information on employment trends in all major occupation and industry groups.

Gottfredson, G., and Holland, J. L. (1996). *Dictionary of Holland occupational codes* (3rd ed.). Odessa. FL: Psychological Assessment Resources.

Holland, J. L. (1985). *Making vocational choices: A theory of vocational personalities and work environments.* Odessa, FL: Psychological Assessment Resources.

Holland, J. L. (1986). New directions for interest testing. In B. S. Plake & J. C. Witt (Eds.), *The future of testing.* Hillsdale, NJ: Erlbaum.

Presents a discussion of the usefulness, validity, and reliability of interest testing. Identifies some of the current trends as well as the critical issues and opportunities in this area.

Journal of Vocational Behavior, 33(3). (1988, December).

This is a special issue on fairness in employment testing.

Kapes, J. T., & Whitfield, E. A. (2001). *A counselor's guide to vocational guidance instruments* (4th ed.). Falls Church, VA: National Vocational Guidance Association.

Provides critical reviews of the major interest inventories, measures of work values, career development inventories, and instruments for special populations.

Kline, P. L. (2000). *Handbook of psychological testing* (2nd ed.). New York: Routledge.

Contains chapters on interest and motivation tests, and psychological tests in occupational and industrial psychology.

Kummerow, J. M. (Ed.). (1991). *New directions on career planning in the workplace.* Palo Alto, CA: Consulting Psychologists Press.

Two chapters provide valuable information for the career counselor: one by Kummerow on using the Strong Interest Inventory and the Myers-Briggs Type Indicator together in career counseling, and one by Mirabile on competency profiling.

Pfieffer Library on Training and Development Resources. San Francisco: Jossey-Bass.

The Pfieffer Library is available in two formats: CD-ROM or a 28-volume looseleaf set. There are six volumes of inventories, questionnaires, and surveys that contain 80 instruments on topics such as individual development, communication, problem solving, groups and teams, consulting and facilitating, and leadership.

Power, P. W. (1991). *A guide to vocational assessment* (2nd ed.). Austin, TX: PRO-ED.

Reviews instruments, techniques, and issues related to vocational assessment of clients with disabilities, including use of work samples and computers, independent living with behavioral assessment approaches, and so on.

Watkins, C. E. & Campbell, V. L. (2000). *Testing and assessment in counseling practice* (2nd ed.). Mahwah, NJ: Erlbaum.

Tests such as the Strong Interest Inventory, the Kuder Occupational Interest Survey, the COPSystem, and the Self-Directed Search are discussed in detail.

12 Personality Testing

Personality includes all the special qualities people have that make them different from each other—charm, energy, disposition, attitude, temperament, cleverness—and the feelings and behaviors they exhibit. Personality assessment is important in describing and understanding behavior; it is also an area of controversy. Several personality theories are presented in this chapter, including psychodynamic, behavioral, humanistic, trait, type, and state theories. In addition, the text covers empirical approaches to personality assessment, such as the criterion group method and the factor-analytic method.

Personality tests are part of the affective domain and are thus not as valid and reliable as most of the aptitude and achievement tests that make up the cognitive domain. They give us a picture of the individual's typical performance. Personality tests are used in clinical settings to identify personal problems and diagnose psychopathologies as well as in counseling and guidance contexts. Just as values and interest tests are important tools in vocational guid-ance, adjustment and temperament inventories are important in personal counseling. Personality tests can help individuals gain insight into their own behavior, and they can be used to evaluate change after therapy, growth groups, and assertiveness training. Personality tests can help describe an individual systematically, diagnose a problem, give an indication of growth or change in behavior, and predict behavior. Such tests are extensively used in research studies.

Workers in the helping professions who plan to use personality tests need more training than is provided in this text. The goal here is to present an overview of the field and a conceptual framework for personality tests. Separate courses are available for individuals who want to develop proficiency in the use of projective and other clinical-level tests. The potential user needs to have experience under the supervision of an experienced examiner. Specialized inservice training is available for many tests and is valuable even for experienced examiners because of the many innovations in the field.

OBJECTIVES

After reading this chapter, you should be able to

✔ Understand the role and importance of theory in personality assessment

✔ Identify and discuss different personality theories

✔ Be familiar with the techniques of measuring personality

✔ Know the advantages and disadvantages of different formats in assessing personality

✔ Identify tests and instruments to assess specific dimensions of personality

✔ Locate and discuss sources of information related to personality assessment

✔ Be cognizant of the issues and problems in personality assessment

ROLE OF PERSONALITY THEORY

Counselors and helping professionals want to identify and measure human characteristics as a way to explain or predict behavior. As such, personality theorists have attempted to discover general principles or laws that explain personality. Some theorists have tried to identify specific types (or fixed categories) of personality; others focused on distinguishing various personality traits. Still others have relied on psychodynamic, humanistic, and behavioral theories to explain personality. The lack of consensus on how personality develops makes the assessment of personality a difficult task. There are many instruments used to assess personality. Most are constructed (1) according to a specific personality theory or (2) empirically by developing a test that identifies individuals of different personality.

The theoretical bases of personality are complex, and there is no single generally accepted theory of personality. However, it remains important for counselors and other professionals interested in psychological assessment to be familiar with the major theoretical approaches that provide a rationale for personality test construction. The personality theories presented in this section include psychodynamic, behavioral, and humanistic as well as trait, type, and state theories. In addition, empirical approaches to personality assessment are presented. Each section provides examples of personality tests that were developed based upon that theory, some of which will be more fully described in subsequent sections of the chapter.

Psychodynamic Approaches

Psychodynamic theorists including Freud, Jung, and Adler have described components of personality. For example, Freud views human personality as the interaction among the id, ego, and superego. Freud also believed that the key to understanding personality was to delve into the unconscious. He felt that most psychological functioning (the interactions of the id, ego, and superego) was in the unconscious realm. Although the unconscious cannot be studied directly, personality can be inferred from behavior (Corey, 2001).

Assessment of personality based upon psychodynamic theories involves some way of understanding a client's unconscious process. Projective techniques have been developed by psychoanalysts to explore the unconscious. A projective technique involves the examinee completing a relatively unstructured task; that is, a task that permits an almost unlimited variety of responses (Anastasi & Urbina, 1997). Through the use of these techniques, clients are thought to project or express their unconscious fears, conflicts, or needs, thereby gaining awareness into the unconscious. A variety of ambiguous stimuli have been used for assessment purposes, including inkblots, pictures, and incomplete sentences. Examinees usually respond in the form of stories, descriptions, completed sentences, or associations. Because an infinite number of possible responses exist for projective tests, scoring is subjective and no specific conclusion can be drawn from any single response. However, well-trained and experienced examiners can draw general impressions and inferences about an individual's personality from the tests. Examples of projective tests include the Rorschach Ink Blot Test, the Thematic Apperception Test (TAT), the House-Tree-Person Test, and the Rotter Incomplete Sentence Blank.

Behavioral Approaches

Traditional behaviorists explain consistency in behavior across time and situation as learned responses that are regulated from the environment. They focus on individuals' learning histories, such as how their behavior was reinforced and how their personality may have been affected by conditioning. They oppose the use of constructs to describe personality because constructs cannot be directly observed or measured. Behaviorism was greatly expanded once internal behaviors, particularly cognitions, were accepted as legitimate foci for study (Thorndike, 1997).

Albert Bandura's social learning theory significantly influenced the development of personality assessment instruments. Social learning theory focuses on the importance of observing and modeling the behaviors, attitudes, and emotional reactions of others as a way of explaining human behavior; psychological functioning is the reciprocal interaction of these reactions. People both influence and are influenced by the social environment, in which learning takes place by observation, imitation, and modeling. For example, people can acquire unusual fears or phobias from observing how others react with fear to specific situations. Unlike traditional behavior theorists, Bandura maintains that learning takes place without reinforcement; however, reinforcement becomes important in determining when learned behavior occurs (Aiken, 2000).

A common behavioral approach to assessment involves the notion that the constructs used to measure personality must be primarily inferred from behavior. Therefore, a common approach to measuring personality is through behavioral observation. Unlike administering a personality test to a client, behavioral observation involves the examiner (or other trained professional) observing the client to see what he or she "does" in a situation. This type of assessment does not focus on generally inferred personality characteristics; rather, the focus is on client behavior. Behaviors are often observed in their natural settings (such as a classroom) and recorded using a rating scale. Examples of rating scales include the Behavioral and Emotional Rating Scale–Revised, the Derogatis Psychiatric Rating Scale, the Gilliam Autism Rating Scale, and the Pupil Rating Scale-Revised.

Humanistic Approaches

Humanistic approaches emphasize the analysis of immediate, personal, and subjective experiences in the understanding of personality. Humanistic theorists are critical of trait theorists (who try to divide personality into a set of components) as well as psychodynamic and behavioral approaches to personality. Instead, humanists stress perceptions, meanings, feelings, and the self. They believe that people constantly create themselves and that the product of this self-creation is the self-concept, an integrated set of self-perceptions and evaluations that are the core of personality (Thorndike, 2001).

Rogers (1951) believed that the person best equipped to assess self-conceptions is the person himself or herself. As such, he was not a great believer of personality assessment instruments. However, a number of self-concept measures have been developed by other authors, including the Tennessee Self-Concept Scale, the Multidimensional Self-Esteem Inventory, the Piers-Harris Children's Self-Concept Scale, Second Edition, and Coopersmith's Self-Esteem Inventory. A renewed interest in self-concept measurement has occurred in recent years, particularly for children and adolescents. Self-concept scores have been shown to correlate with a wide variety of indicators of development and social adjustment. Thorndike (2001) states that "educators often advocate teaching children to view themselves more positively in the hope that better adjustment and higher achievement will follow" (p. 337).

Another instrument derived from humanistic theories is the Personal Orientation Inventory (POI; Shostrom, 1963). The POI is based on Maslow's theory of self-actualization, the view that individuals strive to become all that they can be to actualize their potential. It is a 150-item, forced-choice, self-actualization inventory and includes the following scales: time ratio, support ratio, self-actualization value, existentiality, feeling reactivity, spontaneity, self-regard, self-acceptance, synergy, acceptance of aggression, and capacity for intimate contact.

Trait, Type, and State Theories

Traits were originally studied in an effort to arrive at a comprehensive description of personality. However, just as there is no consensus on the definition of personality, there is no consensus regarding the definition of trait. Traits have been defined as (1) physical entities that are mental structures in personality, (2) a system that initiates and guides behavior, and (3) a relatively enduring way in which one individual varies from another (Allport, 1937; Cattell, 1950; Guilford, 1959). In general, traits are viewed as the characteristics possessed by an individual.

Discussion

The Minnesota Multiphasic Personality Inventory (MMPI-2) was administered during a 90-minute session. No items were omitted. Inspection of David's scores on the validity scales suggest a valid clinical profile of honest responses and an accurate self-presentation. Elevations of individual scales of the MMPI-2 suggest that David experiences moderate levels of psychological distress. The two highest scale scores are Hysteria ($T = 76$) and Social Introversion ($T = 72$). The score on the Hysteria scale indicates specific somatic complaints as well as discomfort in social situations; his somatic complaints are typically anxiety-related. In addition, his score on the Social Introversion scale indicates that his lack of confidence and insecurity are manifest by high levels of anxiety in social situations. He is excessively sensitive and overly responsive to others' opinions and often interprets feedback as self-criticism. As a result, David remains socially introverted and tends to avoid interaction.

California Psychological Inventory. In contrast to the MMPI, which is used primarily with special populations, the California Psychological Inventory (CPI; Gough & Bradley, 1996) assesses typical personality dimensions concerning an examinee's normal behavior patterns, feelings, opinions, and attitudes related to social, ethical, and family matters. The CPI focuses on diagnosing and understanding interpersonal behavior within the general population. It is a pencil-and-paper personality inventory for individuals ages 12 through 70 who have a fifth-grade or higher reading level. The test is easily administered and can be completed in approximately 1 hour.

The CPI's 434 true-false items and 20 folk scales were normed on standardization samples of 6,000 men and 7,000 women of varying age and socioeconomic status. Samples came from high school and college students, teachers, business executives, prison executives, psychiatric patients, and prison inmates. Because the MMPI was used as a basis for its development (over one-third of the CPI items), the CPI is sometimes termed "the sane person's MMPI" (Hood & Johnson, 2002, p. 247). The 20 scales (divided into four clusters) provide scores for 20 common personality traits. The four clusters of scales are presented in Table 12.3.

Standard scores (T scores) have a mean of 50 and a standard deviation of 10. High scores (T scores of 60 or more) indicate psychological health. Lower scores (T scores of 40 or below) indicate psychological inadequacy or distress (except for the femininity-masculinity scale).

Three of the scales, well-being, communality, and good impression, are used to detect "faking bad" or "faking good." A T score of 35 or less on these scales indicates faking bad. If this type of score is obtained, the counselor should ask why the client feels a need to create an impression of serious problems. A T score of 65 on the good impression scale suggests faking good.

Because a number of the 20 scales on the CPI show considerable overlap, three vector scales were developed to facilitate understanding and interpretation of the 20-scale profile. Vector 1 (internality vs. externality) measures interpersonal presentation of self through the capacity for status, dominance, self-acceptance, sociability, and social presence scales. Vector 2 (norm favoring vs. norm questioning) involves interper-

Table 12.3
Scales of the California Personality Inventory.

Scale Clusters	Scales	Descriptors
I. Measures of poise, self-assurance, and interpersonal proclivities	Dominance	Conflict vs cautious
	Capacity for status	Ambitious vs unsure
	Sociability	Outgoing vs shy
	Social presence	Self-assured vs reserved
	Self-acceptance	Positive self vs self-doubting
	Independence	Self-sufficient vs seeks support
	Empathy	Empathetic vs unempathetic
II. Normative orientation and values	Responsibility	Responsible vs careless
	Socialization	Conforms vs rebellious
	Self-control	Over-control vs under-control
	Good impression	Pleases others vs complains about others
	Communality	Fits in vs sees self different
	Well-being	Optimistic vs pessimistic
	Tolerance	Fair minded vs fault finding
III. Cognitive and intellectual functioning	Adjustment via conformity	Efficient and well organized vs distracted
	Achievement via independence	Clear thinking vs uninterested
	Intellectual efficiency	Keeps on task vs hard time getting started
IV. Measure of role and personal style	Psychological-mindedness	Insightful and perceptive vs apathetic and unmotivated
	Flexibility	Likes change vs not changeable
	Femininity/Masculinity	Sensitive vs unsentimental

sonal values assessed by the responsibility, socialization, and self-control scales. Vector 3 (self-realization vs. self-actualization) is assessed by combining scores on achievement via conformance, achievement via independence, intellectual efficacy, well-being, and tolerance scales.

In addition to the 20 folk scales, there are 13 special-purpose or research scales: management potential, work orientation, creative temperament, Baucom's unipolar masculinity scale, Baucom's unipolar femininity scale, Leventhal's anxiety scale, Dicken's scale for social desirability, Dicken's scale for acquiescence, leadership amicability, law enforcement orientation, tough-mindedness, and narcissism (Gough, 1999, 2000).

Except for the MMPI, the CPI is the most thoroughly researched inventory of personality. Test-retest reliability coefficients for all scales except for psychological-mindedness and communality range from .57 to .77. It is one of the most frequently used personality inventories and has been employed in many contexts and research studies. The CPI is rated as one of the best personality inventories currently available.

Millon Clinical Multiaxial Inventory. Theodore Millon developed several instruments including the Millon Clinical Multiaxial Inventory (MCMI-III), which is used to assess personality disorders and clinical syndromes. The inventory has 14 Personality Pattern Scales (categorized by clinical and severe), 10 Clinical Syndrome Scales (categorized by clinical and severe), three Modifying Indices, and one Validity Index:

Clinical Personality Pattern Scales (DSM-IV-TR, Axis II):

1 — Schizoid	6B — Sadistic (Aggressive)
2A — Avoidant	7 — Compulsive
2B — Depressive	8A — Negativistic (Passive-
3 — Dependent	Aggressive)
4 — Histrionic	8B — Masochistic
5 — Narcissistic	(Self-Defeating)
6A — Antisocial	

Severe Personality Pathology Scales:

S — Schizotypal
C — Borderline
P — Paranoid

Clinical Syndrome Scales (DSM-IV-TR, Axis I):

A — Anxiety	B — Alcohol Dependence
H — Somatoform	T — Drug Dependence
N — Bipolar: Manic	R — Post-Traumatic Stress
D — Dysthymia	Disorder

Severe Syndrome Scales:

SS — Thought Disorder
CC — Major Depression
PP — Delusional Disorder

Modifying Indices:

X — Disclosure
Y — Desirability
Z — Debasement

Validity Index:
V — Validity

The MCMI-III has two validity indicators. The W (Weight) factor is a scale that suppresses the distorting effects of either psychological defensiveness and self-enhancement or emotional complaining and self-depreciation. The V (Validity) index is a scale that detects those who fail to cooperate, are unable to comprehend the items, or are too disturbed to answer the items relevantly.

Two computerized interpretations are available from the National Computer Systems and MICROTEST assessment software. The first is a clinical interpretative report that includes the profile of the client and a detailed narrative explaining the psychodynamic relationship between the client's personality patterns of behaving and feeling and the clinical symptoms he or she may be exhibiting (Million & Davis, 1996).

The second is the correctional interpretive report that distinguishes the enduring personality characteristics from the more acute maladaptive symptoms. The report focuses on difficulties the client may have in adjusting to imprisonment, his or her trustworthiness, problems with authority, and general antisocial behavioral tendencies. The report provides implications for management and rehabilitation strategies.

The Millon Behavioral Health Inventory (MBHI) is intended to help mental health workers design a comprehensive treatment plan for adult medical patients. The MBHI provides information on the client's basic coping styles, problematic psychosocial attitudes and stressors, and information on attitudes toward treatment intervention. The 20 scales on the MBHI are classified into four areas: basic coping skills, psychogenic attitudes, psychosomatic correlates, and prognostic indexes. The scales under basic coping styles relate to the way the individual reacts to health care personnel, services, and medical regimens. The scales are titled *introversive, cooperative, confident, respectful, inhibited, sociable, forceful,* and *sensitive.* The six scales under psychogenic attitudes assess problematic psychosocial attitudes and stressors; they are titled *chronic tension, premorbid pessimism, social alienation, recent stress, future despair,* and *somatic anxiety.* The three scales under psychosomatic correlates show the similarities of clients to patients with psychosomatic complications; the scales are titled *allergic inclination, cardiovascular tendency,* and *gastrointestinal susceptibility.* The three prognostic indexes identify possible treatment problems or difficulties: pain treatment responsivity, life threat reactivity, and emotional vulnerability. The total test consists of 150 true-false items and is written at the eighth-grade reading level.

The Millon Adolescent Personality Inventory (MAPI) is geared to assess the specific concerns and behaviors of adolescents. The MAPI provides information on the social functioning of adolescents, including information on their relationships with family and peers, their self-esteem, impulse control, and social tolerance. The 22 scales are grouped under four categories: personality styles, expressed concern, behavioral correlates, and reliability and validity indexes. Here are some items similar to those asked on this test:

T   F   I like to be with people who go to church regularly.

T   F   I feel tense when I think of what I will be expected to do in school this year.

T   F   I worry about my drug habits getting out of control.

Two types of report forms are used—one for clinical use and the other for educational or guidance use.

FORMAT OF TESTS

A wide variety of item formats are used to assess personality dimensions. The MMPI and CPI use a true-false format; the Adjective Checklist presents a list of descriptive words to check; the Work Environment Preference Inventory uses a Likert-type attitude format. The Edwards Personal Preference Inventory has a forced-choice format: The examinee has a choice between two options on an item. On the Allport-Vernon-Lindzey Scale of Values the examinee ranks options in one part of the test.

DIMENSIONS OF PERSONALITY

Many different dimensions of personality exist. Some tests attempt to assess overall personality, whereas others focus on one dimension. Following is a representative sample of topics and tests.

Enneagram

The enneagram is a type system with nine dimensions. Riso (1990) postulates that this ancient system will help individuals unlock their hidden aspects so that they can become freer and better functioning individuals. They believe that the study of one's profile leads to self-understanding and then to the understanding of others. Three levels are present in each type: healthy, average, and unhealthy. A number of questionnaires and instruments have been developed. Riso (1994) has a paired comparison test, the Riso-Hudson Enneagram Type Indicator (see Table 12.4).

Self-Concept Scales

Self-concept has been a popular construct in theories of personality and vocational development. Some of the widely used self-concept measures are listed here:

- The Coopersmith Self-Esteem Inventory assesses attitudes toward self in social, academic, and personal contexts. Both short and longer versions present items (25 to 58) to be answered by choosing "like me" or "unlike me." Specific scales include general self, school-academic, home-parents, social self-peers, and lie. School and adult forms are available.
- The Culture-Free Self-Esteem Inventory, Third Edition (CFSEI-3) is a set of self-report inventories used to determine the level of self-esteem in students ages 6 through 18. It includes three age-appropriate forms: Primary, Intermediate, and Adolescent. All three forms of the inventory provide a Global Self-Esteem Quotient (GSEQ). The Intermediate and Adolescent Forms provide self-esteem

Table 12.4

Types included on the Riso-Hudson Enneagram Type Indicator.

Type	Healthy	Unhealthy
1. Reformer	Idealistic, orderly	Perfectionistic, intolerant
2. Helper	Concerned, helpful	Possessive, manipulative
3. Achiever	Self-assured, ambitious	Narcissistic, psychopathic
4. Individualistic	Creative, individualistic	Introverted, depressive
5. Investigator	Perceptive, analytical	Eccentric, paranoid
6. Loyalist	Likable, dependable	Masochistic, plagued by doubt
7. Enthusiast	Accomplished, extroverted	Excessive, manic
8. Challenger	Powerful, self-confident	Dictatorial, destructive
9. Peacemaker	Peaceful, reassuring	Passive, repressed

scores in 4 areas: Academic, General, Parental/Home, and Social. The Adolescent Form provides an additional self-esteem score: Personal Self-Esteem.

- The Inferred Self-Concept Scale is a 30-item scale in which parents, teachers, or counselors rate dimensions of behavior indicative of an individual's self-concept. This scale can be used with nonverbal or non-English speaking children because no language is required of the child.

- The Multidimensional Self-Esteem Inventory (MSEI) is a 116-item scale measuring components and levels of self-esteem. The highest level is assessed on the inventory by a global self-esteem scale. There are eight component scales at the intermediate level: competence, lovability, likeability, personal power, self-control, moral self-approval, body appearance, and body functioning. There is an identity integration scale providing a measure of global self-concept and a defensive self-enhancement scale that serves as a measure of the individual's defensiveness.

- The Piers-Harris Children's Self-Concept Scale, Second Edition (Piers-Harris 2) assesses self-concept in individuals ages 7 to 18. It has 60 items covering six subscales: Physical Appearance and Attributes, Intellectual and School Status, Happiness and Satisfaction, Freedom from Anxiety, Behavioral Adjustment and Popularity. Test items are simple descriptive statements, written at a second-grade reading level. Children indicate whether each item applies to them by selecting a yes or no response. The test takes 10 to 15 minutes to complete. A Spanish version is available. The Pier-Harris 2 is used in both schools and clinics.

- The Self-Concept and Motivation Inventory (SCAMIN) assesses self-concept in an academic setting, measuring achievement needs, achievement investment, role expectation, and self-adequacy. The four levels are preschool-kindergarten, early elementary (grades 1 through 3), later elementary (grades 3 through 6), and secondary (grades 7 through 12).

- The Tennessee Self-Concept Scale, Second Edition (TSCS:2) measures self-concept in individuals ages 7 to 90 years and is available in Adult and Child Forms. Each form can be group or individually administered in 10 to 20 minutes. The Adult Form, written at a third-grade reading level, is designed for individuals 13 years of age and older. The Child Form, written at a second-grade level, can be used with 7- through 14-year-olds. The TSCS:2 can be hand scored, computer scored, or scored through a mail-in fax service.

Many studies have related self-concept to achievement, minority group membership, and locus of control. Self-concept is believed to be a useful personality construct, although its measurement seems to have continued problems because of the lack of validity and reliability of many of the instruments.

PROBLEMS IN PERSONALITY ASSESSMENT

A number of problems can affect the validity of personality assessment. Many responses to assessment procedures are influenced by variables other than the personality characteristics of the test takers. Psychological, sociological, linguistic, and other variables influence how the examinees respond.

One source of error in personality testing involves systematic biases called *response sets* or *response styles*. Response style is the tendency of the examinee to approach a test in a manner that distorts the test results. One response style is referred to as acquiescence. Acquiescent response style is the tendency of the test taker to accept or agree with statements regardless of the item content. Test constructors can help examinees avoid this response style by making sure the number of items with "yes" or "true" responses equal the number of items with "no" or "false" responses.

The *social desirability* response style is the tendency of the test taker to choose the response that he or she believes to be socially desirable rather than the response that more accurately reflects the individual's behavior or feelings. Sometimes a test taker deliberately and consciously chooses the socially desirable response; the individual may be faking goodness because he or she is defensive about his or her behavior. Sometimes the choice is unconsciously expressed. Extreme degrees of social desirability help to distort results and affect the validity of the interpretation. Some tests such as the Edwards Personal Preference Inventory have attempted to control the social desirability of the items by using forced-choice item matching on the basis of social desirability. Forced-choice item matching requires the respondent to choose between two descriptive terms or phrases that appear equally acceptable but differ in validity (Anastasi & Urbina, 1997). In other words, these paired phrases may be both desirable or undesirable. In addition, some personality tests such as the MMPI have scales that can be used to identify the test taker as a good or bad "faker."

Other response styles include *nonacquiescence* (disagreeing with whatever item is presented), *deviance* (making unusual or uncommon responses), *extreme* (choosing extreme, rather than middle, ratings on a rating scale), and *gambling/cautiousness* (guessing, or not guessing, when in doubt) (Cohen & Swerdlik, 1999, p. 389).

Kline (1993) mentions another potential problem, the influence of ability and attainment on test scores. These variables can be a major source of distortion. He points out that "personality questionnaires are, inevitably, somewhat superficial, are usually transparent and thus easy to fake, and ultimately seem too crude to encapsulate the subtlety and richness of personality" (p. 242).

Another problem in personality assessment involves cultural differences among test takers. This issue specifically concerns whether an instrument, standardized on a representative sample of Americans, "penalizes testtakers from other cultures with higher scores on measures of psychopathology" (Cohen & Swerdlik, 1999, p. 432). A number of studies on the MMPI, for example, have yielded findings in which minority group members tend to present with more psychopathology than majority group members (Montgomery & Orozco, 1985; Whitworth & Unterbrink, 1994). The issue of cultural sensitivity in personality assessment brings up questions regarding an instrument's generalizability and appropriateness.

SUMMARY

Many ways of assessing personality have been described, and different dimensions have been identified. It is important to know what method is best to obtain the desired client information. Personality tests have lower validity and reliability coefficients than achievement and ability tests and produce larger standard errors of measurement. Promising tests and techniques exist, but many procedures and instruments require specialized training and supervision for proper administration, scoring, and interpretation.

QUESTIONS FOR DISCUSSION

1. How important is personality theory in personality assessment? Do tests and assessment techniques have an adequate theoretical foundation?

2. Identify and discuss two personality theories or approaches presented in this chapter.

3. What are the many different ways of measuring personality? Compare the advantages of each approach.

4. Faking is one of the major problems on personality tests. How would you structure a testing situation to minimize faking? Do you believe that everybody fakes on personality inventories? Explain your answer.

5. A wide variety of item content measures dimensions of personality, from food choices to occupations to musical preferences. How important do you think the content of the items is in assessing personality? Another factor is the format of the items. What are the advantages and disadvantages of the different formats? For what groups would each format work best?

6. Do you believe that pencil-and-paper personality inventories give a valid picture of an individual's personality? Would situational tests or observation in naturalistic, everyday settings provide more valid information?

SUGGESTED ACTIVITIES

1. Operationally define a personality construct and devise several strategies to measure the construct. Develop some preliminary instruments and give them to a sample of individuals. What was the reaction of the test takers to the form of the test? Analyze the forms. Which form or type of test was most valid? Most reliable?

2. Identify a personality test of interest to you. Critically analyze the test. Read the reviews of the test in the *Mental Measurement Yearbooks* and *Test Critiques*.

3. Interview workers in the helping professions who use tests and find out which personality tests they use and why. Report your findings to the class.

4. Review the research on one of the current issues in personality testing and write a critical analysis of your findings.

5. Make an annotated bibliography of personality tests, specific test types, or test areas appropriate for your current or future field.

6. In this enneagram exercise, read the adjectives listed in the box and rank them within each group using the following scale. No ties are allowed (each rank must only be used once for each group).

1 = Least like you
9 = Most like you

Group 1	Group 2	Group 3	Group 4
Principled	Orderly	Perfectionistic	Idealistic
Caring	Generous	Possessive	Nurturing
Adaptable	Ambitious	Image-conscious	Pragmatic
Intuitive	Individualistic	Self-absorbed	Withdrawn
Perceptive	Original	Provocative	Cerebral
Engaging	Responsible	Defensive	Security-oriented
Enthusiastic	Accomplished	Excessive	Busy
Self-confident	Optimistic	Assertive	Decisive
Easy-going	Stable	Accepting	Trusting

Reading across each row, add the total points for the 4 scores. Look at your high scores and low scores. Then turn back to Table 12.4 showing enneagram types and look at the description of the nine types. Row 1 gives a score for type 1, row 2 for type 2, and so on.

7. Read the following case and answer the questions at the end.

Case of Salinda

Name: Salinda

Age: 18

Race: African American

Highest grade completed: Grade 10

Family: Mother is a single parent who works as a practical nurse in a local hospital

Salinda's dependents: 2 children, ages 17 months and 3 months

Career goal: Telemarketing

Personality Profile

Measures of Psychosocial Development

	T Score		T Score
Trust	24	Mistrust	55
Autonomy	41	Shame and Doubt	38
Initiative	28	Guilt	64
Industry	42	Inferiority	65
Identity	59	Identity Confusion	69
Intimacy	36	Isolation	62
Generativity	24	Stagnation	61
Ego Integrity	55	Despair	65
Total Positive	38	Total Negative	60

Values Scale

Inner Oriented	*T Score*
1. Ability Utilization	23
2. Achievement	31
3. Aesthetics	42
4. Personal Development	37
5. Altruism	40

Physical Prowess

1. Physical Prowess	57
2. Risk	56
3. Authority	46

Group Oriented

1. Social Interaction	36
2. Cultural Identity	45
3. Social Relations	50
4. Working Conditions	43
5. Variety	31

Physical Activity

1. Physical Activity	49
2. Variety	31

Material

1. Advancement	31
2. Economic Rewards	26
3. Economic Security	35
4. Prestige	33
5. Autonomy	49
6. Lifestyle	31

Checked that she was dissatisfied with her status as a student, occupation, leisure, and community.

On the Adult Career Concerns Inventory she was high on the exploration and implementation stages.

On the Myers-Briggs Type Indicator: ESFP.

Self-Directed Search: SEC

Self-Concept

Self-Esteem Inventory

			Raw Score	*Percentile*	*Standard Score*
1.	(32)	Total	27	63	56
2.	(16)	General	15	78	59
3.	(8)	Social	7	51	53
4.	(8)	Personal	5	50	51

a. How would you describe Salinda's personality?

b. What additional tests would you like to have Salinda take?

c. What other types of information would you like to have to enhance your interpretation of the results?

d. How would you present the test results to Salinda? What would you tell her?

e. Would it make a difference in your interpretation if Salinda were Native American, Asian, Hispanic, or White?

f. Would your interpretation be different if Salinda were seeking career counseling? Personal counseling?

ADDITIONAL READINGS

American Psychiatric Association. (2000). *Diagnostic and statistical manual of mental disorders* (4th ed. Text Revision). Washington, DC: Author.
Provides the description of criteria and codes for psychiatric diagnostic classification.

Bellak, L., & Abrams, D. M. (1997). *The TAT, CAT, and SHT in clinical use* (6th ed.). Boston: Allyn & Bacon.
Provides a history and foundations for projective testing and guides examiners in the use of the Bellak Scoring System for the apperception tests.

Bracken, B. A. (Ed.). (1996). *Handbook of self-concept.* New York: Wiley.
A chapter by Keith and Bracken contains a historical and evaluative review of self-concept instrumentation.

Butcher, J. N. (1990). *MMPI-2 in psychological treatment.* New York: Oxford.
Discusses the use of the MMPI in psychological treatment selection and planning.

Byrne, B. M. (1996). Measuring self-concept across the life span. Issues and instrumentation. Washington, DC: APA.
Discusses multiple models and instruments used to measure self-concept over the life span.

Graham, J. R. (2000). *MMPI-2: Assessing personality in psychopathology* (3rd ed.). New York: Oxford University Press.
The book is a guide to the revised MMPI-2 and discusses the new validity and content scales.

Gross, M. (1962). *The brain watchers.* New York: Random House.
The author tells of some of the misuses of personality testing and even discusses how to cheat on personality tests.

Groth-Marnat, G. (2003). *Handbook of psychological assessment* (4th ed.). New York: John Wiley & Sons.
Contains chapters on the interpretation of projective drawings, the Thematic Apperception Test, the Rorschach, the MMPI, and the California Psychological Inventory. Presents information on the history and development of the tests, their reliability and validity, their assets and limitations, interpretation procedures, and a bibliography of references and resources on each test.

Handler, L., & Hilsenroth, M. J. (Eds). (1998). *Teaching and learning personality assessment.* Mahwah, NJ: Erlbaum.

Covers conceptual models for assessment of different tests and teaching and learning specialized issues in assessment.

Kline, P. (1993). *Handbook of psychological testing.* New York: Routledge.

Reviews psychometric theory and methods and discusses the major types of tests. Presents information on the uses of tests and provides a description and evaluation of some of the major instruments.

Newmark, C. S. (Ed.). (1996). *Major psychological assessment instruments* (2nd ed.). Boston: Allyn & Bacon.

Contains chapters on the MMPI, the Rorschach, the Thematic Apperception Test, the House-Person-Tree Test, the Draw-a-Person Test, and the Bender Gestalt Test along with chapters on the Kaufmann and the Wechsler scales. This is an excellent source on current research, use, and interpretation of these tests.

Rabin, A. I. (Ed.). (1986). *Projective techniques for adolescents and children.* New York: Springer.

Contains chapters on the major projective personality tests used with children, such as the Thematic Apperception Test, the Michigan Picture Test-Revised, the Separation Anxiety Test, the Rorschach, the Hand Test, and the Story and Sentence Completion Tests.

Reilley, R. R., & Reilley, B. A. (1991). *MMPI-2 tutorial workbook.* Austin, TX: PRO-ED.

Contains information on the revised test and is designed for professionals who desire a refresher in the appropriate use of the test. Topics such as computer assessment, report writing, psychometric scaling, and source of information on the MMPI-2 are presented.

Schinka, J. A., & Green, R. L. (Eds.). (1997). *Emerging issues and methods in personality assessment.* Mahwah, NJ: Erlbaum.

The book has three parts: (1) Personality Assessment Instruments: Current Status and Future Research Directions, (2) Continuing Issues in Personality Assessment, and (3) Advances in Statistical Methods for Personality Assessment Research.

Wylie, R. (1990). *Self-concept instruments.* Lincoln: University of Nebraska Press.

13 Clinical Assessment

OVERVIEW

Clinical assessment involves the use of tests or other assessment procedures to gather information about an individual to aid in diagnosis, to predict future behavior, or to determine counseling interventions. For these purposes, tests are typically individualized and given one-to-one. The setting may be in a hospital, mental health clinic, prison, treatment facility, or counselor's office. A number of problems and issues relate to the use of tests for clinical assessment and counseling.

OBJECTIVES

After studying this chapter, you should be able to

✔ Describe the models of clinical assessment

✔ Explain types of tests and techniques that can be utilized effectively

✔ Understand the ethical standards, legal issues, and general standards that need to be followed

✔ Understand the issues and concerns about the use of tests in clinical assessment and counseling

CLINICAL ASSESSMENT

Clinical assessment is the process that counselors and psychologists use to gain information about a client. The examiner is often interested in diagnosing the problems of a client and may also want to describe the client's behavior, predict future behavior, or evaluate therapeutic interventions. Tests and assessment procedures are selected to provide information useful in decision making while taking into account the special background and characteristics of the client. The client may be a child, adolescent, or adult; a patient in a clinic or hospital; an inmate in a prison; or an outpatient in a clinic.

Types of Tests and Assessment Techniques

A wide variety of tests and assessment techniques are available. The choice of which to use is influenced partly by the theoretical orientation of the counselor and partly by the type of decision to be made. In most cases the counselor uses more than one technique, choosing among aptitude batteries, ability tests, personality tests, projective techniques, interview schedules, checklists, rating scales, behavioral observations, and tests for emotional functioning and level of psychopathology. There are several reasons for appraisal:

1. To determine which DSM-IV-TR classification is appropriate
2. To see whether neurological impairment exists
3. To help decide which type of treatment, counseling, or therapy would be most appropriate
4. To prescribe the proper instructional strategies
5. To identify the client's assets, achievement, aptitude, or personality to guide in rehabilitative, therapeutic, or educational planning
6. To determine whether an inmate should be considered for a release program
7. To evaluate the effectiveness of treatment, counseling interventions, and group sessions

Models of Clinical Assessment

One popular model of clinical assessment is the psychodiagnostic model influenced by the theories of Murray and Rapaport. The model is holistic and is intended to describe the client in a variety of ways. The model calls for the use of a number of procedures, the measurement of various areas of psychological functioning, assessment of conscious as well as unconscious levels, use of projective techniques as well as objective personality instruments, interpretation based on scorable responses and symbolic signs, and a description more personal and individualistic than normative (Holt, 1968). The counselor or psychologist is the key individual in this process and has to organize and conceptualize the questions to be asked and decide on techniques. Clinical judgment is crucial.

A second model is psychometric and emphasizes more objective use of tests and assessment instruments. Tests must be reliable and valid for the purposes identified;

the test findings must rely on the criterion validity of the tests rather than the clinical judgment of the examiner. The psychodiagnostic and psychometric positions have been in contention for several decades and are part of the controversy between clinical and statistical prediction (Meehl, 1954).

Rogers (1942) believed that assessment results were not that valuable. He argued against formal assessment, believing that no discovery about a client makes any difference in psychotherapy until the information becomes evident to the client in the course of the therapeutic encounter. Individuals holding to the humanistic approach do not use tests routinely or as a precondition to therapy. If used, the testing process includes the client as a coassessor, rather than an object being studied by a detached examiner. Behavioral psychologists and counselors look for objective behavioral indicators, not tests, to measure traits, drives, motives, and unconscious wishes.

TESTS IN COUNSELING

Many counselors use tests as a tool in working with their clients. Research has shown that standardized tests can be a valuable part of the counseling process.

Counselors tend to use tests to help their clients learn more about their own

1. Occupational or work values
2. Career goals and vocational interests
3. Career development
4. Occupational knowledge and preferences
5. Educational interests
6. Achievement, aptitude, and abilities
7. Problem-solving and coping skills
8. Study skills

Example of the House-Tree-Person Test used in clinical assessment.

9. Relationships with others
10. Attitudes and motives
11. Developmental needs
12. Attitudes toward family, spouse, marriage, and significant others

Counselors use all of the different types of tests and techniques listed in Chapters 8 through 13. They use both formal and informal methods—pencil-and-paper inventories, projective techniques, checklists, situational tests, interviews, simulations, inventories, and work samples. For tests to be an effective tool in counseling, counselors need to be skilled in helping their clients understand and interpret the results. Counselors need to be able to facilitate the appropriate use of the data in decision making. Counselors use tests in all types of settings such as agencies, government, industry, private practice, and schools. Test use is influenced by the setting as well as the background of the counselor and the test taker.

The counselor should also caution the client not to rely solely on the test results but to consider other test scores, observations, and other relevant information on personal and social skills, values, interests, accomplishments, and experiences. The counselor should encourage multiple valid assessments of the client's abilities, interests, and personality. The counselor should look at school or work performance, participation in extracurricular activities, and hobbies. The counselor should also be sure that interpretive materials and illustrations are made relevant to the client.

ASSESSMENT APPROACHES

Interviews

The interview has become an important tool in clinical assessment. The purposes of the initial interview are to (a) determine the suitability of the client for counseling, (b) assess and respond to a client's crises, (c) familiarize the client with the counseling process, and (d) gather sufficient client information to formulate a diagnosis and treatment plan (Seligman, 1996). In addition to the verbal content of the interview, a clinician is often interested in a client's nonverbal behavior or cognitive style. Currently, more attention is being placed on the cognitive areas for knowing and understanding a client.

Structured Interviews.   *Structured interviews* call for the interviewer to ask each interviewee exactly the same questions in the same manner. A specific set of questions is usually read to the client. The advantages of the structured interview are that it ensures that specific information will be collected from all clients, and it does not require as much training because all interviewers have a list of questions in a prescribed order. A sample structured interview schedule, appropriate for use in an alcoholic treatment facility, is shown in Figure 13.1.

```
Name _____  Date _____

Address_____  Home phone _____

_____  Business phone _____

City _____  State _____  Zip _____

Race _____  Sex _____  Height _____  Weight _____  Age _____

Date of birth _____  Place of birth _____

Next of kin _____  Relationship _____

Address _____

Current employment _____  Duration _____  Salary _____

Spouse's employment _____

Other sources of income _____

Referred by _____

Health insurance _____

Current marital status _____  Number of marriages and duration _____

_____

Children (sex and ages) _____

Type of residence_____

Number in household _____  Head of household_____

Church membership _____  Attendance_____

Belief in higher power_____

_____

Current health problems _____

Physical handicaps _____

Serious illness/surgery_____

_____

Current medications_____

Schools attended _____

Years _____  Certificates/diplomas/degrees _____

_____

Vocational and technical training _____

Military service: _____

Army _____  Navy _____  Air Force _____  Marines _____  Coast Guard _____

Length of service_____  Rank _____  Type of discharge _____

VA history_____

Employment history:

Job description                  Dates                        Reasons for leaving

_____

Family history:

Brothers _____Sisters _____Birth order _____

Type of family structure _____

Father's occupation_____  Mother's occupation _____

Description of mother_____

Description of father_____

Description of home life _____

_____

History of drug abuse in family_____
```

Figure 13.1

Outline of a structured psychosocial interview.

Family's attitude toward substance abuse _____
_____
Current relationships with parents _____
Current relationships with siblings _____
Current relationship with spouse _____
Current relationships with children _____
Criminal justice record:
Number of arrests _____
Types _____
Number of convictions _____
Number and duration of times in jail_____
Number and duration of times in prison _____
Number of times on probation or parole _____
Cases/warrants pending _____
Current probation officer _____
Current legal status _____
Alcohol and substance abuse information:
Number of times in detoxification centers _____ Mental hospitals and/or state
hospitals _____ Jail (for substance-abuse-related offenses) _____
Hospital (for medical attention) _____ Shelters (such as Salvation Army) _____
Dates of DWI convictions _____
History of drug use:
Age of first use_____ Substances tried_____
First contact _____ First drinking experience_____
First intoxication _____ First blackout _____ Convulsions _____
Morning tremors_____ Hallucinations _____ DTs _____ Fights _____
Personality change_____
Substances regularly used_____
_____ Choice _____
Frequency of use _____
Attempts to stop substance abuse_____
_____
Support groups attended _____
Pattern of substance abuse:
Daily _____ Weekends _____ Periodic _____ Alone _____ Bars _____ Friends _____
Use in 24-hour period:
At present _____ Substances _____
At peak _____ Substances _____
Date of last drug/substance abuse and amount_____
Overdoses, withdrawals, or adverse reactions_____
_____
Attempted suicides_____
Problems caused by substance abuse:
Job _____
Family_____
Finances _____
Health_____
Sex_____
Loss of control _____

Figure 13.1
Continued

Computerized versions of structured interviews are available. The Structured Clinical Interview for the DSM-IV-TR provides several report options, helps clinicians screen clients on Axis I in approximately 25 minutes, and covers areas such as mood disorders, anxiety disorders, psychoactive substance abuse disorders, somatoform disorders, eating disorders, and psychotic symptoms.

Unstructured Interviews.   In contrast to structured interviews, *unstructured interviews* consist of counselor-made questions with "client responses" and "counselor observations" recorded by the counselor. It is considered unstructured because there is (a) no standardization of questions and (b) no recording of client responses. The advantages of the unstructured interview are that it gives the interviewee a chance to determine what is important to talk about; it allows the examiner to pursue important but unanticipated topics; and it provides an opportunity to judge the interviewee's behavior in an unstructured situation. Counselors may follow an interview outline.

Certain general guidelines should be considered before and during an interview:

1. Have a clear idea of why the individual is being interviewed. The kinds of questions asked depend on the types of inferences, decisions, or descriptions to be made after the interview. Better information results from specific goals.
2. Be concerned about the physical setting or environment for the interview. Interviews will go better if the environment is quiet and comfortable. If the room is noisy or has poor lighting, it may detract from the quality of the information gained. Comfortable and private facilities permit the client to relax without the confidentiality and privacy of the interview being threatened.
3. Establish rapport with the interviewee. Good rapport leads the interviewee to be cooperative and motivated.
4. Be alert to the nonverbal as well as verbal behavior of the client. How a person says something may be as important as what is said.
5. Be in charge and keep the goals of the interview in mind. Have the interview schedule readily available but do not suggest answers. Give the client time to answer and do not become impatient during periods of silence.

During the interview, you will be asking the client many questions on diverse topics to gain information about the client's presenting problem and history. Few of us can remember all of what we hear during an interview, and you may not have time to write extensive notes immediately after the interview session. Therefore, you may elect to take notes during the interview process.

The length of interviews varies depending on the circumstances of the interview and client. For example, interviews of clients in crisis in an emergency room may take as little as 20 minutes, while a full psychological interview in which testing is involved may take up to 4 hours (Seligman, 1996). Most counselors may devote 1 to 2 hours to the interview session in order to gather as much information as possible. Also remember that more information about the client will most likely emerge after the initial interview and during the counseling process itself.

The Unstructured Interview Format.   As stated earlier, clinicians using unstructured interviewing do not have a specific set of questions to ask the client. However, it is important to gather information in some general content areas. The following is a description of some content areas to explore in an interview:

- *Identifying Information*—This section of information includes name, date of birth, sex, age, race/ethnicity, and marital status.
- *Presenting Problem*—This is a brief statement about the problems or concerns that brought the client to counseling. It is helpful when counselors ask, "What brings you here?" or "How can I be of help?" to elicit discussion about the client's concerns. Asking open questions and using reflective responses can help clients be specific about their concerns. Presenting problems can be about the client's psychological, occupational, or social functioning. Counselors need to listen for symptoms that can help with the determination of a diagnosis.
- *History of Presenting Problem*—It is important that counselors assess the history of the problems/symptoms the client is experiencing. The interviewer needs to clearly document the onset, frequency, duration, and severity of each client symptom to differentiate between diagnoses (Wiger, 1999). For example, you would have to know that the client has been depressed for a minimum of 2 years to diagnose dysthymia.
- *Family History*—This part of the assessment focuses on gathering information about the client's family. The history of the client's presenting problem may be related to his or her interaction with significant social systems, the family being the most prominent (Hersen & Van Hasselt, 1998). Gathering information about family history can also help uncover any previous experiences that may be a precipitant of a mental disorder (e.g., child abuse, substance abuse in the family, domestic violence). It can include questions about parents' and siblings' age, education, and occupation; composition of the family during the client's childhood and adolescence; medical and mental health history of family members; and the quality of relationship with family members both past and present (Johnson, 1997).
- *Relationship History*—Relationship history emphasizes information regarding the client's past and current friendships and romantic relationships including marital or other long-term relationship; spouse/significant other's age, education, occupational history; previous marital/nonmarital relationships; number of children; and quality of relationships.
- *Developmental History*—This section involves gathering information about the client's developmental milestones, whether they were met at appropriate ages or whether there were any delays or difficulties (Johnson, 1997). Topics can include information about birth trauma, schooling, and early object relations.
- *Education/Employment History*—Information about educational and occupational history can help determine if the client's issues or problems have impaired the client's functioning both past and present. Ask the client about educational level and professional, technical, and/or vocational training. Find out about the client's work and education-related accomplishments as well as job losses, leaves of absence, and occupational injuries.

- *Medical History*—The client's medical history includes information about previous illnesses and injuries, medications, hospitalizations, and disabilities. It is important in determining whether any possible diagnosis may be related to a medical problem.
- *Substance Use*—The purpose of this section is to assess for possible substance abuse or dependence. Questions include the following:
  - Do you use alcohol or drugs?
  - If yes, what kinds?
  - How often?
  - Has anyone ever expressed a concern that you use too much?
  - Have you ever tried to cut down on your substance use?
  - Do you ever feel guilty about your substance use?
- *Previous Counseling*—Finding out about previous counseling can help in determining a diagnosis for the client. Information about previous counseling may aid in obtaining information about previous diagnoses or the type of treatment the client received. Also, ask if the client has ever been hospitalized for emotional difficulties or is currently on any psychotropic medications. Finding out the medications the client is taking can also help you with a diagnosis.

Interview Checklists.   There are a wide variety of interview checklists available to help clinicians organize the information gained in the interview and help structure the interview. Some examples follow:

- *The Mental Status Checklist*—provides a comprehensive examination of the mental status of the client. There are versions for children, adolescents, and adults.
- *The Personal History Checklist*—facilitates recording personal history during intake sessions for children, adolescents, and adults.
- *The Personal Problems Checklist*—provides a list of common problems for each age group. Versions are available for adults, adolescents, and children.

Interview Schedules.   A number of interview schedules are available for adults with personality disorders. The Personality Disorder Interview IV (PDI-IV) is a semistructured interview for the assessment of the DSM-IV-TR personality disorders. The Hare Psychopathy Checklist–Revised, Second Edition (PCL-R:2) is designed to assess antisocial personality disorder in forensic and psychiatric populations. The Structured Interview of Reported Symptoms (SIRS) assesses malingering and feigning of psychiatric symptoms.

BEHAVIORAL ASSESSMENT

Behavioral assessment centers on the circumstances of behavior rather than the reasons for it. The process relies greatly on observation, especially observation that requires few inferences on the part of the observer. Sometimes clients are required to keep a log of their behavior. Counselors use behavioral assessment in naturalistic and contrived settings, role playing, psychodrama, and interviews. Behavioral assessment is also used in a number of different ways, such as screening, identifying a problem, designing the intervention, monitoring progress, following up, and evaluating cases. A number of strategies are used: interviewing techniques, behavior checklists, observational schedules, self-monitoring procedures, simulation and analogue methods, physiological assessment, and computer-assisted assessment (Ollendick & Greene, 1990).

Behavioral Observation

One of the major methods of behavioral assessment is observation, normally of a specific, observable set of behaviors. Observations can be carried out in different contexts and environments, but a number of factors should be considered (Haynes, 1990; Ollendick & Greene, 1990).

1. Observers should be familiar with the behavioral categories to be studied.
2. Observers should have been trained to use videotapes, films, and other audiovisual equipment.
3. Observers should have a chance to check their observations with other raters and with the standards established in the training sessions.

Several problem areas relate to the observation technique. First is the problem of reactivity. If the client knows he is being observed, his behavior may be quite different from when he is unaware of it. People often play roles to put themselves in a good light. Second, when an observer has to assess a number of individuals over time, fatigue and boredom may occur. In addition, observers may have some unconscious or conscious biases that interfere with objective results. Observer expectations can also influence client behavior.

Two major types of observation are participant and nonparticipant. A group leader responsible for conducting a group but also monitoring the behaviors of individuals in the group is an example of participant observation (Haynes, 1990). In nonparticipant observation the observer does not become a part of the situation. For example, a teacher on playground duty might be able to observe a certain student without her knowing she is being observed, thereby eliminating the problem of reactivity.

Observation can be highly structured. When time sampling is a part of the system, every so often the observer might classify the behavior taking place and record the person responsible for it. The procedures for coding can be simple, requiring just a check by a category, or complex, demanding analysis. Unstructured observation might describe or identify the following components:

1. Purpose and object of the observation
2. Physical environment
3. Acts or events that have taken place
4. Time dimensions
5. Actors or people observed
6. Goals of the persons observed
7. Feelings of the observer

Students of ethnographic observation follow outlines such as this when they are observing. They are interested in naturalistic observation and do not usually have preconceived theories or set observational schedules to follow.

Self-Monitoring

Self-monitoring is a widely used technique in behavioral assessment. It can be used effectively as a therapeutic technique or simply as a data-collecting device to assess low-rate behaviors such as migraine headaches, high-rate or continuous behaviors such as blood pressure, and other behaviors such as eating patterns, smoking, caffeine intake, and the like. It is a reactive type of measurement technique because attention is focused on the targeted behavior, and the individual knows what events are to be observed. It is a valuable strategy to provide accurate information to workers in the helping professions, and it can provide client reinforcement and feedback. The success of the technique depends on the goals of the monitoring, the quality of the instructions given, and the number of behaviors being monitored. The accuracy of this method depends on the motivation and cooperation of the client. A number of recording devices can be used—for example, pocket diaries, golf counters, tape recorders, and phone-answering devices. When using self-monitoring with a client, the counselor should follow these procedures:

1. Give explicit definitions and examples of the targeted events and explain their possible relevance to the problem at hand.
2. Give explicit monitoring instructions on how to record the behavior.
3. Illustrate the use of the form or recording device and provide practice exercises.
4. Ask the client to repeat the target definitions and self-monitoring instructions.
5. Test client understanding of the assignment.
6. Check with the client during the period specified for any questions or problems.

Simulation and Analogue Methods

Often a counselor wants to find out what a person might do in a given situation, testing a hypothesis before the situation develops in reality. This procedure can be used as an evaluation tool to see whether training has had an effect. It also is a means of giving individuals a chance to rehearse or practice a needed skill and is a nonthreatening technique in the therapeutic process. Role playing is often used to evaluate the client's social skills (Haynes, 1990). The procedures are (1) analyze the task the client is to do, (2) develop realistic situations, and (3) provide role-playing opportunities. The technique has the advantage of helping clients distinguish between the form and functions of the behaviors being assessed. It also allows the counselor to assess performance in highly personal and intimate situations, and it can provide a more flexible and individualized assessment.

TESTS THAT ASSESS DSM-IV-TR AXIS I DISORDERS

A number of inventories are widely used for assessing DSM-IV-TR Axis I disorders. These include both personality tests and specialized tests that measure specific symptoms—sometimes called the "specific domain" of personality. The scales of the MMPI-2 and the MCMI-III, discussed in the last chapter, can be used to assess for Axis I disorders.

The Clinical Analysis Questionnaire (CAQ; Krug, 1980) is designed to measure both normal and pathological traits and provides a multidimensional profile of the client. The test has 28 scales, 16 of which measure normal personality traits included on the 16 Personality Factor Questionnaire, 7 of which measure various primary aspects of depression, and 5 of which measure factors identified in the Minnesota Multiphasic Personality Inventory-II pool. The clinical scales are hypochondriasis, suicidal depression, agitation, anxious depression, low-energy depression, boredom and withdrawal, paranoia, psychopathic deviation, psychasthenia, and psychological inadequacy. The test can be administered to individuals 16 and older. A number of second-order factors can be scored by the equations developed through factor analysis: extroversion, anxiety, tough poise, independence, superego, socialization, depression, psychoticism, and neuroticism. The test belongs to the family of factorial-derived tests discussed in Chapter 12.

The Personal Assessment Inventory (PAI) is a 344-item, self-administered, objective inventory used to assess critical clinical aspects of personality. The PAI has 22 nonoverlapping full scales, 4 validity scales, and 11 clinical scales. The clinical scales measure somatic complaints, anxiety, anxiety-related disorders, depression, mania, paranoia, schizophrenia, borderline features, antisocial features, alcohol problems, and drug problems. The treatment scales involve aggression, suicidal ideation, stress, nonsupport, and treatment rejection. The validity scales cover inconsistency, infrequency, negative impression, and positive impression. A short form of the PAI consists of the first 160 items.

A number of other tests, literally hundreds in fact, are available to help mental health counselors assess specific symptoms or treatment issues. Table 13.1 provides a listing of the domain for assessment along with a few relevant tests.

Psychodiagnostic Testing

Clinicians often have been trained to use and interpret certain classic tests in the field such as the Wechsler tests, the Rorschach, the Thematic Apperception Test (TAT), the Sentence Completion Test, the Bender Visual Motor Gestalt Test, and the MMPI-2. Katz (1991) identifies the best tools for assessing different diagnostic categories:

Intellectual functioning—Wechsler tests, Bender-Gestalt II, Draw-a-Person (DAP), Stanford-Binet-V

Brain damaged—Wechsler tests, Bender–Gestalt II, and specialized tests

Psychotic—Rorschach, MMPI-2, MCMI-III, biographical data blank

Neurotics—MMPI-2, Rorschach, TAT, DAP, PAI, MCMI-III

Sociopathic—TAT, MMPI-2, MCMI-III

Passive-aggressive—TAT, Sentence Completion

Schizoid—Rorschach, TAT, DAP, MMPI-2

Katz looks for patterns when he analyzes the test results. For psychotic individuals he might find withdrawn or disturbed behavior exhibited on a test battery. The Wechsler Adult Intelligence Scale-III (WAIS-III) might show variation or disturbed and odd think-

Table 13.1
Assessment instruments listed by domain.

General Symptoms
- Brief Symptom Inventory (BSI)
- Minnesota Multiphasic Personality Inventory-II (MMPI-II)
- Millon Clinical Multiaxial Inventory-III (MCMI-III)
- Outcome Questionnaire 45.2 (OQ-45.2)
- Symptom Checklist 90–Revised (SCL-90-R)

Depression
- Beck Depression Inventory (BDI)
- Children's Depression Inventory (CDI)
- Hamilton Depression Inventory (HDI)

Anxiety
- Beck Anxiety Inventory (BAI)
- Revised Children's Manifest Anxiety Scales (RCMAS)
- State-Trait Anxiety Inventory (STAI)

Behavior Problems
- Child Behavior Checklist (CBCL)
- Child Symptom Inventory: Ages 6 to 12 years (CSI-4)
- Conduct Disorder Scale (CDS)

Eating Disorders
- Eating Disorder Inventory-2 (EDI-2)

Relationship/Family
- Conflict Tactics Scale (CTS)
- Fundamental Interpersonal Relations Orientation-Behavior (FIRO-B)
- Marital Satisfaction Inventory, Revised (MSI-R)

Substance Abuse
- Michigan Alcoholism Screening Test (MAST)
- Substance Abuse Subtle Screening Inventory (SASSI-3)

Suicide
- Beck Scale for Suicide Ideation (BSS)
- Adult Suicidal Ideation Questionnaire (ASIQ)
- Suicidal Ideation Questionnaire (SIQ)

Trauma
- Detailed Assessment of Posttraumatic Stress (DAPS)
- Multiscale Dissociation Inventory (MDI)
- Trauma Symptom Inventory (TSI)
- Trauma Symptom Checklist for Children (TSCC)

ing. On the MMPI-2, the client might score high on the schizophrenia, paranoia, and psychasthenia scales. On the Sentence Completion Test the sentences will show confused, illogical, and bizarre patterns. The TAT might reveal odd elements, bizarre twists, and possible anguish.

Kellerman and Burry (1991) recommend that the data gained through observation, interviewing, and testing be combined to complete the diagnosis. The crucial elements in determining treatment are the individual's level of intellectual functioning, the nature of his or her anxiety, defensive structures, self-image, self-esteem, sexual identity, and the balance between impulse and control.

Neuropsychological Assessment Batteries

Neuropsychological assessment refers to testing for brain damage. Such tests are sensitive to the condition of the brain. Brain damage most often affects the cognitive functions, such as memory, speed in performing skilled activities or psychomotor/perceptual-motor activities, auditory or tactile perception, and visual-spatial skills.

One of the most widely used instruments for neuropsychological assessment is the Halstead-Reitan Neuropsychological Test Battery. This test uses Wechsler intelligence scales, but also includes a number of tests utilized originally by Halstead, some added by Reitan, and several added by others. Some tests within the battery call for tactual performance. For example, the Halstead Tactual Performance Test uses the Seguin-Goddard formboard, but the test taker is blindfolded and has to place all 10 blocks into the formboard using only a sense of touch. The test taker has to do this three times—first, with the preferred hand, then the other, and finally with both hands. On the Klove Roughness Discrimination Test the test taker must order four blocks, each covered with a different grade of sandpaper. The blocks are presented behind a blind, and the test is scored on the time the client takes and the number of errors made with each hand.

Also included in the Halstead-Reitan Battery are visual and psychomotor scales. For example, the Reitan Aphasia Screening Test contains both language and copying tasks. The copying tasks require the test taker to make a copy of a square, Greek cross, a triangle, and a key. The language functions measured are naming, repetition, spelling, reading, writing, calculation, narrative speech, and left-right orientation. The language section is scored by listing the number of aphasic symptoms. The Klove Grooved Pegboard Test requires the test taker to place pegs shaped like keys into a board containing recesses oriented in randomly varying directions. The test taker performs first with one hand and then the other. Some of the other tests on the scale are the Halstead Category Test, the Speech Perception Test, the Seashore Rhythm Test, the Finger Tapping Test, the Trail Making Test, the Perceptual Disorders Test, and the Visual Field Examination. The battery takes 6 to 8 hours to administer.

Another widely used battery is the Luria-Nebraska Neuropsychological Battery. The test has 11 content scales:

1. *Motor functions* measures a wide variety of motor skills.
2. *Rhythm functions* measures nonverbal auditory perception, such as pitch discrimination and rhythmic patterns.
3. *Tactile functions* measures tactual discrimination and recognition.

4. *Vision functions* measures visual-perceptual and visual-spatial skills.
5. *Receptive speech* measures perception of sounds from simple to complex.
6. *Expressive speech* measures ability to repeat sounds, words, and word groups and produce narrative speech.
7. *Writing* measures ability to analyze words into letters and to write under varying conditions.
8. *Reading* measures ability to make letter-to-sound transformations and read simple material.
9. *Arithmetic* measures knowledge of numbers, number concepts, and ability to perform simple calculations.
10. *Memory* measures short-term memory and paired associate learning.
11. *Intellectual processes* measures sequencing, problem solving, and abstraction skills.

The test is shorter than the Halstead-Reitan and helps screen a large number of areas that may be affected by brain damage. There are a variety of tests available from the Benton Laboratory of Neuropsychology. A kit is available, or some tests can be purchased separately. Examples include the Facial Recognition Test, the Judgment of Line Orientation Test, the Pantomine Recognitions Test, the Right-Left Orientation Test, the Serial-Digit Learning Test, the Tactile Form Recognition Test, the Temporal Orientation Test, and the Visual Form Discrimination Test.

Other available tests include the following:

- The Kaufman Short Neuropsychological Assessment Procedure (K-SNAP) was developed by H. S. Kaufman and N. L. Kaufman to measure cognitive functioning of individuals age 11 to 85. The test measures attention and orientation, simple memory, and perceptual skills.
- The Quick Neurological Screening Test, Second Edition (QNST-2) assesses 15 areas of neurological integration as they relate to learning. The scales are control of large and small muscles, motor planning, motor development, sense of rate and rhythm, spatial organization, visual and auditory skills, perceptual skills, and balance orientation.
- The Ross Information Processing Assessment, Second Edition (RIPA-2) is designed to assess any cognitive and linguistic deficits and determine severity levels. The scales on the RIPA-2 are immediate memory, recent memory, spatial orientation, orientation to the environment, recall of general information, organization, and auditory processing and retention.

Interviewing Children and Adolescents

A number of specific interview schedules are designed for use with children and adolescents. The Child Assessment Schedule (Hodges, Kline, Stern, Cytryn, & McKnew, 1982) includes questions about school, friends, activities, family, fears, worries, self-image, mood, somatic concerns, expressions of anger, and thought disorder and also has questions on delusions, hallucinations, and related symptoms. The schedule has been useful in detecting psychopathology in children.

The Diagnostic Interview for Children and Adolescents-IV (DICA-IV) is a computerized diagnostic interview based on the DSM-IV, designed for children and adolescents ages 6 to 17 years. There are two versions of the DICA-IV: the Child/Adolescent Version and the Parent Version. The two versions work independently of each other and are administered separately. However, when used together, the results help to achieve a more complete assessment of the behavior and condition of the youth.

The Child Behavior Checklist (CBCL) is a questionnaire to be answered by parents, teachers, and other caregivers about children. There are two separate forms: One for children between ages 1 1/2 to 5 and one for children between ages 6 and 18. Parents provide information for items covering their child's activities, social relations, and school performance. Results are comprised of DSM-IV-TR-oriented scales including: Affective Problems, Anxiety Problems, Pervasive Developmental Problems, Attention Deficit/Hyperactivity Problems, & Oppositional Defiant Problems and Conduct Problems.

The Trauma Symptoms Checklist for children ages 8 to 16 is available in paper-and-pencil format and has a window's scoring and interpretation version available. The six clinical scales are anxiety, depression, anger, posttraumatic stress, dissociation, and sexual concerns. Two validity scales are also a part of the checklist: underresponse and hyperresponse.

PITFALLS

Fisher (1985) reminds professionals involved in assessment in the mental health field to look carefully at counterproductive behaviors:

1. *Being too sociable or following the "nice-guy" syndrome*—Some examiners are more concerned with being liked than being objective and professional in their tasks.
2. *Being collusive or aloof*—This is the other end of the scale—the opposite of being too sociable.
3. *Being a technician*—Some examiners put more emphasis on the procedures and the techniques than on looking at the whole person.
4. *Being a rescuer*—Some examiners rush to the rescue of their clients (also called the *doctor syndrome*).
5. *Being an opponent*—Some examiners act as though they and their clients are on opposite sides.

CULTURAL ISSUES IN PERSONALITY ASSESSMENT

Counselors assess clients from different ethnic groups and cultural backgrounds. During the assessment process, it is important that counselors take into account the client's cultural frame of reference when evaluating behaviors. The consequence of lack of multicultural perspectives in assessment is identifying culturally normal behaviors as pathological. For example, certain religious practices such as hearing or seeing a deceased relative during bereavement may be misdiagnosed as a psychotic disorder (American Psychiatric Association, 2000).

During the assessment, it is appropriate for you to ask, respectfully, about cultural differences with your client. These questions could be about differences in gender, age, race, ethnicity, religion, or other cultural factors. Sommers-Flanagan and Sommers-Flanagan (1999, p. 389) provided a list of suggestions for exploring cultural differences:

1. Do ask about tribal, ethnic, or background differences that are obvious or are made obvious by information provided by the client.
2. Do ask for clarification if something is not clear.
3. Do accept the client's beliefs regarding the sources of distress: ancestral disapproval, the evil eye, God's wrath, or trouble because of misbehavior in another life. A strong therapeutic relationship must first be established before determining adaptive or maladaptive beliefs.
4. Do remember that patterns of eye contact, direct verbalization of problem areas, storytelling, and note-taking all have culturally determined norms that vary widely.
5. Don't explain away symptoms or insist on interpreting physical complaints psychologically.
6. Don't diagnose prematurely. Seek cultural understanding of even the most "obvious" symptoms.

SUMMARY

Many different assessment models and techniques are used to assess adjustment of clients. Workers in clinical and counseling contexts use tests for a number of purposes. Although the use of clinical testing has declined, many new techniques are used in measuring and evaluating clients. Behavioral assessment techniques such as self-monitoring, behavioral observation, and the use of simulation are widely used in the field because they center on evaluating actual behavior in naturalistic situations.

Several new instruments and techniques, as well as renewed interest in the classical testing procedures, have resulted from computer scoring and interpretation procedures.

Neuropsychological testing has been developed to identify brain damage or organicity. Traditional techniques such as the interview and case study are primary tools of workers in the helping professions.

QUESTIONS FOR DISCUSSION

1. What do you believe the role of testing should be in a mental health setting? What should the goals and objectives be for testing in this context? Some clinicians are opposed to any type of testing in this field. Why do you agree or disagree with their position?

2. What are the advantages and disadvantages of using behavioral assessment techniques? In what types of situations would behavioral assessment procedures be more appropriate than traditional standardized testing?

3. What are the advantages and disadvantages of an interview? What are the different types of interviews and when would you use them? What are the sources of

bias operating in the interview and how would you attempt to correct bias in interview situations?

4. What types of interviews are used in the mental health field? What are some of the problems and issues in the use of the interview technique?

5. What are the uses of the case study? What are the advantages and disadvantages of this approach? When would you use case studies in your work?

SUGGESTED ACTIVITIES

1. Interview psychologists and counselors working in the mental health field and find out what tests and assessment procedures they use and why. Report your findings to the class.

2. Critically review a test used primarily in mental health settings. Read the reviews of the test in different journals and yearbooks.

3. Design a behavioral assessment instrument and try it out on several individuals. Write an analysis of your experiment.

4. Design an interview schedule and try it out on several individuals. Write an analysis of the results.

5. Critically review a software package used in a mental health setting—for example, a biographic data program or a test interpretive package.

6. Write a review of the literature on a topic such as behavioral assessment, case study approach, use of tests in clinical settings, use of tests in counseling settings, or neuropsychological testing.

7. Make an annotated bibliography of tests used in the mental health setting.

8. Study the case of Lawana and answer the questions that follow.

Case of Lawana

Lawana is a 16-year-old who has completed her education through grade 10. She says she doesn't have the energy or desire to go anywhere and adds that when she does go out, she feels anxious and scared.

Background Information:

Lawana's mother is living with a Hispanic man and has been married twice—the first time for 11 years, the second for 1 1/2 years. Lawana has two sisters, age 8 and 12, and an older brother, age 22, who no longer lives with the family. Lawana's mother got pregnant with Lawana during a period of separation from her first husband. Lawana learned about this and maintains regular positive contact with her biological father. She hates her mother's live-in boyfriend, who abuses her when he is drunk. Her mother, who has refused to acknowledge the abuse, believes Lawana's problems are caused by racial prejudice at school. Lawana is earning Bs and Cs in her classes.

   Lawana's mother was concerned enough about Lawana's condition to arrange an appointment at the local mental health clinic for Lawana. Lawana was tested with a number of assessment instruments. Her profile follows.

Personal Assessment Inventory

Validity

Inconsistency	52	Infrequency	50
Positive Impression	40	Negative Impression	57

Clinical

Somatic Complaints	55	Anxiety	68
Anxiety-Related Disorders	65	Depression	45
Mania	45	Paranoia	55
Schizophrenia	56	Borderline Features	57
Antisocial Features	48	Alcohol Problems	50
Drug Problems	48		

Treatment

Aggression	55	Suicidal Ideation	62
Stress	62	Nonsupport	58
Treatment Rejection	40		

Interpersonal

Dominance	48	Warmth	42

Beck Anxiety Inventory: 27 (severe)
Beck Depression Inventory: 42 (moderate)

a. How would you describe Lawana's adjustment? (Remember: On the PAI, the mean *T* score is 50 and the SD is 10.)

b. What additional information about Lawana would you like to have?

ADDITIONAL READINGS

Several good source books on tests are available for special groups and populations. PRO-ED has published an interesting assessment series: S. Joseph Weaver (1984) edited *Testing Children;* Robert G. Harrington (1986) edited *Testing Adolescents;* and Dennis P. Swiercinsky's (1985) collection is *Testing Adults.*

Choca, J.P. (2004). *Interpretive guide to the Millon Clinical Multiaxial Inventory* (3rd ed.). Washington, DC: APA.
Provides guidance to users of the Millon on how to interpret the tests and also examines the design and development of the inventory.

Dean, R. (1986). Perspectives on the future of neuropsychological assessment. In B. S. Plake & J. C. Witt (Eds.), *Buros-Nebraska Symposium on Measurement and Testing: Vol. 2. The future of testing.* Hillsdale, NJ: Erlbaum.
Presents current thinking and future projections on neuropsychological testing.

Golden, C. J. (1990). *Clinical interpretation of psychological tests* (2nd ed.). Boston: Allyn & Bacon.
Provides examples of the clinical application of tests such as the Wechsler scales, the Wide Range Achievement Test, the Peabody Individual Achievement Test, the MMPI—2, the 16 Personality Factor, the Bender Gestalt, and the Halstead-Reitan Neuropsychological Battery.

Groth-Marnat, G. (2003). *Handbook of psychological assessment* (4th ed.). New York: John Wiley & Sons.

Katz, L. (1986). *A practical guide to psychodiagnostic testing.* Springfield, IL: Charles C. Thomas.
    Provides practical suggestions on how to conduct psychodiagnostic testing.

Rogers, R. (2001). *Handbook of diagnostic and structured interviewing.* Chicago: Guilford Press.
    The handbook is designed to help workers in the social and behavioral sciences hone their
    interviewing skills.

Ziskin, J. (1986). The future of clinical assessment. In B. S. Plake & J. C. Witt (Eds.), *Buros-
    Nebraska Symposium on Measurement and Testing, Vol 2. The future of testing.* Hillsdale, NJ: Erlbaum.
    Presents current thinking and future projections on clinical assessment.

14 Assessment of Development

OVERVIEW

Approximately 17% of individuals in the United States 18 years and younger have a developmental disability. Developmental disabilities are a diverse group of severe chronic conditions that are due to mental and/or physical impairments, including impairments in language, mobility, learning, self-help, and independent living. Developmental disabilities can begin anytime during development up to 22 years of age and usually last throughout a person's lifetime. Autism spectrum disorders, cerebral palsy, hearing loss, mental retardation, vision impairment and attention deficit hyperactivity disorder are examples of developmental disabilities.

Counselors need to know characteristic behaviors at the different developmental stages, be able to assess problems, and recommend special educational and counseling assistance. Failure to adapt at one period of development promotes difficulty later. The chapter focuses on not only early development and developmental delays but also development through the life span. Moral development, career development, and psychosocial development are discussed.

OBJECTIVES

After studying this chapter, you should be able to

✔ Discuss the general principles of developmental assessment

✔ Describe the major domains assessed in developmental testing

✔ Explain the advantages and disadvantages of the various assessment devices used to measure aspects of development

✔ Identify some of the major instruments used in developmental assessment

GENERAL PRINCIPLES

Developmental and readiness testing has become increasingly important in the early screening and identification of clients who might need remedial help or further assessment. Children are rapidly developing and this must be considered in assessment and treatment (Yule, 1993). Assessment can be a valuable tool in screening, diagnosis, placement, program planning, and evaluation of programs. Much attention has been placed on identifying preschoolers with disabilities, but many developmental theories now focus on the total lifespan rather than just childhood and adolescence. Developmental assessment is important in understanding cognitive, ego, interpersonal, moral, and psychosocial development as individuals progress through the various stages of their lives.

Developmental assessment needs to focus on both the client and the client's environment. The client plays an active role in shaping an environment that fulfills his or her basic needs. The significant individuals in the client's world need to be identified, and parents, guardians, spouses, friends, and relatives might be needed to provide input to the assessment. Attachments, separations, and losses in a client's life have a dramatic influence. Although age is an important factor in assessment, social factors also must be considered (Yule, 1993).

Current functioning is influenced by previous events, and counselors need to evaluate clients with this in mind. Research points out that conflicts are inevitable and necessary for human development, and some may never be completely resolved.

Developmental assessment focuses on these characteristics:

1. The normality of client functioning in the various domains
2. The historical factors that contributed positively or negatively to the client's functioning
3. The current state of affairs—family, school, or work factors that contribute positively and negatively to the client's functioning
4. The current state of wellness of the client—physical, psychological, and emotional health
5. The expectations of the client and significant others
6. The client's current educational, social, and psychological needs

Yule (1993) reminds helping professionals not to treat any assessment finding in isolation, but to piece it together with other data on the client's overall adjustment. Isolated symptoms should be viewed cautiously and emphasis should be placed on patterns of adjustment and their adaptability and flexibility. Behavior is interpreted in light of developmental norms and environmental factors.

DOMAINS

Developmental tests measure typical skills that should be mastered at certain stages. Preschool tests, for example, assess gross motor, fine motor, language, self-help, social, emotional, and cognitive skills. A number of domains are common to developmental assessment instruments across the lifespan.

- *Communication skills*—verbal and nonverbal, receptive and expressive, listening and comprehension
- *Cognitive skills*—reasoning, thinking, memory; basic achievement in reading, writing, and mathematics; problem solving
- *Physical development*—general growth; motor and sensory; balance, locomotion, walking
- *Emotional development*—temperament, adjustment, emotional expression, self-concept, attitudes
- *Social development*—peer and family relationships, friendships, interpersonal relationships
- *Self-care skills*—basic self-care needs such as drinking, eating, toileting, dressing
- *Independent living skills*—functioning independently in the home and community, including clothing care, cooking, transportation, shopping, money management
- *Work habits and adjustment skills*—working independently, maintaining proper work habits, working with employers and employees, seeking and keeping jobs
- *Adjustment problems*—aggression, hyperactivity, acting out, withdrawal, delinquency, stress, depression

Drawings of people can provide information about a child's developmental level.

METHODS OF ASSESSMENT

The four major techniques of assessment are direct testing; naturalistic observation; interviewing of parents, teachers, or guardians; and multiple measures. Direct testing is not always possible because of the developmental level of a client, a disability, wariness toward the test administrator, or the presence or nonpresence of parents in the case of young children. The performance of these individuals tends to be inconsistent.

Naturalistic observation provides an opportunity to see how a person behaves and performs in normal everyday functioning. The process is time consuming and expensive. A number of structured observation schedules exist, and raters need to be trained to use them so that observations are consistent and properly focused.

Helping professionals use a wide variety of interviewing methods. Computerized versions are designed to elicit specific information; life history schedules help guide the collection of appropriate information from parents. Preschoolers or individuals with certain disabilities are not capable of filling out self-report forms, so interviews with parents or guardians are necessary to determine skills and adaptive behaviors not always modeled in school. The validity of personality tests such as the Personality Inventory for Children, Second Edition, (PIC-2) and self-concept scales such as the Inferred Self-Concept Scale that teachers or parents complete is questionable. Reliability of the data depends on the quality of the scale (content validity) and the accuracy of the people answering the questions.

A variety of informal assessment procedures exist that helping professionals can use to achieve a more global perspective of the problem. Sentence completion techniques can be used to zero in on important concerns at a particular stage of development (e.g., "In school, when the teacher calls upon me, I _____ _____."). Journaling is also used. Individuals are asked to tell how they feel about certain types of experiences, interventions, programs, and the like. A portfolio of these feelings can be kept. Other writing exercises such as stories and poems can also be helpful in understanding the client.

Observing individuals while they are playing games, drawing, and in play therapy or other informal situations can provide information on their cognitive and psychosocial development. Clients can be asked to tell a story about a particular picture or situation, or to complete a story.

Self-monitoring requires the individual to keep a record of certain behaviors, feelings, or worries. A client could keep a record of the number of times he "blew his cool," felt depressed, spoke out in class when not called upon, felt a craving for certain foods, and so on.

Helping professionals get more complete information when they use multiple measures. The process might be more time consuming and expensive, but it allows the counselor to combine information from a number of different sources, individuals, and occasions.

EARLY IDENTIFICATION

Three widely used general batteries to assess preschool children are the Developmental Indicators for the Assessment of Learning-Third Edition (DIAL-3), the Battelle Developmental Inventory, Second Edition, (BDI-2) and the Denver Developmental

Screening Test, Second Edition (DDST-II). DIAL-3 is used to assess motor, language, and concept development, plus self-help and social development of children ages 3 years to 6 years 11 months. In the motor area tests the child is involved in activities like catching a bean bag, jumping, hopping, skipping, building with blocks, touching fingers, and cutting with cutting cards and scissors. The BDI-2 can be given from birth to 7 years 11 months and measures personal, social, adaptive, motor, communication, and cognitive skills. The DDDST-II assesses personal-social, fine motor adaptive, language, and gross motor development in children from birth to age 6.

Some instruments focus on one domain. The Children's Adaptive Behavior Scale is designed to assess a child's adaptability to different social environments. Five areas covered are language development, independent functioning, family role performance, economic and vocational activity, and socialization. The Matson Evaluation of Social Skills can be used with clients age 6 through adult and features both a teacher rating and a self-report form. Some other instruments widely used for assessing preschool children follow:

- The Bayley Scales of Infant and Toddler Development, Third Edition (2005) are useful in monitoring early signs of behavioral problems.
- The McCarthy Scales of Children's Abilities (MSCA, 1972) have 18 subtests and yield 5 scale scores: verbal, quantitative, perceptual performance, memory, and motor. The scales are combined to provide a general cognitive index.
- The Miller Assessment for Preschoolers (1982) measures sensorimotor and cognitive abilities, as well as gross and fine motor functioning. It also has a verbal index.
- The Stanford-Binet Intelligence Scale-V (2003) has 10 subtests. Verbal reasoning, abstract/visual reasoning, quantitative reasoning, and short-term memory scores are available to the examiner.
- The Wechsler Preschool and Primary Scale of Intelligence-Third Edition (WPPSI-III) is a downward extension of the WISC-III. Verbal, performance, and total IQ scores can be computed.

LANGUAGE DEVELOPMENT

The time between birth and age 6 is a crucial period for language development. A number of standardized tests are available to help professionals look at qualitative and quantitative differences. Here are a few examples of the tests available:

- The Houston Test for Language Development, Revised Edition (HTLD-R) measures verbal and nonverbal communication of children from birth to age 6. The HTLD is used for differential diagnosis of problems resulting from emotional deprivation, auditory and motor deficits, and other causes. The test provides a profile of strengths and weaknesses that can be valuable when planning specific interventions.
- The Reynell Developmental Language Scale, Third Edition (RDLS-III) is used to assess slow development in receptive and expressive language areas of children ages 1 to 7 years.

- The Test of Adolescent Language, Third Edition (TOAL-3) identifies problems in both the spoken and written language of adolescents. TOAL-3 provides scores in listening, speaking, reading, writing, spoken language, written language, vocabulary, grammar, receptive language, and expressive language.
- The Test of Language Development-Primary, Third Edition (TOLD-P:3) assesses receptive and expressive vocabulary and expressive grammatical structure by using picture identification, grammatic completion, word definitions, word discrimination, and word articulation. The test can be given to children ages 4 to 8 years 11 months.

COGNITIVE STAGES

Piaget's theory of cognitive development involves four major stages. In the *sensorimotor stage* children from birth to age 2 develop schemes and organized patterns of behavior or thought through sensory and motor activities. The *preoperational stage* occurs between the ages of 2 and 7 when children develop the ability to conserve and decenter—that is, to overcome perceptual centration, irreversibility, and egocentrism in their logical thinking. During the *concrete operational stage* children between ages 7 and 11 develop the ability to use mental operations but have difficulty in manipulating conditions without experience. The *formal operational stage* starts at ages 11 to 12 when children are able to solve problems, work with abstractions, form hypotheses, and engage in mental operations. Children tend to think, perceive, organize, and understand their personal, physical, and social environment differently at various stages of development.

Two tests assess stages of development:

- The Concept Assessment Kit (CAK) measures cognitive development of preschool and primary-grade children. The CAK is a multiple-item task-assessment and oral-response test measuring conservation. Forms A and B measure conservation of two-dimensional space, number substance, continuous quantity, discontinuous quantity, and weight. Form C measures conservation using area and length.
- The Wach Analysis of Cognitive Structures assesses the development of learning ability among young children and suggests activities to stimulate learning and growth. The inventory has 15 clusters of tasks divided into subtests consisting of manipulative, visual-sensory, and body movement actions. The test is culture-free and nonverbal, and has been used with children having language, mental, and hearing disabilities.

The tests focus on how we think and reason. They do not present norms and standard scores like traditional cognitive ability tests and do not have the same level of validity. Some counselors believe this information also provides a frame of reference to look at social and emotional development and is useful in instructional programming.

The case of Deshon shows how school professionals might assess development.

CASE OF DESHON

Deshon

Race/gender: African American male
Date of birth: 8/17/96
Grade: Kindergarten
Present school: San Pablo Elementary

Tests Used

At age 4.5 on 1/27/01:

Developmental Test of Visual-Motor
Integration
Leiter International Performance Scale
Peabody Picture Vocabulary Test-Revised
Preschool Attainment Record
Stanford-Binet Intelligence Scale, Form L-M

At age 5.8 on 4/23/02:

Wechsler Preschool and Primary Scale of
Intelligence-Revised

At age 5.9 on 5/15/02:

(speech and language evaluation)
Bracken Basic Concept Scale
Cultural Evaluation of Language
Fundamentals-Revised
Expressive One-Word Picture Vocabulary
Test
Goldman-Fristoe Test of Articulation
Structured Photographic Expressive
Language Test-II
Zimmerman Preschool Language Scale

At age 6.4 on 12/18/02:

Vane Kindergarten Test
Vineland Adaptive Behavior Scale
Woodcock-Johnson Test of Achievement-
Revised

Reason for Referral

Deshon was originally referred by the Speech
and Hearing Center to obtain a current level of
functioning. His parents noted delays in overall
developmental skills and significant deficits in
the use of speech and language.

Background Information

Deshon's mother reported her pregnancy was
normal and without complications. However, at
the age of 6 months Deshon contracted bacte-
rial meningitis, after which his speech and language skills were severely delayed.

Review of Records

Deshon's initial evaluation by the psychologist
on 1/27/01 (age 4.5) indicated a Stanford-Binet
Intelligence Scale IQ of 54, a Leiter IQ of 79, and
a Peabody Picture Vocabulary Test score of 52.
The examiner noted that the scores obtained
appeared to be somewhat depressed due to significant difficulties in speech and language.
Placement in a preschool program for students
with disabilities was recommended on 3/22/01.

A reevaluation was completed on 4/23/02.
Results of Deshon's performance on the
WPPSI-R were a Verbal IQ of 70, a Performance
IQ of 86, and a Full Scale IQ of 75.

Speech and language assessment was completed in May of 2002. Reported results include
these scores:

Bracken Test of Basic Concepts	50
Cultural Evaluation of Language Fundamentals—Revised	65
Expressive One-Word Picture Vocabulary Test	61

The examiner reports that Deshon evidences
severe delays in expressive language and a severe phonological disorder. Participation in a
program for students with severe language disabilities was suggested.

Testing was also administered on 12/18/02.
The Woodcock-Johnson Test of Achievement—
Revised indicated academic skills at a prereadiness

level comparable to a preschool youngster below 4 years old.

Vane scoring of the human figure drawing yielded an age equivalent of 5.4, which is in the low average range.

Adaptive skills as measured through teacher ratings of the Vineland Adaptive Behavior Scale showed standard scores in the average range.

Sensory Functioning

In the fall of 2002 Deshon passed the vision screening administered at school. During the evaluation he was observed shielding his right eye during drawing activities. Observations were discussed with his parents and periodic screenings at school were suggested.

Results of the hearing screening indicated auditory acuity in the left ear was adequate. He failed to respond appropriately at all frequency levels presented in the right ear. Significant deficits in speech articulation and language were also reported.

Summary and Conclusions

Deshon is a 6-year, 4-month-old youngster who is placed in a full-time program for students with learning disabilities (SLD). He has evi-denced significant deficits in acquisition of basic academic skills, and he also manifests substantial delays in speech and language. Results of formal intellectual assessments indicate overall conceptual skills are within the borderline to low average range, but scores should be interpreted with caution due to his significant difficulties in speech and language. Current academic levels are significantly below that expected of his estimated ability.

Adaptive skills show functioning at a level more typical of a much younger child with the most notable deficits in communication skills. Daily living and self-help skills are an area of relative strength although still rated at the preschool level.

Deshon can be expected to continue requiring a comprehensive, well-structured, individualized educational program. Preferential seating and individual presentation of instructions are suggested. Continued placement in the self-contained SLD program seems the most appropriate and least restrictive to meet his overall educational needs. A meeting of counselors, psychologists, teachers, and parents should be scheduled to consider permanent placement and review current assessment results.

PSYCHOSOCIAL DEVELOPMENT

Erikson developed a theory of personality development based on psychoanalytical, biographical, historical, and anthropological methods of study. He postulates eight stages of psychosocial development. At each stage positive and negative forces produce conflict and a crisis that must be resolved. When the negative forces have a stronger influence than the positive factors, the outcome leads to difficulties in adjustment and development. The developmental crisis that needs to be resolved during the first year is trust versus mistrust. For 2- and 3-year-olds it is autonomy versus doubt; for 4- to 5-year-olds it is initiative versus guilt. Industry versus inferiority is the crisis from 6 to 11 years. Identity versus role confusion takes place during adolescence, whereas intimacy versus isolation occurs during young adulthood. Generativity versus stagnation is the crisis during middle age, and integrity versus despair occurs during old age. The degree and direction of conflict resolution determines the overall health of the individual, but the degree of conflict resolution is relative because no stage conflict is completely resolved. One of the major instruments to assess Erikson's stages is the Measure of Psychosocial Development. The case of Anita illustrates the use of this inventory.

CASE OF ANITA

Ms. Moore was a counselor working with a group of unwed African American teenage mothers. She was eager to find out more about the personality dynamics and conflict resolution of Anita, one of her counselees.

Anita is 16 and will be a senior if she is able to pass her courses. Her pregnancy and the birth of a daughter during the school year have hampered her academically, and she is talking about dropping out of school. Anita comes from a single-parent family. Currently, her grandmother is taking care of her baby while she works part time at Kentucky Fried Chicken. Ms. Moore decided to administer the Measures of Psychosocial Development (MPD) because it is based upon sound personality theory and assesses adolescent and adult personality development. The MPD is a 112-item, self-report inventory that has 27 different scales: 9 positive scales (trust, autonomy, initiative, industry, identity, intimacy, generativity, ego integrity, and total positive), 9 negative scales (mistrust, shame and doubt, guilt, inferiority, identity confusion, isolation, stagnation, despair, and total negative), 9 resolution scales (one for each stage), and a total resolution scale. The test taker responds on a 5-point scale ranging from "Not at all like me" to "Very much like me."

The MPD is easy to score. Ms. Moore just removed the top page of the answer sheet, counted the ratings for each row of items, and recorded the scores on each of the 27 scales on the profile sheet.

Alpha reliabilities ($n = 372$) for the scales ranged from a low of .65 on trust to a high of

.84 on identity confusion. The median coefficient was .74. Test-retest coefficients for 108 individuals were also reported and ranged from a high of .91 on total negative to a low of .67 on inferiority.

The MPD reports construct validity through intercorrelations of the scale and correlation of the MPD with the Inventory of Psychosocial Development and the Self-Description Questionnaire. The author claims the data support the discriminant validity of the positive scales, and that there is moderate support for the negative scales and consistent evidence for convergent validity of the scale. Separate norms are presented for males and females ages 13 to 17, 18 to 24, 25 to 49, and 50 and over. The manual does not provide the means and standard deviations for any of these groups or the standard errors of measurement for the various scales. Despite separate norms, no statistical evidence indicates a gender difference. The norms use T scores with a mean of 50 and a standard deviation of 10.

Anita had the following percentile ranks on the MPD:

Positive Scales	
Trust	03
Autonomy	42
Initiative	27
Industry	24
Identity	14
Intimacy	01
Generativity	11
Ego Integrity	01
Total Positive	03

Negative Scales

Mistrust	79
Shame and Doubt	50
Guilt	35
Inferiority	69
Identity Confusion	65
Isolation	92
Stagnation	38
Despair	96
Total Negative	79

Resolution Scales

Trust versus Mistrust	08
Autonomy versus Shame and Doubt	50
Initiative versus Guilt	46
Industry versus Inferiority	27
Identity versus Identity Confusion	24
Intimacy versus Isolation	01
Generativity versus Stagnation	27
Ego Integrity versus Despair	02
Total Resolution	05

The MPD manual (p. 9) states that high scorers on mistrust perceive the world as inconsistent, painful, stressful, and threatening, and believe that life is unpredictable. They struggle with the burden of questioning whether others are trustworthy. Their basic mistrust may be characterized as a sense of living precariously, of feeling that good things never last, or doubting that needs will be met. High scorers on isolation tend to remain alone and be self-absorbed from fear of ego loss. Isolation occurs if a person's identity is too weak to sustain the uncertainties of intimacy. The individual may be drawn toward intimate relationships but also be frightened by them (p. 10). Commitments and responsibilities seem unreasonable or too restrictive.

High scorers on despair perceive that their lives have been filled with misdirected energies and lost opportunities. They believe there is no time to undo the mistakes of the past and to begin life anew.

MORAL DEVELOPMENT

Piaget studied the moral development of children and identified two broad stages. Kohlberg expanded the two broad stages into three levels, each with two stages. The first level is *preconventional morality* and usually extends to the age of 9. The two stages are punishment-obedience orientation and instrumental-relativist orientation. The second level is *conventional morality* and includes the good boy–nice girl and the law-and-order orientations. This period is typical of youth aged 9 to 20. Level three is *postconventional morality* and includes social contract and universal ethical principle orientation. A number of instruments have been developed to measure moral reasoning:

- The Defining Issues Test is a pencil-and-paper instrument that presents dilemmas about which the client selects preferred responses.
- The Ethical Reasoning Inventory is a paper-and-pencil inventory that consists of six dilemmas from Kohlberg's manual. Questions are followed by two responses and sets of reasons that represent stages of Kohlberg's theory.
- The Moral Judgment Interview and Scoring System uses a structured interview technique that involves a minimum of 21 questions about the client's reasoning regarding three moral dilemmas. Raters are used to match the responses against the stage criteria.

- The Social Moral Reflection Measure is a group-administered version of Kohlberg's manual.

The scoring of some of these tests is tedious, time consuming, and demands careful study of the manuals and criteria for scoring. Reliability of some instruments is moderate. Gilligan (1982) believes that women have a different approach to resolving real-life dilemmas. The question about the criterion-referenced validity of these tests is whether individuals actually behave the way they say they do.

CAREER DEVELOPMENT

Super, Thompson, and Lindeman (1988) postulate a five-stage theory of career development. The first is the growth stage in which the preadolescent develops self-awareness and interests. Children role play and fantasize about different jobs and occupations. The exploratory stage extends from early adolescence to early adulthood and has three phases: crystallization, specification, and implementation. *Crystallization* relates to developing ideas about fields of endeavor and appealing occupations. *Specification* relates to moving from general preferences to choosing a specific career or job. *Implementation* requires pursuing chosen fields.

The establishment stage normally takes place in early to middle adulthood and consists of developmental tasks: stabilizing, consolidating, and advancing. Individuals settle down, support their families, and develop appropriate lifestyles in the stabilizing stage. At the consolidating stage, individuals are concerned with their place in an occupation or in an organization. Workers have the expectation of moving up the ladder and getting ahead financially in the advancing stage. The maintenance stage extends from middle adulthood to later adulthood and consists of three developmental tasks: holding, updating, and innovating. The disengagement stage extends from the early 60s to retirement and has three phases: disengagement, retirement planning, and retirement living.

Super et al. (1988) point out that it is common for individuals to change career paths after becoming established. This requires individuals to reassess life and career plans and go back to previous developmental stages and tasks.

The case of Cindy shows how testing can be used in career development.

CASE OF CINDY

Cindy is a 28-year-old White female. She has been married since June 1995 and has a 6-year-old daughter. Cindy is interested in reentering the job market but is unsure about her employment qualifications and interests. She doesn't know whether to return to school, get vocational training, or begin work wherever employment is available. Cindy maintained a high-C or low-B average throughout high school, but did not particularly like school. After graduation she was employed as a grocery clerk and a retail salesperson but stopped working when her daughter was born. Now Cindy wants to develop her job skills and explore career options. Her husband is employed as a high school teacher and has encouraged her to research her career choices.

Cindy dresses neatly, has good eye contact, and is friendly, verbal, and articulate. She understands the need for career exploration and appears focused and committed to developing an action plan.

The counselor chooses the Adult Career Concerns Inventory (ACCI) as one of the assessment instruments because it is intended for adults rethinking their careers. The ACCI is appropriate for men and women, is written in American English at the eighth-grade reading level, and may be hand- or machine-scored. The test taker is asked to respond to 61 items on a 5-point scale, indicating the amount of current concern toward the statement.

The test manual provides a developmental model for assessment and counseling. The authors present content, concurrent, and predictive validity as well as the factor structure of the instrument. Alpha coefficients are reported for two different groups and range primarily in the .80s and .90s. The authors also present the standard error of measurement.

Cindy's results on the ACCI indicate considerable concern for exploration. Specification had an average score of 5.0, whereas implementation and crystallization were 4.5 and 4.0, respectively. The next highest score was 4.6 on updating. The other scales had scores of 4.0 or less. The disengagement stage had the lowest score.

Here are Cindy's other test results:

Strong Interest Inventory—General Occupational Theme Scores—
Realistic: average
Investigative: moderately low
Artistic: moderately high
Social: moderately high
Enterprising: moderately low
Conventional: moderately low
Academic Comfort: moderately high
Intro/Extroversion: average

Salience Inventory—

Participation:	High salience—home and family, working Moderate—studying Low—leisure, community service
Commitment:	High salience—home and family Moderate—working, studying Low—leisure
Value Expectations:	High salience—home and family, community service Moderate—working, studying
Myers-Briggs Type Indicator:	Extrovert, intuitive, feeling, perceptive (EIFP)

SUMMARY

Counselors' knowledge of assessing developmental readiness has become increasingly important in the early identification and screening of clients with problems. Developmental tests measure the typical skills expected in normal development. Assessment includes physical, social, cognitive, emotional, communication, self-care, and independent living skills as well as work habits and adjustment. Direct testing, naturalistic observation, interviewing, and a combination of these are used to assess these domains. Much emphasis is placed on the early identification of problems and preschool screening. Developmental theories provide a useful framework for understanding critical periods of development.

QUESTIONS FOR DISCUSSION

1. What are the general principles of developmental assessment?

2. List and discuss the major domains assessed in developmental testing.

3. What are the advantages and disadvantages of the various methods of developmental assessment?

4. What are some of the major instruments used in early identification?

5. What contributions have developmental stage theories made to assessment? Do you agree or disagree that developmental theories have little value in the assessment process?

6. Review the case of Deshon, Anita, or Cindy. Do you feel that the counselor used appropriate tests? Why or why not? Did the tests have sufficient reliability and validity for the purposes intended? What is your interpretation of the data and test results given? What additional information would you have found desirable?

SUGGESTED ACTIVITIES

1. Interview counselors and helping professionals about what types of developmental assessment procedures they use and why. Have them identify problems they have had in working in developmental assessment. Report your findings to the class.

2. Visit a Head Start program and inquire about the assessment procedures they use, the cooperating agencies they work with, the incidence of children with disabilities they have identified, and the type of parent education and training that is available. Report this information to the class.

3. Write a paper or give a report on assessing developmental stages, milestones of development, assessment domains, critical issues or problems in preschool assessment, or a similar topic.

4. Select a developmental screening or stage instrument and administer it to an appropriate subject. Write the results and discuss them in class.

5. Write a critical analysis or review of one of the major developmental assessment instruments.

6. Imagine you are a school counselor. What developmental assessment tools and techniques would you use to help understand the following cases?

Case of Jessica

Jessica is in ninth grade and involved in all types of school activities. She is a cheerleader, a member of the basketball team, and a member of the National Honor Society. She has increased the amount of time she spends exercising and jogging. Jessica does these activities every day and is on a stringent diet. She has begun to lose weight. Her mother is concerned and calls you to arrange an appointment.

Case of John

John has just started second grade. He becomes tearful when school or his teacher is mentioned. He procrastinates when getting ready for school in the morning and misses the bus some mornings. His parents have called you because they are concerned about John's behavior.

Case of Isabel

Isabel is a junior in high school. She is concerned because all her friends know what they want to do after high school but she doesn't. She thinks that something is wrong with her and feels she doesn't have the skills and abilities to do much of anything.

ADDITIONAL READINGS

Bagnatto, S. J., & Neisworth, J. (1991). *Assessment for early intervention.* New York: Guilford Press.
  Focuses on the competencies needed for developmental assessment and presents models of team assessment and intervention.

Blau, T. H. (1991). *The psychological examination of the child.* New York: Wiley.
  The book is designed to help the examiner identify anything that might be out of order in the child's development, and deals with what is important to learn about all children and their development.

Cohen, L. G., & Spenciner, L. J. (1994). *Assessment of young children.* New York: Longman.
  Contains chapters on assessing development and assessing adaptive problems.

Newman, B., & Newman, P. (1999). *Development through life.* Pacific Grove, CA: Brooks/Cole.
  Presents developmental characteristics of 14 stages of development based on Erikson and Havighurst.

Reynolds, C. R., & Kamphaus, R. W. (1990). *Handbook of psychological and educational assessment of children: Intelligence and achievement. Vol. 2: Personality, behavior, and context.* New York: Guilford Press.
  Covers a broad base of the domains tested and includes evaluation and treatment of childhood disorders of development, learning, and behavior.

Vance, H. B. (Ed.). (1998). *Psychological assessment of children* (2nd ed.). New York: Wiley.
  Various assessment approaches are critically analyzed.

Vernon, A. (1993). *Developmental assessment and intervention with children and adolescents.* Alexandria, VA: American Counseling Association.
  Provides strategies to assess the normal problems that children and youth face. Case studies are presented along with strategies to help diagnose and remediate the problem.

15 Environmental Assessment

Environmental assessment contributes to the understanding of the dynamics of behavior and is used to determine the impact of environment on the development of the individual, the family, and other groups. Knowledge of a client's environment helps the counselor determine possible intervention strategies and resources that could be used effectively. Ecological psy-chology focuses on specific features of the environment and the interactive effect of individuals within systems. The focus is on not only how situational variables determine the present behavior of individuals and groups but also how these variables influence the direction of personal and social growth over time.

After studying this chapter, you should be able to

✔ Understand the uses of environmental assessment in counseling and in personality appraisal

✔ Describe the dimensions and models of environmental assessment

✔ Explain the instruments and techniques available to helping professionals

✔ Understand the applications of environmental assessment in counseling and educational contexts

THEORETICAL BACKGROUND

Environmental psychology studies the interrelationship between the physical environment and human behavior and experience. *Environmental assessment* is a way of measuring specific environmental factors. For example, one might want to know how the classroom environment affects a student's poor academic performance. Unlike other assessment practices that place the reason for academic problems solely upon the student, environmental assessment takes into consideration environmental factors as a possible cause of academic difficulties. School environmental factors could include, among others, physical setting, teacher/student relationship, curricular and educational materials, and other students' behaviors.

Environmental assessment has roots in the phenomenological approaches to counseling because idiographic approaches are often used by the counselor. Counselors are sometimes interested in discovering the laws or factors that guide the behavior of a certain individual rather than laws pertaining to people in general. Barnett and Zucker (1990) state that this approach stresses the personal and social behaviors and constructs that have validity for the client, such as overt behaviors of concern to the individual or others; covert or internal events that can be reported; central themes, values, and goals; and the impact of behaviors and situations on the individual (p. 145). The approach is concerned with the perceptions, cognitions, and learning of the individuals involved. Wallace and Larsen (1992) point out that this perspective helps the counselor to view children in relation to their total environment.

Environmental assessment also has roots in ecological psychology. Bandura (1986) emphasizes that in social transactions, people become each other's environments (p. 335). Ecological psychology focuses on groups and their adaptation to their environment, and it is characterized by its naturalistic methodology, site specificity, systems concepts, emphasis on long time periods, transdisciplinary emphasis, and evaluation of natural experiments.

A number of important values in this approach have been identified:

1. Knowledge of the environment can help us understand the behavior and adjustment of children and adults.
2. Ecological assessment helps counselors determine possible intervention strategies and resources.
3. Ecological strategies help counselors evaluate outcomes of the assessment-intervention process.
4. Environmental assessment is important to help determine the extent to which a given environment is likely to facilitate positive development.
5. Environmental assessment helps counselors determine the extent to which certain skills are required for successful placement in those environments.
6. Public Law 94–142 requires assessing environments to determine, across multiple dimensions, the extent to which they are normalized and least restrictive.

Barnett and Zucker (1990) state that child, school, family, and relevant community systems should be assessed for multiple perspectives of adjustment pertaining to the referral question, systems problems, and strengths (p. 146). They believe that it is important to consider not only how situational variables influence the present behavior of clients but also how these variables may affect clients' personal and social growth and adjustment at a later time.

Models and Dimensions

Moos (1987) developed a model to assess the dimensions related to the psychosocial characteristics and social climates of environments. He claims that environments have unique "personalities" just as people do (p. 1). His model focuses on relationship dimensions, personal development or personal growth dimensions, and system maintenance and system change dimensions. The relationship dimensions identify the nature and intensity of the personal relationships within the environment. Key concepts in the relationship dimensions across environments are involvement, support, spontaneity, expressiveness, affiliation, and peer cohesion. Personal development dimensions are characterized by autonomy, practical orientation, personal problem orientation, independent-task orientation, competition, self-discovery, and anger and aggression. The exact nature of these dimensions, of course, depends on their underlying purposes and goals. System maintenance and system change dimensions assess the extent to which the environment is orderly, is clear in its expectations, maintains control, and is responsive to change. The scales are called order and organization, clarity, and control. Moos and his coworkers have developed a number of scales to assess environments in a wide variety of settings, such as the family, school, and correctional setting.

Bailey and Wolery (1989) define the environment as including everything that surrounds us and experiences to which we are exposed. They stress seven important components:

1. Physical space—amount of space that is available and the way the space is arranged
2. Organization and supervision of space—space must be organized and well defined according to use or function
3. Materials—environment should contain sufficient materials for those who will be using the environment
4. Peer environment—the number and type of people who are going to share the environment
5. Organization and scheduling—level of organization of the environment, how activities are scheduled, and the roles of the people involved
6. Safety—environment that is free of hazards and has adequate supervision
7. Responsiveness—provides an opportunity to enhance feelings of competency and independence

Moos (1987) points out six ways of identifying characteristics of human environments (p. 1):

1. Ecological dimensions, which include geographical, meteorological, architectural, and physical design variables
2. Behavior settings, which are characterized by both ecological and behavioral properties
3. Dimensions of organizational structure
4. Dimensions identifying the collective, personal, and/or behavioral characteristics of the people living and functioning in an environment

5. Variables relevant to the functional or reinforcement analyses of environments
6. Dimensions related to psychosocial characteristics and social climates of environments

ASSESSMENT STRATEGIES

The strategy used to assess the environment depends on the referral question or the purpose of the assessment. One of the major techniques, direct observation, is preferred to interviewing because clients may have difficulty assessing their own environment. For example, if there is a concern about safety, the observer might want to draw a schematic of the room and plot the activity and movement within the space. For convenience, observers use checklists and rating scales when assessing the salient features of the environment.

Bailey and Wolery (1989) point out that helping professionals should be aware of the complexities of environmental assessment, appreciate the dynamic and interactive nature of environments, focus on functions rather than forms, and be familiar with a variety of strategies. They believe multiple sources of information and multiple measurement strategies should be used.

FAMILY AND HOME ENVIRONMENT

Research has revealed the importance of environmental factors in personal, social, and cognitive growth. The family is one of the most important environments for children and can have a tremendous impact on personal and social growth. Many instruments to assess dimensions of the family environment have been developed. Some of the observational scales used to code different dimensions of family interaction are as follows:

- The Affective Style Measure is used to observe families in situations where the participants discuss problems. The observer codes their interaction in categories, such as criticism, guilt induction, and intrusiveness. The code has been found useful in predicting psychiatric disturbance in adolescents and young adults.
- The Defensive and Supportive Communication Interaction System is a coding system used to observe the defensive and supportive communication in family interaction, family therapy, and marriage therapy. Some of the defensive categories coded are judgmental-dogmatism, indifference, and superiority. Some of the supportive categories coded are emphatic understanding, equality, and spontaneous problem solving.
- The Developmental Environments Coding System (DECS) assesses familial variables predicted by structural-developmental theory to affect ego and moral development. Dimensions such as focusing, competitive challenging, noncompetitive sharing of perspective, avoidance, rejection of the task, distortion, support, and affective conflict are coded.
- The Family Constraining and Enabling Coding System (CECS) is used to analyze transactions in family communication by measuring the frequency of commu-

nication events and their sequences. Constraining categories include cognitive constraining and affective constraining; enabling categories include cognitive enabling and affective enabling.

- The Family Interaction Scales (FIS) is a coding system for observing family interaction and is based on the theories of Jackson and Satir. The purpose of the scale is to promote understanding of individual personal development in the family context. The six major dimensions are agreement/disagreement, clarity, topic, commitment, intensity, and relationship.

Self-report instruments are another approach to measure the family environment. Some of the widely used instruments are as follows:

- The Children's Version of the Family Environment Scale (CVFES) is a downward pictorial extension of the Family Environment Scale and is used with elementary schoolchildren.
- The Colorado Self-Report Measure of Family Functioning–Revised is designed to provide a description of whole-family functioning along 15 dimensions under three general headings—relationship, personal growth, and system maintenance dimensions.
- The Conflict Tactics Scales (CTS) have been used for decades to evaluate violence within families and intimate relationships. Two updated versions of the instrument were developed: the revised Conflict Tactics Scale (CTS 2), which is the recommended form for assessing partner violence, and the Conflict Tactics Scale: Parent-Child Version (CTS PC), which is the recommended form for evaluating child maltreatment and parent-to-child violence.
- The Family Adaptability and Cohesion Evaluation Scales III (FACES III) measures family cohesion and adaptability and perceived and ideal family functioning.
- The Family Assessment Measure, Version III (FAM-III) is a self-report measure that assesses the strengths and weaknesses within a family. It consists of three types of forms: a 50-item General Scale that examines overall family health; a 42-item Dyadic Relationship Scale that examines how a family member views his or her relationship with other family members; and a 42-item Self-Rating Scale that allows each person to rate his or her own functioning within the family.
- The Family Environment Scale (FES) measures the social/environmental characteristics of the family and has three scales: relationship, personal growth, and system maintenance. The FES has 10 subscales: cohesion, expressiveness, conflict, independence, achievement orientation, intellectual-cultural orientation, active-recreational orientation, moral-religious emphasis, organization, and control.
- The Family Evaluation Form (FEF) assesses dimensions of family functioning: family centeredness, conflict and tension, open communication, emotional closeness, community involvement, children's relations, children's adjustment, parenting-nurturance, parenting-independence training, parenting-effective discipline, parenting-strict/punitive discipline, parenting-negative style, husband/wife dominance, marital satisfaction, homemaker role, worker role, financial problems, and extrafamilial support.

- The Family Functioning in Adolescence Questionnaire (FFAQ) measures family functioning in adolescence and has scales such as structure, affect, communication, behavior control, value transmission, and external systems.
- The Family Process Scales (FPS) assesses the interdependence of family members, the dynamic homeostasis in the family, and the family's ability to provide an environment that fosters healthy psychological development and a sense of well-being in its members.
- The Family Relationship Questionnaire (FRQ) measures family functioning in the areas of affect, conflict, and dominance and can be used with culturally and economically different types of families.
- The McMaster Family Assessment Device, Version 3 (FAD) evaluates family functioning on seven dimensions and is used to screen healthy and pathological family functioning. The FAD scales are problem solving, communication, roles, affective responsiveness, affective involvement, behavior control, and general functioning.
- The Self-Report Family Inventory (SFI) assesses dimensions of the family such as health, communication, cohesion, directive leadership, and expressiveness and can be used along with observational instruments in the Beavers System approach to family assessment.

The case of Ann shows how tests of family functioning can be used.

CASE OF ANN

Ann, a 9-year-old in third grade, was not achieving up to the expectations of her mother. She believed Ann was better than a C or D student and that she was lazy and not trying in school. Ann says she likes school but can't keep up with the work and she complains about too much homework. Recently Ann's father, a naval officer, was sent to the Middle East on deployment for at least 6 months. Ann is the oldest of three children. Her mother mentioned the problems of being a navy wife and the sometimes stormy relationship with her husband. Ann's mother works part time as a receptionist for a local business.

One of the tests given to Ann by the counselor was the Family Environment Scale, Children's Version. Ann had no problems taking the test, which includes 30 items. She was asked to select from three pictures on each of 10 scales the one that looks most like her family.

The test appears to have face validity and the pictures seem to represent the scales and constructs measured by the test. The authors report the procedures they used to establish the content validity of the items. The test-retest reliability was .80 over a 4-week interval. The norms are based on a population of 158 children from the Buffalo, New York, area grades 1 through 6. According to the authors, the sample represented approximately 26 per grade, an equal number of males and females, and a number of different nationalities. The religious grouping was primarily Roman Catholic. A norm table is available for converting raw scores to standard scores over the combined grades. No information is provided in the manual on the fixed

Table 15.1
Case of Ann: Results of the children's version of the Family Environment Scale.

Scales	Raw Score	Standard Score
Relationship		
Cohesion	4.0	28
Expressiveness	5.0	43
Conflict	8.0	57
Personal Growth		
Independence	3.5	35
Achievement Orientation	7.0	55
Intellectual/Cultural	2.0	22
Active/Recreational	3.0	22
Moral/Religious	8.0	53
System Maintenance		
Organization	4.5	30
Control	7.5	52

mean and fixed standard deviation of the subscales. Table 15.1 illustrates Ann's scores.

The scales with the highest standard scores were conflict (the amount of openly expressed anger, aggression, and conflict among family members), achievement-orientation (the extent to which school activities are cast into an achievement-oriented or competitive framework), and moral/ religious emphasis (emphasis on ethical and religious issues and values).

The lowest standard scores were on intellectual/cultural orientation (degree of interest in political, social, intellectual, and cultural activities), active/recreational orientation (extent of participation in social and recreational activities), and cohesion (degree of commitment and support family members provide to one another).

SCHOOL ENVIRONMENT

A number of variables are important not only to the attitudes, personal success, and achievement of students but also to a number of nonachievement behaviors such as attendance, social interaction, number of interruptions, and level of questions (McKee and Wilt, 1990). Assessment needs to focus on seating position, classroom design and furniture arrangement, spatial density and crowding, noise, and lighting. Teacher effectiveness research also has identified teacher behaviors that are related to student achievement such as "with-itn-ess," overlapping, signal continuity and momentum, group alerting, and accountability in lessons.

Scales have been developed to measure the psychological attributes of the school environment at all levels from kindergarten to graduate school. Various forms measure the perceptions of groups such as parents, teachers, students, and administrators. Some of the major instruments are described here:

- The Classroom Environment Scale, Third Edition (CES), measures the psychosocial environment of the school on three major dimensions: relationship, personal growth, and system maintenance and change. The scales are involvement, affiliation, teacher support, affiliation, competition, order and organization, rule clarity, teacher control, and innovation.
- The College Characteristics Index (CCI) measures 30 needs. The first nine scales are abasement, achievement, adaptability, affiliation, aggression, change, conjunctivity, counteraction, and deference.
- The College Student Experiences Scale (CSEQ) assesses 14 dimensions of college activities, 8 dimensions of college environment, and 21 estimates of outcomes of colleges. Additional sections call for demographic data and opinions about college.
- The Effective School Battery (ESB) assesses school climate and provides a portrait of the attitudes and other characteristics of a school's students and teachers. It measures and reports on school safety, staff morale, administrative leadership, fairness and clarity of school rules, respect for students, classroom orderliness, academic climate, school rewards, student educational expectations, attachment to school and other aspects of school climate as reflected in teachers' and students' perceptions, behavior, and attitudes.
- The High School Characteristics Index (HCSI) assesses 30 dimensions of the high school environment.
- The Institutional Functioning Inventory (IFI) can be used to compare how administrators, faculty, students, trustees, and so on perceive dimensions of the college environment. The 11 scales are intellectual-aesthetic extracurriculum, freedom, human diversity, concern for improvement of society, concern for undergraduate learning, democratic governance, meeting local needs, self-study and planning, concern for advancing knowledge, concern for innovation, and institutional spirit.
- The School Environment Preference Survey (SEPS) measures work-role socialization as it occurs in the traditional school. SEPS has four scales: self-subordination, traditionalism, rule conformity, and uncriticalness. The test is helpful in planning instructional strategies for students or as an aid in placement in alternative learning environments.

SCHOOL CLIMATE

The National Association of Secondary School Principals (NASSP) developed a model to assess school climate (Howard & Keefe, 1991). The comprehensive model consists of four types of variables: school district and community environment, school input, school climate, and student outcomes. The school district and community environment variables include the population in the area in which the school is located and the percentage of school-age children in the area served by the school. The school input variables include the following: governance of the school (private, public), percentage of minorities enrolled in the school, number of students receiving free or reduced lunches, percentage of students in remedial programs, number of activities for which budgeted resources are available, number of elective courses in the curriculum, average-per-pupil expenditure, principal's attitude toward change, performance of the school's administrative team, average teacher salary, student-teacher ratio, percentage of school employees who are professionals, number of transfers in and out of the school, average daily attendance, number of students whose primary language is English, principal's perception of autonomy of action in the district, principal's perception of participation in school decisions, number of students enrolled in the school, nature of student dress rules in the school, nature of student employment rules in the school, importance of 14 selected school goals, teacher satisfaction, teacher perceptions of autonomy of action in district or school, and teacher perceptions of participation in school decisions.

Two school climate variables include teacher climate and student climate; these are measured by the NASSP Climate Surveys.

There are six student outcomes: total achievement (reading and math scores), percentage of students receiving disciplinary referrals, percentage of students passing all courses, student satisfaction, student self-efficacy (measured by the Brookover Self-Concept of Ability Scale), and percentage of students completing the school year (not dropping out). With the impact of school reform and decentralization of authority, much attention has been placed on the school climate and school environment.

LEARNING STYLES

Learning style is defined as an individual's preferred mode and desired conditions to learn. People differ in how they approach learning. Mann and Sabatino (1985) state that "two individuals with identical IQs, with the same configuration of special abilities, or with exactly the same type and strength of information processing capacities may nevertheless be quite different in the ways that they perceive things, think, solve problems, recall events, come to decisions, play musical instruments, and swing baseball bats" (p. 189).

Assessing learning style has important benefits. It can help us understand how an individual learns and perceives, approaches, interacts, and responds to the learning environment (Keefe & Languis, 1983). Dunn, Dunn, and Price (1987) found that when students are taught with approaches and resources that complement their unique learning styles, their achievement is significantly increased and their attitudes are better. Hargrove and Poteet (1984) believe that one of the most neglected aspects of diagnostic activity with exceptional students is the determination of their unique learning styles (p. 10).

Processing Style

Processing style, an important component of learning style, can be defined as the individual's method of inputting and outputting information. Input is the reception of sensory information from visual, auditory, or hepatic sources. (Hepatic combines the kinesthetic and tactile stimuli.) Processing involves integrating the information with previously learned information. Individuals store the information in short-term memory and then use a variety of memory strategies to store the information in long-term memory. Output involves using a vocal or motor response to a problem or task.

Modality Assessment

Modalities are the specific sensory or motor abilities that are our pathways to learning. Inghram (1980) states that modality assessment is divided into two types—an assessment of acuity and assessment of perception. Assessment of acuity is an attempt to evaluate whether a certain pathway to learning exists. Assessment of perception evaluates the ability to discriminate visually, aurally, tactilely, or kinesthetically to store and recall a stimulus and integrate that stimulus into memory. In summarizing the research on modality preference, Reiff (1992) reports that about 30% will remember what is seen, 30% will remember what is heard, and 30% will use mixed modalities. The remaining 10% remember kinesthetically. Modality strengths vary with age as the child matures and gains experience; eventually, the modalities blend.

Visual Assessment.   Usually perception includes five dimensions (Inghram, 1980, pp. 274–275):

1. Visual discrimination—the ability to identify differences and similarities in stimuli, such as among letters, numbers, words, or graphic forms.
2. Figure/ground—the ability to locate or identify a figure from a background of irrelevant stimuli, such as finding a certain word on a page.
3. Visual memory—the ability to recall a sequence of visually presented stimuli, such as letters or numbers.
4. Visual closure—the ability to make a whole from reduced cues, such as naming an object or scene from an incomplete drawing.
5. Visual motor integration—the ability to utilize perceived visual stimuli to make body movements more effective and efficient, such as a football player weaving downfield to avoid tackles.

Listed here are a number of instruments available to measure both visual acuity and visual perception:

- The Beery-Buktenica Developmental Test of Visual-Motor Integration, Fifth Edition, assesses visual-motor function of children ages 2 to 18.
- The Bender Visual-Motor Gestalt Test, Second Edition, assesses the examinee's ability to reproduce visual stimuli and aids in identifying brain-injured individuals. The Bender Gestalt II is a form of the Bender test for young children.

- The Detroit Tests of Learning, Fourth Edition, Aptitude measure visual attention to letters and visual discrimination.
- The Frostig Developmental Test of Visual Perception, Fourth Edition, measures hand-eye coordination, figure/ground, form constancy, position in space, and spatial relations in children ages 4 to 8.
- The Illinois Test of Psycholinguistic Ability, Third Edition, includes subtests on visual closure, visual sequential memory, and visual association.
- The Keystone Visual Survey Test measures dimensions of visual functioning.
- The Memory for Designs Test measures visual perception of individuals ages 8 and older.
- The Slosson Drawing Coordination Test is used to diagnose visual-perceptual and visual-motor coordination problems and brain damage.
- The Snellen Eye Chart is used to screen visual acuity.
- The Spache Binocular Reading Test is used to screen a child's visual acuity.

Visual perceptual difficulties can be informally assessed by observing a client in different contexts. Any of the following behaviors might signal trouble (Inghram, 1980, p. 281):

Holding paper too close to the face
Holding a book too near or too far away
Having poor eye-hand coordination
Stumbling
Being restless, irritable, or nervous when called on to use eyes for close work
Frowning, scowling, and squinting
Blinking eyes frequently
Shutting or covering one eye
Rubbing eyes frequently

Clients with visual perceptual difficulties may complain about different physical problems when they have to use their eyes. They may state they have a hard time reading what is required. Students with visual perception problems may be clumsy in visual motor tasks such as writing, drawing, cutting, and different types of games involving movement and coordination. Such students are easily distracted and are careless about doing assignments sequentially.

Auditory Assessment.   The auditory modality has four dimensions:

1. *Auditory discrimination*—the ability of the client to distinguish among sounds, such as the sounds of letters or blends.
2. *Sound/ground*—the ability to select an auditory stimulus (e.g., a theme in music) from a background of competing auditory stimuli (e.g., the accompaniment).
3. *Auditory memory*—the ability to recall the sequence of stimuli presented orally, such as following commands and remembering digits.
4. *Auditory blending*—the ability to blend distinct sounds into words.

Any question about auditory acuity should be referred to an audiologist. A number of standardized measures of auditory acuity can be administered by trained examiners. Examples of some of the auditory assessment instruments are included here:

- The Brown, Carlsen, Carstens (BCC) Listening Test, designed for ages 18+, measures a listening skill or skills: recalling items in a sequence, following directions, recognizing transitions, recognizing word meanings, and comprehending lecture material.
- The Goldman-Fristoe-Woodcock Auditory Skills Test Battery contains 12 subtests that assess auditory attention, discrimination, memory, and sound-symbol skills in individuals age 3 to 80.
- The Goldman-Fristoe-Woodcock Test of Auditory Discrimination assesses skills in auditory discrimination, auditory memory, and sound-symbol associations in individuals age 3 to 70+.
- The Illinois Test of Psycholinguistic Abilities, Third Edition, includes subtests on auditory frequency memory and sound blending.
- The Screening Test for Auditory Perception assesses ability of students in grades 1 through 6 to discriminate types of vowels, consonants, rhyming verses, nonrhyming words, and so on.
- The Sequential Tests of Educational Progress: Listening Comprehension (STEP) is designed for grades 4 through college and measures the following skills: plain-sense comprehension, interpretation, and evaluation and application.
- The Wechsler Intelligence Scale for Children IV and the Wechsler Adult Intelligence Scale III include a digit span subtest.
- The Wepman Auditory Discrimination Test assesses the ability of children age 5 to 8 to identify similarities and differences in word pairs.

Many informal ways of identifying auditory problems are used. If the examinee has problems following directions, asks constantly to have items repeated, is distracted easily by extraneous auditory stimuli, or has pronunciation problems, auditory processing problems may be present.

Inghram (1980) identifies seven categories of auditory perception deficits (see Table 15.2).

Motor Assessment.   An individual can learn through using psychomotor abilities. A number of standardized tests measure different types of sensory motor skills. Sometimes self-concept and academic performance can be improved through development of the individual's motor abilities. Improved coordination may improve participation in sports, games, dancing, and so on. Individuals may become more confident or more accepted and feel much better about themselves. Here are some of the tests available in this area:

- The Bruininks-Oseretsky Test of Motor Proficiency, Second Edition, assesses dimensions such as running speed, agility, balance, bilateral coordination, strength, and upper limb coordination and looks at the gross and fine motor coordination of examinees age 4 to 12.
- The Lincoln-Oseretsky Motor Development Scale measures 36 motor development tasks in children age 6 to 14.

Table 15.2
Auditory perceptual deficits.

Deficit	Characteristic Behavior
Signal/ground	Has difficulty attending to what is said because of the presence of competing noise Has difficulty identifying a sound in its word context
Auditory closure	Cannot supply the missing auditory parts Has trouble in retrieving all that is said
Auditory constancy	Has difficulty in recognizing vowel or word sounds from one day to another Cannot recognize rhyming patterns Does not understand sound families
Sound discrimination	Has difficulty in distinguishing and discriminating between sounds that closely resemble each other
General auditory memory	Has difficulty remembering a sound contained in several different words Has immediate memory and can repeat but may forget the next day
Auditory attention	Is unable to remember something that has just been said by someone else Exhibits poor memory for auditory stimuli and is easily distracted
Sequential auditory memory	Cannot recall appropriate word order to constitute acceptable syntax in a sentence Cannot remember simple instructions Has difficulty in recalling appropriate word order

- The Primary Visual-Motor Test assesses visual-motor functions in copying geometrical and representative designs in children age 4 to 8.
- The Purdue Perceptual-Motor Survey–Revised Edition assesses laterality, directionality, and perceptual-motor matching skills in children from preschool to grade 8.
- The Southern California Sensory Integration Tests measure visual, tactile, and kinesthetic perception as well as motor performance in children age 4 to 10.
- The Test of Gross Motor Development, Second Edition (TGMD-2), assesses children from 3–10 years of age in 12 gross motor patterns, e.g., bouncing, catching, and kicking. The TGMD-2 can help identify children who are significantly behind their peers in gross motor skill development.

Modality Preference Assessment. Certain tests and assessment instruments can be used to quickly determine the examinee's modality preference. It is important to determine not only effective modalities but also the modalities that interfere with learning. The Swassing-Barbe Modality Index (Barbe & Swassing, 1979) is used to identify a student's modality strengths. It presents a matching-to-sample task, is individually administered, and takes about 20 minutes. The examiner presents a stimulus sample (circles, triangles, squares, and hearts), and the examinee is asked to reproduce the sample. Testing is conducted with visual, auditory, and tactile stimuli.

The first test in the index is the visual test. The examinee is given several warmup items and is then shown a set of shapes, beginning with three shapes and ending with nine. The test taker is instructed to assemble the shapes in the sequence just seen. Testing is stopped when the examinee makes errors on two consecutive sets. The second test is an auditory test. The names of shapes are read aloud in sequence at the rate of one per second. The examinee is asked to assemble the shapes in the sequence just heard. The third test is a kinesthetic test. The examiner holds a shield so that the examinee can feel but cannot see the shapes. Then the examiner removes the shield and asks the examinee to reassemble the shapes in the sequence just felt. Three separate scores are tallied.

Cognitive Style

Cognitive style is another dimension of learning style. It is the preferred way in which an individual reacts to environmental stimuli; it is used to describe how individuals differ in organizing and controlling a task. Messick (1989) defines cognitive styles as information processing habits that represent an individual's typical modes of perceiving, thinking, remembering, and problem solving. Witkin (1949) identified two component styles: field dependence and field independence. Field-dependent individuals tend not to restructure situations but to accept them as experiences. They are more attentive to social cues, accept other people readily, and like to be with people. Field-independent people prefer to interpret and restructure their environmental situations. They are less attentive to social cues and prefer to work with ideas and abstract principles. Field-independent individuals are more interested in science and mathematics, like to set their own goals, are more internally oriented, and do not require external reinforcement. Reiff (1992) reports that field-independent individuals are global, benefit from cooperative learning, and need strategies to help organize and comprehend material. Field-independent individuals are analytical, more internally motivated, and cognitively flexible, and they like independent projects.

Witkin, Moore, Goodenough, and Cox (1977) found that cognitive style is an important factor in academic learning and social behavior. Three of the widely used tests of cognitive style are listed here:

- The Children's Embedded Figures Test is a 25-item individually administered test of perceptual process and cognitive style for children age 5 to 12.
- The Embedded Figures Test assesses cognitive style in perceptual tasks; it is a 12-item test with cards containing complex and simple figures that requires the examinee to locate and trace a previously seen simple figure within a larger complex figure.
- The Group Embedded Figures Test assesses cognitive style through 25 pencil-and-paper items that require individuals to find one of eight simple figures in complex designs.

Numerous cognitive styles exist. For example, Kagan (1966) identified the impulsive/reflective style. Examinees with an impulsive style give answers quickly, without thinking through the situation, and often make errors. Reflective examinees are just the opposite. Mann and Sabatino (1985) classify cognitive styles into three general categories (p. 191):

1. A cognitive style may simply identify particular characteristics or traits that a person possesses in greater or lesser degree, such as authoritarianism.
2. A cognitive style may indicate placement at a particular point on a cognitive personality dimension whose opposite poles indicate opposing cognitive orientations, such as field independence versus field dependence or reflection versus impulsivity.
3. Certain cognitive styles place individuals within a particular cognitive category, such as analytical, categorical, or relational in their thinking.

Some of the cognitive control styles are leveling-sharpening, scanning-focusing, conceptual-differential, constricted-flexible, and field articulation. Leveling-sharpening is defined by Goldstein and Blackman (1978) as representing the characteristic degree to which current precepts and relevant memory traces interact or assimilate in the course or registration of current precepts and memories (p. 8).

Conceptual Tempo.   Conceptual tempo or reflection-impulsivity, a popular cognitive construct, was studied by Kagan, Rosman, Day, Albert, and Phillips (1964); it relates to the different speeds with which individuals make decisions. Kagan et al. used the Matching Familiar Figures Test to assess reflection-impulsivity. Individuals are presented with 12 pictures and asked to choose the one that most nearly matches a particular picture selected by the examiner. The task requires individuals to scan the alternatives and make a decision. The time taken to respond is considered a measure of the individual's tendency toward reflection or impulsivity.

Reiff (1992) reports that reflective learners think longer before they answer a question and tend to make fewer errors. They spend time deliberating and analyzing the situation. Impulsive individuals fail to attend to tasks, have difficulty considering quick decisions and alternatives to problems, are less systematic in their information search, produce fewer testable hypotheses, underestimate time intervals, are impatient, and want immediate gratification.

Counselors can help reflective learners by allowing them time to thoroughly examine materials, modeling risk taking to show that error is natural, helping them organize proofing of work, providing cooperative learning experiences, and teaching them test-taking skills. Impulsive learners can be helped by organizing materials and assignments into smaller components, providing a nondistracting environment, providing explicit guidelines and directions, and structuring time into smaller segments (Reiff, 1992).

Brain Preference.   Grady (1984) reports that research points toward two hemispheres of the brain. The left hemisphere takes care of linear and sequential operations; the right hemisphere is in charge of simultaneous and visual functions. He concludes that cognitive style is related to hemispheric organization: individuals tend to have a hemispheric preference or dominance (p. 1). Wonder and Donovan (1984) emphasize that the human brain's two halves have different but overlapping skills or ways of thinking. They found individuals with left-brain preferences to be positive, analytical, linear, explicit, sequential, verbal, concrete, rational, active, and goal-oriented. Individuals with right-brain preferences were intuitive, spontaneous, emotional, nonverbal, visual, artistic, holistic, playful, diffuse, symbolic, and physical.

According to Gazzaniga (1985) and Sherrod (1985), people tend to prefer one side of the brain over the other, and that preference affects their approach and attitude toward life and work. Sherrod states that an individual's major and minor dominance could serve as a supplemental clue to a career selection. Left-brain-oriented people tend to prefer career fields such as planning, law, editing, technology, writing, and bookkeeping. Right-brain-oriented people tend to prefer roles such as policymakers, artists, poets, sculptors, politicians, playwrights, and musicians. Two brain preference instruments are identified here:

- The Brain Preference Indicator uses a 36-item multiple-choice self-report format, with selected options scored for left- or right-brain preference.
- Your Style of Learning and Thinking (SOLAT) appears in different forms for children, adolescents, and adults and attempts to measure brain preference through 40 items with three response options per item, one each representing left, right, and integrated ways of functioning.

Figure 15.1 shows sample items representative of those often included on such instruments.

SA	A	D	SD	1. I prefer to be a listener.
SA	A	D	SD	2. Daydreaming helps me solve problems.
SA	A	D	SD	3. I like to do things on the spur of the moment.
SA	A	D	SD	4. I like to follow my hunches.
SA	A	D	SD	5. I like to take risks.
SA	A	D	SD	6. I like to be free to learn without a lot of structure.
SA	A	D	SD	7. I can express myself well verbally.
SA	A	D	SD	8. I remember faces easily.
SA	A	D	SD	9. My mood changes frequently.
SA	A	D	SD	10. I can remember and sing songs I hear on the radio or TV.
SA	A	D	SD	11. I like to print when I take notes.
SA	A	D	SD	12. I like to work in groups.
SA	A	D	SD	13. I am seldom absentminded.
SA	A	D	SD	14. I use gestures to express my feelings.
SA	A	D	SD	15. I prefer hands-on experiences to verbal instructions.
SA	A	D	SD	16. I like to think before I answer so that I use the right words.
SA	A	D	SD	17. I can rely on my intuition.
SA	A	D	SD	18. I can remember slogans I hear.
SA	A	D	SD	19. I like to write down the goals and activities I need to accomplish each day.
SA	A	D	SD	20. I like to learn things by watching how others do them and then imitating.

SA = strongly agree, A = agree, D = disagree, SD = strongly disagree

Figure 15.1
Sample brain preference survey.

LEARNING STYLES: A MULTIPLE INTELLIGENCES APPROACH

Through his theory of multiple intelligences (MI), Gardner (1983) described eight kinds of intelligences, each one representing a different way to learn. MI has had moderate to high influence on the formal curriculum and instructional materials, and almost two decades later, educators around the world are using MI in their classrooms. If you browse the Internet for MI, you will see the large number of states, school districts, and individual schools, not to mention teacher education programs that contain curriculum guides, syllabi, units, and lessons drawing on versions of MI. Some mistakenly think of multiple intelligences as being synonymous with learning styles; however, learning style theories usually refer to personality characteristics or preferences in the process of learning, while multiple intelligences emphasizes the skill of creating a product, providing a service, or problem solving. The learning styles are as follows:

1. Visual-Spatial—think in terms of physical space; learn by drawing, doing jigsaw puzzles, reading maps.
2. Bodily-kinesthetic—use the body effectively; like movement, making things, touching; physical activity, hands-on learning, acting out, role playing.
3. Musical—show sensitivity to rhythm and sound; can be taught by turning lessons into lyrics, speaking rhythmically, tapping out time.
4. Interpersonal—understanding, interacting with others; learn through group activities, seminars, dialogues.
5. Intrapersonal—understanding one's own interests, goals; learn through independent study, introspection, independent reading, diaries, privacy and time.
6. Linguistic—using words effectively; like reading, playing word games, making up poetry or stories.
7. Logical-Mathematical—reasoning, calculating, like to experiment, solve puzzles, ask cosmic questions
8. Naturalist—living things, sensitive to the natural world; learn by exploring nature.

Instruments assessing multiple intelligences include the following:

- The Multiple Intelligence Developmental Assessment Scales (MIDAS) is a self-report measure of intellectual disposition. Designed to examine the dominant intelligences of students in kindergarten through the twelfth grade, it may be completed by either the user or, in the case of a young child, by her/his parent. It takes about 35 minutes to complete the 119 multiple-choice questions that cover eight areas of abilities, interests, skills and activities.
- The Teele Inventory for Multiple Intelligences (TIMI), widely used in schools, is a pictorial instrument that enables educators to discover their students' strengths.

Learning Personalities

Another way to look at differences in learners is through their personality structure. In educational settings, one of the most widely used tests to measure personality type is the Myers-Briggs Type Indicator (MBTI). The test is based upon Jung's theory of psychological types and measures personal tendencies or preferences along four bipolar dimensions: extroversion-introversion, sensing-intuition, thinking-feeling, and judging-perceptive.

Individuals are assigned the initial letter of each bipolar dimension on which they score highest. An individual's type is the combination of the four preferences.

E represents an extrovert who relates more easily to the outer world of people.

I represents an introvert who relates more easily to the inner world of ideas.

S stands for sensing, preferring to work with known facts.

N stands for intuition, preferring to look for possibilities and relationships.

T stands for thinking, basing judgments on impersonal analysis and logic.

F stands for feeling, basing judgment more on personal values.

J refers to judging, preferring a planned way of life.

P refers to perceptive, preferring a flexible, spontaneous way of life.

The MBTI profile sheet presents a quick picture of 16 different combinations of the four dimensions. For example, the INFP has the following characteristics:

1. Full of enthusiasm
2. Loyal
3. Not apt to talk of a continuing relationship until a person is known well
4. Concerned about learning
5. Interested in language
6. Fond of independent projects
7. Apt to undertake too much but will somehow get it done
8. Friendly but not always sociable
9. Not concerned with physical environment
10. Not concerned about possessions

Lawrence (1982) states that individuals must follow their inclinations if the best learning is to take place.

The Murphy-Meisgeier Type Indicator for Children (1987) measures the psychological type of children in grades 2 through 8 using the same four preference scales as the MBTI. The authors provide manuals to help teachers and parents use the information from the test. Characteristics of each type of student are identified and suggested activities are given. Teachers are told that an intuitive student needs opportunities to be creative and original, dislikes routine and taking time for precision, has a seemingly sporadic approach rather than an orderly one, and so forth. Some of the suggested activities for intuitive students are to challenge them with problem-solving activities for which there are multiple solutions; to implement role-playing activities, especially improvisation; and to reduce the number of practice examples that are required for assignments.

Learning Style Inventories

Learning style can be broadly defined as the way in which an individual learns. Dunn (1983) states that learning style represents the "way individuals concentrate on, absorb, and retain new or difficult information or skills" (p. 496). Keefe and Monk (1988) define learning style as the composite of characteristic cognitive, affective, and physiological factors that serve as relatively stable indicators of how individuals perceive, interact with, and respond to learning environments (p. 3). Many learning style inventories are available. One widely used instrument is the Learning Style Inventory (LSI) (Dunn, Dunn, & Price, 1983), which looks at modality preferences as well as other factors. The test authors look at environmental elements that affect learning: sound, light, temperature, and design. An emotional dimension considers factors such as motivation, persistence, responsibility, and structure. Sociological dimensions relate to whether an individual likes to work alone, with peers, in pairs, in a team, with adults, or in a varied situation. Another level considers the physical factors, including intake of food or drink, time of day, and desire for mobility. The final dimension of the model relates to psychological variables: cerebral dominance, impulsivity, and analytical versus global approaches.

- The Learning Style Profile (LSP) is a 128-item pencil-and-paper inventory that was developed under the sponsorship of the National Association of Secondary School Principals. The subscales on the test cover cognitive, affective, and physiological dimensions of learning styles. Cognitive dimensions include perceptual preferences, field independence/dependence, simultaneous/successive, inductive/deductive, active/reflective, thinking/feeling, need for structure, sharpening/leveling, focusing/scanning, narrow/broad, reflective/impulsive, and complex/simple. Affective styles include achievement motivation, risk taking/cautiousness, social motivation, anxiety, persistence, inductive/deductive, thinking/feeling, and need for structure. Physiological dimensions are time-of-day preference, need for mobility, anxiety, and environmental elements such as sound, light, temperature, and design.

Other widely used learning style instruments are listed here:

- The Canfield Learning Styles Inventory assesses individuals from grade 6 to adult in four areas: conditions (peer, organization, goal setting, competition, instructor, detail, independence, authority), content (numeric, qualitative, inanimate, people), mode (listening, reading, iconic, direct experience), and expectation.
- The Learning Efficiency Test, Second Edition (LET-II), measures visual and auditory memory under both ordered and unordered recall. It measures immediate, short-term, and long-term recall.
- The Learning Preference Inventory uses Jung typology: sensing-feeling, sensing-thinking, intuiting-feeling, and extroversion-introversion.
- The Learning Styles Inventory measures student attitude toward nine models of instruction: projects, drill and recitation, peer teaching, discussion, teaching games, independent study, programmed instruction, lecture, and simulation.
- The Learning Type Measure assesses four types of learning styles based on doing/watching and feeling/thinking continuums.

Learning style inventories can also be geared to specific subject areas. One such inventory is the Reading Style Inventory (RSI), a diagnostic reading test that identifies a student's natural learning style in reading. The test takes 20 to 30 minutes to administer and has a diskette available to test, score, and produce computerized individual or group profiles. The RSI matches an individual reading-style diagnosis with the most appropriate reading methods and materials.

Kolb (1976) has a different type of model. He postulates that learning proceeds in four stages:

1. Concrete experience that directly involves the learner
2. Reflective observation in which the learner reflects on experience from different perspectives
3. Abstract conceptualization in which the learner creates generalizations and theories
4. Active experimentation with application of theories to problem solving and decision making

Kolb's Learning Style Inventory is used to assess an individual's personal preferences along the abstract-concrete and active-reflective dimensions. He identifies four major types of learning styles:

1. Convergers, who like to solve specific problems
2. Divergers, who like to organize many relationships into a gestalt and use their imaginative ability to see commonalities
3. Assimilators, who use inductive reasoning to develop theoretical models
4. Accommodators, who like to carry out plans and conduct experiments and who are action-oriented

Graska and Riechmann (in Eisen, 1984) have a different type of conceptualization of learning style. Their instrument measures six types of learning styles: competitive, collaborative, avoidant, participant, dependent, and independent.

Mind Styles.   Gregorc (1982) has yet another conceptualization of learning styles. His scale is called the Gregorc Style Delineator and consists of 10 sets of four words each, which the examinee is asked to rank. The scale is designed to reveal two types of abilities for managing information: perception and ordering.

Gregorc looks at perception as the means by which an individual grasps information. It has two dimensions: abstractness and concreteness. He defines abstractedness as the quality that enables an individual to grasp, conceive, and mentally visualize data through the faculty of reason and to emotionally and intuitively register and deal with inner and subjective thoughts, ideas, concepts, feelings, drives, desires, and spiritual experiences (1982, p. 5). He defines concreteness as the quality that enables an individual to grasp and mentally register data through the direct application of the physical senses. The second type of ability—ordering—also has two qualities: sequence and randomness. Sequence is defined as the quality that helps individuals grasp and organize information in a linear, step-by-step, methodical, predetermined order. Randomness helps individuals grasp and organize information in a nonlinear, galloping, leaping, and multifarious manner. The Gregorc Style Delineator assesses the perception and ordering abilities individuals use to adapt to their everyday environments at work, school, home, or in social interactions.

WORK ENVIRONMENT

A number of approaches measure the work environment. Sometimes the instrument measures the social-psychological dimensions of work; other times the scale might focus on measuring leadership, stress, organizational climate, or attitudes toward the bureaucratic structure. Here is a sample of work environment scales:

- The Leadership Appraisal Survey evaluates how associates view their leader or supervisor and looks at leadership style and components of leadership.
- The Occupational Environment Scale assesses the types of stress people experience in their work environment—role-related stress, responsibility for others, role ambiguity, role insufficiency, role overload, and boundary roles.
- The Organizational Climate Index (OCI) measures the psychological climate of the work setting.
- The Productivity Environmental Preference Survey (PEPS) assesses how workers prefer to function, learn, and perform their work-related or educational activities. PEPS is used for employee placement and for counseling as well as to provide information for office design and layout. It has scales such as sound, temperature, light, design, motivation, responsibility, persistence, structure, self-orientation, and peer orientation.
- The Rahim Organizational Conflict Inventories-II (ROC-II) measure the types of conflict and various styles of handling conflict found within an organization.
- The Work Environment Scale, one of 10 social climate scales developed by Moos and associates, measures three dimensions of work: relationship, personal growth, and system maintenance and system change. The scales are involvement, peer cohesion, supervisor support, autonomy, task orientation, work pressure, clarity, control, innovation, and physical comfort. There are three forms: the real form measures workers' perceptions of existing work environments . . . ; the ideal form measures the workers' perceptions of the ideal work environment; and the expectations form measures workers' expectations about their work settings.

PERSON-ENVIRONMENT-FIT

Person-environment-fit theories stress the need to study the congruence between the client's needs, capabilities, and aspirations and environmental demands, resources, and response opportunities (Holland, 1997). Counselors look for ways that different environmental arrangements and conditions force accommodations in behavior and study the individual-environment interactions. At times counselors focus on whether clients are functioning in the environment as predicted. Person-environment-fit has wide application and is especially important when working with preschool children, students with disabilities who need to be mainstreamed, and workers who are making career-change decisions.

Holland (1997) points out that individuals seek an environment that is reinforcing, satisfying, and congruent with their personality types. Congruence is related to factors such as job and personal satisfaction. Holland developed two instruments that measure personality types—the Self-Directed Search and the Vocational Preference Inventory. These tests are discussed in Chapter 10.

CASE OF SAM

Mr. Brown, a beginning fifth-grade mathematics and science teacher, came to the counselor for help. Sam is causing the teacher "fits" because he acts in an inappropriate manner. The counselor decides to use The Instructional Environment Scale (TIES; Ysseldyke & Christenson, 1987) as the instrument to help understand the situation.

The authors state that TIES systematically describes how a student's academic behavior problems are a function of factors in the instructional environment. TIES is used to gather data on 12 components of effective instruction: instructional presentation, classroom environment, teacher expectations, cognitive emphasis, motivational practice, relevant practice, informed feedback, adaptive instruction, academic engaged time, progress evaluation, instructional planning, and student understanding.

The counselor followed the procedures outlined in the manual and:

1. Conducted a classroom observation and recorded the observations on the green form.
2. Interviewed Sam, the student identified by the teacher as a problem, with the structured interview schedule on page 4 of the green form.
3. Interviewed Mr. Brown and completed page 1 of the green form.
4. Reviewed information from the interviews and observations to see if more information was needed.
5. Observed science and mathematics classes and completed the institutional rating

form on the blue sheet and the summary profile sheet.
6. Provided feedback to the teacher and to the student.

The counselor carefully read the directions for scoring TIES and read the interpretive examples. The manual presents interrater reliabilities ranging from .83 on cognitive emphasis and motivational strategies to .96 on informed feedback and student understanding. The median coefficient was .95.

The authors present evidence on the content validity of the 12 components and support each with evidence from research on effective teaching.

After observing Sam, the counselor asked the teacher whether Sam's performance was typical. Mr. Brown said that Sam put on a big show because he had a bigger audience. The teacher said his instructional goals and expectations were the same for all students. He did not plan for Sam separately and followed the instructional sequence as in the syllabus of the county. Mr. Brown said he taught the class as a whole. He wanted to keep all the students at the same place and did not give Sam any independent assignments or help.

In the interview with Sam the counselor asked about the mathematics and science classes Sam had just attended. Sam said he knew what the teacher wanted him to learn but did not know why he had to learn the "junk." He said, "I will never use this stuff." Sam said he did his homework once in a while if he liked the topic. The boy reported that the teacher asked him questions once in a while, but usually he could not answer them. Mr. Brown yelled at him for being lazy, not completing assignments, and not doing his work neatly. The counselor reviewed the class exercise that had just been assigned and found that Sam had completed 10 of 15 math problems, the first 7 of which were correct. When the problems called for more than one operation, Sam appeared to be confused.

The counselor rated the 12 dimensions of teaching after observing the classes. Each item was rated on a 4-point scale. A rating of 1 indicated that the description was not at all like the student's instructional environment, whereas a rating of 4 indicated that the description was very much like the student's instructional environment. The purpose is to identify instructional strengths and weaknesses and to identify aspects of the environment that are contributing to the student's difficulties. Domains of 1s and 2s suggest areas of difficulty where change is needed for the student to improve academically.

The counselor rated Mr. Brown 4 on instructional presentation, classroom environment, cognitive emphasis, and teacher expectation. Ratings of 3 were given on relevant practice and academic engage time. Scores of 2 were given on motivational strategies, informed feedback, and instructional planning, and 1s were assigned for student understanding, adaptive instruction, and progress evaluation.

SUMMARY

Environmental assessment contributes to the understanding of the dynamics of behavior of children and adults and the work, school, or other type of environment. The environment can be viewed in terms of physical space—how the space is organized and supervised, the materials in the environment, the people, how it is scheduled, its safety, its responsiveness, and so on. The environment can also be assessed from a psychosocial perspective. Research has pointed to the importance of the family and home environment to personal, social, and cognitive growth. Likewise, the school environment and specifically the classroom environment influences the achievement and self-concept of learners. Research on person-environment-fit supports the importance of the congruence between the environment and the individual's potential. Assessing the environment can contribute to a positive learning situation across the lifespan. Lambert and McComb (1998) see improved environment as one of the positive results of reforming schools through learner-centered education. Much of the research on environmental issues focuses on practices in business and industry, family situations, and school contexts.

QUESTIONS FOR DISCUSSION

1. What are the theoretical roots of environmental assessment?

2. Why is environmental assessment valuable to the helping professional?

3. What are some of the major models and dimensions of environmental assessment?

4. What are some of the major strategies used to assess the environment?

5. What approaches are used to measure the family environment?

6. Compare and contrast approaches used to measure the school environment.

7. What approaches are used to measure the work environment?

8. Review the case of Ann. What should the counselor say to Ann's mother when reporting the results of this test? Would you have given Ann this test? From the information provided, how would you rate this test? What other tests would you have given Ann, if any? Why?

9. Review the case of Sam. If you were the counselor, how would you proceed to work with Mr. Brown and Sam to improve the instructional environment as well as Sam's academic performance? Discuss possible strategies with other class members.

SUGGESTED ACTIVITIES

1. Interview family counselors and find out what types of assessment instruments and techniques they use and why. Report your results to the class.

2. Interview school counselors and find out what types of assessment instruments and techniques they use to evaluate the school and classroom environment and why. Report your findings to the class.

3. Administer one of the family, work, or school environment scales, score and interpret the results, and present the report to the class.

4. Write a critical review of one of the major environment instruments.

5. Write a paper on one of the current issues in assessing the environment, such as person-environment-fit or a similar topic.

6. Study the following case of Team X and answer the questions at the end.

Case of Team X

A Fortune 500 company decided that it would change its system and use work teams. The company had a general orientation session on total quality management (TQM) but did not provide any team-building or group skills training, which are crucial elements in TQM. The organization brought in a consultant to try to "fix" the teams when it appeared the experiment resulted in lower, rather than higher, productivity. The consultant gave the Campbell-Hallam Team Development Survey (TDS) to collect baseline data.

  The purpose of the TDS is to stimulate a focused discussion about the team's strengths and weaknesses; to help the team identify, acknowledge, and address its problems; to give team members an opportunity to share their ideas for improving the team; to help the leader see how his or her perceptions compare with those of the rest of the team; to identify training needs; and to provide benchmark data to track the team's progress. Members respond to 93 statements using a 6-point scale ranging from "strongly agree" to "strongly disagree." A sample of the statements follows:

  1. Team members resent being on this team.

2. The team has an excellent idea of the directions needed to accomplish the goals set for it.

There is also a 23-item observation scale that can be used in conjunction with the team member form. This form also uses a 6-point scale and includes statements such as "Group members respect each other."

Here are the results of the Team X group and its leader's scores:

Dimension/Scale	Team Average T Score	Chair's T Score
Resources		
Commitment	50	51
Competence	60	59
Material Resources	45	60
Time and Staffing	45	55
Information	58	60
Resource Use		
Mission Clarity	38	36
Leadership	40	38
Planning/Organization	42	40
Team Unity	62	64
Empowerment	45	52
Individual Goals	47	52
Improvement		
Conflict Resolution	58	53
Innovation	60	55
Team Assessment	48	60
Feedback	43	40
Rewards	38	40
Team Success		
Satisfaction	55	58
Performance	47	45
Overall Index	51	52

The mean T score is 50 and the SD is 10. The authors call 45–55 the midrange, 55–60 high, and 60 or more very high, whereas 40–45 is low and 35–40 very low.

a. What would you identify as the strengths and weaknesses of the team?
b. How do the perceptions of the chair and members correlate?
c. What implications do the data have for training and development?

ADDITIONAL READINGS

Cohen, L. G., & Spenciner, L. J. (1994). *Assessment of young children*. New York: Longman. Chapter 43, "Observing the Child and the Environment," provides an excellent overview of the current instruments and assessment strategies in working with preschool and elementary children.

Grotevant, H. D. (1989). *Family assessment: A guide to methods and measures.* New York: Guilford Press.

Discusses observational measures and self-report measures; presents abstracts of major schedules and instruments used in family assessment.

Lambert, N., & McComb, B. (1998). *How students learn.* Alexandria, VA: American Psychological Association.

Discusses the importance of enhancing the school environment to produce positive learning in classrooms.

Moos, R. H. (1976). *The human context: Environmental determinants of behavior.* New York: Wiley.

Moos presents his psychosocial model of assessing environments.

Touliastos, J., Perlmutter, B. F., & Straus, M. A. (Eds.). (1990). *Handbook of family measurement techniques.* Newbury Park, CA: Sage.

The authors review tests and assessment devices to measure family interaction, intimacy and values, parenthood, roles and power, and adjustment.

16 The Computer in Assessment

OVERVIEW

Helping professionals are seeing tremendous growth in measurement instruments created for administration, scoring, and interpretation by the computer. Some sort of computerized measure is included with many assessment instruments. The Internet is also changing the current landscape and the future of testing by providing 24/7 access, ease of use, immediate scoring, and a more limited need for test administrators, leading to convenience, cost effectiveness, and efficient testing.

Professionals need to be certain that these tests meet the professional standards for educational and psychological testing and be alert to legal and ethical issues involved in the use of computers and assessment.

OBJECTIVES

After studying this chapter, you should be able to understand

✔ the use of computer-based testing

✔ the purpose of adaptive-testing

✔ such technology as Internet-based assessment, electronic portfolios, and computer simulation testing.

✔ professional standards and guidelines for computer-based tests

COMPUTER USES

The computer is currently used in assessment in a number of ways:

1. Test scoring
2. Computing norms
3. Assessing reliability
4. Assessing validity
5. Providing interpretative feedback
6. Computing factor analysis and other statistics needed in testing

Computer programs have been developed for all types of tests including intelligence, achievement, aptitude, personality, career, and other clinical tests (Samson, 1999). Computer technology also helps facilitate and improve all phases of measurement practices. Two major types of testing involving the use of the computer include computer-assisted testing and computer-adaptive testing.

COMPUTER-ASSISTED TESTING

Computer-assisted testing, the administration of test items at a terminal, is one of the most common computer testing applications. Tests administered via computer terminal are not very different from conventional pencil-and-paper tests. Normally, the items are multiple choice and are presented one at a time. The examinees indicate an answer by pressing a key on a keyboard. Light pens are used with some programs. Instructions are presented visually, and test takers can proceed only by pressing the key that the program requests. Practice items give the examinee a chance to become familiar with the format. On some tests examinees are required to check whether they have pressed the key they meant to press. Madsen (1986) lists seven advantages for test administration on a terminal:

1. Relatively low equipment costs are required if the testing volume is low.
2. Computer-assisted tests reproduce closely the instructions and presentation formats of pencil-and-paper versions.
3. Testing on a terminal has proven to be as cost effective as traditional testing after the initial equipment costs are covered.
4. Positive client response to computer-assisted testing is common.
5. Evidence is beginning to show that computer testing does not affect the reliability of the instrument over a wide range of special clients and situations.
6. The collection of ancillary test data is now possible on variables such as response time and scales.
7. Adaptive testing, in which selection of the next question is based on the test taker's responses to previous items, is a near perfect example of computer-assisted testing adjusted to suit the needs of individuals.

Watkins and McDermott (1991) summarize the advantages of computer-assisted testing: the ability to do interactive testing, more efficient use of staff time, more efficient scoring, reduced error rate, and potential assistance to persons with visual or auditory disabilities. Kline (1993) believes the first and greatest advantage of computer-assisted testing over traditional testing is that it allows for almost immediate feedback of results. In addition, he notes, administration procedures are always the same. He also states that in cases where skilled examiners are in short supply, the prewritten interpretation can be valuable. Kline also points out that computer-assisted tests can facilitate the testing of individuals with disabilities, who can use special keyboards.

As limitations, Watkins and McDermott (1991) note that computer-assisted tests depersonalize the client, interface poorly with clients, reduce efficiency with difficult clients, compromise the confidentiality of clients possibly at risk, cannot discriminate between normal and pathological responses, and may introduce bias into testing.

Madsen (1986) also lists several limitations of computer-assisted test administration, such as increased cost and scheduling problems, problems of some test takers in using the equipment, difficult or impossible adaptation of certain types of tests and item formats, and lack of normative data for computer-assisted tests. Kline (1993) states that some clients, particularly older adults and those with intellectual handicaps, may have difficulty with computer-administered tests. In addition, some counselors believe that a primary tenet of counseling is to establish rapport with the client, and a computer cannot do this.

Jackson (1985) points out some differences between conventional and computerized administration:

1. Method of presentation of stimulus material—only one nonverbal item might be present on the screen rather than several on a page in conventional administration.
2. Type of task required of the test taker as a result of computer presentation. The computer may not be programmed to review previous responses.
3. Method of recording responses.
4. Method of score interpretation. (p. 7)

One other difference is that more information can be gained through computer administration. Green (1984) indicates that the computer can time each response and produce a response rate in addition to the number of correct answers.

COMPUTER-ADAPTIVE TESTING

Computer-adaptive testing is a form of computer-assisted testing. It is based on a model known as Item Response Theory (IRT). The goal of IRT is to describe both (1) the properties of test items (are they difficult or easy? are they informative?), and (2) the ability of the examinees. It is called a latent model because an individual's ability is not measured directly; rather, ability is only measured indirectly by looking at the various items the subject answers on a test.

Computer-adaptive testing involves the use of IRT, as well as the powerful features of computer technology, to present the test taker with a test specifically tailored for his or her individual ability level (Kline, 2000). The computer quickly locates the examinee's ability level, then tailors the questions to that level in order to obtain a more precise ability level. The first question is usually selected close to the passing level. If the test taker answers the question correctly, a more difficult item is presented next. All items are calibrated to a benchmark scale and the same cutoff for pass score is used for all test takers (Van der Linden & Ashley 2000).

The advantage of computer-adaptive testing over traditional testing is its ability to choose the test taker's next test item based upon the answer of the last item. Using computer-adaptive testing, clients have a more personalized learning experience in a controlled environment. Computer-adaptive testing provides sensitivity to the needs of users with disabilities, and the differential item function ensures equality and fairness in testing. Calibrated test items (items that are graded to a common difficulty scale) are another advantage of computer-adaptive testing. The test taker typically answers fewer items, has more time per question, can cancel responses, and scores are reported much more quickly.

Computer-adaptive testing can use the computer's capabilities to provide formats not generally used in pencil-and-paper tests. On a case write up, for example, the client could edit and make changes in the case study, which could result in more accuracy with fewer items and less testing time required. Test administration can be scheduled at the test taker's convenience, and not every test taker has to take or finish a test at the same time. Students have a new way to demonstrate their skills and test administrators can gather demographic information that might be potentially valuable in program development, instructional planning, and eliminating time pressures.

DIFFERENCES BETWEEN CONVENTIONAL AND COMPUTER TESTS

One of the major advantages for computer presentations of ability, aptitude, and achievement tests is that the format makes possible individualization of the tasks to be measured. Item banks can be developed, and the computer can be programmed to select items from the set so that each test taker could get a different test. Two types of formats—adaptive and nonadaptive—are used. On adaptive tests the item selection is sequential; that is, the items are selected on the basis of how the test taker performed on the previous items. An estimate of the examinee's skill level is made after each item response and is the basis for selection of the next item. The method gives rough approximations and requires a number of responses before the precision improves. One advantage is the climate created by the process: high-ability individuals are not bored by lots of easy items, and low-ability test takers are not frustrated by questions that are too difficult. Green (1984) concludes that computer tests can be more precise, moving estimates up and down the scale until a sufficiently accurate ability estimate is found—often after half the number of items a conventional test would need (p. 10).

In nonadaptive testing the items are selected at random from the item bank so that each test taker gets a different test form. This method has been used to simplify test security and repetitive testing. It also reduces the advantage of coaching on specific item content. This approach is useful when individuals have to be retested, such as on minimum-level skills tests. However, the item pool must be large so that the items presented on the retake are not likely to have been included on the first test. One problem with this approach is equivalence. If the item bank contains items that are homogeneous in content and of approximately equal difficulty, the tests will be fairly parallel and equal.

THE GRADUATE RECORD EXAMINATION (GRE)

The Graduate Record Examination (GRE) is an adaptive test used for graduate admissions, fellowship selection processes, and other approved purposes. There are two separate types of the GRE: the GRE General Test, which consists of three sections (verbal reasoning, quantitative reasoning, and analytical writing), and the Subjects Test (from 8 different academic areas including psychology, physics, and literature in English). The Subjects Test is required less often than the General Test. Scores on the GRE General Test are reported in standard scores and have a mean of 500 and a standard deviation of 100. The GRE shows high internal consistency reliabilities of .90 or above.

The GRE General Test is an example of an aptitude test that is administered primarily on computer, the paper-and-pencil version being available only where computers are not. Because of the flexibility of computer administration, test takers can schedule to take the test on a first-come first-serve basis at numerous sites around the world. As an adaptive test, examinees are presented with questions of average difficulty, after which the computer selects questions based on the difficulty level of the questions answered correctly and incorrectly. Each correct answer leads to a more difficult question, whereas an incorrect answer is followed by an easier one.

COMPUTER-AIDED PERSONALITY TESTING

Computer-aided personality testing is receiving as much attention as computer applications of testing in the cognitive areas. Jackson (1985, p. 5) lists the following advantages of computer-aided personality testing:

1. The saving of time of the counselor or psychologist
2. The possibility of using trained assistants to monitor test administration
3. The short time lag between administering the test, scoring it, and interpreting it
4. The elimination of human scoring errors
5. The programming capability of the computer to combine rules and complicated processing
6. The standardization of interpretations, eliminating different points of view
7. The potential for systematically collecting and developing normative databases
8. The ability of the computer to perform complex scoring procedures
9. The ability to use computer-based assessment with special populations for whom standard pencil-and-paper procedures are not feasible

The widespread availability of microcomputers has made possible not only online presentation of stimulus material but all types of programs for scoring and interpreting the test data. Studies have been made with computer-assisted testing of psychiatric patients and individuals with physical disabilities at all age levels. Programs have been developed to aid psychiatric diagnosis; diagnosis of alcoholism, type A behavior, and personal construct systems; and personal decision making and career guidance.

EVALUATING COMPUTER-BASED ADAPTIVE TESTING

Green (1984) lists five main psychometric criteria for evaluating computer-based adaptive testing: unidimensionality, reliability, validity, quality of the item parameters, and equating. Unidimensionality relates to the domain being measured. In ability and aptitude testing, items should be homogeneous and should correlate highly with the total score. The test or scale usually yields one score. However, evidence should be presented that the domain is unidimensional and measures primarily one dimension.

Reliability for these tests is computed by the use of an internal consistency reliability index. McBride and Martin (1983) found that twice as many items are needed on a conventional test to get the same reliability as on a computer-adaptive test. Content, predictive, and construct validity of these tests is computed in the same way as for a paper-and-pencil test. It is important to look at how the content validity of the items was studied.

The quality of parameters relates to the quality of the reliability indexes of the items, and the estimate of the item parameters appears to require a large number of cases and items (Green, 1984, p. 15). Because not all items are used with each test taker, those items selected can affect reliability significantly. Items with low reliability dilute the estimate of time parameters of items with good reliability.

Green (1984) identifies two aspects to equating. Because each individual's test is unique, the tests must be certified as equivalent. This task demands that the test be unidimensional with a small error of measurement and that the item responses fit the item-response theory model. The second is being able to equate the computer-adaptive test score with the conventional test score. The Educational Testing Service (ETS) publication *Computer Based Testing: From Multiple Choice to Multiple Choices* (1994) gives these advantages of computer-adaptive testing:

1. Mastery levels can be demonstrated faster and the test can be terminated (licensure or certification) once a test taker has reached the criterion level of mastery.
2. Testing is more interesting and positive. The test provides questions at a level that is consistently appropriate and challenging to the test taker.
3. Testing time is shortened by focusing on the test taker's ability level.
4. Increased psychometric precision is possible over a broad range of proficiency.

In assessing computer-assisted and computer-adaptive tests, the form included in Figure 16.1 might be useful. Moreland (1992) summarizes four important factors in assessing computer-assisted test interpretations: the credentials of the system author, the

Test title _____

Description of test _____

Description of scales _____

Potential uses _____

Publisher's address _____

        Phone _____

Author qualifications _____

Hardware requirements _____

     K _____

     Additional equipment _____

System availability   Trial period available _____ Yes   Cost

_____ Apple   _____ No   _____ Number of users

_____ IBM   _____ Software cost per user

_____ Other_____   _____ Supplemental costs (other systems,
                                                          additional hardware)

Materials provided

_____ Handbook or guidebook   _____ Videocassettes

_____ Technical manual   _____ Training package

_____ User's manual   _____ Other_____

_____ Discs

Populations to be served

_____ Primary/preschool   _____ Young adult

_____ Elementary (K–6)   _____ College/community college

_____ Middle school (7–9)   _____ Adult

_____ High school (10–12)   _____ 65+

_____ Special populations (specify)_____

Potential users   Sophistication required

_____ Administrators   _____ High

_____ Counselors   _____ Medium

_____ Psychologists   _____ Low

_____ Teachers

_____ Students/examinees

Features available on software

_____ Test scoring   _____ Measures of variability

_____ Test score interpretation   _____ Record-keeping features

_____ Item analysis, difficulty, discrimination _____ Individual records

_____ Reliability information   _____ Accumulated record keeping

_____ Descriptive statistics   on individuals

Figure 16.1
Form to evaluate computer testing programs.

Features available on software *(continued)*

_____ Group records
_____ Capability of adding other data
_____ Measures of central tendency

_____ Tabular presentations
_____ Graphic presentations

Administration features

_____ Self-administered
_____ Randomly generated

_____ Can add local items
_____ Computer-adaptive

Technical characteristics (1 = excellent, 2 = good, 3 = poor)

_____ User friendliness
_____ Display
_____ Documentation
_____ Storage capacity
_____ Clarity of score
_____ Clarity of reports
_____ Ability to change scores
_____ Response time between input and feedback
_____ Reliability data
_____ Parallel forms
_____ Content validity
_____ Predictive validity

_____ Ease of operation
_____ Ease of input/entry
_____ Printing/graphics
_____ Flexibility
_____ Profiles
_____ Error checking
_____ Reading level
_____ Help options
_____ Internal consistency
_____ Standard error measurement
_____ Construct validity
_____ Concurrent validity

Item selection/presentation

_____ Access to directions
_____ Type of item selection

_____ Skipping features

    _____ Random
    _____ Adaptive

    _____ Sequential
    _____ Feedback

Display conventions

_____ Format
_____ Headings

_____ Color
_____ Highlighting

_____ Menus

Answering/scoring

_____ Answer registration methods   _____ Backup and changing answers   _____ Error hopping

Norms

_____ Computer-assisted-adaptive format
_____ Appropriateness
_____ Types of scores

_____ Pencil-and-paper format
_____ Adequacy of sample

Figure 16.1
Continued

documentation of the system, the scholarly review of the system, and the tryouts of the system.

INTERNET-BASED ASSESSMENT

It is difficult to estimate the number of assessment-related websites currently available on the Internet other than to say that the number is large and increasing (Buchanan, 2002). Internet-based assessment webistes vary in content, quality, and function. Some seek to adhere to high standards of professionalism of psychological assessment. Others appear unprofessional and unconcerned with ethical and security issues. The motivation for development of many of these sites is easy to understand. Commercial assessment sites can make more money because the Internet offers easy access to large numbers of participants. Researchers benefit from Internet-based assessment: they have access to large numbers of participants; the costs associated with traditional assessment methods, such as publishing and distributing paper surveys, mailing materials to study participants, and data collection and entry are eliminated; and the costs to develop, publish, and maintain Web-based surveys are significantly lower. Musch and Reips (2000) identified some of the advantages Internet-based assessment brings to psychologists. The main advantages reported are the following:

1. The large population access
2. Less costs
3. The possibility of providing the tools around the clock, without any time limitation
4. The completely voluntary participation, which usually improves respondents' motivation

Concerns about the reliability and validity of the data collected through the Internet remain, although previous research indicates no significant difference between traditional and Internet-based testing. Another concern is that although many people have access to the Internet, not everyone does, which can be a confounding variable in a research study in terms of population sample. Questions regarding test security remain, and it is nearly impossible to positively identify a person taking an online assessment if the test is not taken at a special site. Another issue is that of providing feedback/results to participants; specifically, the inability of having human contact with a clinician/researcher while the participant is receiving and processing test results.

COMPUTER SIMULATION IN TESTING

Computer simulation is the technique of representing the real world through a computer program. Interactive software programs allow individuals to explore new situations, make decisions, acquire knowledge based on their input, and apply this knowledge to control the ever-changing simulation state. Simulations have been in use for many years to assess performance in different environments. It has been a prominent, long-established technique for conducting training and assessing the readiness of individuals, crews, teams, groups, and units to perform military operations. Devices used for computer simulations range from plastic mock-ups to laptop computers to full-motion aircraft simulators. All sectors—educational, industrial, and the military—use techniques ranging from simulated device operation to role-playing in order to prepare and assess personnel. A simulated environment can never be quite like "the real thing"; however, assessment problems associated with experiments in the real world can be avoided in a simulated environment. Simulations can be used to investigate problem-solving skills, perhaps allowing the student to explore a range of options. It has been suggested that computer simulations may be used for intelligence assessment (Kroner, Plass, & Leutner, 2005).

Computer simulations provide a range of flexible assessment tools, suitable for individual or group exercises, under open or closed conditions. Rather than taking individuals through a series of test items, assessments involving computer simulations would immerse them in situation like the ones for which they are being selected or prepared. In addition, it has the potential to be more convenient and more accepted by participants, to improve participants' interest and motivation, and to allow for adaptive testing.

PROFESSIONAL STANDARDS AND GUIDELINES

In *Guidelines for Computer-Based Tests and Interpretations*, the American Psychological Association (1998) suggests that automated tests be used as only one of several sources of information about clients. Shertzer (1986) recommends that professional training standards be changed so that all graduate students in the helping professions take a course in computer applications with emphasis on computer-assisted testing and become familiar with the APA guidelines. He calls for five main objectives to be gained:

1. Basic computer literacy
2. Knowledge of information sources
3. An objective and evaluative attitude toward computer-based tests
4. Understanding of the individual's right to privacy
5. Knowledge of and experience with computer-assisted testing

Because of accelerated advances in computer technology—touch screens, voice recognition, rapid access to data—our knowledge of computer hardware and software needs to keep pace. The field is evolving in its methods and standards. Green (1991) sees the standards as a living document that provides us with an important start but that will require frequent revision.

Standards for Educational and Psychological Testing (AERA et al., 1999) also addresses the issue of computer-assisted and computer-adaptive testing. The standards call for adaptive tests to provide estimates of the magnitude of errors of measurement based on the analysis of the results from repeated administrations using different items. Alternate form estimates of reliability are necessary to provide an independent check on the magnitude of errors in measurement in adaptive testing. The guidelines caution against concurrent comparisons between paper-and-pencil and adaptive forms as estimates of the alternate for reliability; however, if the variance in the methods is small, the tests can be considered parallel.

The standards also suggest that the author needs to provide in the manual the rationale and supporting evidence for procedures used in selecting items for administration, deciding when enough items have been presented, and scoring the test.

The scaling, norming, score comparability, and equating procedures used in adaptive testing need to be reported. The authors are responsible for providing specific information about the methods of equating the different forms of the test, as well as studies checking the adequacy of equating procedures.

The environment for the administration of computer-adaptive tests calls for the items displayed on the screen to be legible and free from glare, with the terminal properly positioned. The novelty of presentation should be watched because it might have an unknown effect on the test administration.

Green (1991) recommends that a good strategy is to use the system, enter a set of responses, and examine the results and their interpretation. Counselors should review similar systems at the same time so they can compare how the systems react to the same response pattern.

SOURCES OF INFORMATION

Many sources of information on software exist in this field. Journals publish reviews or articles and research on computer-assisted and computer-adaptive testing. Professional organizations that address computerized testing are concerned with standards and provide useful information to users. Computer networks, reference and resource books, ERIC documents, and annotated bibliographies are plentiful. Several sources are identified at the end of this chapter.

Other resources that might be helpful to helping professionals include Assessment Abstracts Online at *http://www.parinc.com*. McMinn and Scanish have developed the Rorschach Trainer Version I for Windows.

Several companies provide online administration, scoring, and interpretation of major assessment and outcome measures for use by clinicians. For example, Optaio is a service through the Psychological Corporation. Unlimited monthly use of standardized assessment instruments is available for monitoring patient progress over time. Available instruments include the following:

Beck Anxiety Inventory

Beck Depression Inventory II

Beck Hopelessness Scale

Beck Scale for Suicide Ideation

Brown Attention Deficit Disorder Scale

Butcher Treatment Planning Inventory

Devereux Scales of Mental Disorders

Eating Inventory

Rust Inventory of Schizotypal Cognitions

ETS has developed ACCUPLACER, a system that offers colleges and universities a comprehensive program for testing, placement, advisement, and research. The placement tests for the system use computer-adaptive testing in seven assessment areas: reading comprehension, sentence skills, levels of English proficiency, arithmetic, elementary algebra, college-level mathematics, and supplemental skills. CRASMS is the placement, advisement, and management component. It can be programmed to tell the students their college placement scores and what they mean as well as when their first class starts and who their advisors are.

COMPUTER OPTIONS

Several programs are available to help individuals computerize their own tests. These programs address the following:

1. How the items are presented to the test takers—in high-resolution text, color graphics, special characters, and even foreign alphabets
2. How the test is designed—conventional format (everyone gets the same item), sequential (testing continues until the examiner can make a decision), adaptive (maximum information)
3. How the narrative score interpretation is presented—in the test maker's own words and style or geared to the specific need of the test taker or tester
4. How the data is stored
5. How the data is scored—including what type of statistical analysis is completed

ADVANTAGES AND DISADVANTAGES OF COMPUTER APPLICATIONS

These are some of the major advantages of computer applications:

1. Quick, easy, and economical collection of information
2. Improved scoring accuracy
3. Possible alternate formats
4. Faster feedback to the tester and test taker
5. Reduced time spent on routine tasks, such as intake, interviewing, and initial assessment
6. View of computer-assisted testing and interpretation as legitimate and important
7. Endless computer applications
8. Item-response theory allows for individuals to get different sets of items

Disadvantages of computer applications include the following:

1. Computer interpretations are confounded because no allowances are made for the client's emotional state, physical disabilities, or other pertinent characteristics.
2. Some traditional instruments may not be easily adapted to computer formats. Computer-assisted tests have different psychometric properties than the paper-and-pencil tests they replace. For example, reading tests that require oral reading may be a problem, although in the future speech recognition will be sophisticated enough to be used for this purpose.
3. Normative data may be inadequate for computer-assisted or computer-adaptive tests.
4. The equipment can be expensive, and multiple scoring problems might arise with inadequate equipment.
5. Adequate client-screening procedures need to be developed to identify clients in crisis, who may be unable to concentrate or respond to a computer-assisted interview or assessment.
6. Costs in equipment, training, and time may not be worthwhile.

7. Computers lack human involvement—some individuals see the computer as cold and inhuman. The computer does not recognize when the examinee is tired or has limited attention span. Most of the time the computer program is not able to handle probes.
8. Clients may see a threat to the confidentiality of test data; computers have the potential to collect, store, and recall much intimate information.
9. The standards for obtaining these tests are not strictly monitored.
10. A substantial investment of money is needed by publishers to develop this type of testing.

It is important to remember that the examiner does not have access to decisions or rules the authors have developed or selected. The computer can be guided to make decisions, but someone has to program the computer, providing the information or rules for decision making. Individuals in the helping professions certainly need to develop computer literacy, but that literacy may not be sufficient to evaluate computer rules and procedures. Consequently, it is necessary to be cautious in the use of computerized reports with clients. Some individuals advocate using the computer for what it can do best—quickly process and store information—and humans for what they can do best: think, interpret, and interact.

SOFTWARE FOR TEST DEVELOPMENT

A number of software programs have been developed to help the examiner construct tests:

- Iteman assesses data using the Rasch model of test analysis.
- Microcat is a computerized testing system to support the entire test process. It can create and maintain an item bank, develop and print forms, and develop and administer computerized test forms from conventional to adaptive versions.
- Testpak consists of two software programs—one for criterion-referenced tests, the other for norm-referenced. The packages analyze, disaggregate, and report data in combination with other student information and can produce a variety of reports for teachers, administrators, and parents. The tests are analyzed using the classical theory of test item analysis.

TRENDS AND ISSUES

We have gone through several generations of computer applications. Initially paper-and-pencil tests were programmed for the computer. Now, new formats and types of items are possible, and computer-based simulations can be used in training and testing of problem solving. Many developments in computer and video technology have occurred in the past 25 years, and we can anticipate even greater impact on the field of testing in the future.

It appears that computer-adaptive testing is increasing. The National Council on Licensure Examinations reported that the Nurses Licensing Testing, for example, has a computer-adaptive form. The Graduate Record Examinations, the Professional Assessment of Beginning Teachers, and the examinations of the National Council of Architectural Registration Boards all have computer-adaptive forms available. The Educational Testing Service uses the Sylvan Technology Centers to administer its computer-adaptive versions of tests. Convenience is a strong argument for these types of tests: Clients have a choice of time and date and have a more personalized learning experience in a controlled environment. They receive preliminary scores immediately and final results much faster than before. Computer-adaptive testing in this context provides equal access, sensitivity to the needs of users with disabilities, and test security. The differential-item function ensures equality and fairness in testing.

As computer-based assessment becomes more prevalent in clinical practice, continued research is needed into its limitations and benefits. Improvements must continue to be made in the quality of computer- and Internet-based tests. More research is needed on how viewing diagnoses from computerized interpretive reports can influence clinical decision making. Studies are needed to better understand how a computer aversion or attitudes towards computers might influence the outcome of computerized tests from a cross-cultural standpoint.

Kyllonen (1997) foresees the merging of technology and theory in the development of future aptitude batteries. The process would include computer delivery, item generation technology, multidimensional adaptive technology, comprehensive cognitive abilities measurement, and a latent factor center design. Merging of these latest advances will help develop the prototype test format for the next generation. In 1998 the APA session on testing trends had sections on computerized test item banking: a revolution in item analysis and test construction.

SUMMARY

Computer technology has been used in all phases of testing. Many tests now have computer-assisted versions. Computer-assisted testing allows for more efficient use of staff, more efficient and reliable scoring, and greater flexibility in testing individuals with disabilities. Disadvantages include depersonalization of the client and poor interfaces of the client with the computer. The issue of confidentiality is also of concern.

Computer-adaptive testing is becoming more widely available to assess the aptitude and achievement of test takers. Many tests provide computer-generated interpretations of tests. Helping professionals are seeing a tremendous growth in the instruments being adopted, adapted, and created for administration, scoring, and interpretation by the microcomputer. Users need to be certain that these tests meet the professional standards for educational and psychological testing and be alert to the legal and ethical issues involved with computer testing.

QUESTIONS FOR DISCUSSION

1. Do you agree with Meier and Geiger's (1986) recommendation that all graduate students in the helping professions complete a course in computer applications in human services, with special emphasis on computer-assisted testing? Why or why not?

2. In what ways are computer-assisted assessment and traditional assessment techniques alike? In what ways are they different?

3. Should assessing be left to the computer and interpretation to the human service professional? Defend your position on this issue.

4. What do you see as future trends in this field? Do you believe that there will be marked acceptance of the new technologies and innovative approaches in computer assessment? Why or why not?

5. Adaptive testing is not a new concept but has been adapted for use with the computer. One of the advantages of computer-adaptive testing is that it saves time. Do you believe the results of such approaches will be as valid or reliable as those of traditional testing? Why or why not?

SUGGESTED ACTIVITIES

1. Take a computer-assisted test. Evaluate your experience and report the findings to the class.

2. Interview test takers who have taken computer-adaptive tests and identify their attitudes toward the experience. What aspects did they like best? What aspects did they like least?

3. Make an annotated bibliography of computer-adaptive and computer-assisted tests that are currently available in your field.

4. Get three or four computerized reports of test results. Analyze them according to criteria such as understandability, attractiveness of format, readability, and psychometric properties.

5. Devise a rating scale to evaluate computer-assisted or computer-adaptive tests and select an instrument to evaluate with your scale. Compare the traditional test form with the computerized form. Are there marked differences in the two versions?

6. Read the following case study and answer the questions at the end.

Case of Lu

Lu is upset to learn that the professional licensing examination is a computer-adaptive test now, which will be given at the XYZ Technology Center. She complains to you, her counselor, saying: "At my age, I hate computers, I don't use one. . . I don't want one! How can they really say that the results are the same as before? The exam used to be 6 hours and now you say it will take me only 2 hours. How can they cover all the knowledge we are supposed to have in a 2-hour period? Also, I don't type or speak 'computerese' . . . I will be at a disadvantage!"

a. How would you answer Lu's concerns?

b. How would you help her prepare for the testing and alleviate her anxiety?

ADDITIONAL READINGS

These journals publish research on observational techniques and instruments:

Behavior Research Methods and Instrumentation
Computer Living
Computers in Human Behavior
Computers in Human Services
Computers in Psychiatry/Psychology
Counseling Psychologist
Educational and Psychological Measurement
International Journal of Man-Machine Studies
Journal of Counseling and Development
Journal of Educational Measurement
Journal of Occupational Psychology
Measurement and Evaluation in Counseling and Development
Psychiatric Annals

Maddux, C. D., & Johnson, L. (1998). Computer-assisted assessment. In H. B. Vance (Ed.), *Psychological assessment of children* (2nd ed., pp. 87–105). New York: Wiley.

Moreland, K. L. (1992). Computer-assisted psychological assessment. In M. Zeidner & R. Most (Eds.), *Psychological testing: An inside view* (pp. 343–376). Palo Alto, CA: Consulting Psychologists Press.
Provides the reader with an overview of what is happening in computer-assisted testing.

Parshall, C., Spray, J., Kalohn, J., & Davey, T. (2002). *Practical considerations in computer-based testing*. New York: Springer.
Evaluates the different types of computer testing such as computer-based testing, innovative item types, computerized fixed tests, automated test assembly, computerized adaptive testing, and so on. Evaluates each type on item format, test security, time limits, guessing issues, content coverage, cost, and the like.

Wainer, H. (2000). *Computerized adaptive testing: A primer* (2nd ed.). Hillsdale, NJ: Erlbaum.
Topics such as history, system design and operation, item pools, item-response theory, item calibration and proficiency estimation, scaling and equating, reliability and measurement precision, validity, and future challenges are discussed.

17 Working with Diverse Populations

OVERVIEW

Counselors need to be cognizant of the issues involved in assessing members of diverse populations. In this chapter, the term "diverse populations" refers to individuals with disabilities, disorders, or impairments, as well as to ethnic minorities. Assessment instruments are often criticized for being biased and unfair for use with diverse populations. Some of the issues that give rise to these criticisms are common to people with disabilities and those who are ethnically in the minority: the normative bases of tests, diverse individuals' lack of experience in test taking, the cultural membership of the examiner, and the fact that tests developed by the majority cultural group sometimes require those taking these tests to access information that might not be as readily available to members of nonmajority cultures as it is to members of the majority culture.

OBJECTIVES

After studying this chapter, you should be able to

✔ Identify the standards for testing diverse populations

✔ Identify the major tests and assessment techniques used with individuals from diverse populations

✔ List the goals and objectives and explain the issues and problems of working with diverse groups

✔ Identify factors that help in understanding various ethnic groups

✔ Describe assessment instruments, techniques, and procedures that are appropriate for use with various ethnic groups

STANDARDS FOR TESTING PEOPLE WITH DISABLING CONDITIONS

Standards for Educational and Psychological Testing (AERA et al., 1999) identifies standards for testing people with disabling conditions. The majority are intended primarily for test authors who are modifying tests to use with diverse groups.

Test authors are required to have psychometric expertise and experience in working with these groups, and test publishers should caution examiners about the use and interpretation of the test with clients with special needs until it has been fully validated. Authors should conduct pilot tests on people who have similar disabilities to check on the appropriateness and feasibility of the modifications, and should include a careful statement of steps taken to modify the test so that users will be able to identify any changes that may alter its validity.

Test authors should use empirical procedures to establish time limits for modified forms and explore the effects of fatigue. They also should provide validity and reliability information on the modified forms as well as on the unmodified forms.

Clearly, it is important for the user to study the manual and evaluate the technical information to determine whether the modifications are valid and reliable for the group in question. In addition, counselors and psychologists working with clients who have special needs should know what alternate tests and modes are available and appropriate for these persons. Clients need to be informed of the availability of these other instruments and to be given a chance to take them. Those who are interpreting the test results need to know which set of norms should be used. Regular norms are used when the examiner needs to compare the test performance of the individual with disabilities with the general population. Special norms are appropriate when the examiner is looking at how the individual performs in relation to peers with the same disabling condition.

The needs of examinees with impairments should be considered carefully. Individuals with hearing impairments need interpreters who sign the instructions and items for them. Some tests have videocassettes with the directions and items presented in sign language. For individuals with visual impairments, large-print versions, braille forms, and forms on cassette recorders are available. Most national testing programs have provisions for individuals with special needs to have more time to complete tests.

Both content and format of tests have to be revised for people from diverse groups. Most publishers have expert panels who review the appropriateness of test items to eliminate bias.

Testing Linguistic Minorities

For many non-English-speaking groups, English is a second or third language. Tests written in English may become tests of language proficiency for these individuals, rather than measures of other constructs. Of course, it is sometimes important and necessary to have tests that measure English proficiency—especially for educational diagnosis and placement. Tests not meant to measure proficiency in English are sometimes translated into the appropriate native language. However, there may be problems in translation, and the content and words might not be appropriate or meaningful to the group being tested.

Standards for Educational and Psychological Testing (AERA et al., 1999) includes seven standards relating to the testing of linguistic minorities. The selection and use of appropriate tests need to be reviewed carefully. A number of standards are intended primarily for the test authors and publishers, but should be taken into consideration by the test user. If the test is modified, the changes should be spelled out in the manual in addition to specifications for test use. The reliability and validity of the test for the intended linguistic group are also important. If two versions of dual-language tests exist, evidence of the comparability of the forms should be included. The standards also caution users not to require a greater level of proficiency of the test in English than the job or profession requires—a significant concern in developing and selecting employment, certification, and licensing examinations. Another standard is extremely important to users; it cautions users to not judge English language proficiency on the basis of test information alone. Many language skills are not adequately measured by multiple-choice examinations. The counselor needs to use observation techniques and perhaps informal checklists to assess proficiency more completely.

The Code of Fair Testing Practices in Education (Joint Committee, 1999) calls for tests to be developed in ways that make them fair for test takers of different races, gender, ethnic background, or with disabling conditions. Test users are asked to evaluate the procedures used by test developers to avoid potentially insensitive content or language; review the performance of test takers of different races, gender, and ethnic background when samples of sufficient size are available; and evaluate how performance differences may be caused by inappropriate characteristics of tests. When necessary and feasible, test administrators are to use appropriately modified forms of tests or administration procedures for test takers with disabling conditions and then interpret standard norms with care in light of the modifications that were made.

IDEA

The Individuals with Disabilities Education Act (IDEA) exemplifies the current philosophical and social attitudes toward people with special needs. IDEA's predecessor, Public Law 94-142 was passed by Congress in 1975 and has been amended three times, most recently in 2004. The law guarantees individuals with disabilities age 3 to 21 appropriate educational opportunities in the least restrictive environment. The law also sets standards for the types of assessment materials and procedures used. Assessment must not discriminate against an individual on the basis of race or culture. Furthermore, test and assessment materials should do the following:

1. Be provided and administered in the examinee's language or other mode of communication
2. Be validated for the specific purpose for which they are to be used
3. Be administered by trained personnel according to specifications in the manual
4. Yield useful information in specific areas of educational need
5. Give an accurate picture of what is to be assessed, such as aptitude and achievement, rather than reflecting the examinee's impaired skills

6. Be utilized and interpreted by a multidisciplinary team of persons, including at least one teacher or specialist in the area of the disability

The targeted student should be assessed in all areas related to the suspected disability; the testing should not be confined to academic performance, but should also include health, vision, general intelligence, communication skills, and emotional status. In other words, a single criterion cannot determine the most appropriate educational program for a test taker.

PRESCHOOL EVALUATIONS

In recent years there has been an effort to identify children with disabilities prior to kindergarten. Five important assessment domains for this group include cognitive skills, motor skills, communication skills, play and social skills, and self-care skills.

An annotated list of preschool assessment instruments and tests is provided here:

- The Bayley Scales of Infant and Toddler Development, Third Edition, are used to assess the mental and psychomotor development of children from 2 to 30 months of age and to aid in the diagnosis of normal or delayed development.
- The Cattell Infant Intelligence Scale measures intellectual development of children from 3 to 30 months by assessing verbalizations and motor control.
- The Dallas Preschool Screening Test is used to assess the learning disabilities of children between the ages of 3 and 6; it measures auditory, language, motor, visual, psychological, and articulation development.
- The Denver Developmental Screening Test, Second Edition (DDST-II) is used to evaluate a child's personal, social, fine motor, gross motor, language, and adaptive abilities. The test is appropriate for use as a screening tool with children from birth to age 6.
- The Developmental Assessment for the Severely Handicapped is an observation scale used to assess the progress of children with severe disabilities from birth to 9 years of age (developmental age). The scale provides information on the sensorimotor, language, preacademic, daily living, and socioemotional areas used to establish individual education programs.
- The Kent Infant Development Scale (KID Scale) uses a 252-item inventory to assess the developmental age of infants and young children chronologically or developmentally under 1 year of age. The test measures cognitive, language, motor, self-help, and social skills.

DuBose (1982) reminds us that neither Gesell nor Piaget studied children who were impaired or were developing more slowly than their peers. Thus, this paucity of developmental information makes it harder for examiners to assess preschool children with disabilities. Some of the behaviors to be noted and considered are described in Table 17.1

Public Law 99-457, the Education of the Handicapped Act Amendments of 1986, focuses on identifying and developing programs for infants and toddlers with disabilities. The purpose of the law is to facilitate the development and implementation of

The following tests are used especially for autism:

- The Autism Screening Instrument for Educational Planning, Second Edition provides an assessment and educational planning system for autism and developmental delay. The scale looks at sensory, relating, body concept, language, and social self-help; samples vocal behavior; assesses interaction and communication; and determines learning rate.
- The Behavior Observation Scale for Autism assesses the presence of behaviors characteristic of autism.
- Childhood Autism Rating Scale (CARS) is a 15-item scale designed to distinguish mild to moderate from severe autism. It is suitable for use with any child over 2 years of age.
- The Gilliam Autism Rating Scale helps identify and diagnose autism in individuals age 3 to 22 and estimates the severity of the problem. The scales are stereotyped behaviors, communication, social interaction, and developmental disturbances.

Anxiety Disorders.   Anxiety disorders take different forms in childhood and adolescence but are characterized by intense subjective distress and maladaptive patterns of cognition and behavior. For children and adolescents these might be separation anxiety, overanxiety, and avoidant disorders. For adults they may take the form of generalized anxiety disorders, panic disorder, phobic disorders, and the like. Strauss (1993) suggests the use of multimodal assessment such as structured interviews, self-report inventories, parent and teacher checklists, client observations, and physiological measurements. Major self-report inventories include the Revised Children's Manifest Anxiety Scale and the Fear Survey Schedule for Children-Revised. A number of rating scales contain items dealing with anxiety and withdrawal.

One of the most widely used tests to measure anxiety in adolescents and adults is the State-Trait Anxiety Inventory. It provides two different types of assessment of anxiety: how individuals feel at a particular time (state) and how individuals normally perceive a situation.

Conduct Disorders.   Individuals with conduct disorders show patterns of antisocial behavior, often exhibit impaired functioning at home and school, and are viewed as unmanageable by parents and teachers. The child or adolescent may exhibit the following behaviors: stealing, truancy, property destruction, use of weapons, physical cruelty, arson, and similar actions. Helping professionals assess the disorder with a variety of techniques, including self-report inventories such as the MMPI Adolescent and MCMI-III or reports by others such as the Sutter-Eyberg Student Behavior Inventory–Revised. There are a number of direct evaluative systems such as the Parent Daily Report. Peer evaluations are also sought through sociometric techniques. Kazdin (1993) reports that each method has its strengths, methodological weaknesses, and sources of bias, and he advocates the use of multiple measures for accurate assessment.

Attention-Deficit Disorder.   Although its cause is unknown, attention-deficit disorder involves multiple areas of functioning and is a complex and chronic disorder of the brain. Rapport (1993) recommends multimodal assessment, which includes structured and semistructured interviews such as the Diagnostic Interview for Children and Adolescents, Fourth Edition (DICA-IV); and the Diagnostic Interview Schedule for Children-Revised (DISC-R); checklists and rating forms such as the Child Behavior Checklist (CBC) and observations of classroom behavior, intellectual and achievement testing, and neurocognitive testing such as the Conners' Continuous Performance Test (CPT) or the Matching Familiar Figures Test (MFFT).

The Brown Attention Deficit Disorder Scale (ADDS), is designed to assess ADD in adolescents and adults. The five scales are activating and organizing work, sustaining attention and concentration, sustaining energy and effort, managing affective interference, and utilizing working memory and assessing recall. The Conners' Rating Scale–Revised (1996) assesses a broad range of psychopathological and problem behaviors including attention-deficit hyperactivity disorder (ADHD). There are two forms: a short form for teachers, which measures oppositional behavior, cognitive inattention problems, and hyperactivity, and a long form for parents and helping professionals, with 59 items.

Eating Disorders.   Two major eating disorders, anorexia nervosa and bulimia nervosa, are characterized by a morbid overconcern with weight and physical appearance. In anorexia nervosa the client starves herself or himself to a point of emaciation, strives for thinness, and has a fear of becoming fat. Bulimia clients also strive for thinness but have strong urges to overeat, which leads to binges followed by self-induced vomiting, laxatives, fasting, and other similar behavior. Gardner and Parker (1993) advocate multimodal assessment and starting out with an initial interview. Sometimes a medical examination is necessary to determine if weight loss is due to some underlying physical disorder. Garner and Parker provide an outline of a clinical interview checklist that includes items dealing with demographic features and treatment history, weight-controlling behavior, binge eating and eating behavior, attitudes toward weight and shape, physical symptoms, and psychological and interpersonal factors.

There are a number of self-report inventories, such as the Eating Disorders Inventory-3, that assess features common in anorexia nervosa and bulimia. The scales are drive for thinness, ineffectiveness, body dissatisfaction, maturity, fear, interceptive awareness, impulse regulation, social insecurity, and asceticism. The inventory also assesses three dimensions of eating behavior important in recognizing and treating eating-related disorders: cognitive control of eating, disinhibition, and hunger.

Hearing Impairment

Individuals differ in their degree of hearing impairment as well as the age of onset of the impairment. Audiologists screen individuals with hearing losses that range from mild to profound; such losses can be caused by a number of factors. Normally, examinees with hearing deficits have had a pattern of retarded speech and language development and problems in social development. Some have poor control of their impulses, and do not have a strongly developed sense of responsibility. They often misinterpret the feelings and behaviors of others and may be significantly behind their peers in educational achievement.

Intelligence tests that do not demand oral language are preferable for this group. Examiners must be careful in reaching conclusions during observations. Individuals who exhibit behavior characteristic of people with learning disabilities, behavior disorders, or mental retardation may be suffering from a hearing loss that leads to those similar behaviors. Simeonsson (1986) identified three major purposes of assessment of individuals with hearing impairments to assess the cognitive competency and achievement discrepancy, to assess the cognitive and linguistic discrepancy, and to assess personal and social functioning.

Many individual differences exist within this group, and it is important to take into consideration the etiology of the impairment as well as the developmental history of the individual. The following guidelines pertain to assessment of individuals with hearing impairments. Bradley-Johnson and Evans (1991) point out that testing should be supplemented with interviews, review of school records, and use of classroom observation.

- Be sure that any individual with problems speaking or understanding spoken language has a hearing evaluation.
- Keep the test environment controlled and free from distraction; an individual with a mild hearing loss may be distracted by extraneous noise.
- Avoid visual distractions, especially if the examinee is reading lips.
- If necessary, have an interpreter help communicate with the examinee.
- Allow the interpreter and the person with a hearing impairment to arrange seating to enhance the lines of communication.
- Have more than one test or approach to measure the construct in question.

Vance (1998) recommends assessing adaptive behavior of all students with disabilities or suspected disabilities along with observations conducted in different settings.

Visual Impairment

Visual impairment may be caused by injury or disease that reduces the individual's central vision, accommodation, binocular vision, peripheral vision, or color vision. The impairment affects normal patterns of cognitive, affective, and psychomotor development. Preadolescents and adolescents with visual impairments often have problems in social development that cause lower self-concepts. Psychologists and educators assess aptitude and achievement of individuals with visual impairments by adapting standard instruments to meet their needs. Chase (1986) points out that test administrators need to become familiar with the nature of the visual disorders and their impact on development. Testers must be aware of the

1. Effects of distracting noise in a testing situation
2. Need for additional time to complete tasks, if the test is in braille or large type
3. Need to structure the testing environment and let the examinee become familiar with the objects by handling them
4. Need to describe the setting for the examinee

5. Need for several breaks or multiple sessions

Specialized tests are available for assessing children and adults with visual impairments. The Hill Performance Test of Selected Positional Concepts measures the spatial concepts of children age 6 to 10 with visual impairments. The Reynell-Zinkin Scales provide a profile of six areas for children up to 5 years old: social adaptation, sensorimotor, exploration of environment, response to sound/verbal comprehension, expressive language, and nonverbal communication.

Individuals Who Are Gifted or Talented

Often educators think of individuals who are gifted or talented as having a high level of intellectual ability. Terman (1954) operationally defined gifted as those individuals who score in the top 1% on the Stanford-Binet or have IQs of 130 or above. The official definition by the U.S. Department of Education is "children or youth who give evidence of high performance capability in areas such as intellectual, creative, artistic, or leadership capacity, or in specific academic fields, and who require services or activities not ordinarily provided by the school in order to fully develop such capabilities."

Examiners of individuals who are gifted and talented have relied on group and individual intelligence tests, survey achievement batteries, and the ratings of teachers, parents, and even the students themselves. Here are some of the scales used to assess these individuals:

- The Creativity Attitude Survey for grades 4 through 6 assesses confidence in one's own ideas, appreciation of fantasy, theoretical and aesthetical orientation, openness to impulse expression, and desire for novelty.
- The Creativity Checklist is given to counselors, parents, and teachers to rate eight dimensions of creative behavior, such as fluency, flexibility, resourcefulness, constructural skill, ingenuity, and independence. It can be used with individuals from kindergarten to adulthood.
- The Gifted and Talented Evaluation Scales contain a 50-item rating scale of behaviors characteristic of students who are gifted and talented to be completed by teachers and parents or those having knowledge of the students. The scale is for students age 5 to 18.
- The Group Inventory for Finding Creative Talent (GIFT) surveys the creative interests and attitudes of students in grades K through 6.
- The Group Inventory for Finding Interests: Gifted and Talented Screening Form assesses the creative interests and attitudes of students in grades 6 through 12.
- The Scales for Rating the Behavioral Characteristics of Superior Students, Revised, are completed by teachers, parents, or guidance counselors to measure various dimensions of gifted behavior—learning, motivation, creativity, leadership, art, music, drama, planning, precise communication, and expressive communication.
- The Screening Assessment for Gifted Student, Second Edition has two forms, one for elementary students age 5.0 to 8.11 and one for middle- or upper-grade

students age 7.0 to 12.11. Student aptitude is measured by a reasoning test and achievement by an information test. The middle- and upper-grade version measures creativity with a divergent production subtest.

- Thinking Creatively in Action and Movement (TCAM) is a nonverbal movement test used to assess the creativity of children age 3 to 8.
- Thinking Creatively with Sounds and Words measures the ability of individuals to create images for words and sounds. There are two forms, one for grades 3 through 12 and one for adults.
- The Torrance Tests of Creative Thinking assess the ability of individuals to visualize and transform words and meanings.
- The Watson-Glaser Critical Thinking Appraisal measures the individual's ability to think critically and includes dimensions such as inferences, recognition of assumptions, deduction, interpretation, and evaluation of arguments.

Examiners testing individuals who are gifted should not be influenced by stereotypical attitudes. Who is tested and what tests are given depends partly on the operational definition of gifted. It can pertain to exceptional academic achievement, extraordinary creativity, special talents, superior intelligence, or some other variable. Examiners should remember that students who are gifted and talented can have the same testing problems that other students have. They may not want to do well because of peer pressure, they may be bored and frustrated, or they may come from disadvantaged environments and may be overlooked by teachers and administrators.

STANDARDS FOR MULTICULTURAL ASSESSMENT

Because of increasing diversity in our society, the assessment community must continue striving to assure fair and equitable treatment of individuals regardless of race, ethnicity, culture, language, age, gender, sexual orientation, religion, or physical ability. This is especially important given the increased emphasis placed on assessment spawned by national and state legislation and educational reform initiatives. Professionals need to maintain an awareness of the various assessment standards associated with multicultural assessment.

Technical Considerations

The Code of Fair Testing Practices in Education (Joint Committee, 1999) calls for examiners to make sure the test content and norming groups are appropriate for test takers from different racial, ethnic, or linguistic backgrounds. The counselor is to select tests that have been developed in ways that attempt to make them as reliable and valid as possible for test takers of different race, gender, or ethnic backgrounds. Counselors should review the data from the manual on the performance of these test takers. The groups must be of sufficient size.

The section on Evaluation, Assessment, and Interpretation from the *ACA Code of Ethics* (ACA, 2005) also emphasizes the importance of caution when selecting assessments for culturally diverse populations to avoid the use of instruments that lack appropriate psychometric properties for the client population.

Standards for Educational and Psychological Testing (AERA et al., 1999) emphasizes the importance of reviewing the criterion-related evidence of validity when recommending decisions that have an actuarial as well as a clinical impact. Because many tests are translated from one language or dialect to another, the reliability and validity for the uses intended in the linguistic groups must be established. The examiner also needs to review any studies of the magnitude of predictive bias due to differential prediction for groups for which previous research has established a substantial prior probability of differential prediction for the type of test in question.

Administration and Scoring

The *ACA Code of Ethics* (ACA, 2005) emphasizes the need for counselors to consider the client's personal or cultural context, the level of the client's understanding of the results, and the impact of the results on the client when explaining test scores. *Standards for Educational and Psychological Testing* (AERA et al., 1999) reminds examiners that linguistic modification recommended by the test publishers should be described in detail in the test manual. Testing should be designed to minimize threats to the reliability and validity of the test that can arise from language differences.

Use and Interpretation

The Code of Fair Testing Practices in Education (Joint Committee, 1999) reminds examiners that when interpreting the scores of these groups, they must take into consideration differences between the norms and the scores of test takers and the familiarity of the test takers with the specific questions on the test. In addition, parents and guardians need to know their rights and what procedures they need to follow if they have problems with the assessment.

The *ACA Code of Ethics* (ACA, 2005) notes the effects of age, color, culture, disability, ethnic group, gender, race, language preference, religion, spirituality, sexual orientation, and socioeconomic status on test administration and interpretation, and the importance of placing test results in proper perspective with other relevant factors.

Standards for Educational and Psychological Testing (AERA et al., 1999) explains that in educational, clinical, and counseling situations, test administrators and users should not attempt to evaluate test takers whose special characteristics such as age, disability, or linguistic, generational, or cultural backgrounds are outside the range of their academic training or supervised experience.

Multicultural Counseling Competencies and Standards (Sue, Arrendondo, & McDavis, 1992) includes three standards related to multicultural assessment:

1. Culturally skilled counselors must be aware of the potential bias of assessment instruments and, when interpreting findings, keep in mind the client's cultural and linguistic characteristics.
2. They also need an awareness and understanding of how culture and ethnicity may affect personality formation, vocational choices, manifestations of psychological disorders, help-seeking behavior, and the appropriateness of counseling approaches.
3. Counselors must not only understand the technical aspects of the instruments but also be aware of the cultural limitations.

The bottom line is that counselors need training and experience in assessing these clients, as well as the cultural awareness to protect the welfare of the diverse clients with whom they are working. The ACA's *Code of Ethics* (2005) instructs counselors to provide specific orientation or information to the examinees prior to and following test administration so that the results of testing may be placed in proper perspective with other relevant factors such as the effects of socioeconomic, ethnic, and cultural factors on test scores. Counselors then proceed with caution when attempting to evaluate and interpret the performance of minority group members or other persons who are not represented in the norming groups on which the instrument was standardized.

TEST BIAS

Test bias is the difference in test scores that is attributable to demographic variables (e.g., gender, ethnicity, and age). An item or subtest is labeled biased when empirical evidence shows that it is more difficult for one group member than another, the general ability level of the two groups is held constant, and no reasonable rationale exists to explain the group differences on the same items.

Reynolds and Brown (1984) list six dimensions of bias: inappropriate content, inappropriate standardization samples, examiner and language bias, inequitable social consequences, measurement of different constructs, and differential predictive validity.

Children who are bilingual with limited English skills have trouble understanding oral and written directions in addition to the vocabulary and the syntax of the test items. Often they have a hard time giving correct verbal responses, and they may have trouble discriminating among sounds that are not part of their primary language.

Test Taker Bias Factors

Oakland (1982) advises awareness of points of bias during assessment of culturally different or minority-group individuals. Some potential bias centers around the test taker:

Language—The examinee's ability to understand and communicate in English is very important. Conventional measures that require a high level of competence in English are not appropriate.

Test wiseness—The examiner cannot assume that examinees can understand directions, comply with proper test-taking procedures, and be involved and attentive during testing.

Motivation and anxiety—The examiner may find an examinee who refuses to cooperate or is too anxious. The examiner needs to consider the attitudinal characteristics of examinees and attempt to get them to do their best.

Cultural differences—Minority examinees may come from restricted environments in expectations, language experiences, formal and informal learning experiences, and upbringing. The examiner needs to understand the background of the examinees and whether the test is appropriate. (pp. 153–154)

Examiner Bias Factors

The examiner may introduce bias in several ways. The examiner needs to recognize personal bias and how it may influence interpretation of results. This requires treating each individual with dignity and respect and pursuing the best interests of the examinee. Baruth and Manning (2003) have identified some of the common barriers to effective multicultural counseling:

1. The counselor makes erroneous assumptions about cultural assimilation.
2. There is a difference in class and cultural values.
3. There are language differences and both cultural or socioeconomic class misunderstandings.
4. The counselor believes stereotypes about culturally different people.
5. The counselor fails to understand his or her own culture.
6. There is little understanding of the client's reasoning structures.
7. There is a lack of cultural relativity among counselors.

DEVELOPING GREATER MULTICULTURAL UNDERSTANDING

In developing an action plan to increase their multicultural understanding, counselors can use research on the multicultural counseling process, case studies in the literature, experiences of other counselors they are working with, their own experiences with culturally diverse clients, and other firsthand experiences with various ethnic groups (Draguns, 1989; Nuttall, Romero, & Kalesnik, 1992). For counselors, the first step is to develop greater self-awareness and comprehension of their own cultural group. They need to comprehend their own environmental experiences in the mainstream culture and reflect on their sensitivity toward their personal beliefs and values. Specific training in working with certain groups provides greater confidence and knowledge of the group.

Counselors need to develop an awareness and comprehension of the history and experiences of the cultural group with which the client is currently identifying or encountering. In general, the counselor must develop perceptual sensitivity toward the client's personal beliefs and values (Baruth & Manning, 1991).

Ethical Principles

Ethical standards of working with culturally diverse clients require counselors to have cultural knowledge based on research and experience. They also must understand their own cultural background and be able to go beyond their own biases and prejudices. Counselors must respect the diverse values and beliefs of clients as they affect their view of the world and psychosocial functioning. Counselors must also be aware of the impact of social, environmental, and political conditions on problems and interventions. They must be advocates and stand against racism and discrimination. In assessment they need to use multisource, multilevel, and multimethod approaches to assess the capabilities, potentials, and limitations of the clients (APA, 2002). During assessment and counseling, counselors need to be careful and active listeners, be genuine, and demonstrate verbally and nonverbally that they understand what they are communicating. They should show that they care about clients and their situations and are working to help them achieve a realistic solution.

Etic and Emic Perspectives

Etic perspective emphasizes the universal qualities among human beings by examining and comparing many cultures from a position outside those cultures. *Emic perspective* is culture-specific and examines behavior from within a culture, using criteria relative to the internal characteristics of that culture (Dana, 1993). From the etic perspective, assessment involves comparing individuals' scores to a norming group and comparing different individuals from different cultures on a construct assumed to be universal across all cultures.

Dana (1993) includes as etic measures a broad spectrum of instruments to measure psychopathology, personality measures, and major tests of intelligence and cognitive functioning. Included as etic personality measures are the California Psychological Inventory and the Eysenck Personality Questionnaire. Included in the intelligence/cognitive functioning area are the Wechsler Intelligence Scales, the System of Multicultural Pluralistic Assessment, the Kaufman Assessment Battery for Children, the McCarthy Scales of Children's Abilities, and the Stanford-Binet Intelligence Scale. Other single-construct tests for identification of psychopathology are the State-Trait Anxiety Scale, the Beck Depression Inventory, and the Michigan Alcoholism Screening Test. The MMPI is also on this list; it has been translated into 150 languages and has reported applications in 50 countries. The other tests listed have also been translated into other languages, mainly Spanish.

Emic methods include behavior observations, case studies, studies of life events, picture story techniques, inkblot techniques, word association, sentence completion, and drawings. Most of these methods are classified as projective. These tests can provide a personality description of the individual that reflects the data and mirrors the culture and ethnic group (Dana, 1993). The analysis demands that the examiner have more knowledge of the culture but aids the understanding of the individual in a cultural context. Thematic apperception test versions include the Tell Me a Story Test, designed for Spanish-speaking populations, and the Thompson Modification of the Thematic Apperception Test, a 10-card version of the TAT for African Americans.

Sentence completion methods have been used with many different cultures. The items can be designed to assess the social norms, roles, and values of clients from different cultures. Here are examples of some of the items:

The thing I like most about America is _____.

Anglos _____.

If I could be from another culture or ethnic group, I _____.

There are not always formal scoring systems for the different emic tests.

Acculturation

The degree of acculturation to the dominant society and the extent to which the original culture has been retained provide valuable information in interpreting assessment results. Dana (1993) has developed a checklist to record acculturation information. One item relates to the phase of the acculturation process and has five levels: precontact, contact, conflict, crisis, or adaptation. Another item relates to the mode and has four categories: assimilation, bicultural, traditional, marginal. Dana also looks at group membership—whether the group consists of native peoples, immigrants, refugees, ethnic groups, or sojourners. The sociocultural pattern is recorded by looking at settlement patterns, status, status mobility, support network, and group acceptability.

For Americans, two instruments can provide information on the moderating variables that affect assessment interpretation: the Developmental Inventory of Black Consciousness Revision 2 (DIBC) and the Racial Identity Attitude Scale (RIAS). The DIBC has four stages: preconsciousness, confrontation, internalization, and integration. The RIAS also has four stages: preencounter, encounter, immersion-emersion, and internalization. Another useful scale is the African Self-Consciousness Scale (ASC), which has four dimensions: awareness of Black identity; recognition of survival priorities and affirmative practices, customs, and values; active participation in defense of survival, liberation, and the like; and recognition of racial oppression (Baldwin & Bell, 1985).

Dana (1993) advises counselors to use moderator variables whenever there is evidence that a client is not representative of an Anglo-American cultural background. A counselor can get an idea of whether the client is identifying with a culture of origin rather than with the dominant Anglo-American culture by asking questions such as those shown in Figure 17.1 on page 362.

Strategies

Because each client is unique, the examiner needs to be alert to important behavioral signals. Certain behavior may affect the reliability and validity of the test. Appropriate examiner responses are summarized in Table 17.2.

Table 17.2
Critical behavior indicators and possible examiner responses.

Behavior	Response
Is silent	Establish rapport. Give nonverbal and performance test first, get other indexes of individual behavior.
Says "don't know"	Don't assume client cannot respond.
Is shy and reserved; lowers eyes	Observe client in other situations, spend time establishing rapport, start with nonverbal and untimed tests, provide reinforcement, try to motivate client.
Uses wit or popular language	Be firm and positive, be sure examinee knows why the test/instrument is being given.
Interrupts the test or asks questions	Be firm but allow some dialogue, be sure the examinee knows the purpose of the test.
Is inattentive and restless	Structure test environment, keep examinee involved.
Is uncertain about how to respond	Rephrase question, make meaning clear.
Watches the examiner rather than listening to the questions	Be firm, be sure questions are clear, be sure there are no distractions in test situation. If the responses are inappropriate, question further.
Performs poorly on timed tests	Recognize a culture not oriented to the value of time, avoid drawing conclusions about individual performance until untimed measures have been tried.
Shows poor knowledge of vocabulary	Try other ways of measuring the examinee's expressive vocabulary, question individual in primary language.
Is unmotivated to take test	Explain purpose and value of test to client and family, try techniques to motivate client performance.
Scores poorly on information items	Recognize that some items might be biased and not a part of the examinee's culture, ask examinee to clarify any unusual responses.
Is afraid of embarrassing or dishonoring family	Initiate test-wise session, practice session, or some type of warmup.
Is quiet and does not ask questions or interact	Establish rapport, explain examiner's role and purpose of the test, ask client to repeat the question if no answer is given or the answer is inappropriate.
Is afraid of a male examiner	Observe examinee, establish rapport before testing.

1. What is your country of origin?
2. What was your reason for coming to the United States?
3. How long have you been in the United States?
4. Was any parent, grandparent, or relative in this country before you came?
5. What language do you speak in your home?
6. What languages can you speak? How well?
7. Is your family in the United States?
8. Do you have friends from your country here?
9. Are there people from your country living near you?
10. Where do you live? A house, apartment, room?
11. What education or schooling did you complete?
12. Are you currently going to school or taking classes somewhere?
13. Are you currently working? Where? What do you do on the job?
14. What type of work did you do before coming to this country?
15. Have you had any problems since coming here?
16. Have you had any conflicts on the job, at school, or at home?
17. What kind of problems have you had adjusting to life in the United States?

Figure 17.1
Interview schedule for assessing multicultural clients.

SUMMARY

Psychometric criteria have an important role in diagnosing mental retardation, learning disabilities, and giftedness, and they are used as a secondary tool in diagnosing behavioral and emotional disorders. Clinical judgment is also considered an important factor in the diagnosis of exceptionality, especially in the realm of communication impairment and behavior and emotional disorders. Biomedical information is extremely important when studying visual, auditory, and motor impairment. Examiners need to be aware of the specific standards and guidelines for testing diverse populations. They need to be experienced and knowledgeable in working with the diverse group in question.

Many factors can bias the assessment of multicultural groups and individuals and lead to possible sources of misinterpretation. Legal and professional standards call for nonbiased, nondiscriminatory assessment, validation of tests for a specific purpose, and use of multiple sources of information and multiple windows to view and understand diversity. Emic approaches provide this window and increase the credibility of the assessment. Moderating variables such as the degree of assimilation of the majority culture are also important in understanding the individual.

QUESTIONS FOR DISCUSSION

1. How might the following examiner variables affect the validity of the test results?

    a. personal bias and expectation

    b. difficulty in understanding what the examinee says

    c. lack of knowledge of the particular disability

    d. lack of experience testing and working with the particular exceptionality

    e. lack of special communication skills (e.g., American Sign Language)

    f. lack of knowledge of the client's first language

    g. lack of knowledge of the specific ethnic group

2. Do you think it is acceptable to adapt and modify a standardized test to accommodate the special needs (disability or ethnic) of the examinee? Why or why not?

3. How important do you feel the environment is in the testing of individuals with disabilities? How would the following factors affect the validity of the test results:

    a. lighting in the room,

    b. noise level of the testing environment,

    c. physical features of the room,

    d. artificial nature of the setting, and

    e. positioning needs of the examinee?

4. How do labels and diagnostic criteria affect the types of tests given and the validity of the results? Critics have faulted the designations for not reflecting the presence of a disability or the degree of impairment. How should the examiner address this problem?

5. A large number of individuals have impairments in more than one area. What procedures should the examiner follow to ensure proper diagnosis and placement? How important do you feel these concerns are in affecting students with impairment during testing?

6. What personality characteristics do counselors need to have when testing a member of a minority group?

7. Compare and contrast your culture with that of another ethnic group. What are the similarities? What are the differences?

8. What are the different dimensions of bias that an examiner must be alert to?

SUGGESTED ACTIVITIES

1. Interview psychologists who work with diverse populations and find out what tests they use and why. Report your findings to the class.

2. Review a videotape of a testing session of an individual with a disability. Were there deviations from standard procedures? In what ways did the examiner test the individual differently from the norm?

3. Interview individuals with special needs and find out their experiences and reactions to testing. Report your findings to the class.

4. Review the public laws and court decisions related to assessing individuals with special needs. Write a summary of the legislation and the court decisions.

5. Locate a test that has been adapted and standardized for use with a diverse population. Compare the adaptation with the original version. How was the test modified? Why? How do the two sets of norms compare?

6. Interview a psychologist who assesses a number of multicultural clients and find out what tests he or she uses and why. Report your findings to the class.

7. Make an annotated bibliography of tests designed for administration to one of the following groups: Hispanics, Asian Americans, African Americans, or Native Americans.

8. Interview counselors who work with diverse groups and find out how they developed their cultural knowledge and awareness.

9. Locate public laws and court decisions related to assessing minority group members. Write a summary of the legislation and court decisions.

10. Locate a test that has been adapted for a certain minority or ethnic group. How was the test modified? How do the two sets of norms compare? How does the reliability compare?

11. Study these nine brief cases and answer the questions that follow.

Case of Maria

Maria, who is 12 years old, has dropped from 100 to 75 pounds in the last 6 months. She refuses to eat with the family. Fights take place at mealtime because of her eating habits.

a. How would you classify Maria?
b. What additional information would you like to have about her?
c. What methods would you use to assess Maria or individuals like Maria?

Case of Jonathan

Jonathan had a Full Scale IQ of 76 on the WISC-IV with a Verbal Comprehension Index score of 75, Perceptual Reasoning of 90, Working Memory of 74, and Processing Speed of 85. He was easily frustrated and impulsive in the tasks he was required to do. He couldn't sit still except on the performance items that interested him. His teacher checked "poor" on the following items on a learning profile checklist:

Quality or neatness of handwriting

Completeness of assignments

Quality of reading skills

Quality of speaking skills

She also noted that he completes his work in a hasty, careless fashion.

a. How would you classify Jonathan?

b. What additional information would you like to have on him?

c. What methods would you use to assess Jonathan or individuals like him?

Case of Roberto

Roberto is an 11-year-old boy from a blended family. He lives with his mother, stepfather, and the stepfather's two children. He had a 121 Full Scale IQ on the WISC-IV. His grades were excellent, but lately his disruptive and aggressive behavior has led to frequent suspensions and lower grades. His mother reports that he is unmanageable at home and is increasingly oppositional and angry. When Roberto gets angry, he breaks dishes and starts fires. At school he has been accused of stealing money. When he gets angry, he beats up on any student who happens to be near him.

a. How would you classify Roberto?

b. What additional information about him would you like to have?

c. What methods would you use to assess Roberto or individuals like Roberto?

Case of Mindy

Mindy is a 9-year-old girl who is normal in intelligence but refuses to go to school. She says she is afraid to leave home because she worries that her mother will leave her or die. She tells her mother she can teach her at home. She often enters her parents' bedroom at night and sleeps on the floor.

a. How would you classify Mindy?

b. What additional information about Mindy would you like to have?

c. What methods would you use to assess Mindy or individuals like her?

Case of Chan

Chan's mother is concerned because he shows a lack of affection and little interest in interacting with his peers and parents. His language appears to be delayed. The counselor observing Chan in class noted he had problems communicating and interacting with his classmates.

a. How would you classify Chan?

b. What additional information would you like to have about him?

c. What methods would you use to assess Chan or individuals like him?

Case of Jamir

Jamir is a 15-year-old African American. Assessment using Gardner's Typology shows that he has high musical and kinesthetic intelligence. His family moved into the city from a suburban area because of the father's job change. He attends an inner-city high school with a magnet program in engineering and mathematics because his parents don't want him to be bused to another school 30 minutes away. The school he attends has limited programs in fine arts and music and few resources. One of Jamir's friends was shot by a gang in a shopping center, and another classmate died from a drug overdose. Jamir has started to withdraw and shows signs of depression. He becomes sick on school days. His parents want you to test Jamir and help him.

a. What type of assessment procedures and instruments would you use with Jamir?

b. What factors and issues do you feel need to be addressed?

c. What additional information would you like to have about Jamir?

Case of Claudia

Claudia is a 14-year-old bilingual Latina referred to the child study team because of her truancy, lack of motivation, and negative attitude toward her teachers and school. She has been placed in an English as a Second Language class with many students who have negative motivation and poor skills. Often she tells her parents she is going to school but instead skips and goes to the local mall. However, she does well academically when she is in class. One of her teachers says: "She is like all of the other problem students we have in this program: no interest, no discipline, and no motivation."

a. What type of tests would you give to Claudia and why?

b. What factors might tend to bias Claudia's test results?

c. What additional information about Claudia would you want to have?

Case of Tobeka

Tobeka, a 6-year-old African American, has entered first grade but is having considerable academic difficulties. She has been referred for a multifactor evaluation by the school's multidisciplinary team. Her mother has refused to let Tobeka be tested until she can examine the tests that will be used. You have met with the mother to explain why the tests will be given and have discussed what tests will be administered.

a. What factors were involved?

b. What test standards were involved?

c. What was your ethical responsibility?

Case of Janie

Janie, an 8-year-old Native American of the Penobscot tribe, has been referred to a multidisciplinary team by her guidance counselor and teachers for evaluation of her avoidant behavior and assessment of her intellectual potential. She refuses to participate in her reading group, cries often, and usually fails to follow directions. Her teacher says Janie isolates herself from others in the class and refuses to participate. Her mother has indicated that the other students make fun of Janie.

a. What issues should you consider before you meet with Janie?

b. What important professional standards for multicultural assessment should be considered in this case?

c. What assessment techniques and procedures would you use?

ADDITIONAL READINGS

Aylward, G. P. (1994). *Practitioner's guide to developmental and psychological testing.* Austin, TX: PRO-ED.

Discusses the psychological tests that are used to assess children with developmental delays, poor school performance, and behavioral problems.

Bradley-Johnson, S., & Evans, L. D. (1991). *Psychoeducational assessment of hearing-impaired students: Infancy through high school.* Austin, TX: PRO-ED.
Discusses the issues and procedures related to the assessment of students with hearing impairments and reviews the tests and subtests commonly used with this population. Presents a checklist of procedures to use before, during, and after testing.

Burns, E. (1998). *Test accommodations for students with disabilities.* Springfield, IL: Charles C. Thomas.
Discusses the impact of accommodation on validity and reliability. Chapters cover test accommodation, scheduling, test scores, and the like.

Canino, I. A., & Spurlock, J. (1994). *Culturally diverse children and adolescents: Assessment, diagnosis, and treatment.* New York: Guilford Press.
The authors guide clinicians in learning how to determine the impact of cultural differences, poverty, discrimination, and acculturation issues when assessing children and adolescents; numerous clinical vignettes illustrate the constructs.

Cookson, P. W., & Halberstam, J. (1998). *A parent's guide to standardized tests in school: How to improve your child's chances for success.* New York: Learning Express.
Chapter 8 discusses children with special needs and is an excellent source for parents.

Dana, R. H. (1993). *Multicultural assessment perspectives for professional psychology.* Boston: Allyn & Bacon.
Presents a comprehensive model for multicultural assessment and a specific review of instrumentation used to assess African Americans, Hispanics, Asian Americans, and Native Americans.

Geisinger, K. F. (1992). *Psychological testing of Hispanics.* Washington, DC: American Psychological Association.
Discusses differential psychology and psychological testing of Hispanic people.

Hamayan, E. V., & Damico, J. S. (Eds.) (1991). *Limiting bias in the assessment of bilingual students.* Austin, TX: PRO-ED.
Problems in the education and assessment of students with limited English proficiency are identified.

Hilliard, A. G. (Ed.). (1991). *Testing African American students.* Morristown, NJ: Aaron.
The contributors discuss issues such as African American culture and psychological assessment, the impact of testing on African Americans, and issues in professional practice.

Mash, E. J., & Terdal, L. G. (Eds). (1997). *Assessment of childhood disorders* (3rd ed.). New York: Guilford Press.
Discusses assessment of behavior disorders, emotional and social disorders, developmental and health-related disorders, children at risk, and problems of adolescence.

Pierangelo, R., & Giuliani, G. (1998). *Special educator's complete guide to 109 diagnostic tests.* West Nyack, NY: The Center for Applied Research in Education.

Rapoport, J. L., & Ismond, D. R. (1996). *DSM-IV-TR training guide for diagnosis of childhood disorders.* New York: Routledge.
This comprehensive source focuses on the roles, issues, and techniques of the school psychologist.

Reynolds, C. R., & Gutkin, T. B. (1999). *Handbook of school psychology* (3rd ed.). New York: Wiley.

Rogers, M. R. (1998). Assessment of culturally linguistically diverse children and youth. In H. B. Vance (Ed.), *Psychological assessment of children* (pp. 358–384). New York: Wiley.
Rogers discusses professional preparation as well as psychometric considerations important in assessing children.

Rossetti, L. M. (1990). *Infant-toddler assessment: An interdisciplinary approach.* Austin, TX: PRO-ED.
Discusses the assessment of high-risk infants and toddlers and includes sample questionnaires and evaluation instruments.

Simeonsson, R. J. (1986). *Psychological and developmental assessment of special children.* Boston: Allyn & Bacon.
Identifies dimensions and issues in assessing children from diverse groups such as children with hearing impairments, visual impairments, motor impairments, and autism, and children who are hospitalized and chronically ill.

Vance, H. B. (Ed.). (1998). *Psychological assessment of children* (2nd ed.). New York: Wiley.
Part III of the text focuses on assessing diverse populations. There are chapters on developmental assessment of infants and preschoolers, culturally and linguistically diverse children and youth, diagnosis and assessment of autistic disorders, vocational assessment of learners with special needs, and assessing children with mental retardation.

18 Assessment Issues in Education

OVERVIEW

There are many goals, purposes, and people included in school testing programs. The purposes range from identifying individuals with special needs to determining whether students have mastered the graduation requirements set by the district, county, or state. Decisions about testing programs should be formulated by committees of administrators, teachers, students, counselors, psychologists, and citizens. The first step is to identify the types of information gained from the testing that would be important for the various groups. Not all the purposes and outcomes questions about school assessment programs will be answered, but baseline data are important in evaluating the curriculum and quality of education.

School testing programs include a wide variety of tests that range from scholastic aptitude to vocational aptitude. Many of the tests must be individually administered and require an examiner who has the proper credentials and competencies. To maintain accreditation, schools are required to systematically conduct surveys. Most schools conduct high-stakes testing as required by state and federal authorities. There are a number of legal and philosophical issues involved in this type of testing.

Test-taking skills have become an important topic in schools. Schools are focusing on helping individuals improve their test performance through two main approaches: better content preparation and better test-taking skills. A number of strategies can be used to help students maximize their test performance, such as coaching by administrators, teachers, and counselors; increasing test wiseness; offering workshops and seminars on test-taking skills; accessing information sources on various tests; and so on.

OBJECTIVES

After studying this chapter, you should be able to

✔ Critique high-stakes testing programs

✔ Discuss the goals of an assessment program

✔ List and describe the types of tests that should be administered and why

✔ Discuss the roles and responsibilities of school personnel involved in testing programs

✔ List and discuss the different strategies to help individuals maximize their test performance

✔ Identify and analyze the different factors related to test performance

✔ Evaluate the sources of help available to assist individuals in improving their test performance

HIGH-STAKES TESTING

Accountability through high-stakes testing has become a major issue in the reform of school systems through the United States. Paris (2000) defines high-stakes tests as all academic achievement tests that are used to make important decisions about the evaluation of students from kindergarten through grade 12. These decisions include promotion (or retention) and graduation.

In recent years, high-stakes tests have been used as an indicator of the educational impact of a school (Thorn & Mulvenon, 2002). The policy of high-stakes testing in education has gained popularity at the state and federal levels. In fact, on January 8, 2002, President Bush signed into law the No Child Left Behind Act of 2001. This law contains the most sweeping changes to the Elementary and Secondary Education Act (ESEA) since it was enacted in 1965. It changed the federal government's role in K–12 education by requiring America's schools to describe their success in terms of what each student accomplishes. The act contains four basic education reform principles: stronger accountability for results, increased flexibility and local control, expanded options for parents, and an emphasis on teaching methods that have been proven to work.

As a result of this act, states have created policies to reward schools that score well on high-stakes tests. Merit-based awards, clear accountability and public visibility, and financial incentives for educators are purported benefits of high-stakes tests. Yet, many criticize the use of these tests in education. Paris and Urdan (2000) cite a number of concerns:

- Teachers feel pressured or coerced to get their students to achieve at higher levels on tests in order to receive merit pay or promotion.
- The curriculum is often narrowed as teachers prepare students for high-stakes tests. Test content and skills tend to be taught to the exclusion of nontested content (Shepard, 2000).

- Teachers who put effort into their jobs but are not rewarded because of students' test scores may become embittered. They may leave a position at a low-achieving school to teach at a "rich school" or to teach at grade levels that are not affected by test scores.
- High-stakes testing is biased against urban, rural, and poor schools that have large populations of low-socioeconomic, minority, or disadvantaged students who are typically at risk of obtaining lower test scores.
- Low-socioeconomic schools that do not perform as well on the high-stakes test may be denied the resources and finances they so desperately need to improve student learning.

Although one purpose of high-stakes testing is to aid in making decisions on grade retention, a recent National Research Council report (Heubert & Hauser, 1999) states that it is especially hazardous to retain children based on low test scores. Often, such children are stigmatized and fail to benefit from that treatment. Evidence indicates that children who have been retained in a grade display a heightened tendency to become a high school dropout (Roderick, 1993). Grade retention often is more deleterious than helpful to a child (Jones, 2001).

Other difficult questions also arise when tests are used as a sole determinant of a child's progress in school (Jones, 2001). What accommodations are provided for students with visual impairments or who are in special education classes? What special efforts are dedicated to helping students who fail to pass the tests? Will teachers simply "teach to the test" and focus on preparing students for the tests at the expense of other important educational objectives, such as encouraging creativity and the students' natural curiosity?

With the emphasis on high-stakes testing in education, AERA (2001) states the following in a position paper:

1. High-stakes decisions should not be based on a single test.
2. All students should have adequate resources and opportunity to learn.
3. Each separate use of the test must be validated.
4. Full disclosure of negative consequences needs to be considered.
5. Alignment between the test and the curriculum should be documented.
6. Validity of the passing score must be demonstrated.
7. Appropriate attention to language differences among examinees must be considered.
8. Appropriate attention to students with disabilities must be evaluated.
9. Careful attention must be paid to explicit rules for determining which individuals are going to be tested.
10. Sufficient reliability for each intended use must be documented.

Experts in large assessment programs recommend that the results be reported by gender, race, ethnic group, income level, and evaluation purposes.

Because testing is an extremely important part of the accountability movement, experts recommend that more research be conducted on large-scale testing programs. In addition to more research, the experts also recommend increased accountability for student performance, more focus on what works, reduced bureaucracy, increased feasibility, and more empowering of parents.

STUDENT ASSESSMENT PROGRAMS

The primary purposes of student assessment programs are to provide information needed to improve the public schools by enhancing the learning gains of all students and to inform parents of the educational progress of their public school children. Over the past 10 years, responding both to federal legislation (the No Child Left Behind Act) and local pressure to improve learning, states have been developing or amending their accountability systems. Virtually every state now has standards for student learning, most have aligned student assessment programs with those standards, and many are currently developing data collection and reporting systems to support their accountability decision making.

The latest revision of the Elementary and Secondary Education Act (ESEA), the No Child Left Behind Act (NCLB), makes substantial changes to state standards and testing and brings far-reaching changes to how states measure student progress. According to NCLB, all students must perform at a "proficient" level or above on state reading and math assessments by 2013–2014. States must develop their own accountability system to assess student performance. The primary method is standardized achievement tests. A typical student assessment program is delineated in Figure 18.1.

Grade Level	Test/Inventory
Kindergarten	School Readiness Uniform Screening (SRUSS)
Grades K–3	Reading Diagnostic Assessments
Grades 3–10	State standardized achievement test in reading, writing, sciences, and mathematics
Grade 10	Preliminary Scholastic Assessment Test (PSAT) PLAN Tenth-Grade Assessment
Grade 11	SAT ACT
Optional Tests in High School	College Placement Test (CPT) ASVAB GED
Other K–12 Tests	National Assessment of Educational Progress (grades 4, 8, and 12) TIMSS-R (8th grade) Special studies sponsored by the U.S. Department of Education Personal Fitness
Community College Tests	College Entry-Level Placement Test

Figure 18.1
Sample student assessment program.

Under the federal "No Child Left Behind" law (NCLB), the National Assessment of Education Progress (NAEP) has a new role in efforts to improve student achievement. While state participation in NAEP testing previously had been voluntary, NCLB now requires all states to participate annually in NAEP 4th and 8th grade reading and math tests. However, the NAEP scores are not included in measuring whether schools make NCLB's "adequate yearly progress"—the annual improvement required in the percent of students who score at the proficient level on state tests. NAEP is viewed as an independent measure of a state's success in meeting NCLB's goals; thus, no consequences to states or schools occur based on NAEP scores. Because the NCLB requirement for "adequate yearly progress" allows each state to set its own standards and decide which tests to use, and because state tests and standards vary widely, NAEP will provide a national benchmark so the public can see how students in their state do on state tests compared to the NAEP. If there are wide differences (as there are in most states), then NCLB envisions this creating a dialogue within the state about why such differences exist.

Scholastic Aptitude Tests

Many school districts administer scholastic aptitude tests. Some districts use these tests only as a rough screening for the gifted program; others give scholastic aptitude tests with survey achievement tests. Counselors, teachers, and parents find the test information useful because it describes students' cognitive abilities and is helpful for college and vocational planning. Nonetheless, these tests have been criticized because of their cultural bias and misuse.

Multifactor Aptitude Tests

Four of the most widely used multiaptitude tests are the Armed Services Vocational Aptitude Battery (ASVAB), the General Aptitude Test Battery (GATB), the Differential Aptitude Test (DAT), and the Career Aptitude Placement Survey (CAPS). Some school districts administer an aptitude test in the 10th grade. Civilian counselors working with the ASVAB visit high schools and administer the test to all high school students who want to take the test for educational and vocational guidance purposes. They meet with armed services personnel only if they request an interview.

Career Guidance Tests

A wide variety of career guidance tests are used in the schools, especially at the middle school and high school levels. General interest batteries are often given at both levels. In addition to interest tests, schools often administer career decision and maturity scales that help the school district evaluate the educational and vocational needs of the students. The American College Testing Service has developed a system called WorkKeys to assess the abilities of noncollege students so that businesses can better evaluate these individuals. The assessment includes performance tests, records of education, training, and work experience.

NEEDS ASSESSMENTS

A number of different instruments have been developed to assess the needs of students. Some measure primarily social, psychological, and emotional needs, whereas others measure guidance and instructional needs. A variety of such instruments are available from major publishers, but many schools prefer to develop their own based on specific programs and community characteristics. Figure 18.2 shows an example of a career guidance needs assessment instrument.

Developmental Model

Schools need to design systems that are appropriate to meet their needs. The sample model included in Figure 18.1 looks only at standardized and external testing. A complete testing program includes methods to identify and plan for students who have special needs and a way to assess areas of development not measured by standardized tests. For examples of the types of testing some school districts use to assess students with special needs, see Table 18.1.

Read each phrase and then decide the importance of that activity to you. Circle the appropriate number to the left of each phrase, using the scale that follows. Also circle the item number of any area in which you would like to have assistance from the counselor.

    0 if you feel the item is not important
    1 if you feel the item is of some importance to you
    2 if you feel the item is of moderate importance to you
    3 if you feel the item is of great importance to you

0	1	2	3	1. Knowing what jobs are available locally that I can enter immediately after graduating from high school
0	1	2	3	2. Knowing how to apply for a job
0	1	2	3	3. Knowing how to write a résumé
0	1	2	3	4. Knowing how to dress for and what to say in an interview
0	1	2	3	5. Learning more about my career interests
0	1	2	3	6. Learning more about the training and education required in my career interest areas
0	1	2	3	7. Talking with people employed in my career interest areas
0	1	2	3	8. Arranging for work experience in my career interest fields
0	1	2	3	9. Learning more about my values and the way they relate to my career choice
0	1	2	3	10. Learning about what courses I should take if I want to enter certain career fields

Figure 18.2
Example of a career guidance needs assessment instrument.

Table 18.1

Identification of exceptional students.

Exceptionality	Tests and Procedures
Mental disability	Slosson Intelligence Test–Revised Third Edition (score of 75 or below)
	Public school version of the American Association of Mental Deficiency's Adaptive Behavior Scales
	Devereux Behavior Rating Scale
	Wechsler Intelligence Scale for Children (WISC-IV), Wechsler Preschool and Primary Scale of Intelligence (WPPSI-III), or Stanford-Binet Intelligence Scale, Fifth Edition
	Leiter International Performance Scale
	Peabody Picture Vocabulary Test, Third Edition
	Vision, hearing, speech, and language screening
	Medical, social, and psychological data
Emotional disability	California Test of Personality–Revised Edition
	Wide Range Achievement Test, Third Edition
	Slosson Intelligence Test Revised Third Edition
	Draw-a-Person Test, Kinetic Family Drawing Test
	Children's Apperception Test
	Burks's Behavior Rating Scales
	Behavioral observations
	Complete social history
	Documented and dated evidence of two conferences
	Documented and dated evidence of two interventions or adjustments that have been tried but have not been successful
	Vision, hearing, speech, and language screening
Specific learning disabilities	Slosson Intelligence Test Revised Third Edition
	WISC-IV, WPPSI-III, Stanford-Binet-5
	Peabody Picture Vocabulary Test, Third Edition
	Wide Range Achievement Test, Third Edition
	Bender Visual Motor Gestalt Test, Third Edition
	Survey achievement test results
	Peabody Individual Achievement Test–Revised
	Behavioral observations
	Documented and dated alternatives attempted
	Summaries of two conferences held
	Vision, hearing, speech, and language screening
	Woodcock-Johnson Psycho-Educational Battery, Third Edition
	Work samples
	Attendance record
	Social, psychological, and medical history
Gifted	Slosson Intelligence Test Revised Edition
	Renzulli Rating Scale
	WISC-IV, WPPSI-III, Stanford-Binet-5
	Survey achievement test results

TEST-TAKING SKILLS

Skills tests are important to the schools because they hold both the students and the schools accountable. Besides mastering the knowledge and cognitive objectives of the tests, more schools are focusing efforts on teaching students how to study, hoping that these skills will translate to other subject areas. The two main approaches used in helping students improve their test performance are better content preparation and better test-taking skills. The next several sections outline the strategies used to accomplish these goals.

Stress Reduction

Learning can be increased if stress is reduced. Stress is defined as a force that can cause strain or distortion in the individual. Teaching test-taking skills is one approach to reducing stress on tests; many of the large test publishers have practice examinations and study guides available to help orient students. Another approach is to improve students' knowledge base. One way to do this is to help teachers improve the quality of their instruction. Effective teachers use analytical and synthetic approaches to the subject matter, organize the material to make it clear, and establish rapport with their students (Whitman, Spendlove, & Clark, 1986, p. 1).

Feedback is an important factor in improving future performance and alleviating stress. Five steps are essential for effective feedback:

1. Help students know where they stand.
2. Set specific objectives, and state the evaluative criteria for successful performance.
3. Provide written comments on papers, tests, and homework assignments.
4. Test frequently.
5. Talk individually with the learners about the quality of their work.

TEST ANXIETY

Test anxiety is the general feeling of uneasiness, tension, or foreboding that some individuals experience in testing situations. Excessive anxiety can have a detrimental effect on individual performance (Sarason, 1980; Tobias, 1979; Tyron, 1980). When individuals feel pressure to achieve high scores on a test, their anxiety level may increase (Deffenbacher, 1978). In reviewing the literature on anxiety and test performance, Goldman (1971) found that individuals with high levels of anxiety tend to do worse on cognitive tests. Wine (1980) concluded that individuals with high test anxiety worry about not doing as well as they would like to do on a test. This mind-set leads to their failure to concentrate on or attend to the test. Individuals with low test anxiety, on the other hand, do not worry and are able to concentrate on their test performance. Zeidner and Most (1992) conclude that maximum performance tests (e.g., problem-solving, situational, and critical-thinking exercises) tend to evoke anxiety in the test takers. High anxiety levels impede performance and lead to cognitive interference and task-irrelevant thinking (Saklofske, Kowalchuk, & Schwean, 1992). Spielberger and Vagg (1995) conclude that test anxiety is a situation-specific trait, with worry and emotionality being its major components. Worry is not correlated with achievement, whereas emotionality is.

Measures of Test Anxiety

Several published instruments are designed to measure test anxiety. The Test Anxiety Inventory is a 20-item paper-and-pencil test to measure two major components of test anxiety: worry and emotionality. The inventory can be given to students and adults in grade 10 and higher and is similar in structure to the A-Trait scale of the State-Trait Anxiety Scale. It can also be self-administered.

The Suinn Test Anxiety Behavior Scale (STABS) and the Test Anxiety Profile (TAP) by Oetting and Cole measure test anxiety. The STABS is a 50-item paper-and-pencil test for individuals in grade 7 to adulthood. Clients rate their anxiety concerns on a 5-point scale, ranging from "not at all" to "very much." The test items concern clients' experiences related to academic testing situations. The TAP is a 77-item paper-and-pencil test measuring individual feelings about six academic testing situations: multiple-choice exams, mathematics exams, essay exams, unannounced tests, talking in front of a class, and tests with time limits.

The classic test in the field is the Children's Test Anxiety Scale (CTAS), which contains 30 items. Feld and Lewis (1969) have identified four components discovered through factor analysis of the CTAS: test anxiety, remote school concerns, poor self-evaluation, and somatic signs of anxiety. Test anxiety is measured by questions such as "Do you worry a lot before you take a test?" and "While you are taking a test, do you usually think you are doing poor work?" To assess remote school concerns, the test includes questions such as "When you are in bed at night, do you sometimes worry about how you are going to do in class the next day?" and "After you have taken a test, do you worry about how well you did on the test?" Poor self-evaluation is measured by questions such as "When the teacher is teaching you about reading, do you feel that other children in the class understand him or her better than you?" and "Do you sometimes dream at night that other boys and girls in your class can do things you cannot do?" To measure somatic signs of anxiety, there are questions such as "When you are taking a test, does the hand you write with shake a little?" and "When the teacher says that she is going to find out how much you have learned, do you get a funny feeling in your stomach?"

Strategies to Help Test Anxiety

Gonzales (1995) concludes from his research that reduction in test anxiety leads to improvement in the academic performance of students. Cognitive therapeutic approaches and systematic desensitization are found to be effective. Cognitive therapy focuses in this case on the worry aspect of the testing situation and desensitization on the emotional part. Hembree (1988) reviews the correlates, causes, effects, and treatment of test anxiety. The test examiner must be attentive to the examinee's needs. Examinees should be motivated to do their best on tests but should not be made anxious. Sometimes, however, pressure comes not from the psychologist, counselor, or teacher but from the parents. Currently in our educational system tests have assumed too much importance in some states. They are used as the sole criterion to judge whether a student should be promoted to the next grade or allowed to move from one level to another.

The examiner should consider these strategies in test administration:

1. To be sure examinees understand test instructions, check with them, asking whether they understand. In a group test, circulate around the room to see if students are following directions and recording their answers properly.
2. To establish rapport and an environment that is relaxed and as stress-free as possible, before the test create a learning-oriented environment. Examinees may need to be taught more effective study habits and may need more time to prepare for tests. Tests can be an interesting learning experience as well as a motivational one. At test time be friendly and positive but follow standardized procedures. Ensure that examinees have the proper physical facilities, space to work, proper lighting, ventilation, and so on.
3. To remove some of the pressure from major tests and exams, conduct group or class sessions on how to take a test, give the examinees practice tests, and provide a list of guidebooks and study guides that are available for an upcoming test.

Relaxation Techniques

The object of relaxation exercises is to help test takers practice mind calming. The following is an example of what a test administrator might say before a test:

Sit down and get very comfortable. Close your eyes and take a deep breath. Exhale and let your body and mind relax completely. Breathe in again, and as you breathe out, feel even more relaxed. Forget about everything except what I am saying. Listen carefully. Continue to breathe deeply and slowly. You should begin to feel more and more relaxed.

You are sitting in a lounge chair on the beach. It is not too warm or too cold. The temperature is just right. Everything is very peaceful and pleasant. You see the waves coming onto the beach. They are a beautiful blue, and the sun is a brilliant yellow. You feel nice and warm and relaxed all over. Take a deep breath in the nice clear air. You lose track of time. The sky becomes a deeper blue.

Now that you are relaxed, think positively of yourself. Say, "I can remember all I need to know on the test." Say it several times. Say, "I will know the right answers." Say, "I am alert; my mind is powerful."

IMPROVING TEST SCORES

As we have discussed, two of the main approaches to improving test scores are better content preparation and better test-taking skills. Counselors can help individuals become more familiar with types of items and testing procedures. The goal of any consulting session is ultimately a valid performance measure of the individual who is being tested.

Coaching

Coaching is a method used by administrators, teachers, and counselors to help test takers improve their test performance. Prell and Prell (1986) state that although there is no universally accepted definition for coaching, the term is popularly used to mean training test takers to answer specific types of questions and provide the information required by a specific test. Coaching is sometimes referred to as teaching to the test.

The topic of coaching has been the object of much attention lately. Considerable controversy has surrounded coaching to improve performance on the SAT. Alderman and Powers (1980) reported that almost one-third of the high schools surveyed offered special programs for students taking the SAT. Many commercial seminars are also available. Researchers have reported that short high school training programs help examinees gain on average 10 points on the SAT verbal section and 15 points on the mathematics section (Messick, 1980; Messick & Yungeblut, 1981). It should be understood, however, that gains of 20 to 30 points result from getting just two to three more items correct. Stockwell, Schaeffer, and Lowenstein (1991) wrote about the phenomenon in their book, *The SAT Coaching Coverup: How Coaching Courses Can Raise Scores by 100 Points and Why ETS Denies the Evidence.* Cronbach (1984) concludes that the research stimulated by the SAT controversy indicates the following factors:

1. Many different types of coaching programs are in operation in the schools.
2. A key variable in the success of such programs is client motivation and prior preparation.
3. Because most studies have not used true experimental designs, it is difficult to compare an experimental group with a control group.

Of significance are concerns about the social, philosophical, and ethical aspects of coaching. Some social scientists believe that individuals from lower socioeconomic groups are at a disadvantage because they cannot afford to participate in such programs. Wigdor and Garner (1982) conclude that there may be a considerable advantage to preparing test takers for an examination if it measures abilities and knowledge that are educationally worthwhile.

Strategies to Increase Test Wiseness

Millman, Bishop, and Ebel (1965) define test wiseness as "a subject's capacity to utilize the characteristics and formats of the test and/or test-taking situation to receive a high score" (p. 710). Test wiseness is independent of the examinee's knowledge of the subject matter that the items are designed to measure. Millman et al. identify two major dimensions of test wiseness—elements dependent on the test construction or purpose, and elements independent of that construction or purpose. Four major categories of concern for increasing test wiseness are use of time, avoidance of errors, strategies for guessing, and use of deductive reasoning.

Spielberger and Vagg (1995) conclude that the most effective treatment of test-anxious students is to allow students to discuss and practice their newly learned coping skills. Treatment provided in groups is more effective than what individuals receive in a one-to-one session. Most students who suffer from test anxiety need instruction on how to study as well as on how to take tests. Vagg and Spielberger advocate a two-stage strategy. First, focus on reducing test anxiety during the test; then help students use their existing coping skills more effectively.

Strategies to increase test wiseness include becoming familiar with the test before test day. It is always best to know as much as possible about what to expect before arriving at the test center. Once students know what to expect on the test, they should practice taking the test. In general, test takers feel more knowledgeable and have less anxiety when they receive instructions about how to take a test. This reduces errors caused by unfamiliarity with test procedures and lead to scores that better reflect an examinee's knowledge and abilities.

Special strategies apply to each type of item format. For example, test takers on multiple-choice tests are cautioned to examine carefully all of the options or responses before attempting to choose the correct answer. If the examinee stops when she sees a correct answer—say, option A—she could miss reading options B, C, D, and E, which might also be correct. Option E might read, "All of the above." At other times options may be similar and vary only slightly; usually these options can be eliminated. The examinee has a better chance of getting a higher score if options known to be incorrect can be eliminated and the choice is made from among the remaining alternatives. Sometimes an option resembles the stem—uses the same names, words, or phrases; usually such options should be selected. Correct answers are often longer and perhaps stated more precisely or specifically than the other alternatives.

Prell and Prell (1986) conclude that the most important aspect of test wiseness is its relationship to test validity. Test wiseness is considered a source of variance on tests that reduces the validity. The goal is to maximize the variance due to the knowledge and abilities measured by the test and not penalize test takers who are not test wise. Urman (1983) found that a lack of test wiseness can penalize test takers and that the bias against test takers who are not test wise extends to standardized tests. Prell and Prell conclude that student performance on tests will become a more accurate reflection of actual knowledge if test wiseness techniques are taught to students.

Application of Test Wiseness to Teacher-Made Tests

More attention has focused recently on training in test wiseness to help improve test takers' performance on standardized tests, but that knowledge will also help, even more dramatically, with teacher-made tests. Chiodo (1986) provides rules that instructors should follow to reduce student anxiety and improve test wiseness of students on teacher-made examinations:

1. Review the scope of the exam. The instructor should tell the learners in advance the general areas that the test will cover and the relative importance of each.
2. Use practice tests. The instructor should give the learners samples of the types of items they will face and sample answers for essay and short-answer questions. Sample items help learners become familiar with the language the instructor uses.
3. Be clear about time limits. Learners need to know how long the test will take and whether extra time will be allowed.
4. Announce what materials and equipment the learners need to bring to the testing situation—pencils, calculators, notebooks, blue books, and the like.
5. Review the grading procedures. Test takers need to know how the test will be scored and interpreted and how much the test will count.
6. Review the policies on makeup exams and retakes. The instructor needs to spell out the rules prior to the testing period. Test takers should know whether they may take a makeup test if they have a legitimate reason for missing class or whether they may retake the test if they do not do well.
7. Provide study help. Students might benefit from a study guide for the test or some formal review sessions.
8. Make some provisions for last-minute questions. Some test takers come up with questions on the day of the test or even during the testing. The instructor needs to have an established procedure for handling these questions.
9. Allow for breaks during long exams. Test takers should have a chance to stand up or stretch or go to the restroom if needed.
10. Coach students on test-taking skills. The examiner should remind learners to survey the whole exam before they start and plan their time efficiently. Test takers need to understand the directions and be reminded to answer those questions they are sure of first.

WORKSHOP ON TEST-TAKING SKILLS

A workshop or seminar for individuals on test-taking strategies might last for several sessions, depending on the test to be taken. These sessions should focus on behavior before the test, behavior during the test, general strategies for taking tests, specific strategies for certain types of items or domains, and content review. Here is an outline of a possible series of workshops on test-taking strategies:

A. Session 1—Behavior before the test
   1. Get psychologically ready for the test.
   2. Attend any orientation sessions.
   3. Read informational brochures on the test.
   4. Check domains and objectives to be measured.
   5. Determine review and study strategies.
   6. Secure study guides and previous exams if available.
   7. Check into availability of review or study groups.
   8. Think positively; pep yourself up.

  B. Session 2—Day of the test
    1. Get a good night's rest, eat properly, dress comfortably.
    2. Be early, don't rush, allow time.
    3. Try relaxation techniques.
    4. Concentrate on task, avoid being distracted, block feelings of anxiety.
    5. Develop a positive mind-set toward the test.
  C. Session 3—Behavior during the test
    1. If permitted, skim the test before starting to gain a general overview of the tasks to be accomplished.
    2. Decide how much time to allocate to each part of the test.
    3. Keep an eye on the time.
    4. Read the test critically.
    5. Read directions carefully as well as sample questions and answers.
  D. Session 4—Objective test/multiple choice
    1. Work quickly and accurately but read the whole item.
    2. Read the directions carefully.
    3. Watch for more than one correct answer and options such as "all of the above."
    4. Read every word in the stem of an item and don't skim.
    5. Eliminate implausible options.
    6. Identify clues in the item stems of questions.
    7. Identify clues in the options or answer choices.
    8. Know the rules for guessing.
    9. Know how standardized tests arrange items.
    10. Look for key words or clues that may be in the item.
    11. Don't be afraid to guess.
    12. Don't be afraid to change your answer.
    13. Be confident and don't get flustered.
    14. Know how to answer verbal analogy items.
    15. Know how to answer reading comprehension items.
    16. Know how to answer mathematical and quantitative reasoning items.

OTHER FACTORS

A number of factors can affect test-taking behavior and thus test scores:

1. Anxiety
2. Bluffing
3. Past experience
4. Response set and positional preferences
5. Reading comprehension
6. Speaking ability, enunciation, and voice
7. Spelling and grammar
8. Penmanship and fluency

  Anxiety was discussed earlier in this chapter and can affect all four major types of tests—objective, essay, oral, and performance. Bluffing occurs mainly on essay or oral examinations and can bias an individual's score. Test takers with good verbal facility quite often can express themselves well but must be sure to spend some time organizing their answers, using good topic sentences or opening statements.

Past experience can also influence results. Many test takers are exposed to a test type or item type with which they have had no experience. Alternate forms, if available, may be given to examinees in this situation. Sometimes testing in general has not been a part of an individual's cultural or educational experiences. This type of test taker might profit from attending sessions on how to take tests.

Response set and positional preferences affect individual performance, especially on personality tests. In general, a good standardized test in the cognitive area randomizes correct answers. If 100 items have four options each, each option should serve as the correct answer approximately 25% of the time.

Teacher-made tests often reveal unconscious patterns, such as having more items true rather than false. Examinees should be informed that correct answers will follow a random pattern, and any guessing should take that pattern into consideration.

A major criticism of group tests is that they demand reading comprehension skills. Most test authors, however, try to keep the verbal level of the item simple so that the items measure knowledge or application rather than reading comprehension. Counselors should check an examinee's reading level before arbitrarily administering a test. In some cases a test may have to be administered orally, or a nonverbal test may have to be given.

Voice, enunciation, and oral expression are also factors that can affect an individual's performance on an oral test. Many times, practice or rehearsal sessions and role playing can help individuals learn to present themselves better on oral examinations.

Spelling and grammar, penmanship, and fluency are important factors on essay tests. Errors in spelling and grammar detract from the ideas being presented and influence rater judgment negatively. On the other hand, good penmanship and fluent expression create a positive expectation in raters and encourage high ratings.

INFORMATION ON TEST TAKING

One of the major sources of information on test taking is the test publisher. Many publishers have brochures, study guides, and practice exercises available for their tests. A representative bibliography is included at the end of this chapter. The quality of publisher aids varies, however; some are well done, some are not. The following outline should guide the helping professional who must develop an awareness brochure for a scholastic aptitude test:

A. General statement and misconceptions about preparing for tests
    1. The test measures innate ability, and there is no way to prepare for the test.
    2. A system can be developed to help improve test scores.
B. General statement of what research says about different factors related to test performance
    1. Previous educational experiences are an important factor in test performance.
    2. Generic skills in verbal reasoning and fluency and mathematical analysis and reasoning—the skills necessary for success in academic programs—are measured by scholastic aptitude tests.

C. General statement of what type of preparation has helped individuals improve their test performance
    1. Test companies and educational publishers often have sample tests and study guides available for test takers.
    2. Special short- or long-term courses in a given area might be considered.
    3. Courses in test-taking strategies might be of help to some individuals.
D. General statements about test-taking strategies
    1. Test performance is only one indicator of potential; previous achievement and other factors are also valid indicators. Therefore, test takers ought not be overwhelmed by the importance of the test.
    2. Test takers should become knowledgeable about the tests they plan to take.
    3. Test takers should practice taking sample tests.
    4. Test takers should develop the proper mental and psychological mind-set.
    5. Test takers should develop time-management skills and apply the principles to taking tests.
    6. Test takers should learn strategies for problem solving and guessing on tests.
    7. Test takers should learn to be careful and check their work.
E. Specific strategies for answering verbal and mathematical types of questions should be discussed.
F. An annotated bibliography of resource information (books, guides, and audiovisuals) should be available.

Most test publishers provide brochures on how to take tests, practice tests, purposes and scope of the test, and so on. For example, for the National Teachers Examination ETS has available a bulletin of information, a descriptive booklet on the NTE Core Battery, and descriptive leaflets for the specialty area tests. These guides include a previously administered form of the test, rationale for the answers, test-taking strategies, and an explanation of scoring procedures. They also include a separate answer sheet and answer key. ETS (1988) has developed a test-taking tip sheet to provide general information on test taking. Other tip sheets have been developed on analytical, reading, verbal, and quantitative questions and preparing for achievement tests. The tip sheet provides the following suggestions on test taking:

Be a Good Consumer

1. Get information about tests from the test publisher. Often there are available copies of tests that have been previously given.
2. Know what the test covers and does not cover.
3. Plan to be successful the first time you take the test.

Before the Test

1. Become familiar with the types of questions.
2. Assess your strengths and weaknesses.
3. Develop practice and study strategies.
4. Become familiar with the directions and organization of the test.
5. Learn whether you will be penalized for guessing.
6. Study your guessing pattern.

During the Test

1. Arrive at the test site early.
2. Work carefully.
3. Answer the questions immediately.
4. Decide what questions you might respond to if you have enough time and the questions you will not respond to because you have no idea of the answer.
5. Answer every question if there is no penalty for guessing.
6. Keep focused. Don't let others distract you.

After the Test

1. Cancel your test performance if you had unforeseen health, family, or emotional problems.
2. Review your results on the test along with your goals and aptitude.
3. Plan to take the test again if necessary.

Test Alert

Test Alert (1990) is an instructional program of test-taking strategies published by Riverside Publishing Company. The purpose of the program is to introduce primary school students to effective techniques for taking standardized tests. The goal of Test Alert is to help students achieve test scores that accurately reflect their achievement. The program focuses on strategies for test taking, not on a review of the content being tested. Level A is for grades 1 and 2 and is organized into five lessons, one for each day of the school week. Each lesson takes 35 to 45 minutes. The five lessons are Good Listening, Good Guessing, A Closer Look at Numbers, A Closer Look at Words, and Using Clues. Level B is for grades 3 and 4; Level C is for grades 5 and 6. The 10 lessons at levels B and C each take approximately 45 minutes. A list of strategy categories follows:

Mechanics of Test Taking

Lesson 1 Reordering Information and Answers

Lesson 2 Pacing Yourself

Lesson 3 Making Good Guesses

Reading Strategies

Lesson 4 Recognizing Main Ideas

Lesson 5 Drawing Conclusions

Mathematics Strategies

Lesson 6 Improving Computation Skills

Lesson 7 Solving Word Problems

Lesson 8 Understanding Math Units

Language Strategies

Lesson 9 Ordering Ideas

Lesson 10 Developing Paragraphs

The lessons include a focus exercise—an entertaining activity that demonstrates the major concepts of the lesson. Discussion questions, activity booklets, and a teacher's guide are available. The session ends with a trial test in which questions are presented in both timed and untimed formats.

LEARNING STYLES

A learning style is defined as an individual's preferred mode and desired conditions to learn. People differ in how they approach learning. As noted earlier, Mann and Sabatino (1985) conclude that two individuals with the identical IQ and with the same configuration of special abilities or with the same type and strength of information processing abilities may nevertheless be quite different in the ways that they perceive things, think, solve problems, recall events, come to decisions, play musical instruments, and swing baseball bats (p. 189). Dunn, Dunn, and Price (1983) found that when students are taught with approaches and resources that complement their unique learning styles, their achievement is significantly increased and their attitudes are better. See a full discussion on this topic in Chapter 15, "Environmental Assessment."

PROCESSING STYLE

Processing style, a component of learning style, can be defined as the individual's method of inputting and outputting information. An individual inputs sensory information from visual, hepatic, and auditory sources. Hepatic combines kinesthetic and tactile stimuli. The individual then integrates the information with previously learned information and stores it in long-term memory. Output involves using vocal or motor responses to solve a problem or accomplish a task.

SUMMARY

Testing takes place from early childhood to adulthood. Even children less than 2 years old are required to take tests in a literacy program. The Stanford Binet-5 reports that adults up to 90 years old can be tested also. Almost all 50 states have school testing programs. In some states, students must pass a high school level examination, and in other states, achievement tests are given at each grade level.

A wide variety of types of tests are given to students, such as career awareness tests, multiaptitude tests, interest tests, and vocabulary tests. There are individual tests that a counselor or psychologist has to administer, score, and interpret. The test administrator needs to be able to critically evaluate the tests used.

Some schools have sessions on test anxiety and provide workshops for students. Some reviewers are critical of testing programs because they feel teachers might teach to the tests so that the students will pass. Others feel that traditional multiple-choice tests are best. People question the value of tests that do not utilize performance measurement and authentic assessment.

Often we neglect to prepare individuals properly to take tests. We fail to teach not only test-taking skills but also study skills. Many tests now have practice exams and study guides. Practice in test taking is helpful for those with limited recent experience. The goal of tests is to obtain a true measure of individual performance. Factors such as self-concept, self-confidence, and achievement motivation can affect actual test performance as well as participation in test-taking programs.

QUESTIONS FOR DISCUSSION

1. Study Figure 18.1, a sample school testing program. What tests would you add or drop? Why?

2. Study Table 18.1, which lists tests and procedures for identifying students with special needs. Do you see any tests that would be inappropriate for the use suggested in the table? For example, would you use the Slosson Intelligence Test as an initial screen to identify individuals with mental disabilities?

3. Teachers may feel that they are under tremendous pressure because of achievement testing. They may dislike the standardized achievement battery selected for their district because it does not measure what they are teaching. In such a situation what steps should the district administrators take to ensure the best test selection and gain the support of district teachers?

4. What types of nonintellectual or noncognitive tests should be included in the school testing program?

5. Should intelligence tests or scholastic aptitude tests be given to students every 2 to 3 years along with achievement tests? Why or why not? Should all students be required to take some type of personality test, such as the California Test of Personality? Why or why not?

6. Should counselors, psychologists, and teachers make sure that sessions on test-taking skills are conducted prior to all major examinations? Why or why not?

7. Study guides have been published for all of the major national testing programs. How would you go about evaluating these guides? Would you recommend a specific one or series, or would you just tell the client that a number of sources are available in most bookstores? Explain your approach.

8. If an individual came to you for advice about a $1,400 series of seminars in preparation for the Graduate Record Examinations, what would you tell that person?

9. Do you think that anxiety plays a significant role in test performance? Should we try to assess anxiety before and during testing situations? Why or why not?

10. Have you taken seminars in test-taking strategies or sessions on how to improve your performance on a nationally administered examination? What was your evaluation of the seminar or session? Do you believe your performance improved as a result of the seminar?

SUGGESTED ACTIVITIES

1. Interview a school counselor to find out what tests are part of that school's testing program. Report your findings to the class or in a written paper.

2. Assume that you are a school's director of testing and have received the printout that follows. It summarizes the performance of the first-grade students on a recently administered test. In addition to those numbers, you know that the district required a passing score of 80%. Draft the communication piece that you would send to teachers, parents, and students.

Objective	Students Tested	Number Failed	Number Passed	Percent Passed
Recognize basic vocabulary	156	24	132	84.6
Recognize Dolch words	156	0	156	100.0
Identify word meanings in context	156	6	150	96.1
Identify rhyming words	156	8	148	94.8
Identify long/short vowels	156	30	126	80.8
Write uppercase and lowercase alphabet	156	5	151	96.7
Discriminate beginning sounds	156	18	138	88.4
Associate ending sounds	156	46	110	70.5

3. Review the school report card for high school students for High School X. If you were asked to summarize the information for the Parent-Teacher Association, what would you say?

School Report Card

	School Percent	District Percent	State Percent
White	78	53	60
Black	14	41	23
Hispanic	3	2	14
Asian	5	3	2
Indian	0	1	1

By Gender	Male Percent	Female Percent
	49	51

	School Percent	District Percent	State Percent
School Attendance Rate	85	92	91
School Mobility	33	45	34
(beginning of year compared with enrollment at end of year)			
Students with mild disabilities (SLD, EMR, Visual, Physical)	5.0	7.0	6.0
Students with moderate disabilities	1.0	2.0	1.0
Limited English proficiency	1.0	2.0	5.0

Dropouts	Male No.	Female No.	School Percent	District Percent	State Percent
White	40	25	4.0	5.0	4.0
Black	14	7	8.0	4.0	5.0
Hispanic	0	2	4.0	5.0	6.0
Asian	0	2	2.0	2.0	2.0
Indian	0	0	0.0	6.0	6.0

Suspended from School					
White	162	136	16.0	16.0	11.0
Black	69	56	37.0	21.0	20.0
Hispanic	7	9	25.0	20.0	11.0
Asian	11	8	16.0	10.0	6.0
Indian	0	0	0.0	14.0	13.0

Staff	No.
Teachers	98
Administrators	8
Support Staff	40

Degree	School Percent	District Percent	State Percent
Bachelor's	59	58	55
Master's	40	40	41
Specialist	0	1	3
Doctorate	1	1	1

Teaching Experience	Percent	Racial/Ethnic Group	Percent
First Year	0	White	88
1-3	16	Black	8
4-9	19	Hispanic	2
10-19	19	Asian	2
20+	40	Indian	0

High School Competency Test Grade 11
Communications (passing percentage)

	School	District	State
White	95	94	95
Black	80	82	78
Hispanic	82	83	79
Asian	96	83	86
Indian	70	86	89
Unknown	67	76	78

Mathematics

White	89	86	87
Black	61	53	54
Hispanic	56	73	67
Asian	71	84	86
Indian	70	71	79
Unknown	67	56	62
SAT average	900	996	880

Expenditure per Student

Regular	$3400	$3581	$3826
Exceptional	9020	7417	8429
At risk	3600	3497	4294
Vocational	4400	5111	4590

4. Write a position paper on one of the issues related to school testing programs.

5. Many computer programs are available to help individuals prepare for standardized tests. Review one of these programs. Was it more effective than a book or programmed text designed to accomplish the same purpose?

6. Prepare an annotated bibliography of sources to help an individual prepare to take one of the major standardized tests.

7. Administer one of the tests designed to measure test anxiety, and discuss the results with the class.

8. Read the following brief cases and answer the questions at the end of each.

Case of Carolyn

Carolyn needs to take the SAT to complete her file so she will be considered for admission to the college for which she is applying. She says, "I don't have time to go to the test prep sessions at school. It's just an aptitude test, and either I have it or I don't."

a. Do you agree with Carolyn?
b. What approach would you use to help her?

Case of Helen

Helen is a 20-year-old college senior enrolled in elementary education. She has a 3.0 grade point average on a 4-point system. She has to take 2 years of a modern language and is currently taking Spanish 200. Whenever she has a test in class, she becomes nauseous and faints. She does not report the same feeling when she takes tests in other courses.

a. What do you think is Helen's problem?
b. What approach would you use to help her?

Case of Jorge

Jorge is from Mexico and has the equivalent of a high school education. He has worked as a short-order cook in a fast-food business for the past 5 years and wants to better himself. He wants to enter the local state university and major in business but has been told that he has to take the SAT or ACT. He has been out of school for 7 years and is quite concerned that he won't be admitted.

a. What is Jorge's problem?
b. How would you help him?

Case of Mary

Mary is a 43-year-old displaced homemaker. She has raised her family and was a full-time mother and housewife until her recent divorce. She now wants to become economically independent. She graduated from college with a degree in history when she was 20 years old. To get a current teaching certificate, she is required to take a teacher examination. She failed her first attempt, must take the test over again, and is seeking help.

a. What do you hypothesize is her problem?

b. What strategies would you use to help her?

ADDITIONAL READINGS

Read the results of your state testing program and President Bush's position statement titled No Child Left Behind.

Buros Institute of Mental Measurements. (1994). *Psychological assessment in schools.* Lincoln, NE: Author.

Discusses tests most frequently used in the assessment of youth.

Crestline, published by CSE/CRESST, 10920 Wilshire Boulevard, Suite 900, Los Angeles, CA 90024-6511; *http//:www.cse.ucla.edu.*

Crestline is the newsletter of the National Center for Research on Evaluation, Standards, and Student Testing.

Dobbin, J. E. (1986). *How to take a test: Doing your best.* Princeton, NJ: ETS.

Written in nontechnical language and covering topics such as study techniques, practical test-taking strategies, rules of thumb about guessing, and interpretation of scores, the book also provides practice in answering reading comprehension, sentence completion, synonym and antonym, analogy, and mathematics questions.

Educational Testing Service. On your own: Preparing to take a standardized test [Video]. Princeton, NJ: Author.

This interactive video program intersperses test-taking tips with interactive classroom exercises. (Order from Info-Disc Corporation, 4 Professional Drive, Suite 134, Gaithersburg, MD 20879.)

Glatthorn, A. A. (1998). *Performance assessment and standards-based curricula: The achievement cycle.* Larchmont, NY: Eye on Education.

The book is a very readable introduction to standards-based curricula and authentic learning.

Hembree, R. (1988). Correlates, causes, effects and treatment of test anxiety. *Review of Educational Research, 58*(1), 47–77.

Hembree critically reviews the research literature on test anxiety and identifies significant findings.

Jaegar, R. M. (1994, April). What parents want to know about schools: A report on school report cards. *Evaluation Perspectives, 4*(2), 2–3.

Plake, B. S., & Witt, J. C. (Eds.). *Buros-Nebraska Symposium on Measurement and Testing, Vol 2: The future of testing.* Hillsdale, NJ: Erlbaum.

Read two chapters in Part II, "Educational and Academic/Professional Directions": Nancy Cole's "Future Directions for Educational Achievement and Ability Testing" and Ronald Berk's "Minimum Competency Testing: Status and Potential."

Reitz, R. (Ed.). (1989). *Test anxiety.* Bloomington, IN: Phi Delta Kappa.

The book is a collection of articles on components of test anxiety, attributes of test-anxious students, assessment of treatment strategies, and test anxiety treatment programs.

Sapp, M. (1993). *Test anxiety.* Lanham, MD: University Press of America.
Reviews research design and instruments used in anxiety research.

Spielberger, C. D., & Vagg, P. R. (Eds.). (1995). *Test anxiety: Theory, assessment, and treatment.* Washington, DC: Taylor & Francis.
The text has four sections: text anxiety theory and measurement, antecedents and correlates and the consequences of anxiety, research on the treatment of anxiety, and theory-based treatment of test anxiety.

Tyron, G. S. (1980). The measurement and treatment of test anxiety. *Review of Educational Research, 50,* 343–372.
Representative test-taking guides are listed here.

19 Communicating Test Results

OVERVIEW

There are a variety of methods that professionals use to communicate test results to clients. Written test reports are probably the most widely used method. Many test publishers provide computer scoring and interpretation and computer-generated test reports. Often clients have problems reading and understanding the reports without having individual feedback sessions with a counselor. Even with the help of the counselor, such factors as client readiness, motivation and attitude, and negative test results can affect the client's ability to accept test results.

OBJECTIVES

After studying this chapter, you should be able to

✔ Identify important standards from AERA, NCME, and APA that apply to test selection

✔ Be familiar with methods of communicating written reports

✔ Compare models of reporting test results

✔ Discuss strategies to communicate results to clients, parents, and professionals

✔ Recognize the different methods of reporting and disseminating test results

✔ Identify approaches that increase communication with parents, students, and teachers

TEST REPORTS

Counselors often give a variety of tests. Most of the recently published tests have computer scoring and analysis programs. Other test reports can only be scored and interpreted by counselors and psychologists who have been trained to administer and score these "C" level tests, such as the Wechsler tests and the TAT. The client in many cases is asked to be involved in test interpretation.

Written Reports

Writers need to pay attention to punctuation, capitalization, and spelling as well as grammar. A clear, concise report that students and parents can understand is essential. A system approach includes three steps: planning, writing, and editing. Many parents may not understand the tests that were selected to be used in diagnosis and remediation. According to the Standards (1999), the test user is obligated to make the report readable.

Purpose of Written Reports

According to Ownsby (1992), not all authors agree on what should be included in the report. Ownsby feels that the report should serve several purposes: describe the client who is being assessed and his or her problem, provide a record of evaluation, record results for further use, act as a means of communication, and recommend an appropriate course of action. Ownsby also recommends looking at the context of the report while writing it.

Dimensions of Reports

Many publishers provide written reports of test results, making it easier for the client to score and interpret the test results. School districts often provide parents with interpretative results of their children's performance, such as profiles and descriptions of their scores. Examiners need to be concerned with the mechanics of writing these reports. For example, the writer needs to pay attention to punctuation, capitalization, and spelling as well as grammar. To produce a clear, concise report that students and parents will understand, writers should follow the three steps of planning, writing, and editing.

MODELS OF ASSESSMENT

Nail (1996) identified three models for writing psychological reports: the test-oriented model, the domain-oriented model, and the hypothesis-oriented model.

Test-Oriented Model

In the test-oriented model, results are discussed on a test-by-test basis. Each test is listed by title, and the results for that test are presented. The examiner makes little or no effort to contrast data from the various tests. The method makes clear the source of each set of data and causes the test taker to focus on the tests rather than on the client's adaptive functioning. There is a danger, however, that the examiner will use low-level skills to analyze the results. The method also ignores the role of the counselor as interpreter of test results.

Domain-Oriented Model

In the domain-oriented model the results are grouped according to abilities or functional domains such as intellectual ability, interpersonal skills, psychological stress, coping techniques, motivational factors, and the like. When there are no specific referral questions, the model is useful in reports dealing with newly admitted patients, in neuropsychological reports, and in monitoring treatment progress. A problem with this model is that the reader is presented with a lot of information. Known as a "shotgun" approach, the domain-oriented model allows helping professionals to assess functioning over a wide area, but may overwhelm the counselor with data that have little relevance to the evaluation.

Hypothesis-Oriented Model

In the hypothesis-oriented model the results are focused on possible answers to the referral questions. The examiner presents a hypothesis and then the data that support or refute the hypothesis. The strength of the model lies in its efficiency and narrow focus. The examiner integrates data from the history, mental status exam, and behavioral observations from all the tests. The weakness of the model is that the tester may not report all the data that might be valuable to the evaluation.

LEVELS OF REPORTS

Nail (1996) identifies three levels of reports:

Level 1 Copied out of manual level

No effort to personalize the evaluation

Limited generalizability

Blind interpretation of the test data

Level 2 Minimum level of conceptual input used

Only confirmed data used

Level 3 Personalized interpretation

Integrates all available information

Represents the highest level of conceptualization

In level 3 the examiner provides suggestions for intervention based on the client's strengths and coping skills. The psychologist and counselor must identify the information that needs to be clearly communicated in the report. Clinical assessment can provide useful information and has four purposes:

1. Diagnosis and screening
2. Problem descriptions and case conceptualization
3. Selection of treatment procedures
4. Evaluation of treatment outcomes and progress

The clinical information sources that provide help to the counselor in writing the report are as follows:

1. Clinical interviews
2. Observation
3. Interviews with significant others
4. Psychological testing
5. Self-reports
6. Medical records
7. Physiological measurement

A thorough assessment helps the tester to conceptualize how best to help the client. As indicated previously, the decision to help the client is influenced by the client's motivation, intelligence, personality, and coping style. Another dimension to consider is skill level. The theoretical orientation of the counselor is also very important. For example, some counselors have a Jungian or Rogerian orientation. A counselor with a set orientation like this would tend to use the methodology advocated by his or her role model.

GUIDELINES FOR COMMUNICATING TEST RESULTS

The AAC (2003) position statement *Responsibilities of Users of Standardized Tests* lists four key elements: the counselor must know the test manual, know the limits of the test, know informed consent procedures, and protect the client's right to privacy.

As was mentioned previously, examiners need to know the information that is contained in the test manual and be prepared to explain difficult concepts. It is important to get clients to understand the limits of a test. When appropriate, the standard error of measurement can help to emphasize that the test results are not absolute; results provide approximations of where true scores might fall. Test results can be influenced by various sources of bias, which may affect the interpretation of the scores. The test taker needs to understand that test data represent just one source of information.

Shertzer and Linden (1979) provide a good summary of the principles needed to guide test interpretation:

1. Select the most valid test available for the purpose.
2. Be skilled and competent in interpreting the test results.
3. Interpret test data in light of the other available information.
4. Present results in terms of probabilities rather than certainties.

5. Be certain that test data help meet a need, and present the results objectively and impersonally. Encourage the client to make her own interpretation and express her own reactions.
6. Results from tests in which clients can vary their responses at will must be interpreted with special care.
7. Realize that the client may react emotionally and even irrationally to the test results, and temper the approach with knowledge of the individual.
8. Use both group and individual approaches to help clients engage in self-appraisal and planning. (p. 501)

Goldman (1971) believes that the counselor needs to look at the process, and he agrees that the first key step is selecting the correct test. In addition, counselors constantly need to sharpen their interviewing skills. The posttest interview gives an opportunity to deal with interpretation and use it in planning and decision making. Counselors need to keep up with the literature on reporting test results.

Lien (1971) adds several other dimensions that should be considered:

1. Be sure that both the examiner and examinee have a clear and immediate goal in mind that serves as the basis of the test report.
2. Avoid specific reporting of derived scores such as standard scores and percentile ranks, if possible.
3. Concentrate on increasing understanding rather than posing as an expert.
4. Recognize that the client may be helped to understand the data, but may not necessarily accept the results.
5. Never compare one client with another.
6. Be sure that your client or others needing the test information understand the interpretation.

Garfield and Prediger (1982) suggest certain steps and procedures that a counselor should consider in interpreting test results; these are included in the checklist in Figure 19.1.

Informed Consent

Certain responsibilities relate to informed consent. The test taker should be informed what will be done with the test results and who will use them. The examiner should also discuss with the test taker any circumstances that could affect the validity or reliability of the results. The consent of the examinee must be obtained before test results are used for any purpose other than that advanced prior to the testing. The examiner also needs to protect the examinee's right of privacy and all information needs to be accurate.

STANDARDS FOR REPORTING TEST RESULTS

Professional standards and codes of ethics emphasize the importance of how test results are reported. Some of these standards focus on requirements of test authors and

Prior to Testing

_____   Read in the manual the suggestions for interpreting the test.
_____   Check to see whether interpretation procedures are substantiated by the psycho-
             metric evidence found in the manual.
_____   Review with the client the purposes of the testing.
_____   Explain the strengths and limitations of the test.
_____   Explain how the test is scored.
_____   Discuss who receives the test results and how they are used.

During the Reporting Session

_____   Have client discuss personal reactions to and feelings about the test.
_____   Examine whether any factors such as race, age, gender, or disabling conditions
             have influenced the test results.
_____   Seek additional information to explain any discrepancies or inconsistencies that
             become evident.
_____   Translate the results into language the client can understand.
_____   Emphasize strengths and objectively discuss weaknesses.
_____   Allow sufficient time for client to assimilate the results.
_____   Listen attentively to what client says.
_____   Observe nonverbal as well as verbal cues.
_____   Check to see whether the examinee understands the test results.
_____   Correct any misconceptions.
_____   Encourage client to further research or study the meaning of the results.
_____   Provide some alternatives for the test taker to consider, based on the test information.
_____   Schedule follow-up sessions, if needed, to facilitate understanding, planning, or
             decision making.

Figure 19.1
Checklist of steps and procedures for test interpretation.

publishers. The test manual, for example, should contain information that will facilitate test interpretation. As a matter of fact, all test materials including computerized reports should be designed to facilitate test interpretation. Other standards focus on special types of tests, such as certification and licensing examinations. Reports are to be given promptly to applicants. Test takers who fail should be told their scores and the cutoff score required to pass the test. Applicants should be informed of their performance on all parts of the test for which scores are produced. In addition, rules and procedures used to combine scores or other assessments to determine the overall outcome should be reported to the test taker.

Furthermore, the rights of the test taker must be taken into consideration and procedures to handle test irregularities most be employed. Some testing organizations offer the test taker the option of prompt and free retesting or arbitration of the dispute.

Standards call for the clinician to share with clients the test results and interpretations. The clinician is directed to provide information about the range of error for such interpretations when this information will be beneficial to the client. The test information is to be expressed in language that the client or client's legal representative can understand.

METHODS OF REPORTING TEST RESULTS

There are six major methods of reporting test results: individual sessions, group sessions, written reports, computer-generated reports, video approaches, and oral reports. The role and function of the test taker and counselor vary with each approach.

Individual Sessions

Counselors often use individual interpretation sessions to present test results to clients. How the scores are reported is a function of the counselor's theoretical orientation. Counselors who are more client-centered are apt to present clients with raw and derived scores and encourage the clients to join in the process of interpreting the scores. Counselors might direct more attention to how the clients feel about their scores and interpretations. Counselors who are more direct may review the purpose of the testing, present the results, clarify what the scores mean, and discuss the implications of the results.

When a client interprets and reacts to his own scores, the counselor may gain new insight into the client. By participating in the discussion of the test results, the client may become more accepting of the results and may use the information in decision making. Some counselors argue that the more the client participates, the more understanding and learning takes place. Other counselors believe that individual sessions are time consuming and unproductive.

Group Sessions

Group sessions are used frequently to provide interpretation of client test results. Clients with particular learning or personality styles prefer group and social interaction; such clients often learn from each other as well as from the counselor. Most tests now provide interpretive material that the counselor can highlight effectively and efficiently in group sessions. This approach is usually more economical. The counselor can work with a small or large group and can use overhead transparencies, filmstrips and tapes, or videotapes to present material. Such aids are less likely in a one-on-one situation. The use of group sessions does not preclude offering individual sessions if a client needs further help processing the information.

Written Reports

More and more test publishers are providing some sort of written report of the test results. With many tests, clients score themselves, plot the scores on a profile, and have immediate interpretation of the results. School districts often provide parents with interpretive reports of their children's performance on survey achievement testing. Both the language and interpretation are simplified.

Written reports are not valuable to all individuals. Many students and parents have problems reading and understanding test reports even when the language is simple. Many written reports present profiles of scores that are helpful for test takers who have difficulty visualizing test results. Some individuals find written reports impersonal and have aversions to them. Many computerized forms of test interpretation are now available. Computerized reports may be effective in presenting basic facts but probably are ineffective in changing a person's established belief system.

Computer-Generated Test Reports

Advancement in computer technology and the increasing presence of computers in school and clinical settings is changing the way professionals conduct assessments, including the method of providing interpretive feedback. Numerous computer programs convert test results into extensive narrative reports – the issue is whether these computer-generated reports are valid. The majority of studies conducted on the accuracy of computerized narrative reports have found the reports to be appropriate. However, most professionals believe that computer-generated reports should be viewed as valuable adjuncts to, rather than substitutes for, clinical judgment.

There are advantages to using computer-generated test reports: the reports may be more comprehensive than individual clinicians' reports, they save the clinician time in preparing reports, and the reports may provide more objective information. Ethical concerns also exist about counselor misuse of computer-generated test reports. Unqualified counselors may use these reports to compensate for a lack of training and experience. In addition, counselors may come to depend more on the computer based reports rather than their own clinical judgment.

Video Approaches

A current trend is to combine the technology of the computer with that of video equipment. Scores on certain scales can key individualized reports back to clients, providing audio as well as visual presentation. The presentation can appear more professional and be checked for accuracy before it is used with clients. In addition, the analysis can be more complete and thorough because the rules are built into the program.

Oral Reports

Often the examiner makes an oral report to parents and guardians. The complexity of the report depends upon the familiarity of the parents or client with the concepts and terms used. It is the responsibility of the counselor to translate the information into language the parents can understand. To maximize the effectiveness of the report, parents and guardians need to do the following (Shore, Brice, & Love, 1992, p. 110):

1. Ask for definitions of unfamiliar terms.
2. Request examples to support any generalizations that the examiner makes.
3. Offer examples of the examinee's behavior that contradict test results.
4. Have the examiner repeat the parts they didn't understand when presented.
5. Ask for a summary before leaving the session.

Parents should make a list of questions to ask the examiner, such as the following:

1. What tests did my child take?
2. What were my child's strengths on each test? Weaknesses?
3. Are there any recommendations or suggestions on how I might help my child?

PROBLEM AREAS

Counselors may face a number of problems in disseminating test information. Some of the more common problems are discussed here.

Acceptance

The goal of the feedback session with clients often is getting them to accept the test results and incorporate that information into their decision making. Negative results frequently prompt resistance of the test takers to change their self-concepts to align with test data. They often resist accepting valid and genuine information about themselves.

Counselors can enhance acceptance of the test information by

1. involving the clients in decision making and general selection of tests prior to the testing
2. establishing rapport with the clients so that they trust the counselor and are relaxed in the sessions
3. spending sufficient time with the clients in interpreting the results—not overwhelming them with too much data
4. translating the results into language that the clients can understand
5. showing the validity of the information for the decision(s) to be made

Readiness of the Client

The critical factor in the acceptance of the data is client readiness. Test takers who believe that they have a specific need for counseling about the test results and want to learn what meaning data have for them will more readily accept the information presented. If the information is damaging to a client's self-concept or ego, the counselor might have to work on getting that client to extend his or her acceptance. The counselor can use these techniques to help the client become ready:

1. Have several sessions prior to the report session to build understanding and acceptance.
2. Allow the client to bring up the topic; don't immediately begin the session with test interpretation.
3. Focus on the test rather than on the client.
4. Try to engage the client actively in the learning and planning process both before and after the testing.

Negative Results

Often the results are not what the client wanted, desired, or expected. The client may have failed to pass a certification or licensing examination or to achieve the minimum score for admission to college. Certain results are a threat to the client's self-concept. On a personality test a client may turn up with high scores on the lie scale and become defensive. Or the client may tend to be overly truthful and may have a high score on a neuroticism scale. The test administrator should consider the following:

1. Explain the rationale for cutoff scores and the validity of the established procedures.
2. Gain an understanding of the test taker's perceptions and feelings; see the whole person complete with irrationalities and blind spots.
3. Accept the test taker's right to argue with test implications, without necessarily agreeing with the test taker.
4. Be genuine and express personal feelings, perhaps disagreeing with the clients' views and goals, and point out the consequences of a particular course of action.
5. Identify other information about the client that supports or does not support the test data.
6. Discuss the implications of the data and the importance of that information for decision making.

Flat Profiles

Many times an individual's pattern of scores has no highs or lows but is just a flat profile. On aptitude and achievement tests this would indicate a similar level of performance in all areas. It might be above average, average, or below average. On interest or career guidance inventories, especially if the client is undecided about future goals, the data are not extremely helpful. Response set might be a factor on a test, with the individual ranking everything high, average, or low. Holland (1979) believes there are major problems in counseling individuals with flat profiles. In the case of flat profiles on interest and career guidance tests, counselors can ask clients to read the descriptions of the six Holland types and rank the three types most characteristic of themselves (Miller, 1985) and discuss the clients' expectations, relevant past experiences, previous work activities, and misconceptions and stereotypes.

In the case of flat profiles on aptitude and achievement tests, counselors can look at the interests, values, and career goals and assure the clients that their profiles are not abnormal. The counselor should discuss what an individual considers his or her goals to be and what he or she can do acceptably. A good procedure is to investigate the individual's performance on previous tests to determine whether this pattern is typical.

Motivation and Attitude

Test results are more significant to clients who are motivated to take a test, come in and discuss the results, and have a positive attitude toward the value of the data. Some clients have a negative attitude toward testing prior to the test and maintain that attitude afterwards. Some clients become negative after they see that the test results are not what they expected.

Workers in the helping professions should recognize that tests can aid clients in developing more realistic expectations about themselves and can be valuable in decision making. However, some clients put too much weight on the results and become overdependent on test data to solve their problems. Other clients use test results as a way of escaping from their feelings and problems. Counselors interpreting test results need to be aware not only of a client's motivation to take or not take a test but also his or her attitude toward the test. Other important information is the immediate goal for the interpretation of the test results and the client's desire to be involved in decision making about the type of test to be taken and the dissemination of test results.

COMMUNICATION OF TEST RESULTS TO THE PUBLIC

When test results are released to the news media, those responsible for releasing the results should provide information to help minimize the probability of misinterpretation. A current movement toward accountability has influenced the use and reporting of test data by the schools. Administrators like to use standardized and criterion-referenced test data to show that the schools are accomplishing the educational goals of society. However, many people have trouble understanding the concepts used in measurement and the many different types of derived scores test makers report. Test data, when properly presented, can be a useful tool in interpreting the school system for the community. Shertzer and Linden (1979) advocate that emphasis be placed on interpretive reporting of group results to show what the scores signify in terms of progress toward the realization of school objectives and vocational plans (p. 504).

General Guidelines

Communication with the public should follow these general procedures:

1. Communication should take place before and after testing. News releases can announce a test, and letters and cards can be sent to the parents or guardians. An example of such a letter is shown in Figure 19.2. Reports of test results can be made through the local media or can be presented at PTA or community meetings.
2. Because most citizens are not familiar with test jargon and statistical terms, the results should be presented as simply as possible while still remaining accurate and honest.
3. Percentile bands or stanines can be reported graphically or visually using handouts, transparencies, or slides.
4. Data should be presented in summary form—for example, by grade rather than by teacher.
5. Statistical and measurement terms can be defined in nontechnical language with examples provided.
6. The public is not stupid and should not be treated with condescension.

Dear Ocean School Parents and Guardians:

Can you believe it? We have only 9 weeks left in the school year! The time has passed quickly, but there is still much to accomplish. We are confident that with your cooperation we will attain the goals set for this year. We want this to be the best year ever for our children.

As you may know, our school board has adopted promotional criteria for students in grades K through 8. The criteria are based in part on the Stanford Achievement Test and the Essential Skills Tests. We will begin administering the Stanford Achievement Test next week. The first day of testing will be Monday, April 5. The test will be given over a 2-week period. This time includes makeup testing for children who might be absent, although we hope that every child will be present on testing days and will arrive at school on time. Nonetheless, we do not want any children who are ill to take the tests, so those students will have an opportunity to be tested later.

The Essential Skills Tests will be administered in early May. These tests measure a child's progress in mathematics and reading. We will send home a reminder before the tests.

You can help your child(ren) do well on these tests by following some simple suggestions:

1. Each child should have a good night's rest prior to a testing day. We suggest 10 hours of sleep.
2. Each child should have a good, well-balanced breakfast before coming to school on a testing day.
3. Conflicts and arguments should be avoided. A child's emotional state has great influence on performance.
4. No child should feel anxious about the test. Pressure has a negative effect.

If you have any questions or suggestions, please do not hesitate to contact the school office, in person or by telephone. We have appreciated your assistance and support throughout the year.

Sincerely yours,
Ocean School Guidance Counselor

Figure 19.2
Sample letter of information for parents.

Any oral or written report should include the following components:

1. A general description of the tests or testing program
2. Uses of the test results
3. Types of skills and competencies measured
4. Types of scores reported and the meaning of those scores
5. Type of norms used
6. Definitions and examples of the summary statistics and measurement concepts needed to understand the presentation
7. The results with appropriate comparisons (national, state, district, and school; year-to-year changes; or grade by grade)
8. Factors that might have influenced the results

An oral presentation requires time for questions. The examiner should be prepared to answer the following types of questions about major issues:

- Are these tests biased against minority and disadvantaged students?
- Why do we test so much?

- Why are some schools in the system achieving higher results than others in the system?
- Are teachers influenced by the test results?

THE TESTER AS CONSULTANT: LEGAL CONSIDERATIONS

When testers act as counselors they need to be aware of legal requirements, which can be very specific in many situations. The Buckley Amendment became the Family Education Rights and Privacy Act (PL 93-380) and gave parents the opportunity to see all the information affecting the evaluation, placement, or programming of their children. The law covers all personally identifiable educational records collected, maintained, or used. Parents have the right to demand changes in a record if they find the information to be inaccurate, and their consent must be obtained before test scores and records can be released. These rights transfer to the individual at age 18 or to students attending postsecondary schools. Schools are responsible for informing parents of their right to access records and are required to hold a hearing if errors are thought to be included in the records.

When a client is being assessed for placement, the examiner should remember that the parents probably have useful information. In the screening and placement of students under PL 94-142, the counselor must document contact with the parents and the information received from them. The counselor is required to provide the parents written notice of any proposed change in client identification, evaluation, or placement. Each evaluation procedure and test to be used must be described in writing. Communication must be in a form that is understandable to the parents and in their native language. If the parents are deaf, the information must be transmitted in sign language.

ETHICAL STANDARDS FOR CONSULTATION

Principle 8 of the American Psychological Association's *Ethical Principles of Psychologists and Code of Conduct* (2002) calls for psychologists to make every effort to promote the welfare and best interests of their clients and to guard against the misuse of assessment results. Principle 5 states that psychologists have a primary obligation to respect the confidentiality of information obtained in the course of their work and should reveal information to others only with the consent of the individual involved or that person's legal representative. The exception to this principle occurs when its exercise would result in clear danger to the individual or to others.

CONSULTING WITH PARENTS

Parents are an important resource in improving children's capacity to cope with the demands of their environment. When parents want to be involved, helping professionals should identify the skills, values, and possibilities of the parents relative to helping their children. *Principles for Professional Ethics* (National Association of School

Psychologists, 1992) calls for psychologists to recognize the importance of parental support and obtain it prior to working with a child. Psychologists should secure continued parental involvement through frank and prompt reporting of evaluation findings. They are responsible for telling parents what records consist of, what kind of information goes into the report, who receives the report, and what steps are used to protect the information.

Dustin and Ehly (1984) propose a simple five-step model that involves establishing rapport or phase-in, obtaining information and identifying the problem, providing information for implementation, conducting follow-up and evaluation, and terminating the relationship. The counselor discusses the implications for the child, helps establish goals for the parents, and selects strategies that will be most beneficial to the client and family.

The *Code of Fair Testing Practices in Education* (Joint Committee, 1999) states that the counselor should tell test takers or their parents or guardians how the test scores will be kept on file and indicate to whom and under what circumstances test scores will be released. Parents should also be informed of how to register complaints and have problems resolved about testing. Counselors need to provide parents and guardians with information about the rights of the test taker and discuss whether they can obtain copies of tests and completed answer sheets, retake tests, have tests rescored, or cancel scores.

Brown, Wyne, Blackburn, and Powell (1979) propose a more elaborate model, consisting of seven steps that can be modified to convey test results to parents:

1. Establish a good working relationship.
2. Assess the family and parent dynamics and environment.
3. Check the validity of assumptions about the family and parents.
4. Explain the test results.
5. Discuss the implications for the child.
6. Establish goals for the parents and select strategies.
7. Involve the child in the conference with the parents.

The consultation can be done with a single parent, a couple, or a group of parents.

Explaining Test Results to Parents

Most parents have little knowledge about testing. Even if various facets of the testing program are explained initially, the examiner should review for parents the purposes of the testing, using nontechnical language. Actual test results might be visually presented through graphs and profiles to help parents understand. Reports need to be comprehensible as well as informational. In reporting specific types of scores, the examiner should be sure that parents understand the type of score being discussed. They should be told the limitations of the test, and the standard error of measurement should be explained.

The examiner should walk the parent through the interpretation, being patient and understanding but honest. Working with parents may identify a need for parent education in some group sessions on measurement topics and issues. Goldman (1971) points out that those who work with children and adolescents find that parents rather than the children are most in need of the information provided by tests (p. 438). However, he believes that counselors cannot assume parents will be reasonable and objective about the test report; they may have unreasonable aspirations, blind spots, and defense mechanisms for themselves or about their children. It is important to spend enough time with parents, perhaps more than one session, to deal with their feelings and attitudes.

Sattler (1992) proposes a four-stage model for working with parents:

1. *Initial phase of the interview*—It is important to have both parents or guardians present at the report session to permit the counselor a more objective assessment of the facts and a chance to get the parents or guardians to share in the responsibilities of the test results. The examiner needs to establish rapport and recognize that parents may have experienced many frustrations and hardships in their family life. They should be encouraged to talk; what they have to say is important. The examiner should assess parents' interest in the test results, their attitudes toward their child's condition, their handling of problems with the child, and their goals and expectations for the child.

2. *Communicating diagnostic findings*—The examiner should set the ground rules for the information sharing and should refuse to side with either the parent or the child. Parents should be encouraged to participate in the session and should be warned that some of the information shared might at times arouse conflict, hostility, or anxiety. They should be free to express their feelings, just as the examiner is honest in portraying the results. The hope is that the parents will develop realistic perceptions and expectations for their child.

3. *Discussion of specific recommendations*—The examiner should check to see that the parents have fully understood the test results and their implications. The parents may want specific recommendations or program suggestions, and the examiner should be prepared to provide these.

4. *Termination of the interview*—Parents may be unable or unwilling to accept the results of the evaluation. The examiner should accept that difficulty and perhaps provide the names of other professionals or agencies in case the parents want to get a second opinion. The examiner should also be available to see the parents again if necessary and desirable.

Parent–Examiner Conferences

In preparing for a parent conference, it is important for the examiner to gather all pertinent information, including a report of the standardized tests taken by the child and an interpretation of the results. The examiner should also be prepared to record additional information from the parents that might facilitate work with the child. Parents might be asked to describe how the student feels about school, teachers, counselors, testing, grading, or peers. They might also elaborate on the student's special interests. The examiner might have on display the work of other students so that the parents can see not only what books and materials are being used, but also what level of work is expected. The examiner should end the conference on a positive note, thanking the parents for their interest and scheduling another appointment if necessary.

Types of Questions Parents Ask About Tests

Parents tend to ask a number of questions about test scores and reports. Here are some typical questions and some points to include in a response.

- *What is a standardized test?* "Standardized" refers to conditions under which the test was developed, resulting in a number of standards of performance that are representative of a wide sample of test takers. It also refers to conditions under which the test is administered, usually in a uniform manner so that all test takers receive the same directions, same time to take the test, and so on.
- *How was the test administered?* It was administered by individuals trained and experienced in giving tests such as teachers, counselors, and psychologists.
- *How are the tests scored, reported, and recorded?* Tests are usually sent back to the publisher to be computer scored. Individual and group reports are sent back to the school district or examiner. Many testing services provide labels on which results are recorded and which can be fastened to the cumulative record or file of the individual. Individual profiles and test summaries are sent to parents; class, grade, and district profiles are sent to the schools.

Often parents ask questions about specific scores used for different tests. The examiner should be prepared to explain scores such as national percentile ranks, grade equivalent scores, stanines, local norms, and standard scores. Specific questions may relate to many areas.

- What do these scores really mean?
- What is wrong with grade equivalent scores?
- Why are our school's scores below the national norms?
- Why do you test so much?
- How do you use the scores?
- How accurately do the tests predict success?
- Is there a relation between the scores and a child's achievement in class?
- How much do scores vary and why?
- What is scholastic aptitude?
- What is intelligence?
- What kinds of questions were asked on this test?
- Who will see the test results?
- Can test scores be improved with coaching?
- Is the test fair to members of my race, gender, or ethnic group?

Other Areas of Concern to Parents

Parents also may want to know what to do if they disagree with the results of the testing. For example, the examiner says the child is not ready for kindergarten and the parents think the child is, or the parents think the child should be placed in the gifted program and the examiner doesn't agree. They could be advised of avenues they might take, such as pursuing an independent evaluation on their own, recognizing that the school district may not reimburse them for the evaluation and that it may be difficult to have the client tested with the same tests. Shore, Brice, and Love (1992) remind parents that the people involved in the process are trying to do what is in the best interest of the test taker. Parents should use the information gained from the assessment and discussion with the examiner to make an informed decision about what is best for their child.

Parents may want to know whether test results really matter. The examiner should elaborate on the testing objectives and point out that our society is concerned with accountability. In addition, test results are often a major criterion for promotion or admission to a specific program. Parents should take test results seriously and be supportive of testing programs. They should encourage their children to do their best and praise them for doing as well as they can. Parents' attitudes toward a testing program influence how children view that program.

Parents are sometimes concerned about the anxiety caused by tests and want to know about techniques to help reduce that anxiety. Many bookstores offer audiotapes detailing relaxation techniques. The examiner needs to emphasize that some anxiety is useful, but too much is a problem. Parents should be warned to respond to test anxiety in a realistic manner and not to overreact to test scores.

Parents might ask whether the tests are culturally biased. Many attempts have been made to eliminate as much bias as possible in most test instruments. The essential-skills and minimum-level skills tests are based upon what the students are supposed to learn in schools. Scores would be biased only if individuals did not have an equal opportunity to learn the material included on these tests. Standardized tests use panels of experts to review the items for sexual bias, cultural bias, and bias against individuals with disabilities. On scholastic aptitude tests, the item responses for various groups are compared to see if there are differences in how minority and majority groups respond to the test items. However, even with these attempts, some bias might still be operating in the testing situation and may distort a person's true score.

Parents may be concerned about whether scores are fixed or changeable. They need to be reminded that a test measures a sample of behavior at a particular time, using items from a given domain. Tests scores do change; they can go up and down. There may be some ups and downs in the child's test profile from year to year or subtest to subtest. Sometimes a poor performance happens because a student may not be skilled in the areas measured by the test. Most children perform better in some areas than in others. Parents need to understand the dynamics at work and refrain from hasty value judgments.

Parents may also be concerned about whether students ought to be given their own test results. In most cases students should be provided feedback on their performance in words and terms they can understand. The information can help them understand their own strengths and weaknesses and make more realistic educational and vocational choices.

Parents may wonder whether their children are overachievers or underachievers. Overachievers are students who achieve better in the classroom than scholastic aptitude tests predict. These students usually have a positive attitude toward school, internal orientation, and high motivation. The label has been greatly criticized by educators and psychologists from a theoretical and practical standpoint. Underachievers perform below the prediction of a scholastic aptitude test. Many students with learning disabilities have normal aptitude but achieve a standard deviation or more below the average for their grade or age.

The Informing Interview

In the informing interview the counselor attempts to communicate assessment results with the parents or guardians. The goal of this session may be partly educational and motivational for the parents and partly therapeutic (Gabel, Oster, & Botnik, 1986). When problems identified are mild or less deviant, parents are more accepting of the results and are less anxious. When the problems are severe, the parents or guardians may become angry, defensive, or blame themselves and others. When parents are defensive, communication is usually ineffective.

Gabel and colleagues (1986) suggest that the initial statement and explanation of the problem should be in nontechnical terms. Later the counselor may use medical and psychological terms as support for the assessment. Certain terms, such as *mental retardation* and *brain damage,* might stand as an emotional block to communication if not adequately clarified and explained.

The counselor needs to be alert to what questions the parents asked as well as what questions they did not ask. What questions were they really asking? What questions should they have asked? The counselor may want to address practical questions that concern the client such as schooling, therapy, and counseling needs and the like.

Parents as Test Interpreters

Testing companies usually provide self-interpretative report forms for parents, but most parents still have questions about what the test scores mean. A workshop for parents might help them understand and interpret test results properly. Boehm and White (1982) provide four guidelines for parents who present test results to their children (pp. 138–139):

1. Inform the child about areas of strength or areas needing development.
2. Find out whether the child understands what the test scores mean (e.g., children often confuse the meaning of *percentile* with *percentage*).
3. Avoid judgment of an individual's worth. The student whose score is high is no better as a person than the student whose score is low.
4. For a student who is having difficulty, offer to find out the reasons why and try to help.

Overall, parents need to maintain open communication with their children. Test results should be shared constructively, and steps should be outlined to help with any problem area. Parents also need to listen to their children's view of a test or test result.

Consulting with Teachers

Teachers may also need consultation about test use and interpretation. They have to administer and score both local and standardized tests, and they need to know the practical implications of the scores for their students.

Again, the first step for the examiner is to establish a working relationship. Brown, Pryzwansky, and Schulte (1995) call for a relationship of mutual trust, open communication, genuineness, and positive regard. The teacher is seeking ways to help a student and wants to have the test results interpreted into language that is easy to understand. The consultation is often for the purpose of establishing a plan of action for a particular student.

Caplan and Caplan (1993) identified four types of problems that arise in teacher consultation:

1. The teacher lacks skills and competencies needed to work with students.
2. The teacher is not objective and unbiased.
3. The teacher lacks confidence and perceives personal deficiencies.
4. The teacher lacks the ability to conceptualize the student's problem.

The National Education Association (NEA) and the National Council or Measurement in Education (NCME) have asserted that student assessment is an essential part of teaching and that good teachers cannot exist without good student assessment. Teachers need to acquire skills and abilities to select, develop, apply, use, communicate, and evaluate student assessment information.

Problems that might interfere with the success of the consultation process might be identified by observing the teacher in class, or by listening carefully to what the teacher has to say.

"Shandra has a low IQ. It is impossible to motivate her."

"Keanu comes from a bad family. He will be just like his brothers and not amount to anything."

"Will scored at the 34th percentile. He did not do well at all."

Part of the problem may be that the teacher does not know enough about basic measurement concepts. This topic could be addressed in a group situation, perhaps through inservice education. If the teacher is biased, the examiner may have to use confrontation and report the objective data collected through observation and feedback. Teacher expectations have a tremendous influence on what happens in the classroom; they should be realistic and communicated regularly and effectively.

Goals should be set for the teacher consultation; they help focus attention on strategies. The collaborative model of consultation calls for strategies to be developed jointly by the consultant and teacher. The theoretical orientation of the consultant partly determines the strategies to be used. Neo-client theory might stress human relation skills, such as problem solving and effective communication, whereas behavior theory might focus on selective use of reinforcement strategies.

The National Association of School Psychologists (1992) calls for establishing professional relationships with school personnel. Standard IV relates to the need of the school psychologist to have a working understanding of the goals, processes, and legal requirements of the educational system and to be familiar with the organization, instructional materials, and teaching strategies of the school. Effective communication skills are essential, and the school psychologist is reminded that the findings and recommendations need to be put into language that is readily understood by the school staff.

Indirect Delivery Model

Gutkin and Curtis (1982) propose an indirect service model that includes these steps that will help teachers and parents and other professionals understand, interpret, and use assessment results more effectively:

1. Develop an open, trusting relationship. Rapport must be established.
2. Establish a collaborative, coordinate relationship. Both parties should have equal authority in the decision-making process.
3. Involve the consultee in the consultation process. The consultant is responsible for helping the consultee become active in the process.
4. Encourage the consultee to accept or reject suggestions. The consultee cannot be forced to accept strategies.
5. Maintain a voluntary relationship. Principals should not force teachers into consultation.
6. Maintain confidentiality. The information shared should be kept confidential.

In this model the consultant may plan to collect data from observations, interviews, and standardized tests if both the consultant and consultee believe such information would be useful. Any tests selected and administered should address specific problems identified in the case.

Problem-Solving Consulting Model

A problem-solving approach helps the parties involved clarify and define the problem of the client and facilitates the analysis of forces that will lead to more effective problem solving. Helping professionals can use brainstorming of alternate strategies, evaluate and choose among the alternatives, and then specify the responsibilities of the consultee and consultant. The strategy then must be implemented and evaluated for effectiveness. The process can be recycled if necessary and the steps repeated (Gutkin & Curtis, 1982, p. 805).

When the purpose of the consultation focuses on mental health issues, Caplan (1963, 1970) and Caplan and Caplan (1993) proposed a model that includes the focus as well as the goal of consultation. The two major goals are remediation and prevention. The focus may be on individual cases or on administrative programs. Caplan (1970) advocates a consultee-centered case consultation because the primary goal is to improve the consultee's capacity to function effectively in this category of case, in order to benefit many similar clients in the future. Because of the educational emphasis, the consultant uses the discussion of the current case situation not to understand the client, but to understand and remedy the consultee's work difficulties as manifested in this example (p. 125).

CONSULTING WITH OTHER PROFESSIONALS

Many times an examiner is required to communicate test results to other professionals, such as principals, psychologists, social workers, correctional officers, and judicial staff members. Not all of these professionals understand test information. Again, it is important to work cooperatively to establish good rapport and a working relationship based on mutual respect and recognition of joint proficiencies. Communication skills remain an important variable.

Explanations should be clear and unambiguous. The APA's (2002) *Ethical Principles of Psychologists and Code of Conduct* (Principle 8) calls for the examiner to indicate any reservations regarding test validity or reliability because of assessment circumstances or inappropriate norms. Psychologists and counselors are cautioned to ensure that assessment results and interpretations are not misused by others.

In reporting to other professionals, examiners are faced with a variety of decisions. Goldman (1971) provides some basic guidelines for presenting test information to other professionals:

1. Find out exactly what information the recipient needs, what he or she plans to do with it, and what qualifications he or she has.
2. Make sure ethical and legal procedures are followed, such as securing a client's written permission to release information.
3. Check to see whether procedures have been established for test information. Normally a policy is already in force.
4. Aim the report as directly as possible to the particular question asked. This practice saves time and provides clear communication of needed information.

EVALUATION OF THE CONSULTANT

Parents, teachers, and other professionals might be asked to evaluate the work of the consultant. Questions such as these are helpful:

1. Did the consultant help you better understand the problem that prompted the testing?
2. Did the consultant help you understand the test results better?
3. Did the consultant provide you with practical suggestions for utilizing the test results?
4. Were you satisfied with the consultant's style in relating to you?
5. Were you happy with the services provided by the consultant?
6. What could be done to improve the services?

A checklist or rating form for consultees might pose questions like these:

1. How many times have you met with the consultant this year?

   1   2   3   4   5   6   7   8   9   10 or more

2. How helpful was the consultant to you?

   Not helpful 1   2   3   4   5   6   7 Extremely helpful

3. How knowledgeable was the consultant about testing?

   Slightly 1   2   3   4   5   6   7 Extremely

SUMMARY

Dissemination of test results is a function of communication. Knowledge of what to communicate requires a thorough background in test interpretation and an understanding of the test manual and the purposes of the test. Group and individual counseling sessions need to be administered prior to testing as well as after testing has been completed. In many types of testing programs, parents and the community need to be informed. It is advantageous to develop a systematic program to inform test users, parents, teachers, and the public about testing. The examiner needs a thorough knowledge of ethical and legal aspects and must be able to translate the test results into language clients can understand.

Consultation demands a knowledge of not only the problem situation but also different models of interaction. The consultant needs to know the ethical and legal standards as well as strategies to work with teachers, parents, and other professionals. Communication skills are an important part of the consultation process. In addition, the consultant should include in the process a mechanism for evaluation of his or her services.

QUESTIONS FOR DISCUSSION

1. Which type of test interpretation do you feel is more accurate—group versus individual, computer-based narratives, or standard test profiles?

2. Do you agree that individuals interpreting tests should be extremely careful about interpretation of test results for women, older individuals, minority group members, and individuals with disabilities? Why or why not? Does the type of test influence the need for caution?

3. What role do you believe counseling theory should have in the interpretation of test results? Should the interpretation be based on a given theory? Defend your position.

4. What are the major problem areas in disseminating results to parents? The community? The test taker? How would you go about evaluating the effectiveness of dissemination efforts?

5. If you could choose the way you were to receive your test results, what system would you choose? Why?

6. Clients value tests more if they see the need for the test information. Are the attitudes of test takers more important than the system chosen for interpreting results?

7. What do you think are the main issues and problems that consultants face in working with parents, teachers, and other professionals regarding testing results?

8. How important is the role of the consultant for people in the helping professions? What skills does a consultant need?

9. How would you handle a teacher or parent who became excessively dependent on your services and solutions? What should the role of the consultant be in such a case?

10. What model of consultation would you choose if you were asked to work with individuals on testing problems or results? What factors would influence your choice? Would underlying psychological theories be a factor in your decision?

11. Goldman (1971) states that parents are most in need of the information provided by tests. Do you agree with this statement? What kind of program should be established to help parents better understand the test results of their children?

SUGGESTED ACTIVITIES

1. Review the literature on methods and techniques of test interpretation.

2. Talk with the persons responsible for test interpretation and dissemination in several school districts. Assemble a notebook or folder of sample news releases and examples of the districts' letters to parents, students, and teachers.

3. Interview psychologists and counselors who use tests frequently. Find out the systems they use to report test results to their clients and their approaches to problems such as flat profiles, individuals who are disappointed with test results, and so on. Report your findings to the class.

4. Devise a rating scale to evaluate different types of media presentations for disseminating test results.

5. Videotape how you would handle test interpretation sessions with a client who (a) is not ready to accept the results, (b) had a flat profile with all low scores, or (c) has a really negative attitude toward testing.

6. Devise a workshop for a group of individuals in your field who work with tests and need help in communicating test results.

7. Interview workers in the helping professions who use tests and find out how much time they spend in consultation. Have them discuss the model of consultation they use. Ask them what steps they follow in the consultation process. Also, ask them what types of problems they have had in their roles as consultants. Report your results to the class.

8. Compare the major models of consultation on test results. Identify studies and articles in the literature that deal with test results and test problems.

9. Set up a model consultation program for a consultant who is working with teachers, parents, or other professionals on testing problems and results.

10. Role play a situation in which you have to consult a helping professional on testing problems or results.

Examples: A teacher might want to know how she can help her students improve their test scores. She is afraid that she will lose her job if the class does not do well on achievement tests. Or a doctor might want to know whether a child shows any signs of learning disabilities and how that information could be relayed to the child's parents.

11. Write a paper on the skills a consultant needs to be effective with testing problems and results.

12. Design an instrument to evaluate the work of a consultant on testing problems.

13. Review the brief case studies and answer the questions that follow.

Case of M. W.

M. W.'s mother was very concerned when she received her second-grader's scores on the Comprehensive Test of Basic Skills. M. W. scored at the 99th percentile on math but only at the 81st on reading. M. W. was at the 94th percentile on the word attack scale and the 95th on vocabulary, but at the 45th on language and 54th on science. M. W. had been tested for the gifted program and was accepted by virtue of a 133 score on the Stanford-Binet. M. W.'s mother can't make any sense out of the test scores and wants the teachers and counselors to help her daughter improve her scores.

a. What approach would you use with M. W.'s mother?

b. What would you tell her about the test results?

You have been asked to be a consultant on a training and development project. The project involves work with unemployed workers; you are to help explain how to use and interpret different career instruments. The previous consultant who left recently had convinced the project managers to use the Self-Directed Search (SDS) and the Myers-Briggs Type Indicator (MBTI).

a. How would you go about developing your role as a consultant?

b. What steps would you follow?

c. The project participants want you to consult with them on how to interpret the two tests. One individual wants you to guide him through the process of analyzing, interpreting, and reporting back to the client the results on the SDS and MBTI. His case is of Albert Smith, a 23-year-old White male who dropped out of school in the 10th grade. He is enrolled in a high school equivalency program in conjunction with the project. Albert has had numerous jobs in the food service industry but has not been able to hold on to them. He has a wife and three children and realizes that he needs further training and education to support his family. On the MBTI he is an ISFJ. On the SDS he is an ARS. How would you proceed?

ADDITIONAL READINGS

Alpert, J., & Silverstein, J. (1985). Mental health consultation: Historical, present, and future perspectives. In J. R. Bergan (Ed.), *School psychology in contemporary society: An introduction.* Columbus, OH: Charles E. Merrill.
This chapter presents a good overview of the field and gives information on where it has been and where it is going.

Brown, D., Pryzwansky, W. B., & Schulte, A. C. (1995). *Psychological consultation: Introduction to theory and practice* (3rd ed.). Boston: Allyn & Bacon.
Presents a good overview of different theories and approaches to consultation. Several chapters deal with evaluation, ethical and legal considerations, and training consultants. The last chapter contains a good discussion of issues in consultation.

Caplan, G., & Caplan, R. B. (1993). *Mental health consultation and collaboration.* San Francisco: Jossey-Bass.
Stresses the theory and practice of mental health consultation and the nature and purpose of mental health collaboration.

Gutkin, T. B., & Curtis, M. J. (1982). School-based consultation: Theory and techniques. In C. R. Reynolds & T. B. Gutkin (Eds.), *Handbook of school psychology* (pp. 519–561). New York: Wiley.
This chapter is especially valuable and useful for individuals who work in the school environment.

Harmon, L. W. (1989). Counseling. In R. Linn (Ed.), *Educational measurement* (3rd ed.). New York: Macmillan.
The chapter discusses and illustrates some measurement applications to counseling and issues related to such applications.

Miller, M. J. (1985). Counseling Region 99 clients. *Journal of Employment Counseling, 22,* 70–76.
Offers a strategy for clients who possess a flat profile and are positioned in Region 99 on the "World of Work Map."

Nail, G. (1996). Some thoughts on psychological report writing. Available at *http:// www.misresource.com/theory.html.*

Shore, M. F., Brice, P. J., & Love, B. G. (1992). *When your child needs testing: What parents, teachers, and other helpers need to know about psychological testing.* New York: Crossroad.
Covers topics such as why psychological testing is needed, how to begin, what the child should be told, how to interpret the results, how to handle disagreements, and the issue of confidentiality.

Standardized tests and our children: A guide to testing reform in New York. New York Public Interest Research Group, 9 Murray St., New York, NY 10007.

Appendix: Test Publishers and Distributors

Academic Therapy Publications
20 Commercial Boulevard
Novato, CA 94949
800-422-7249
fax 888-287-9975
www.academictherapy.com

American Guidance Services
4201 Woodland Road
Circle Pines, MN 55014-1796
800-328-2560
fax 800-471.8457
www.agsnet.com

Alpine Testing Solutions
560 South State Street, Suite H-2
Orem, Utah 84058-6397
801-226-4283
fax 801-223-9069
www.alpinetesting.com

Assessments.com
512 East Edgehill Drive
Bountiful, UT 84010
877-277-3778
www.assessments.com

Center for Credentialing & Education, Inc. (CCE)
3 Terrace Way, Suite B
Greensboro, NC 27403
336-482-2856
fax 336-482-2852
www.cce-global.org

Chronicle Guidance Publications, Inc.
66 Aurora Street
Moravia, NY 13118-3569
800-899-0454
fax 315-497-3359
www.chronicleguidance.com

The College Board
45 Columbus Avenue
New York, NY 10023
212-713-8000
www.collegeboard.com

Consulting Psychological Press (CPP) and Davies-
   Black® Publishing
1055 Joaquin Rd., Suite 200
Mountain View, CA 94043
800-624-1765
fax 650-969-8608
www.cpp-db.com

Educational Testing Service
Rosedale Road
Princeton, NJ 08541 USA
609-921-9000
fax 609-734-5410
www.ets.org

EdITS
P.O. Box 7234
San Diego, CA 92167
800-416-1666
fax 619-226-1666
www.edits.net

Graduate Management Admission Council
1600 Tysons Blvd., Ste. 1400
McLean, VA 22102
703-749-0131
fax 703-749-0169
www.gmac.com/gmac

Harcourt Assessment, Inc.
19500 Bulverde Road
San Antonio, Texas 78259
800-211-8378
fax 614-885-2323
www.harcourtassessment.com

IDS Publishing Corporation
P.O. Box 389
Worthington, Ohio, 43085
phone/fax: 614-885-2323
www.idspublishing.com

Institute for Personality and Ability
    Testing, Inc.
1801 Woodfield Drive
Savoy, IL 61874
800-225-4728
fax 217-352-9674

Pearson Assessments
One Lake Street
Upper Saddle River, NJ 07458
800-627-7271
fax 800-632-9011
www.pearsonassessments.com

Performance Assessment Network (pan)
11590 North Meridian Street, Suite 200
Carmel, IN 46032
877-449-TEST
fax 317-566-3271
http://www.pantesting.com

PRO-ED
8700 Shoal Creek Boulevard
Austin, TX 78757-6897
800-897-3202
fax 800-397-7633
www.proedinc.com

Psychological Assessment Resources, Inc.
16204 N. Florida Avenue
Lutz, FL 33549
800-331-8378
www3.parinc.com

Psychological Services Bureau, Inc.
2246 Ivy Road, Suite 15
Charlottesville, VA 22903
877-932-8378
www.psbtests.com

Psychological Services Inc. (PSI)
2950 N Hollywood Way, Suite 200
Burbank, CA 91505
800-367-1565
fax 818-247-7223
www.psionline.com

Psychtest.com
1574 Golf Road
Point Roberts, WA 98281
604-464-7919
fax 604-941-1705
www.psychtest.com

Riverside Publishing
425 Spring Lake Drive
Itasca, IL 60143-2079
800-323-9540
fax 630-467-7192
www.riverpub.com

Slosson Educational Publications, Inc.
PO Box 280, 538 Buffalo Road
East Aurora, NY 14052-0280
888-SLOSSON
fax 800-655-3840
www.slosson.com

Valpar International Corporation
PO Box 5767
Tucson, AZ 85703
800-633-3321
fax 262-797-8488
www.valparint.com

Western Psychological Services
12031 Wilshire Blvd.
Los Angeles, CA 90025-1251
800-648-8857
fax 310-478-7838
www.wpspublish.com

Glossary

Ability test An ability test measures the present level of functioning and can provide an estimate of the future performance of an individual on specific tasks or domains in cognitive or psychomotor areas. See also *Achievement test* and *Aptitude test.*

Abstract reasoning A nonverbal measure of reasoning ability. It involves the ability to think logically and to perceive relationships in abstract figure patterns.

Accountability Both students and teachers are being required to show that students have mastered course or grade objectives. Minimum-level skills, essential skills, survival skills, and other types of achievement tests are used to provide evidence of mastery.

Achievement test An achievement test measures the degree or extent of the knowledge, information, skills, and competencies that a person has acquired through training, instruction, or experience. There are survey achievement tests as well as subject-related tests.

Acquiescence response set Some test takers have a tendency to select positive responses (e.g., "true" or "yes") on attitude and personality tests.

Adaptive testing This procedure adjusts the test questions presented according to an individual's responses to previous items on the test. Test items can thus be geared to the individual's ability or achievement levels, and test takers may start and finish at different levels.

Adjustment test An adjustment test is one of the major types of personality tests. Such tests measure the ability of an individual to function normally in society and achieve personal needs.

Affective domain The affective domain covers dimensions of personality such as attitudes, motives, emotional behavior, temperament, and personality traits.

Age norms Age norms for a particular test provide the median score made by test takers of a given chronological age. In addition to intellectual and social age, many tests provide information on typical characteristic behavior of individuals at given age levels.

Alternate forms For many achievement and aptitude tests it is necessary to have more than one form of the tests available. Alternate forms are constructed according to the same blueprint—that is, with the same set of objectives, the same type of items, and similar difficulty and discrimination values for the test items. The two forms also have similar statistical characteristics; the means, standard deviations, and correlations with other measures should all be approximately equal.

Alternate-forms reliability This type of reliability requires correlating the scores of individuals on one form with the scores they acheived on the second form. This coefficient provides evidence of the equivalence of the two forms as well as the stability of the individual's performance.

Alternative assessment Alternative assessment emphasizes assessing performance of the test taker through portfolios, interviews, observations, work samples, and the like instead of through multiple-choice norm- or criterion-referenced examinations.

Anecdotal records Anecdotal records require a series of observations of an individual(s). The observer should provide an objective description of the behavior observed and an interpretation of the situation. School psychologists are often required to record two observations of the child along with test information.

Aptitude test An aptitude test is used to provide an estimate of future performance on tasks that may or may not be similar to the tasks measured on the test. Aptitude tests are used to assess the educational readiness of individuals to learn or become proficient in a given area if education or training is provided. Aptitude tests may contain the same type of items as achievement tests.

Arithmetic mean See *Mean.*

Assessment procedures Assessment procedures are the methods that enable one to appraise or estimate the attributes of a person, group, or programs. The tools of assessment can include checklists, inventories, observational schedules, needs assessments, rating scales, and all types of tests.

Attenuation Attenuation is a phenomenon that takes place in the statistical determination of correlation and regression. The correlation or regression is reduced because of the imperfect reliability of one or both of the measures being correlated or compared.

Attitude Attitude is a dimension of the affective domain and one aspect of an individual's personality. Attitude is reflected in reactions to events, other individuals, objects, or institutions.

Authentic assessment This type of assessment focuses on assessing realistic tasks or activities that relate to the performance on a domain or set of constructs being measured.

Basal age Basal age is the age at which the test taker passes all of the items on a given test.

Basic skills Many achievement tests are designed to measure the basic skills required to be successful in school; these are usually reading, writing, and arithmetic competencies. Such skills are necessary for the student to learn other subjects, such as science and social studies.

Battery A battery is a set of tests usually standardized on the same population. Survey achievement tests are one example of a battery. A battery facilitates comparison of a test taker's performance in different areas.

Behavioral assessment Behavioral assessment focuses on the more objective and observable components of behavior and uses a wide variety of techniques, such as observation, checklists, and self-monitoring.

Behavioral objectives Behavioral objectives require counselors and teachers to specify desired behavioral outcomes in objective, observable forms and to identify the conditions of measurement.

Bias Bias in testing results in scores that are higher or lower than they would be if the measurement were more reliable and valid. The error caused by bias is systematic rather than random.

Bimodal distribution A bimodal distribution is a frequency distribution with two modes or high points.

Biographic inventory A biographic inventory is a questionnaire or survey instrument used to obtain information about the individual's educational, social, medical, and work experiences. It is one of the tools used by counselors and employment psychologists.

Buckley Amendment The Buckley Amendment is federal legislation that gives individuals and their parents or guardians rights to access information, including the results of standardized tests.

Ceiling A ceiling is the level or point at which a test taker fails a test or subtest.

Central tendency Central tendency relates to the typical or average score in a distribution. The three measures of central tendency are the mean, median, and mode. Any one of these statistics summarizes the typical or average performance of a group.

Central tendency error An error of central tendency occurs when the rater avoids all the extreme judgments, both high and low, and rates all items in the middle.

Checklist A checklist is a list of words, phrases, or statements describing the behavior of an individual or situation. The rater checks the presence or absence of the item.

Clerical ability The abilities required in satisfactorily carrying out office duties. Although the number and types of abilities measured may vary from test to test, a clerical test usually assesses such abilities as filing, coding, verbal, arithmetic, and checking.

Coaching Coaching occurs prior to the administration of a test and involves short-term instructional activities designed to help test takers increase their test scores. Sessions often include instruction on test-taking strategies and control of test anxiety.

Coefficient alpha Coefficient alpha is a reliability coefficient that measures the internal consistency of a test. The coefficient is the expected correlation of one test form with an alternate form that contains the same number of items.

Coefficient of determination The coefficient of determination is computed by squaring the correlation coefficient. It provides an estimate of the proportion of variance in one variable that is predictable from the other variable.

Coefficient of equivalence The coefficient of equivalence is used to compute the reliability of alternate forms of a test, based either upon two administrations or on a single administration with odd and even items constituting separate forms.

Coefficient of internal consistency The coefficient of internal consistency is based upon one testing and provides an estimate of the homogeneity of test items. The split-half and Kuder-Richardson methods provide coefficients of internal consistency.

Coefficient of stability A coefficient of stability provides a picture of how consistent an individual's scores are over a period of time. The test-retest method and alternate forms provide some information on the stability of scores over time.

Cognitive domain The cognitive domain encompasses the different levels individuals use in perceiving, thinking, and remembering. These levels are knowledge, comprehension, application, synthesis, analysis, and evaluation.

Cognitive style Cognitive style refers to the strategies or approaches an individual prefers to use in cognitive activities. Some of the styles discussed in the text are internal and external locus of control, field independence-field dependence, and reflectivity-impulsivity.

Competency test A competency test is an achievement test that assesses a test taker's level of knowledge or skill in some defined domain.

Computer-assisted testing Computer-assisted testing refers to testing that is presented on the computer rather than in a test booklet.

Computer-based interpretation Computer-based interpretation is a method of providing the interpretation of test scores according to algorithms built into the computer program. The test user is provided with score reports and narrative statements about the results.

Computer-based testing The administration of test items at a computer, i.e., computer-assisted testing.

Computer-generated test reports Written test reports or narrative summaries generated by a computer program or the Internet.

Computer simulations The technique of representing the real world through the use of a computer simulation program. Rather than taking individuals through a series of test items, assessments involving computer simulations would immerse them in situations like the ones for which they are being selected or prepared.

Concurrent validity Concurrent validity is one type of criterion-referenced validity. Test scores are compared with a criterion measure obtained at about the same time, and the coefficient describes their relationship.

Confidence interval The confidence interval, or confidence band, is marked by two points that define with specified probability the range that includes an individual's true score.

Consequential validity Consequential validity focuses on the consequences of giving a test and relates to all phases—administration, scoring, interpretation, construction, uses, and so on.

Construct A construct is a theory or concept used to explain data in an orderly way. In a psychometric sense it is a psychological attribute or trait.

Construct validity Construct validity is the extent to which a test measures the intended psychological trait or attribute.

Content validity Content validity is the degree to which a test measures a defined body of knowledge. This type of validity is extremely important for achievement tests.

Convergent validity Convergent validity is the degree to which a test correlates highly with other measures designed to assess the same construct.

Correlation Correlation is a statistic used to measure the strength and direction of the association between two sets of scores. Coefficients range from $+1.00$ to -1.00. A correlation of $+1.00$ indicates a perfect positive relationship between the scores, a correlation of .00 indicates no relationship between the scores, and a correlation of -1.00 indicates an inverse relationship.

Covariation Covariation refers to the variance that two or more tests or variables have in common.

Criterion-referenced tests Criterion-referenced tests are designed to assess a rather limited range of objectives or goals. They are usually used as mastery tests to assess whether an individual can demonstrate a specific skill or objective.

Criterion-referenced validity Criterion-referenced validity is based on the correlation of test scores with some type of criterion measure.

Cronbach's alpha Cronbach's alpha is a procedure for estimating the internal consistency of a test based on parts of the test. It is one of the procedures used to compute reliability.

Crystallized intelligence Crystallized intelligence is one of the types of intelligence in Cattell's model. The term refers to the part of intelligence acquired through experience and education.

Culture-fair tests Culture-fair tests are designed to be fair to all types of cultural and socioeconomic groups. These tests attempt to include only content to which all groups have been exposed during maturation.

Decision theory Test users are interested in making decisions and predictions on the basis of test results. Such predictions can be classified as positive, false positive, negative, and false negative. Decision theory is also used in selecting a test—to identify the types of information needed and the types of information already available.

Derived scores A derived score is a score into which a raw score is converted by some type of mathematical operation. Percentile ranks, standard scores, stanines, and grade-equivalent scores are all derived scores.

Descriptive statistics Descriptive statistics are used to summarize characteristics of a group of scores—for example, central tendency and dispersion or variability of scores. The mean, median, mode, variance, and standard deviation are descriptive statistics.

Deviation IQ The deviation IQ is the score that compares an individual with her age or grade group. The fixed mean is usually 100, and the standard deviation is 15.

Diagnostic tests A diagnostic test is an achievement test, most often in mathematics and reading, used to identify the strengths and weaknesses of the individual. Such tests include a wide range of items on a given skill or objective.

Differential prediction Differential prediction is used in situations of criterion-referenced validity. It indicates the degree to which a test that is used to predict individual attainment yields different predictions for the same criteria for groups with different demographic characteristics, prior experience, or treatment.

Discriminant validity Discriminant validity is the degree to which a test does not correlate with tests that measure other constructs.

Domain sampling Domain sampling refers to a given area from which sample items are taken.

Often criterion-referenced tests are called domain-referenced tests. The three major domains are cognitive, affective, and psychomotor.

Electronic portfolios A collection of a student's work used to demonstrate his or her skills and accomplishments. It is a means of organizing, summarizing, and sharing artifacts, information, and ideas about teaching and/or learning, along with personal and professional growth reflections, on computer. The portfolio and information contained in it can be stored digitally on a computer hard drive or some sort of removable media (pen drive, floppy disk, CD, etc.).

Environmental assessment A way of measuring specific environmental factors that impact human behavior and experience.

Equivalence reliability Equivalence reliability estimates the extent to which two or more forms of a test are consistent. In split-half reliability, the test is subdivided into two parts—for example, odd items versus even items. In parallel forms the scores from Form X of a test are correlated with the scores from Form Y to provide an estimate of the equivalence of the forms.

Equivalent forms Test makers may construct more than one form of a test to measure the same objectives with items of similar difficulty.

Error of measurement Error of measurement refers to the discrepancy between an individual's observed score and his or her true score.

Evaluation Evaluation is the process an individual uses to judge information from one or more sources. That process may focus on test data as well as observations and other sources.

Factor The term *factor* can describe a psychological construct, such as verbal, spatial, or numerical aptitude. It can also represent the covariance of various subtests that tend to cluster together; that is, it represents their intercorrelations or intersections.

Factor analysis Factor analysis is a statistical multivariate procedure used to analyze the intercorrelations or covariance of variables. The method results in the identification of a reduced number of factors needed to explain the intercorrelations of variables.

False negative A false negative is a type of error in which an individual is predicted to fail but actually succeeds if given a chance.

Field dependence Field dependence is one of the dimensions of cognitive style that relates to an individual's dependence on body cues in space perception.

Field independence Field independence is a dimension of cognitive style that relates to an individual's dependence on body cues in space perception but independence from the surrounding visual field.

Finger dexterity The ability to move the fingers and manipulate small objects with the fingers rapidly and accurately.

Fluid intelligence Fluid intelligence is one of the two types of intelligence identified by Cattell. It is the inherited dimension of intelligence and includes problem-solving and thinking ability.

Forced choice Some interest and personality tests use the forced choice method, whereby the test taker is required to select one or more items from two or more similar or related options. This method helps to control for response set.

Frequency distribution A frequency distribution is a way of organizing and arranging data in a table. Scores are usually grouped in fewer intervals to summarize overall performance.

***g* factor** The *g* factor is a generalized intelligence factor that is measured in most intelligence tests; tests that yield one score are following the *g*-factor approach. Spearman was the leading theorist of this conceptual model.

Grade equivalent scores Grade equivalent scores are a type of derived test score used primarily by survey achievement tests. A raw score is translated into the grade level for which the achieved score is the real or estimated mean or median.

Group test A group test can be given to more than one test taker in a single setting by one test administrator.

Halo effect Halo effect is the tendency of a rater to let the ratings in other areas of a scale influence the ratings in areas that cannot be observed or are difficult to rate.

Histogram A histogram is a bar graph that provides a picture or description of scores.

In-basket technique The in-basket technique requires the examinee to take action on a series of problem situations presented through correspondence, memos, and other documents found in a sample in-basket.

Informed consent Informed consent requires test takers to give their consent before being tested; it is legally and ethically required. Test takers

are to be told what the purposes of the test are, who will have access to the scores, and how the results will be used.

Intelligence test An intelligence test measures dimensions of aptitude and ability that are needed for success in educational and vocational fields. There are both individual and group tests.

Interest inventory An interest inventory assesses an individual's likes and dislikes, preferences, and interests. This information is then related to occupational fields and clusters and can sometimes be compared to individuals working in given occupational fields.

Internal consistency Internal consistency is a method of estimating reliability that is computed from a single administration of a test. The coefficients reflect the degree to which the items are measuring the same construct and are homogeneous. Cronbach's alpha and the Kuder-Richardson formulas are measures of the internal consistency of a test.

Interpretative report Most interest, aptitude, and achievement tests provide not only a summary of the test scores but also information that helps test takers interpret and understand those scores.

Interrater reliability Two or more observers rate the same subjects and then correlate their observations to come up with interrater reliability.

Interval scale The interval scale is one of the four measurement scales and can be used to classify and order measurements. It plots equal distances between score points but does not have a true zero point. Examples of interval scales include IQ, Celsius, and Fahrenheit scales.

Ipsative measurement Ipsative measurement is a type of item format, such as forced choice or ranking, in which the variables (options or items) are compared with each other. Ipsative comparisons are only intraindividual and are not appropriate for normative interpretation.

Item bias An item is said to be biased when the average expected score on the item for the group in question is substantially higher or lower than it is for the overall population and when this difference results from factors that the item is not intended to measure.

Item response theory (IRT) IRT is an alternative theory to classical measurement theory and was developed from concepts originating in the 19th century in mathematics and psychology. An early example is how Binet placed the items on his test, and is today in a modified way the basis of computer-adaptive testing.

Job analysis The general process of identifying the abilities, competencies, knowledge, and skills needed to perform jobs is called job analysis.

Kuder-Richardson 20/21 The K-R 20 and 21 formulas are used to compute reliability in one administration of a test. They are internal consistency measures. K-R 20 provides an estimate equal to the mean of all possible split-half coefficients. K-R 21 can be substituted for K-R 20 if the item difficulty levels are similar.

Least restrictive environment Public Law 94–142 calls for the placement of each individual with disabilities in the most normal situation in which that individual can be successful.

Leniency error When a person is rated higher on an item than she should be rated, an error of leniency is operating.

Likert scale A Likert scale is an attitude scale that asks people to rate the intensity of their agreement with certain statements.

Locus of control Rotter identifies a cognitive and perceptual style that relates to how individuals perceive themselves as being controlled. The two ends of the continuum are external and internal, with external indicating reliance on external reinforcement and a belief in chance and fate.

Manual dexterity The ability to move the hand easily and skillfully. Ability to work with the hands in placing and turning motions.

Mean The mean is the arithmetic average of a set of scores. It is equal to the sum of the scores divided by the number of scores. The mean is one of three statistics used to indicate central tendency.

Measurement Measurement is the process used to assign numerals to objects or constructs according to rules so that the numbers have quantitative meaning.

Mechanical aptitude The ability to learn about and use tools, machines and equipment. Mechanical ability tests typically measure a person's ability to use various tools and materials as well as spatial reasoning.

Mechanical reasoning The ability to understand basic mechanical principles of machinery, tools, and motion.

Median The median is the 50th percentile or the midpoint of a distribution.

Minimum-level competency test A minimum-level competency test measures the essential or minimum skills that school systems and states have defined as a standard to be met.

Mode The mode is the most frequently occurring score or number in a set of scores.

Motor coordination The ability to coordinate eyes and hands or fingers rapidly and accurately in making precise movements with speed; ability to make a movement response accurately and swiftly.

National norms National norms give the average or median performance of a probability sample representative of the whole country. Most survey achievement batteries and scholastic aptitude tests report national norms.

Nominal scale The nominal scale is a scale that can be used to classify data into mutually exclusive and exhaustive categories.

Nonacquiescence response set A tendency for test takers to disagree with whatever item is presented on attitude or personality tests.

Nonverbal test In a nonverbal test the test taker is not required to respond to the tasks verbally, and items are not presented in a written format. The examinee may be shown pictures and asked to point to a specific one. Or the test taker may be asked to manipulate materials, copy block or bead designs, assemble puzzles, and so on.

Norm groups Norm groups are composed of the individuals on whom a test is standardized. These groups provide the basis for interpreting scores.

Norm-referenced test A norm-referenced test presents score interpretation based on a comparison of individual performance with that of other individuals in specified groups.

Normal curve The normal curve is a smooth, bell-shaped curve that is symmetrical around the mean; the curve can be computed with the use of an equation. Most educational and psychological variables, such as achievement and intelligence, have a normal, bell-shaped distribution.

Objective test An objective test has a predetermined scoring key. Multiple-choice tests are an example of such a test.

Observational techniques Observational techniques are used to look at the behavior of the test taker—sometimes during the examination, sometimes in naturalistic situations. In behavior assessment self-observation is sometimes used; the client is asked to keep a log or diary of his or her behavior. Situational tests require raters to observe individual behavior during the test.

Ordinal scale An ordinal scale requires an individual to rank-order measurements.

Parallel forms See *Alternate* and *Equivalent forms.*

Percentile rank Percentile rank places a score in a distribution by identifying the percentage of scores that fall at or below the given score. A percentile rank is a type of derived score used on most norm-referenced tests.

Performance test A performance test requires the test taker to engage in some process, such as manipulating physical objects, rather than marking an answer on an answer sheet.

Personality inventory A personality inventory measures one or more dimensions of personality, such as attitude, adjustment, temperament, and values. The test taker is usually presented with a wide variety of behaviors and asked if they are characteristic of him or her.

Portfolio A portfolio is a collection of products produced by the person, such as the papers, themes, tests, and book reports of a student in language arts or a collection of products produced by a person in a fine arts class.

Predictive validity Predictive validity is a form of criterion-referenced validity in which test scores are compared with performance that is measured sometime in the future. The predictor variable is the test, and the criterion variable is the future performance, often on the job or in school.

Predictor A predictor is a measurable characteristic—such as a test score, previous performance, rating, or observation—that is correlated with a criterion variable to indicate future success or failure.

Primary standards Primary standards are the essential and fundamental characteristics that should be met by all tests before they are used.

Profile A profile is a graphic representation of individual or group scores. It provides a picture of the relative magnitude of scores.

Projective techniques Projective techniques are one method of assessing personality. The test taker gives free response to a series of stimuli, such as inkblots, pictures, or incomplete sentences. It is assumed that individuals will project their own perceptions, feelings, and attitudes in their answers.

Psychomotor ability The ability to perform body motor movements (e.g., movement of fingers, hands, legs, body) with precision, coordination, or strength. It can include multi-limb coordination (ability to make quick specific or discrete motor movements of the arms or legs), arm-hand steadiness (ability to precisely and skillfully coordinate arm-hand positioning in space), manual dexterity (ability to make precisely coordinated movements of a hand, or a hand and the attached arm), finger dexterity (ability to make precisely coordinated movements of the fingers), visual-motor skills (eye-hand coordination) and static strength (ability to exert muscular force to move, push, lift, or pull a heavy or immobile object).

Psychomotor test A psychomotor test measures fine and gross motor skills. The psychomotor domain—unlike the cognitive and affective domains—organizes and classifies psychomotor behaviors in terms of the amount of concentration required.

Public Law 94-142 Public Law 94-142, the Education of All Handicapped Children Act, was passed in 1975 and established the requirements for free and appropriate education for all children with disabilities. It also restricts the use of tests and assessment procedures with individuals with disabilities.

Quarterile Quartile is a term referred to in percentile measure. The total of 100% is broken into four equal parts: 25%, 50%, 75%, and 100%.

Questionnaire A questionnaire is similar to a structured interview; it contains a list of questions on a topic or issue. A questionnaire is usually administered to a group of individuals to find out about their attitudes, beliefs, behaviors, and so on.

Range Range is a statistic used to measure the variable or spread of the scores. It is the difference between the highest and lowest score in a distribution.

Rapport Rapport is a warm and friendly relationship or interpersonal environment. An examiner wants to ensure valid results by establishing this type of positive environment and thereby encouraging the proper motivation and cooperation of the test taker.

Rating scale A rating scale is a measure that requires the rater to estimate the value of a person or thing or assess the presence of some trait or characteristic. Sometimes the scale calls for self-ratings; at other times ratings are given by peers, teachers, parents, and so on.

Ratio scale   The ratio scale has equal units of measurement and has a true zero point. Time, height, and weight are examples of measurements that use the ratio scale. Most educational and psychological variables cannot be measured on the ratio scale.

Raw score   Raw score is the unadjusted number of correct answers.

Readiness test   A readiness test measures the extent to which the test taker has acquired the skills and knowledge necessary to learn a more complex skill.

Regression   Regression is a statistical technique used to help individuals predict x when they know y and the relationship between x and y. A linear equation can be compared to predict criterion scores with one or more predictor variables.

Reliability   Reliability refers to the degree to which test scores are consistent, dependable, or repeatable. Reliability is a function of the degree to which test scores are free from errors of mea-surement.

Response set   Response set refers to the tendency of a test taker to respond to test items in a stereotyped or fixed way. The test taker may consciously or unconsciously choose the most socially desirable answers or perhaps true rather than false options.

Scatter plot   A scatter plot is a bivariate graph that shows the paired values of two variables being correlated.

Scholastic aptitude test   A scholastic aptitude test measures the cognitive skills necessary for success in school. It is used to predict how well individuals will do in educational contexts.

Scoring rubrics   A rating system that determines at what level a student is successful or not successful. Rubrics provide explicit criteria for the individual to demonstrate in order to meet educational objectives of a particular assignment/ project. Each objective is evaluated using terms such as "below expectations," "meets expectations," or "exceeds expectations."

Screening test   A screening test makes broad categorizations as a first step in a selection or diagnostic process in school or industry.

Situational test   A situational test is a performance test in which an individual is placed in a realistic but contrived situation and then is rated on his or her role competence and problem-solving abilities.

Skewness   Skewness is the degree of asymmetry in a frequency distribution. In positively skewed distributions the scores are piled up at the lower end of the distribution, to the left of the mode. In a negatively skewed distribution the scores are piled up at the high end of the distribution, to the right of the mode.

Social desirability response set   The social desirability response set is active when an individual tries to portray himself or herself in a socially desirable light. The individual fakes "good" instead of putting down what is truly descriptive of his or her behavior.

Space relations   The ability to visualize a three-dimensional object from a two-dimensional pattern and to visualize how this object would look if rotated in space—the ability to "think in three dimensions."

Spatial relationships   Spatial skills help people to figure out maps and interpret technical drawings.

Spearman-Brown prophecy formula   The Spearman-Brown formula is used to estimate the reliability of a test if the test length is increased. Theoretically, a longer test samples more behavior and covers more items from the measured domain, thereby increasing the reliability of the test.

Speeded test   A speeded test measures performance by the number of tasks performed in a given time period. Clerical speed and accuracy, typing, and coding tests are examples of this type of test.

Split-half reliability   Split-half reliability is a method of computing the reliability of a test from one administration of the test. An internal analysis coefficient is obtained by using one-half of the items on the test for one score and the other half for the second score. These scores are then correlated and corrected for a full-length test, using the Spearman-Brown formula. The method provides an estimate of alternate-form reliability.

Standard deviation   The standard deviation is the square root of the variance; it is a statistic that describes the spread or dispersion of scores. Standard deviation is used with a derived score as an index of how far above or below the mean the score falls.

Standard error of measurement   The standard error of measurement is the standard deviation of the errors of measurement associated with the test scores for a specific group of test takers.

Standard score A standard score describes the location of an individual's score within a set of scores. Its distance from the mean is expressed in terms of standard deviation units. Such a score is used in norm-referenced measurement contexts.

Standardized test A standardized test is administered under standard directions and conditions.

Standards-based assessment Standards-based assessment is based upon state or national standards and is characterized by emphasis on what students should be able to do as a result of their schooling. Items on tests emphasize what students should be able to demonstrate in real-world situations.

Stanines Stanines are a 9-point scale having a mean of 5 and a standard deviation of 2. All but stanines 1 and 9 are one-half standard deviation in width. They are used to describe an individual's position relative to the norming group.

Statistics Statistics is an area of mathematics focusing on the collection, organization, and interpretation of numerical data. A statistic is a number used to describe some characteristic, such as the central tendency or variability of a set of scores.

Sten scores A STEN score is a standard score from a distribution in which most of the scores (almost 99%) have a range from 1 to 10 (which gives it it's name, *Sten,* meaning *Standard Ten*). Mean = 5.5, SD = 2.

Subtest A subtest is a grouping of items measuring the same function.

T score A *T* score is a derived score on a scale usually having a mean score of 50 and a standard deviation of 10.

Terman's study Louis Terman began a study in 1921 in which he found that IQ was higher than average for people with athletic abilities, good health, relationship satisfaction, career success, and good mental health.

Test anxiety Test anxiety is a psychological state of stress and fear caused by testing situations. Although some anxiety may be beneficial, extreme test anxiety can disrupt performance.

Test bias The difference in test scores that is attributable to demographic variables (e.g., gender, ethnicity, and age).

Test-retest reliability Test-retest methods require giving the same test to the same group of examinees on two different occasions and correlating the two sets of scores. The resulting coefficient gives an indication of the stability of the results.

True score The true score in classical test theory is the average of the scores earned by an individual on an unlimited number of perfectly parallel forms of the same test.

Usability Usability refers to the practical factors that must be considered in selecting a test—for example, cost, time, ease of administration, and ease of scoring.

User's guide The user's guide contains a statement of the purpose of the test, its content, and appropriate uses. The guide often contains information on how to administer, score, and interpret the test.

Validity Validity is the degree to which a certain inference from a test is appropriate or meaningful.

Variance Variance is the average squared deviation from the mean or the standard deviation squared. The statistic is a measure of variability or dispersion of the scores.

Verbal test A verbal test is a test requiring oral or written responses to test items.

z score A *z* score is a type of standard score in which the mean is 0 and the standard deviation is 1. A *z* score represents the raw score in standard deviation units.

References

Aiken, L. R. (1985). *Psychological testing and assessment* (3rd ed.). Boston: Allyn & Bacon.

Aiken, L. R. (1996). *Rating scales and checklists.* New York: Wiley.

Aiken, L. R. (2000). *Psychological testing and assessment* (10th ed.). Boston: Allyn & Bacon.

Aiken, L. R. (2003). *Psychological testing and assessment* (11th ed.). Boston: Allyn & Bacon.

Alderman, D. L., & Powers, D. E. (1980). The effects of special preparation on SAT-verbal scores. *American Educational Research Journal, 17,* 239-253.

Allport, G. W. (1937). *Personality: A psychological interpretation.* New York: Henry Holt.

American Association of Counseling and Development (AACD). (1980). *Responsibilities of users of standardized tests.* APGA Policy Statement. Falls Church, VA: Author.

American Association on Mental Retardation. (1993). *Manual on terminology and classification in mental retardation.* Washington, DC: Author.

American Counseling Association. (2003). *Standards for qualifications of test users.* Alexandria, VA: Author.

American Counseling Association (2005). *ACA code of ethics.* Alexanderia, VA: Author.

American Educational Research Association, American Psychological Association, and National Council on Measurement in Education. (1999). *Standards for educational and psychological testing.* Washington, DC: Authors.

American Psychiatric Association. (2000). *Diagnostic and statistical manual of mental disorders* (4th ed.). text revision. Washington DC: Author.

American Psychological Association. (1950). Ethical standards for the distribution of psychological tests and diagnostic aids. *American Psychologist, 5,* 620-626.

American Psychological Association. (2002). *Ethical principles of psychologists and code of conduct* (Rev. ed.). Washington, DC: Author.

Anastasi, A., & Urbina, S. (1997). *Psychological testing* (7th ed.). Upper Saddle River, NJ: Prentice Hall.

Ary, D., Jacobs, L. C., & Razavieh, A. (1997). *Introduction to research in education* (5th ed.). Stamford, CT: Wadsworth.

Association for Assessment in Counseling, American Counseling Association. (2003). *Responsibilities for users of standardized tests* (3rd ed.). Alexandria, VA: Author.

Bailey, D., & Wolery, M. (1989). *Assessing infants and preschoolers with handicaps.* Upper Saddle River, NJ: Merrill/Prentice Hall.

Bailey, R. C., & Siudzinski, R. M. (1986). *The FAST profile instruction and reference manual: The Florida Analysis of Semantic Traits Profile.* Dallas, TX: BALI Screening Company.

Baker, F. B. (1989). Computer technology in test construction and processing. In R. L. Linn (Ed.), *Educational measurement* (3rd ed.). New York: Macmillan.

Baldwin, J. A., & Bell, Y. R. (1985). The African Self-Consciousness Scales: An Africentric personality questionnaire. *Western Journal of Black Studies, 9*(2), 65-68.

Bandura, A. (1986). *Social foundations of thought and action: A social cognitive theory.* Upper Saddle River, NJ: Prentice Hall.

Bannatyne, A. (1971). *Language, reading, and learning disabilities.* Springfield, IL: Charles C. Thomas.

Bannatyne, A. (1974). Diagnosis: A note on the recategorization of the WISC scaled score. *Journal of Learning Disabilities, 7,* 272-273.

Barbe, W. B., & Swassing, R. H. (1979). *Teaching through modality strengths: Concepts and practices.* Columbus, OH: Zaner-Bloser.

Barnett, D., & Zucker, K. R. (1990). *The personal and social assessment of children.* Boston: Allyn & Bacon.

Barrios, B. A. (1993). Direct observation. In T. H. Ollendick & M. Hersen (Eds.), *Handbook of child and adolescent assessment.* Boston: Allyn & Bacon.

Baruth, L. G., & Manning, M. L. (2003). *Multicultural counseling and psychotherapy: A lifespan perspective*. (3rd ed.). Upper Saddle River, NJ: Merrill/Prentice Hall.

Battle, J. (1992). *Culture free self esteem inventory.* Austin, TX: Pro-Ed.

Bersoff, D. N., & Hofer, P. J. (1991). Legal issues in computerized testing. In T. B. Gutkin & S. L. Wise (Eds.), *The computer and the decision-making process.* Hillsdale, NJ: Erlbaum.

Binet, A., & Simon, T. (1916). *The development of intelligence in children* (E. S. Kite, Trans.). Baltimore: Williams & Wilkins.

Boehm, A. E., & White, M. A. (1982). *The parents' handbook on school testing.* New York: Teachers College Press.

Bracken, B. A., & McCallum, R. S. (1998). *Universal nonverbal intelligence test.* Chicago: Riverside.

Bradley-Johnson, S., & Evans, L. D. (1991). *Psychoeducational assessment of hearing-impaired students: Infancy through high school.* Austin, TX: PRO-ED.

Brown, D., Pryzwansky, W. B., & Schulte, A. C. (1995). *Psychological consultation: Introduction to theory and practice* (3rd ed.). Boston: Allyn & Bacon.

Brown, D., Wyne, M. D., Blackburn, J. E., & Powell, W. C. (1979). *Consultation: Strategy for improving education.* Boston: Allyn & Bacon.

Brown, F. G. (1983). *Principles of educational and psychological testing* (3rd ed.). New York: Holt, Rinehart & Winston.

Buchanan, T. (2002). Online assessment: Desirable or dangerous? *Professional Psychology: Research and Practice, 33,* 148–154.

Butcher, J. N., Perry, J., & Hahn, J. (2004). Computers in clinical assessment: Historical developments, present status, and future challenges. *Journal of Clinical Psychology, 60,* 331–345.

Byham, W. C., & Thornton, G. C., III. (1986). Assessment centers. In R. A. Burke (Ed.), *Performance assessment.* Baltimore: Johns Hopkins University Press.

Campbell, D. T., & Fiske, D. W. (1959). Convergent and discriminant validation by the multitrait and multimethod matrix. *Psychological Bulletin, 56,* 81–105.

Caplan, G. (1963). Types of mental health consultation. *American Journal of Orthopsychiatry, 33,* 470–481.

Caplan, G. (1970). *The theory and practice of mental health consultation.* New York: Basic Books.

Caplan, G., & Caplan, R. B. (1993). *Mental health consultation and collaboration.* San Francisco: Jossey-Bass.

Carroll, J. B. (1998). *Human cognitive abilities: A survey of factor analysis studies.* New York: Cambridge.

Cattell, R. B. (1950). *Personality: A systematic, theoretical, and factual study.* New York: McGraw-Hill.

Cattell, R. B. (1963). Theory of fluid and crystallized intelligence: A critical experiment. *Journal of Educational Psychology, 54,* 1–22.

Cattell, R. B., Eber, H. W., & Tatsuoka, M. M. (1970). *Handbook for the 16PF.* Champaign, IL: Institute for Personality & Ability Testing.

Chase, J. B. (1986). Psychoeducational assessment of visually impaired learners. In P. J. Lazarus (Ed.), *Psychoeducational evaluation of children and adolescents.* New York: Grune & Stratton.

Chiodo, J. J. (1986). The effects of exam anxiety on grandma's health. *Chronicle of Higher Education, 32*(23), 68.

Clarke, M., Madaus, G., Horn, C., & Ramos, M. (2001). The marketplace for educational testing. *National Board on Educational Testing and Public Policy Statements, 2*(3), 1–11.

Cohen, R. J., & Swerdlik, M. E. (1999). *Psychological testing and assessment: An introduction to tests and measurements* (4th ed.). Mountain View, CA: Mayfield.

Connolly, A. J. (1988). *Manual for the Keymath–Revised.* Circle Pines, MN: American Guidance Services.

Cook, M., & Cook, M. (1988). *Personnel selection and productivity.* Chicago: Dryden.

Corey, G. (2001). *Theory and practice of counseling and psychotherapy* (6th ed.). Stamford, CT: Wadsworth.

CRESST. (1994, February). *Portfolio assessment.* Los Angeles: Author.

Cronbach, L. J. (1951). Coefficient alpha and the internal structure of tests. *Psychometrika, 16,* 297–334.

Cronbach, L. J. (1971). Test validation. In R. L. Thorndike (Ed.), *Educational measurement* (2nd ed., pp. 443–507). Washington, DC: American Council on Education.

Cronbach, L. J. (1994). *Essentials for psychological testing* (3rd ed.). New York: Harper & Row.

Dana, R. H. (1993). *Multicultural assessment perspectives for professional psychology.* Boston: Allyn & Bacon.

Das, J. P., & Naglieri, J. A. (1996). *The cognitive assessment system.* Chicago: Riverside.

Deffenbacher, J. L. (1978). Worry, emotionality, and task-generated interference in test anxiety: An empirical test of attentional theory. *Journal of Educational Psychology, 70,* 248–254.

Doll, E. (1935). *Vineland adaptive behavior scales.* Circle Pines, MN: American Guidance Services.

Draguns, J. G. (1989). Dilemmas and choices in cross-cultural counseling: The universal versus the culturally distinctive. In P. B. Pedersen, J. G. Draguns, J. Lonner, & J. E. Trimble (Eds.), *Counseling across cultures* (3rd ed.). Honolulu: University of Hawaii Press.

DuBose, R. F. (1982). Assessment of severely impaired young children: Problems and recommendations. In J. T. Neisworth (Ed.), *Assessment in special education.* Rockville, MD: Aspen Systems.

Dunn, R. (1983). Learning style and its relation to exceptionality at both ends of the spectrum. *Exceptional Children, 40,* 496–506.

Dunn, R., Dunn, K., & Price, G. E. (1983). *Learning style inventory.* Lawrence, KS: Price Systems.

Dustin, D., & Ehly, S. (1984). Skills for effective consultation. *School Counselor, 31,* 23–29.

Educational Testing Service. (1988). *Test-taking tip sheet: General.* Princeton, NJ: Author.

Educational Testing Service. (1994). *Computer-based testing: From multiple choice to multiple choices.* Princeton, NJ: Author.

Eisen, J. (1984). Researchers examine learning styles. *APA Monitor, 15*(5), 34.

Embretson, S. E. (2004). The second century of ability testing: Some predictions and speculations. *Measurement, 2*(1), 1–32.

English, H. B., & English, A. C. (1958). *A comprehensive dictionary of psychological and psychoanalytical terms.* New York: Longman.

Equal Employment Opportunity Commission, Civil Service Commission, Departments of Labor and Justice. (1996). Uniform guidelines on employee selection procedures. *Federal Register, 43,* 38289–33309.

Erdberg, P. (1985). The Rorschach. In C. S. Newmark (Ed.), *Major psychological assessment instruments.* Boston: Allyn & Bacon.

Exner, J., & Weiner, I. B. (1995). *The Rorschach: A comprehensive system. Vol. 3: Assessment of children and adolescents* (2nd ed.). New York: Wiley.

Feld, S. C., & Lewis, J. (1969). The assessment of achievement anxieties in children. In C. P. Smith (Ed.), *Achievement-related motives in children.* New York: Russell Sage Foundation.

Fischer, R. J. (1994). The Americans with Disabilities Act: Implications for measurement. *Educational Measurement, 13*(3), 17–26, 37.

Fisher, C. T. (1985). *Individualized psychological assessment.* Monterey, CA: Brooks/Cole.

Fisher, T. H. (1993). Perspectives on alternate assessment: What's happening nationally. *Research Bulletin—Florida Educational Research Council, 25*(1), 11–16.

Flanagan, J. C. (1954). The critical incidents technique. *Psychological Bulletin, 51,* 327–358.

Florez, J. (1991, January, February). Quoted in Assessing instruments. *Science Agenda, 4,* 6–7.

Ford, V. (1973). *Everything you wanted to know about test-wiseness.* Princeton, NJ: Educational Testing Service.

Frederiksen, N., Saunders, D. R., & Wand, B. (1957). The in-basket test. *Psychological Monograph, 71*(9).

Friedman, T., & Williams, E. B. (1982). Current uses of tests for employment. In A. K. Wigdon & W. R. Garner (Eds.), *Ability testing: Uses, consequences, and controversies* (Part 2). Washington, DC: National Academy Press.

Fuchs, D., & Fuchs, L. S. (1986). Test procedure bias: A meta-analysis of examiner familiar effects. *Review of Educational Research, 56*(2), 243–262.

Gabel, S., Oster, G. D., & Botnik, S. M. (1986). *Understanding psychological testing in children.* New York: Plenum.

Gardner, H. (1983). *Frames of mind: The theory of multiple intelligences.* New York: Basic.

Gardner, H. (1993). *Multiple intelligences: The theory in practice.* New York: Basic Books.

Gardner, P. M., & Parker, P. (1993). Eating disorders. In T. H. Ollendick & M. Hersen (Eds.), *Handbook of child and adolescent assessment.* Boston: Allyn & Bacon.

Garfield, N. J., & Prediger, D. J. (1982). Testing competencies and responsibilities: A checklist for counselors. In J. T. Kapes & M. M. Mastie (Eds.), *A counselor's guide to vocational guidance instruments* (2nd ed.). Alexandria, VA: National Vocational Guidance Association, American Personnel and Guidance Association.

Gatewood, R., & Perloff, R. (1990). Testing and industrial application. In G. Goldsten & M. Hersen (Eds.), *Handbook of psychological assessment.* New York: Pergamon.

Gatewood, R. D., & Feild, H. S. (1990). *Human resource selection.* Chicago: Dryden.

Gazzaniga, M. S. (1985). *Social brain: Discovering the networks of the mind.* New York: Basic Books.

Gilligan, C. (1982). *In a different voice: Psychological theory and women's development.* Cambridge: Harvard University Press.

Glatthorn, A. A. (1998). *Performance assessment and standards-based curricula.* Larchmont, NY: Eye on Education.

Goldman, L. (1971). *Using tests in counseling* (2nd ed.). Pacific Palisades, CA: Goodyear.

Goldstein, G. (1984). Comprehensive neuropsychological assessment batteries. In G. Goldstein & M. Hersen (Eds.), *Handbook of psychological assessment.* New York: Pergamon.

Goldstein, K. M., & Blackman, S. (1978). *Cognitive styles: Five approaches to theory and research.* New York: Wiley.

Gonzales, H. P. (1995). Systematic desensitization, study skills counseling and anxiety coping training in the treatment of anxiety. In C. D. Spielberger & P. R. Vagg (Eds.), *Test anxiety: Theory, assessment and treatment* (pp. 117–132). Washington, DC: Taylor & Francis.

Gooding, K. (1994, April). Teaching to the test: The influence of alternative modes of assessment on teachers' instructional strategies. Paper presented at the annual meeting of the American Educational Research Association, New Orleans.

Gottfredson, G., & Holland, J. L. (1996). *Dictionary of Holland occupational codes* (3rd ed.). Odessa, FL: Psychological Assessment Resources.

Gough, H. G. (1999). *CPI: Introduction to Form 434.* Palo Alto, CA: Consulting Psychologists Press.

Gough, H. G. (2000). The California Psychological Inventory. In C. E. Watkins & V. L. Campbell (Eds.), *Testing and assessment in counseling practice* (pp. 45–71). Mahwah, NJ: Erlbaum.

Gough, H. G., & Bradley, P. (1996). *CPI manual.* Palo Alto, CA: Consulting Psychologists Press.

Grady, M. P. (1984). *Teaching and brain research.* New York: Longman.

Graham, J. R. (1990). *MMPI-2 in psychological treatment.* New York: Oxford University Press.

Graziano, W. G., Varca, P. E., & Levy, J. C. (1982). Race of examiner effects and the validity of intelligence tests. *Review of Educational Research, 52*(4), 469–497.

Greaud, V. A., & Green, B. F. (1986). Equivalence of conventional and computer presentation of speeded tests. *Applied Psychological Measurement, 10,* 23–34.

Green, B. F. (1984). *Computer-based ability testing.* Washington, DC: American Psychological Association, Scientific Affairs Office.

Green, B. F. (1991). Guidelines for computer testing. In T. B. Gutkin & S. L. Wise (Eds.), *The computer and the decision-making process.* Hillsdale, NJ: Erlbaum.

Gregorc, A. F. (1982). *Gregorc style delineator: Developmental, technical, and administrative manual.* Maynard, MA: Gabriel Systems.

Groth-Marnat, G. (1984). *Handbook of psychological assessment.* New York: Wiley.

Groth-Marnat, G. (1997). *Handbook of psychological assessment* (3rd ed.). New York: Van Nostrand Reinhold.

Guilford. J. P. (1950). Three faces of intellect. *American Psychologist, 14,* 469–479.

Guilford, J. P. (1967). *The nature of human intelligence.* New York: McGraw-Hill.

Gutkin, T. B., & Curtis, M. J. (1982). School-based consultation: Theory and techniques. In C. R. Reynolds & T. B. Gutkin (Eds.), *Handbook of school psychology.* New York: Wiley.

Hammer, A. L. (1992). Test evaluation and quality. In M. Zeidner & R. Most (Eds.), *Psychological testing: An inside view.* Palo Alto, CA: Consulting Psychologists Press.

Hammer, E. F. (1985). The House-Tree-Person Test. In C. S. Newmark (Ed.), *Major psychological instruments.* Boston: Allyn & Bacon.

Hansen, J. C. (1986). Computers and beyond in the career decision-making process. *Measurement and Evaluation in Counseling and Development, 19*(1), 48–52.

Hansen, J. C. (1990). Interest inventories. In G. Goldstein & M. Hersen (Eds.), *Handbook of psy-*

chological assessment (2nd ed.). New York: Pergamon.

Hargrove, L. J., & Poteet, J. A. (1984). *Assessment in special education: The educational evaluation.* Upper Saddle River, NJ: Prentice Hall.

Haring, N. G. (Ed.). (1982). *Exceptional children and youth* (3rd ed.). Upper Saddle River, NJ: Merrill/Prentice Hall.

Harrington, T. F., & O'Shea, A. J. (1993). *The Harrington & O'Shea career decision making system, revised.* Circle Pines, MN: American Guidance Service.

Harris, W. G. (1999). *Association of test publishers.* www.testpublishers.org.

Hartshorne, H., & May, M. A. (1928). *Studies in deceit* (Vol. 2). New York: Macmillan.

Haynes, S. N. (1990). Behavioral assessment of adults. In G. Goldstein & M. Hersen (Eds.), *Handbook of psychological assessment* (pp. 423–466). New York: Pergamon.

Hembree, R. (1988). Correlates, causes, effects and treatment of test anxiety. *Review of Educational Research, 58*(1), 47–77.

Herr, E. L., & Cramer, S. H. (1984). *Career counseling through the life span* (2nd ed.). Boston: Little, Brown.

Herrnstein, R. J., & Murray, C. (1994). *The bell curve.* New York: Free Press.

Heubert, J. P., & Hauser, R. M. (Eds.). (1999). *High stakes: Testing for tracking, promotion, and graduation.* Washington, DC: National Academy Press.

Hirsh, S., & Kummerow, J. (1990). *Introduction to type in organizations* (2nd ed.). Palo Alto, CA: Consulting Psychologists Press.

Hodges, K., Kline, J., Stern, L., Cytryn, L., & McKnew, D. (1982). The development of a child assessment interview for research and clinical use. *Journal of Abnormal Child Psychology, 10,* 173–189.

Holland, J. L. (1979). *Professional manual for the self-directed search.* Palo Alto, CA: Consulting Psychologists Press.

Holland, J. L. (1985). *Self-directed search.* Odessa, FL: Psychological Assessment Resources.

Holland, J. L. (1986). New directions for interest testing. In B. S. Plake & J. C. Witt (Eds.), *Burns-Nebraska Symposium on Measurement and Testing. Vol. 2: The future of testing.* Hillsdale, NJ: Erlbaum.

Holland, J. L. (1997). *Making vocational choices: A theory of vocational personalities and work environments* (3rd ed.). Upper Saddle River, NJ: Prentice Hall.

Holt, R. R. (Ed.). (1968). *Diagnostic psychological testing* (Rev. Ed.). New York: International Universities Press.

Hood, A. B., & Johnson, R. W. (2001). *Assessment in counseling: A guide to the use of psychological assessment procedures* (3rd ed.). Alexandria, VA: American Counseling Association.

Hood, A. B., & Johnson, R. W. (2002). *Assessment in counseling: A guide to the use of psychological assessment instruments* (3rd ed.). Baltimore, MD: American Counseling Association.

Horn, J. L. (1989). Cognitive diversity: A framework for learning. In P. L. Ackerman, R. J. Sternberg, & R. Glaser (Eds.), *Learning and individual differences: Advances in theory and research.* New York: Freeman.

Howard, E. R., & Keefe, J. W. (1991). *The Case-IMS School Improvement Process.* Reston, VA: National Association of Secondary School Principals.

Hurt, S. W., Reznikoff, M., & Clarkin, J. F. (1995). The Rorschach. In L. E. Beutler & M. R. Berren (Eds.), *Integrative assessment of adult personality.* New York: Guilford Press.

Inghram, C. F. (1980). *Fundamentals of educational assessment.* New York: Van Nostrand.

Jackson, D. N. (1985). *Computer-based personality testing.* Washington, DC: American Psychological Association, Scientific Affairs Office.

Jensen, A. R. (1980). *Bias in mental testing.* New York: Free Press.

Johnson, B. (1996). *The performance assessment handbook. Vol 2: Performances and exhibitions.* Princeton, NJ: Eye on Education.

Johnson, M. E., & Holland, A. L. (1986). Measuring clients' expectations: The 15 Personal Problems Inventory. *Measurement and Evaluation in Counseling and Development, 19*(3), 151–156.

Joint Committee on Testing Practices. (1999). *Code of fair testing practices in education.* Washington, DC: Author.

Jones, E. R. (1998). *Web-based teaching.* Paper presented at the 1998 Meeting of the Southwestern Social Science Association. Corpus Christi, TX.

Jones, J. W., & Dages, K. D. (2003). Technology trends in staffing and assessment: A practice note. *International Journal of Selection and Assessment, 11,* 247–252.

Jones, L. V. (2001). Assessing achievement versus high-stakes testing: A crucial contrast. *Educational Assessment, 7*(1), 21–28.

Jung, C. G. (1910). The association method. *American Journal of Psychology, 21,* 219–269.

Jung, C. G. (1918). *Studies in word association.* London: Heinemann.

Kachigan, S. K. (1986). *Statistical analysis: An interdisciplinary introduction to univariate and multivariate methods.* New York: Radius.

Kagan, J. (1966). Reflection-impulsivity: The generality and dynamics of conceptual tempo. *Journal of Abnormal Psychology, 71,* 17–24.

Kagan, J., Rosman, B. L., Day, D., Albert, J., & Phillips, W. (1964). Information processing in the child: Significance of analytic and reflective attitudes. *Psy-chological Monograph, 78,* 1.

Kamphaus, R. W., Petoskey, M. D., & Morgan, A. W. (1997). A history of intelligence test interpretation. In D. P. Flanagan, J. L. Genshaft, & P. L. Harrison (Eds.), *Contemporary intellectual assessment* (pp. 32–48). New York: Guilford Press.

Kapes, J. T., & Whitfield, E. A. (2001). *A counselor's guide to vocational guidance instruments* (4th ed.). Columbus, OH: National Career Development Association.

Katz, L. (1991). *A practical guide to psychodiagnostic testing* (2nd ed.). Springfield, IL: Charles C. Thomas.

Kaufman, A. S. (1976). Verbal-performance IQ discrepancies on the WISC-R. *Journal of Consulting and Clinical Psychology, 44,* 739–744.

Kaufman, A. S. (1990). *Assessing adolescent and adult intelligence.* Boston: Allyn & Bacon.

Kaufman, A. S., Kamphaus, R. W., & Kaufman, N. L. (1985). The Kaufman Assessment Battery for Children (K-ABC). In C. S. Newmark (Ed.), *Major psychological assessment instruments.* Boston: Allyn & Bacon.

Kaufman, A. S., & Kaufman, N. L. (1983). *Kaufman assessment battery for children.* Circle Pines, MN: American Guidance Service.

Kaufman, A. S., & Kaufman, N. L. (2004). *Kaufman assessment battery for children* (2nd ed.). Circle Pines, MN: AGS.

Kazdin, A. E. (1993). Conduct disorders. In T. H. Ollendick & M. Hersen (Eds.), *Handbook of child and adolescent assessment.* Boston: Allyn & Bacon.

Keefe, J. W., & Languis, M. L. (1983, August). Operational definitions. Paper presented to NASSP Learning Styles Task Force, Reston, VA.

Keefe, J. W., & Monk, J. S. (1988). *Manual to learning style profile.* Reston, VA: National Association of Secondary School Principals.

Keesling, J. W., & Healy, C. C. (1988). USES General Aptitude Battery. In J. T. Kapes & M. M. Mastie (Eds.), *A counselor's guide to career instruments* (2nd ed.). Alexandria, VA: National Career Development Association.

Kellerman, H., & Burry, A. (1991). *Handbook of psychodynamic testing: An analysis of personality in the psychological report.* Boston: Allyn & Bacon.

Kelly, E. L., & Fiske, D. W. (1951). *The prediction of performance in clinical psychology.* Ann Arbor: University of Michigan Press.

Kline, P. (1993). *Handbook of psychological testing.* United Kingdom: Routledge.

Kolb, D. A. (1976). *Learning Style Inventory.* Boston: McBer.

Koppitz, E. M. (1968). *Psychological evaluation of children's human figure drawings.* New York: Grune & Stratton.

Koppitz, E. M. (1975). *The Bender Gestalt Test for Young Children. Vol. 2: Research and applications, 1963–1973.* New York: Grune & Stratton.

Koppitz, E. M. (1982). Personality assessment in the schools. In C. R. Reynolds & T. B. Gutkin (Eds.), *Handbook of school psychology* (pp. 273–295). New York: Wiley.

Korchin, S. J., & Schuldberg, D. (1981). The future of clinical assessment. *American Psychologist, 36*(10), 1147–1158.

Kovacs, M. (1982). The longitudinal study of child and adolescent psychopathology. Part 1: The semi-structured psychiatric interview schedule for children. Unpublished manuscript.

Krechevsky, M. (1994). *Project Spectrum preschool assessment handbook.* Cambridge: Harvard Project Zero.

Kroener, S., Plass, J. L., & Leutner, D. (2005). Intelligence assessment with computer simulation. *Intelligence, 33,* 347–368.

Krug, S. E. (1980). *Clinical analysis questionnaire.* Champaign, IL: Institute for Personality & Ability Testing.

Kyllonen, P. C. (1997). Smart testing. In R. F. Dillon (Ed.), *Handbook on testing* (pp. 347–371). Westport, CT: Greenwood.

La Greca, A. M., & Stringer, S. A. (1985). The Wechsler Intelligence Scale for Children–Revised. In C. S. Newmark (Ed.), *Major psychological assessment instruments.* Boston: Allyn & Bacon.

Lambert, N., & McComb, B. (1998). *How students learn.* Alexandria, VA: American Psychological Association.

Lawrence, G. (1982). *People types and tiger stripes* (2nd ed.). Palo Alto, CA: Consulting Psychologists Press.

Lien, A. J. (1971). *Measurement and evaluation of learning* (2nd ed.). Dubuque, IA: Brown.

Loehlin, J. C., Lindzey, G., & Spohler, J. N. (1975). *Race differences in intelligence.* San Francisco: Freeman.

Lyman, H. B. (1998). *Test scores and what they mean* (6th ed.). Boston: Allyn & Bacon.

Machover, K. (1949). *Personality projection in the drawing of the human figure.* Springfield, IL: Charles C. Thomas.

Maddux, C. D., & Johnson, L. (1998). Computer assisted assessment. In H. B. Vance (Ed.), *Psychological assessment of children* (2nd ed., pp. 87–105). New York: Wiley.

Madsen, D. H. (1986). Computer applications for test administration and scoring. *Measurement and Evaluation in Counseling and Development, 19*(1), 6–14.

Mann, L., & Sabatino, D. A. (1985). *Foundations of cognitive process in remedial and special education.* Rockville, MD: Aspen Systems.

Marcus, L. M., & Schopler, E. (1993). Pervasive developmental disorders. In T. H. Ollendick & M. Hersen (Eds.), *Handbook of child and adolescent assessment.* Boston: Allyn & Bacon.

Matey, C. (1984). Leiter International Performance Scale. In D. J. Keyser & R. C. Sweetland (Eds.), *Test critiques* (Vol. 1, pp. 411–420). Kansas City, MO: Test Corporation of America.

Maxmen, J. S., & Ward, N. G. (1995). *Essential psychopathology and its treatment* (2nd ed.). New York: W. W. Norton.

McBride, J. R., & Martin, J. T. (1983). Reliability and validity of adaptive ability tests in a military setting. In D. J. Weiss (Ed.), *New horizons in testing.* New York: Academic Press.

McDaniel, C., & Gysbers, N. C. (1992). *Counseling for career development: Theories, resources, and practices.* San Francisco: Jossey-Bass.

McKee, P., & Wilt, R. (1990). Effective teaching: A review of instructional and environmental variables. In T. B. Gutkin & C. R. Reynolds (Eds.), *Handbook of school psychology* (2nd ed.). New York: Wiley.

McMinn, M. R., Ellens, B. M., & Soref, E. (1999). Ethical perspectives and practice behaviors involving computer-based test interpretation. *Assessment, 6,* 71–78.

Meehl, P. E. (1954). *Clinical versus statistical prediction.* Minneapolis: University of Minnesota Press.

Meier, S. T., & Geiger, S. M. (1986). Implications of computer-assisted testing and assessment for professional practice and training. *Measurement and Evaluation in Counseling & Development, 19*(1), 29–34.

Merz, W. R., Sr. (1984). Kaufman Assessment Battery for Children. In D. J. Keyser & R. C. Sweetland (Eds.), *Test critiques* (Vol. 1, pp. 393–405). Kansas City, MO: Test Corporation of America.

Messick, S. (1980). *The effectiveness of coaching for the SAT: Review and reanalysis of research from the fifties to the FTC.* Princeton, NJ: Educational Testing Service.

Messick, S. (1989). Validity. In R. L. Linn (Ed.), *Educational measurement* (3rd ed.). New York: Collier Macmillan.

Messick, S., & Yungeblut, A. (1981). Time and methods in coaching for the SAT. *Psychological Bulletin, 89,* 191–216.

Meyer, P., & Davis, S. (1992). *The CPI application guide.* Palo Alto, CA: Consulting Psychologists Press.

Miller, M. D., & Seraphine, A. E. (1993). Can test scores remain authentic when teaching to the test? *Research Bulletin—Florida Educational Research Council, 25*(1), 21–29.

Miller, M. J. (1985). Counseling Region 99 clients. *Journal of Employment Counseling, 22,* 70–76.

Millman, J., Bishop, C. H., & Ebel, R. L. (1965). An analysis of test-wiseness. *Educational and Psychological Measurement, 25,* 707–726.

Millon, T., & Davis, R. D. (1996). *Disorders of personality: DSM-IV and beyond.* New York: Wiley.

Miner, M. G. (1976). Selection procedures and personnel records. (Personnel Policies Forum Survey No. 112). Washington, DC: Bureau of National Affairs.

Montgomery, G. T., & Orozco, S. (1985). Mexican Americans' performance on the MMPI as a function of level of acculturation. *Journal of Clinical Psychology, 41,* 203–212.

Moos, R. (1987). *Social climate scales: A user's guide* (2nd ed.). Palo Alto, CA: Consulting Psychologists Press.

Moreland, K. L. (1992). Computer assisted psychological assessment. In M. Zeidner & R. Most (Eds.), *Psychological testing: An inside view.* Palo Alto, CA: Consulting Psychologists Press.

Moss, P. A. (1998). The role of consequences in validity theory. *Educational Measurement, 17*(23), 6–12.

Munsterberg, F. (1955). Relationships between some background factors and children's interpersonal behavior. Unpublished doctoral dissertation, Ohio State University, Columbus.

Musch, J., & Reips, U.-D. (2000). *A brief history of web experimenting.* In M. H. Birnbaum (Ed.), Psychological experiments on the Internet (pp. 61–85). San Diego, CA: Academic Press.

Myers, I. B., & Briggs, K. C. (1962). *The Myers-Briggs Type Indicator.* Princeton, NJ: Educational Testing Service.

Nail, G. (1996). Some thoughts on psychological report writing. Available at http://www.misresource.com/theory.html.

National Association of School Psychologists. (1980). *Standards for the provision of school psychological services.* Washington, DC: Author.

National Association of School Psychologists. (2000). *Principles for professional ethics.* Besthesda, MD: Author.

National Board for Certified Counselors. (2005). *Code of ethics.* Greensboro, NC: Author.

National Council on Measurement in Education. (1994, February). *Alternate assessment standards.* Washington, DC: Author.

National Council on Measurement in Education. (1995). *Code of professional responsibilities in educational measurement.* Washington, DC: Author.

National Council on Measurement in Education, American Association of School Administrators, National Association of Secondary School Principals, National Association of Elementary School Principals. (1994). *Competency standards in student assessment for educational administrators.* Washington, DC: Author.

National Council of Teachers of Mathematics. (1993). *Assessment standards for school mathematics.* Reston, VA: Author.

Nevo, B., & Jaeger, R. S. (1993). *Educational and psychological testing: The test taker's outlook.* Toronto: Hogrefe & Huber.

Newmark, C. S. (Ed.). (1996). *Major psychological assessment instruments.* Boston: Allyn & Bacon.

Nuttall, E. V., Romero, J., & Kalesnik, J. (1992). *Assessing and screening preschoolers: Psychological and educational dimensions.* Boston: Allyn & Bacon.

Oakland, T. (1982). Nonbiased assessment of minority group children. In J. T. Neisworth (Ed.), *Assessment in special education.* Rockville, MD: Aspen Systems.

Oakland, T. D., & Parmelee, R. (1985). Mental measurement of minority group children. In B. B. Wolman (Ed.), *Handbook of intelligence: Theories, measurements, and applications.* New York: Wiley.

Ollendick, T. W., & Greene, R. (1990). Behavioral assessment of children. In G. Goldstein & M. Hersen (Eds.), *Handbook of psychological assessment* (2nd ed., pp. 403–422). New York: Pergamon.

Olsen, F. (2001). Getting ready for a new generation of course-management systems. *Chronicle of Higher Education, 48*(17), A25.

OSS Assessment Staff. (1948). *Assessment of men.* New York: Holt, Rinehart & Winston.

Paris, S. G. (2000). Trojan horse in the schoolyard: The hidden threats in high-stakes testing. *Issues in Education, 6*(1, 2), 1–16.

Paris, S. G., & Urdan, T. (2000). Policies and practices of high-stakes testing that influence teachers and schools. *Issues in Education, 6*(1, 2), 83–107.

Perloff, R., Craft, J. A., & Perloff, E. (1984). Testing and industrial application. In G. Goldstein & M. Hersen (Eds.), *Handbook of psychological assessment.* New York: Pergamon.

Piacentini, J. (1993). Checklists and rating scales. In T. H. Ollendick & M. Hersen (Eds.), *Handbook of child and adolescent assessment.* Boston: Allyn & Bacon.

Piaget, J. (1970). *The science of education and the psychology of the child.* New York: Orion.

Prell, J. M., & Prell, P. A. (1986, November). *Improving test scores—teaching test-wiseness: A review of the literature.* Research Bulletin of the Center on Evaluation, Development, and Research. Bloomington, IL: Phi Delta Kappa.

Rapport, M. D. (1993). Attention deficit hyperactivity disorders. In T. H. Ollendick & M. Hersen (Eds.), *Handbook of child and adolescent assessment.* Boston: Allyn & Bacon.

Reiff, J. C. (1992). *Learning styles.* Washington, DC: National Education Association.

Reiling, E., & Taylor, R. (1972). A new approach to the problem of changing initial responses to multiple choice questions. *Journal of Educational Measurement, 8,* 177–181.

Reynolds, C. R., & Brown, R. T. (1984). Bias in mental testing. In C. R. Reynolds & R. T. Brown (Eds.), *Perspectives on bias in mental testing.* New York: Plenum.

Riso, D. R. (1990). *Understanding the enneagram: The practical guide to personality types.* Boston: Houghton Mifflin.

Riso, D. R. (1994). *Using the enneagram for personal growth.* Boston: Houghton Mifflin.

Roderick, M. (1993). *The path to dropping out: Evidence for intervention.* Westport, CN: Auburn House.

Rogers, C. R. (1942). *Counseling and psychotherapy.* Boston: Houghton Mifflin.

Rogers, C. R. (1951). *Client-centered counseling,* Boston: Houghton Mifflin.

Rossetti, L. M. (1990). *Infant-toddler assessment.* Austin, TX: PRO-ED.

Rotter, J. B. (1966). Generalized expectancies for internal versus external control of reinforcement. *Psychological Monographs, 80,* 609.

Rotter, J. B., & Rafferty, J. E. (1950). *Manual: The Rotter Incomplete Sentence Blank.* New York: Psychological Corporation.

Ryan, K. (2002). Assessment validation in the context of high-stakes assessment. *Educational Measurement: Issues and Practices, 21,* 7–15.

Saklofske, D. H., & Kowalchuk, V. L., & Schwean, V. C. (1992). Influences on testing and test results. In M. Zeidner & R. Most (Eds.), *Psychological testing: An inside view.* Palo Alto, CA: Consulting Psychologists Press.

Sampson, J. P., Jr., & Pyle, K. R. (1983). Ethical issues involved with the use of computer-assisted counseling, testing, and guidance systems. *Personnel and Guidance Journal, 61,* 283–287.

Sarason, I. G. (Ed.). (1980). *Test anxiety: Theory, research, and application.* Hillsdale, NJ: Erlbaum.

Sattler, J. M. (1988). *Assessment of children* (3rd ed.). San Diego, CA: Author.

Sattler, J. (2001). *Assessment of children: Cognitive applications.* San Diego, CA: Sattler.

Schmidt, F. L., & Hunter, J. E. (1981). Employment testing: Old theories and new research findings. *American Psychologist, 36*(10), 1128–1137.

Seligman, L. (1996). *Diagnosis and treatment planning in counseling* (2nd ed.). New York: Plenum Press.

Shapiro, E. S., & Cole, C. L. (1993). Self-monitoring. In T. H. Ollendick & M. Hersen (Eds.), *Handbook of child and adolescent assessment.* Boston: Allyn & Bacon.

Shavelson, R. J., Hubner, J. J., & Stanton, G. C. (1976). Self-concept: Validation of construct interpretations. *Review of Educational Research, 46,* 407–442.

Shepard, L. A. (2000). The role of assessment in a learning culture. *Educational Researcher, 29*(7), 4–14.

Sherrod, B. (1985, November). Jobs for left brainers; jobs for right brainers. *Career World,* 19–21.

Shertzer, B. (1986). Integrating computer-assisted testing and assessment in the counseling process: A reaction. *Measurement and Evaluation in Counseling and Development, 19*(1), 27–28.

Shertzer, B., & Linden, J. D. (1979). *Fundamentals of individual appraisal: Assessment techniques for counselors.* Boston: Houghton Mifflin.

Shore, M. F., Brice, P. J., & Love, B. G. (1992). *When your child needs testing: What parents, teachers, and other helpers need to know about psychological testing.* New York: Crossroad.

Shostrom, E. L. (1963). *Personal Orientation Inventory.* San Diego, CA: EdITS.

Simeonsson, R. J. (1986). *Psychological and developmental assessment of special children.* Boston: Allyn & Bacon.

Simon, A., & Boyer, E. G. (1974). *Mirrors for behavior III: An anthology of observation instruments.* Wyncote, PA: Communications Materials Center.

Skiba, R. J., Knesting, K., Bush, L. D. (2002). Culturally competent assessment: More than nonbiased tests, *Journal of Child and Family Studies, 11*(1), 61-78.

Slosson, S. W., & Callisto, T. A. (1984). *Observational analysis.* East Aurora, NY: Slosson.

Spearman, C. (1927). *The abilities of man.* London: Macmillan.

Spielberger, C. D. (1970). *Manual for the state-trait anxiety inventory (Form Y).* Palo Alto, CA: Consulting Psychologists Press, Inc.

Spielberger, C. D. (1983). *Manual for the State-Trait Anxiety Inventory (STAI).* Palo Alto, CA: Consulting Psychologists Press.

Spielberger, C. D., & Vagg, P. R. (Eds.). (1995). *Test anxiety: Theory, assessment, and treatment.* Washington, DC: Taylor & Francis.

Sternberg, R. J. (1980). Factor theories of intelligence are all right, almost. *Educational Researcher, 9,* 6-13.

Sternberg, R. J. (1985). *Beyond IQ: A triarchic theory of human intelligence.* Cambridge: Cambridge University Press.

Sternberg, R. J. (1986). *Intelligence applied: Understanding and increasing your intellectual skills.* San Diego: Harcourt Brace Jovanovich.

Sternberg, R. J. (1990). T & T is an explosive combination: Technology and testing. *Educational Psychologist, 25*(3, 4), 201-222.

Sternberg, R. J. (Ed.). (2000). *Handbook of intelligence.* New York: Cambridge University Press.

Stiggins, R. (1987). Design and development of performance assessments. *Educational Measurement, 6*(3), 32-42.

Stockwell, S., Schaeffer, B., & Lowenstein, J. (1991). *SAT coaching coverup: How coaching courses can raise scores by 100 points or more and why ETS denies the evidence.* Cambridge, MA: Fair Test.

Stoddard, G. D. (1943). *The meaning of intelligence.* New York: Macmillan.

Strauss, C. C. (1993). Anxiety disorders. In T. H. Ollendick & M. Hersen (Eds.), *Handbook of child and adolescent assessment.* Boston: Allyn & Bacon.

Strong, E. R. (1927). Vocational Interest Test. *Educational Record, 8,* 107-121.

Sue, D. W., Arrendondo, P., & McDavis, R. J. (1992). Multicultural counseling competencies and standards: A call to the profession. *Journal of Counseling and Development, 70.*

Super, D. E., & Crites, J. O. (1962). *Appraising vocational fitness by means of psychological tests* (Rev. ed.). New York: Harper & Row.

Super, D. E., Thompson, A. S., & Lindeman, R. H. (1988). *Manual to Adult Career Concerns Inventory.* Palo Alto, CA: Consulting Psychologists Press.

Suzuki, L. A., Short, E. L., Pieterse, A. & Kugler, J. (2001). Multicultural issues and the assessment of aptitude. In L. A. Suzuki, J. G. Ponterotto, & P. J. Meller, (Eds.). *Handbook of multicultural assessment* (2nd ed.), (pp. 359-382). San Francisco: Jossey-Bass.

Tallent, N. (1992). *Psychological report writing* (4th ed.). Upper Saddle River, NJ: Prentice Hall.

Ten Brink, T. D. (1974). *Evaluation: A practical guide for teachers.* New York: McGraw-Hill.

Tenopyr, M. L. (1981). The realities of employment testing. *American Psychologist, 36*(10), 1120-1127.

Terman, L. M. (1954). The discovery and encouragement of exceptional talent. *American Psychologist, 9,* 221-230.

Test Alert. (1990). Chicago: Riverside.

Test Users Training Work Group of the Joint Committee on Testing Practices. (1993). *Responsible test use.* Washington, DC: American Psychological Association.

Thomas, M. (1937). Méthode des histoires à compléter pour le dépiste des complexes et des conflits affectifs enfantins. *Archives Psychologie, 26,* 209-284.

Thorn, A. R., & Mulvenon, S. W. (2002). High-stakes testing: An examination of elementary counselors' views and their academic preparation to meet this challenge. *Measurement & Evaluation in Counseling & Development, 35*(3), 195-206.

Thorndike, E. L. (1927). *The measurement of intelligence.* New York: Teachers College Press.

Thorndike, R. L., & Hagen, E. P. (1959). *Ten thousand careers.* New York: Wiley.

Thorndike, R. M. (2005). *Measurement and evaluation in psychology and education.* (7th ed.). Merrill/Prentice Hall.

Thornton III, G. C., & Byham, W. C. (1982). *Assessment centers and managerial performance.* New York: Academic Press.

Thurstone, L. L. (1938). *Primary mental abilities* (Psychometric Monograph No. 1). Chicago: University of Chicago Press.

Tobias, S. (1979). Anxiety research in educational psychology. *Journal of Educational Psychology, 71*, 573-582.

Tyron, G. S. (1980). The measurement and treatment of test anxiety. *Review of Educational Research, 50*, 343-372.

Urman, H. (1983). The effect of test-wiseness training on the achievement of third or fifth grade students. Paper presented at the annual meeting of the National Council on Measurement in Education, Montreal.

Valencia, R. R., & Aburto, S. (1991). The uses and abuses of educational testing: Chicanos as a case in point. In R. R. Valencia (Ed.), *Chicano school failure and success: Research and policy agendas for the 1990s.* Basingstoke, England: Falmer.

Vance, H. B. (Ed.). (1998). *Psychological assessment of children* (2nd ed.). New York: Wiley.

Vernon, P. E. (1960). *The structure of human abilities* (Rev. ed.). London: Methuen.

Wallace, G., & Larsen, S. C. (1992). *Educational assessment of learning problems: Testing for teaching* (2nd ed.). Boston: Allyn & Bacon.

Walsh, W. B., & Betz, N. E. (2000). *Tests and assessment* (4th ed.). Upper Saddle River, NJ: Prentice Hall.

Watkins, M. W., & McDermott, P. A. (1991). Psychodiagnostic computing: From interpretive programs to expert systems. In T. B. Gutkin & S. L. Wise (Eds.), *The computer and the decision-making process.* Hillsdale, NJ: Erlbaum.

Wechsler, D. (1958). *The measurement of adult intelligence.* Baltimore: Williams & Wilkins.

Whitman, N. A., Spendlove, D. C., & Clark, C. H. (1986). *Increasing students' learning: A faculty guide to reducing stress among students* (ASHE-ERIC Executive Higher Education Report No. 4).

Whitworth, R. H., & Unterbrink, C. (1994). Comparison of MMPI-2 clinical and content scales administered to Hispanic and Anglo-Americans. *Hispanic Journal of Behavioral Sciences, 16*, 255-264.

Wigdor, A. K., & Garner, W. R. (Eds.). (1982). *Ability testing: Uses, consequences, and controversies* (2 vols.). Washington, DC: National Academy Press.

Wine, J. D. (1980). Cognitive-attentional theory of test anxiety. In I. G. Sarason (Ed.), *Text anxiety: Theory, research and application.* Hillsdale, NJ: Erlbaum.

Witkin, H. A. (1949). Perception of body position and of the position of the visual field. *Psychological Monographs, 63*(1, no. 302).

Witkin, H. A., Moore, C. A., Goodenough, D. R., & Cox, P. W. (1977). Field-dependent and field-independent cognitive styles and their educational implications. *Review of Educational Research, 47*, 1-64.

Wonder, J., & Donovan, P. (1984). *Whole brain thinking: Working from both sides of the brain to achieve peak job performance.* New York: Morrow.

Wylie, R. C. (1990). *Self-concept instruments.* Lincoln: University of Nebraska Press.

Ysseldyke, J. E., & Christenson, S. L. (1987). *Instructional environment scale.* Austin, TX: PRO-ED.

Yule, W. (1993). Developmental perspective and psychopathology and influences in child behavioral assessment. In T. H. Ollendick & M. Hersen, *Handbook of child and adolescent assessment* (pp. 15-25). Boston: Allyn & Bacon.

Zeidner, M., & Most, R. (1992). *Psychological testing: An inside view.* Palo Alto, CA: Consulting Psychologists Press.

Test Index

Name Index

Subject Index

Note: Italicized page numbers indicate illustrations.